When at Times the Mob Is Swayed

When at Times the Mob Is Swayed

A Citizen's Guide to Defending Our Republic

Burt Neuborne

THE
NEW
PRESS

NEW YORK
LONDON

Requests for permission to reproduce selections
from this book should be mailed to:
Permissions Department, The New Press, 120 Wall Street,
31st floor, New York, NY 10005.

Published in the United States by The New Press, New York, 2019
Distributed by Two Rivers Distribution

ISBN 978-1-62097-358-5 (hc)
ISBN 978-1-62097-359-2 (ebook)
CIP data is available.

The New Press publishes books that promote and enrich public discussion and understanding of the issues vital to our democracy and to a more equitable world. These books are made possible by the enthusiasm of our readers; the support of a committed group of donors, large and small; the collaboration of our many partners in the independent media and the not-for-profit sector; booksellers, who often hand-sell New Press books; librarians; and above all by our authors.

www.thenewpress.com

Composition by dix!
This book was set in Electra LT Std

Printed in the United States of America

2 4 6 8 10 9 7 5 3 1

For my wife, Helen—

My brilliant friend for sixty years

So when at times the mob is swayed
To carry praise or blame too far
We may choose something like a star
To stay our minds on and be staid.

—Robert Frost, "Choose Something like a Star," 1916

CONTENTS

When at Times the Mob Is Swayed

1

How Good Are the Brakes on the Democracy Train?

In more than fifty-five years of practicing law, I've sued every American president since Lyndon Johnson, most of them more than once. When I wasn't suing presidents, as national legal director of the American Civil Liberties Union and founding legal director of the Brennan Center for Justice, I sued governors, mayors, police chiefs, FBI directors, generals, school boards, city council members, judges, cops, and any other government official I could get my hands on who appeared to be violating the Constitution.

The constitutional enforcement business was pretty good. I never experienced a shortage of customers. Much of the time the judicial system worked just as advertised, shielding vulnerable targets from unfair abuse at the hands of the politically powerful. I've learned from bitter experience, though, that without an excellent set of constitutional brakes, American democracy can quickly morph into an angry, fearful mob—a runaway political train fully capable of crushing anyone in its path.

Faced, as we are these days, with a charismatic, authoritarian president named Donald Trump, whose genius for creating scapegoats, bending the truth, and fomenting divisiveness poses a profound threat to many of our constitutional values, it's long past time to check the brakes on the twenty-first-century American Democracy Express. Are the brakes strong enough to stop a runaway Trumpist train fueled by racism, misogyny, envy, and fear?

The short—and disturbing—answer is that the brakes on the first-class cars, especially the gilded private cars at the head of the train, are still in pretty good shape. But if you're traveling in coach, or riding outside because you can't afford a ticket, you run a serious risk of being the victim of an ugly train wreck—because the brakes on the low end of the Democracy Express are in terrible shape. I hope that you will treat this book, in part, as a warning from your neighborhood constitutional cop about the faulty brakes; and, in part, as a repair manual for folks willing to get their hands dirty fixing them.

I am confident that sustained political and legal effort can get us back on track. My most important message, though, is that there is no constitutional mechanic in the sky ready to swoop down and save American democracy from Donald Trump at the head of a populist mob. The fate of American democracy is up to us.

The legendary group of Founders—George Washington, James Madison, John Adams, John Jay, and Alexander Hamilton—who built the railroad were so concerned about runaway democratic trains that they installed a dual braking system—internal and external. In 1787, they designed an "internal" set of self-checking electoral brakes designed to prevent an overheated electoral majority from picking up too much speed in any one direction. As a backup, in 1791, they installed a second, "external" set of brakes empowering independent, politically neutral judges, headed by the Supreme Court, to slow or stop the democracy train if, despite the internal brakes, the electoral majority threatened to run roughshod over vulnerable individuals and groups.

The sad truth is that, today, neither braking system is working well enough to stop a runaway populist train fueled by racism, religious intolerance, and ideological fervor from jumping the constitutional tracks and harming the weak and poor. Anyone who tells you differently either doesn't understand how the brakes work, doesn't care who gets run over, or is working for Vladimir Putin.

THE INTERNAL BRAKES

The Founders' internal brakes haven't been overhauled in more than two hundred years. They are in dreadful shape. As originally designed, the internal brakes relied on multiple, relatively equal voting blocs with differing, often conflicting, interests to check each other automatically. The theory was that the interaction of competing voting blocs would prevent any single group of voters from accumulating enough governing power to run roughshod over the losers.

As a matter of history, the Founders' internal electoral braking system worked tolerably well for a long time, with the tragic exception of the Civil War. Today, though, the Founders' electoral brakes are in shambles. Instead of a self-regulating system based on checks and balances, two dominant political parties—Republican and Democratic—provide a ready path for a single, ideologically linked group of voters to gain complete control of the government and, once in power, to abuse that control by crushing their opponents, along with any other scapegoats that happen to get in the way.

The Founders were remarkable visionaries who literally invented the idea of a mass democracy governing a large geographical area. Much of this book is devoted to their brilliant political innovations. The one thing the Founders didn't foresee, though, was the crucial role of political parties in organizing and operating the democratic process. In fact, the Founders hated the idea of political parties, disparagingly calling them "factions." It turns out, though, that you can't run a mass representative democracy without some coordinating mechanism to organize the process. That's where political parties come in—like it or not.

For most of our national history, the Founders' failure to have anticipated the need for political parties didn't do much harm to their internal braking mechanism because nineteenth- and twentieth-century American political parties tended to be either small regional groupings capable of checking each other, or "big tents" that included a bewildering array of self-checking interests crossing ideological, economic, and racial fault lines. Once upon a time, liberal Republicans were to the left of conservative Democrats, and just as many blacks supported the Republican Party, the party of Abraham Lincoln, as supported the Democrats, long the party of racial segregation.

Today, the Republican and Democratic parties have evolved into competing ideological brand names, functioning as closed political silos with virtually no points of overlap. Too often, adherents of each party demonize their political opponents, receive their political information from diametrically opposed media outlets, and view politics as an apocalyptic struggle between right and wrong. Even worse for the internal braking system, today's political parties also predictably divide by particularly incendiary criteria such as race, religion, ethnic origin, and economic status, setting the stage for ferocious partisan competition to win bitterly contested elections by narrow margins, followed by ruthless efforts to ram an ideological agenda down the throats of the electoral losers. Thus, instead of organizing a self-checking mechanism governed by compromise, our current hyper-partisan political parties function as accelerants, enabling extreme partisans to set the throttle at full speed without caring much who gets run over.

I'm confident that the current hyper-partisan nature of the Republican and Democratic Parties can be ameliorated by tweaking the rules governing the nomination process, which currently artificially empower the parties' extreme wings. As we'll see, the democracy repair manual in chapter 3 calls for changing the nominating ground rules to do a better job of reflecting the preferences of moderates in each party, and even opening the way for potential third-party challenges to the current legally protected political duopoly enjoyed by the Republican and Democratic parties.

The unforeseen impact of ideologically defined political parties is not, however, the only reason the Founders' electoral brakes don't work anymore. The real problem is much deeper. The Founders imagined a fair representative democracy where a diverse body of elected "representatives" would accurately reflect the mosaic of American life. In twenty-first-century America, however, the Founders' ideal of fair political representation has all but fallen apart. In fact, it's hard to imagine a system of electoral representation more unfair, unequal, and distorted than ours that would have the chutzpah to call itself a real democracy.

We start with the appallingly undemocratic United States

Senate, where Wyoming, with fewer than 600,000 residents, elects the same number of senators as California, with 40 million residents—a one-person one-vote distortion of sixty-five to one—and where, in a worst case scenario, senators representing only about 18 percent of the country's population can cast 51 percent of the votes in the chamber. Current reality is not quite that bad. In the 116th Congress, Republican senators representing just under 40 percent of the population control the upper chamber. That's not as undemocratic as it could be, but it's nothing to be proud of if you believe in political equality and majority rule.

It would be bad enough if the Senate's representational distortion were random. But it's far from random. It's structurally biased against urban America, where 80 percent of Americans live, including the vast bulk of Americans of color. Face it. Under the existing Senate structure, sometimes it feels as though New York City is a colony of Wyoming.

How did such a distortion of the Founders' democratic dream come about? We all remember the story of the "Connecticut Compromise," where the smaller states agreed to a House of Representatives based on population in return for a Senate where each state would have "equal suffrage" regardless of population. Madison accepted the Connecticut Compromise, but he understood that equal state representation in the Senate regardless of population contravened the principles of representative democracy. In 1787, the Confederation Congress had provided in the Northwest Ordinance that future states formed from the territories would each have about the same population. Despite the compromise with principle, Madison reluctantly went along with the Connecticut Compromise because he believed that modestly overrepresenting several of the original smaller states in the Senate would protect a politically weak minority against possible oppression by the politically powerful majority.

The original compromise with principle was modest. In 1790, Delaware, with about 60,000 residents, elected the same number of senators as Virginia, with more than 750,000 people. Since almost half of the 750,000 Virginians were enslaved people who could not vote, the actual representational deviation was about 6.5 to 1. The one thing Madison never imagined, though, was that a 6.5-to-1 representational deviation in 1790 would metastasize tenfold into a sixty-five-to-one deviation today, empowering a rural, predominantly white minority of the national voting population to dictate policy in the Senate to the nation's urban majority.

As with the need for political parties, here's what the Founders did not—and could not have—foreseen. Over more than two hundred years, the United States has evolved from a small agricultural nation hugging the Atlantic coast with fewer than 4 million people (more than one-third of whom were enslaved) into the world's preeminent industrial and financial power with more than 326 million people spanning the North American continent. Massive, densely populated urban centers dedicated to finance and industry emerged in many states; while other, more sparsely populated states remained primarily rural and agricultural. But, no matter how the national population has grown, and has ebbed and flowed from state to state, from farm to factory, and from town to city, the Constitution's mandate that each state continue to elect the same number of senators regardless of population currently awards an enormous representational advantage to the folks living in rural America. This edge is particularly dramatic when it comes to electing presidents via the distorted Electoral College and confirming Supreme Court justices in the malapportioned Senate.

Short of scrapping the entire Constitution and starting over, though, there's probably nothing that can be done about the profoundly undemocratic Senate. The 1787 Constitution has only three explicitly non-amendable provisions: a right to import enslaved people until 1808; a ban on per capita taxation (to protect slave owners against being taxed out of existence); and the right of each state to enjoy "equal suffrage" in the Senate. While, under Article IV of the Constitution, it would be theoretically possible—and perfectly constitutional—for states with large urban populations such as California, Illinois, Texas, Florida, Pennsylvania, and New York (the six states currently suffering a 20-1 representational deficiency in the Senate) to divide like paramecia into multiple states with two senators each giving urban America fairer Senate representation, don't hold your breath waiting for the moving parts to align. Congress would have to grant permission and the affected states would have to agree on boundaries. Although it's happened five times in the nation's history—Vermont from New York (1791); Kentucky from Virginia (1792); Tennessee from North Carolina (1795); Maine from Massachusetts (1820); and West Virginia from Virginia (1863), I doubt that we have the will or ability to act as modern Founders to rescue the Senate from its current undemocratic swamp. While I hope I'm wrong, I'm afraid that we will almost certainly limp into the future with the Founders' internal electoral brakes warped by the utter collapse of fair and equal legislative representation for urban America in the United States Senate.

The drastic imbalance in the Senate translates into a troubling representational imbalance in the Electoral College, established by the Founders to choose the president indirectly in place of a nationwide popular election. Under the Founders' system, voters in each state choose presidential electors, who then meet in Washington, DC, as the Electoral College to select the president. It takes a majority vote in the Electoral College to win the presidency. The Constitution awards each state as many electors as it has representatives in Congress. That's fine when it comes to members of the House of Representatives, all of whom are allocated according to a state's population. But it's a representational disaster when applied to the Senate, which, as we've seen, is radically unrepresentative. The net result is to tilt the Electoral College toward the same sparsely populated rural states that benefit from the Senate's failure to reflect democratic principles of one-person one-vote.

That means there is no guarantee that the winner of the national popular vote will become president. In fact, twice in the last sixteen years, Republican candidates for president—George W. Bush in 2000 and Donald Trump in 2016—have won a majority in the Electoral College while losing the national popular vote. Can you imagine what we would say about another nation's democratic legitimacy if that country chose powerful presidents who had been repeatedly rejected by a clear majority of the voters?

When you combine the representational unfairness in the Senate with the representative distortion in the Electoral College, you emerge with Donald Trump, a minority president who lost the national election by three million votes, representing a Republican Party that lost the popular vote in six out of the last seven national elections—1992, 1996, 2000, 2008, 2012, and 2016—empowered to appoint Neil Gorsuch and Brett Kavanaugh as swing Supreme Court justices, who are then confirmed by fifty-one Republican senators representing fewer than 40 percent of the nation's population. What would Washington, Madison, and Jefferson think about such sustained representational failure?

And it gets even worse. The one place where the Founders' internal electoral braking system should still work is the House of Representatives, elected every two years to provide an accurate mirror of the incredibly diverse society it is intended to "represent." Since 1962, under Article I, Section 2 of the Constitution and the one-person one-vote principle of *Baker v. Carr*, every member of the House of Representatives must represent an equal number of constituents (currently, about 700,000 persons). So, ideally, the House should function as the Founders' classic self-limiting democratic institution, a body fairly representing diverse interests of relatively equal political weight, no one of which can dominate the others. The result should be a legislative body characterized by shifting coalitions, moderation, and compromise.

There's only one catch. The representational integrity of the House of Representatives has been poisoned by an epidemic of excessive partisan gerrymandering—the hyper-partisan drawing of distorted electoral maps designed to lock large numbers of rural and suburban Republican candidates into office, while systematically depriving their Democratic opponents of fair representation in the Congress and the state legislatures. Democrats would love to do it, too, of course, but, except for Maryland, they have lacked the opportunity in recent years.

In many Republican-controlled states, like North Carolina, the boundaries of congressional districts have been carefully drawn so that reliably Republican voters are strategically spread over numerous districts, with just enough Republican votes in each district (usually 55 percent or so) for Republican candidates to be the overwhelmingly likely winners. In such a Republican-leaning district, every Republican vote is important. Democratic voters in the same state are frequently packed into overwhelmingly Democratic urban districts (as much as 80 percent Democratic), where the Democratic candidate predictably wins by an overwhelming majority, but where many of the Democratic votes are "wasted" because they are not needed to win. It's called "packing and cracking."

Given the current Republican gerrymandered district boundaries, in order for the Democratic Party to elect 50 percent of the House of Representatives, the Democrats must garner between 55 and 60 percent of the total national congressional vote. The Founders would wince. As the 2018 congressional elections demonstrate, it's possible for the Democrats to overcome the built-in headwinds and win a majority in the House of Representatives, but it's also important to note how strong the gerrymandering headwinds can be—in North Carolina, for example, in spite of winning statewide, the Democrats couldn't flip a single Republican district, leaving the Republican Party with ten of thirteen congressional seats in a state that voted Democratic.

Worse, in recent years, five Republican justices on the Supreme Court have virtually invited cynical politicians to remain in power by making it as hard as possible for many poor people (often of color) to vote at all. That's where phony voter ID requirements, felon disenfranchisement, and voter registration purge statutes come from. Under the current Supreme Court, the representational breakdown in the House may even get worse. Stay tuned for: (1) Supreme Court acceptance of even more ruthless partisan gerrymanders; (2) Supreme Court approval of an avalanche of phony anti-fraud devices, such as voter ID requirements and purge statutes; and (3) Supreme Court acceptance of efforts by Republican-controlled states to apportion House seats on the basis of citizenship instead of the historical basis of residence, further diminishing the representation of urban America, where large numbers of noncitizens reside (that's why Republicans are trying to add a citizenship question to the 2020 census).

Stay tuned, as well, for a ferocious rearguard defense of felon disenfranchisement in Florida, where for years it has denied the ballot to 25 percent of the black male electorate. The predictably racially discriminatory impact of felon disenfranchisement is what has enabled predominantly rural white Republican voters to retain control of a rapidly urbanizing state. It almost certainly decided the 2000 presidential election.

In 2018, more than 64 percent of Florida's voters overwhelmingly rejected felon disenfranchisement, but there is, as yet, no plan for how to restore the many thousands of historically disenfranchised voters to the rolls. Republican election officials are already making noises about how important it is to slow down the implementation of the referendum. And it's only a matter of time until Republican politicians in Florida and elsewhere try to condition the restoration of voting rights to convicted felons on payments of court fees beyond the reach of poor voters.

Sadly, instead of being a showcase for the Founders' self-checking internal braking system, the current House of Representative has been turned into a partisan swamp. When you add the representational distortions in the Senate and the Electoral College to the gerrymandered House of Representatives, it's as though the Constitution's great Preamble has been hijacked to read: *We, a rural minority of the people, do hereby ordain and establish this blueprint for governing the urban majority.*

Face it: as far as the weak and poor are concerned, there are no longer any reliable self-checking internal brakes on the Founders' train. If anything, today's train is geared to run over the poor folks who live in urban America.

THE EXTERNAL BRAKES

The Founders didn't rely solely on internal brakes. Somewhat reluctantly, they introduced a backup external braking system, empowering independent, politically neutral judges to slow or stop a runaway democratic train. The good news is that the external brakes still work much of the time, especially when personal autonomy—the right to be left alone—is at stake. The bad news is that the external braking mechanism is so damn complex, with so many moving parts, that it has ceased to be reliable in many settings, especially when the right of the weak to equal treatment is at stake.

The Supreme Court is not shy about touting the Court's constitutional brakes as a state-of-the-art, fail-safe system capable of stopping even a runaway populist train traveling at breakneck speed. According to the warranty printed on the back of the train ticket, riding on the American Democracy Express is a relatively risk-free proposition because "when at times the mob is swayed / to carry praise or blame too far," a politically neutral, life-tenured Supreme Court, sworn to enforce constitutional checks on the tyranny of the majority, can be trusted to slow or stop the train before it causes too much damage. The Supreme Court even promises to perform prophylactic maintenance on the braking system by stopping government officials—especially officials of the national government—from acquiring dangerous unilateral power over the train's throttle.

Like too many warranties these days, the Supreme Court's earnest assurances that it is standing by to apply politically neutral brakes on a runaway electoral majority by enforcing the constitutional text isn't entirely accurate. In fact, it comes close to being downright false and misleading. The warranty doesn't tell you that the precise meaning of the most important rights-bearing provisions of the Constitution—including the First Amendment's forty-five-word protection of religion, speech, and press; and the Fourteenth Amendment's guarantee of the "equal protection of the laws"—is almost always up for grabs.

That's nothing new, of course. The meaning of the Constitution's text has always been deeply contested. What is new is the utter breakdown of the internal electoral brakes and the emergence of an immensely powerful president who expresses utter contempt for the very ideas of toleration and mutual respect that undergird our constitutional republic.

The Supreme Court's warranty doesn't tell you that the justices who actually operate the brakes are more divided than ever these days about how to interpret the Constitution's ambiguous text. In the many important Supreme Court cases where the constitutional text is ambiguous, binding Supreme Court precedent is either absent or confusing, and/or prime constitutional values such as autonomy (the right to be left alone) and equality (the right to be treated the same) point in different directions, Republican justices have, over the years, tended to read the ambiguous constitutional text to favor the right of individuals to be left alone, repeatedly protecting the powerful from a host of government regulations aimed at protecting the vulnerable. Democratic Supreme Court justices have tended to read the same ambiguous constitutional text to advance the equality-based interests of the weak, often at the expense of the autonomy of the strong. Despite the Supreme Court's sincere promise of political neutrality, Republican justices are more likely to read the Constitution from the top down, insulating big business, rich campaign spenders, political bosses, dominant racial groups, dominant social groups, insiders, police, the military, and men from government regulations designed to rein in their power. Democratic Supreme Court justices more often read the same text from the bottom up to protect the equality interests of racial and ethnic minorities, gays, women, political and religious dissenters, the poor, immigrants, people seeking the vote, outsiders, consumers, and targets of government suppression.

Don't get me wrong. I am not asserting that Supreme Court justices consciously advance a partisan agenda, although sometimes, as in *Bush v. Gore* (the 5–4 case where five Republican justices gave George W. Bush the presidency in 2000 despite his loss of the popular vote and quite possibly his loss of the crucial Florida vote), it looks like that's what's happening. Nor do I believe that Supreme Court justices consciously align themselves with the strong or the weak. In fact, I believe that almost all the justices who have served in the modern era would pass lie-detector tests about their nonpolitical commitment to "equal justice under law"—the aspirational motto carved on the façade of the Supreme Court building. But the Supreme Court's braking mechanism is so complex, so dotted with branching points requiring the exercise of discretion and choice, that in a close case, I believe that a justice's deeply held values will inevitably affect her views about the relative persuasiveness of the lawyers' arguments.

The truth is that we have two competing Constitutions—one red, one blue—that blink on and off like neon signs depending on which political party controls the Supreme Court. Partisan control of the Supreme Court has flipped only twice since the Civil War: Republicans controlled the Court from 1865 to 1937; Democrats controlled it from 1937 to 1972; Republicans regained control in 1972 and have held it ever since, most recently by unconstitutionally refusing even to consider Merrick Garland, President Obama's moderate Democratic nominee to replace Antonin Scalia. That's really all you need to know to understand the zigs and zags of American constitutional jurisprudence over the past 150 years. Not in every case, every time. But enough cases and enough times to establish an unmistakable pattern.

So, before you put too much trust in the external constitutional brakes on the Democracy Express, it's a good idea to check on whether the justices operating those brakes are dressed in red or blue. As the legal fate of Donald Trump's successful effort to ban millions of Muslims from traveling to the United States demonstrates, knowing which political party controls the Supreme Court will tell you more about whether, when, and for whom the runaway train will be stopped than the constitutional text, the constitutional lawbooks, and all the history tomes in your library.

Most importantly, whatever the Supreme Court's echo chamber says, it's crucial to remember that, over time, it's the people—the passengers on the train—who have the power to decide whether Republican or Democratic justices operate the brakes. I believe that each presidential election and every Senate election operate, in part, as rolling constitutional conventions where the people have a chance to choose between a red Constitution enabling the strong and a blue Constitution protecting the weak. That's why it was so galling to watch a minority president—who lost the presidential election by more than three million votes, who may well hold office only because of his contempt for campaign finance laws and his dalliance with Russian intelligence services, and who represents a political party that has lost the popular vote in six of the last seven national elections—nominate two swing Supreme Court justices likely to cement the red Constitution into place for a generation, who were promptly confirmed by a majority of the Senate representing fewer than 40 percent of the people.

The Supreme Court's vaunted brake warranty also doesn't tell you that it may not apply to runaway populist trains traveling at dangerously high speeds. Despite the Supreme Court's lofty rhetoric, the justices have rarely acted in the teeth of a broad national consensus. Overwhelming patriotic support for World War I translated into Supreme Court decisions affirming criminal convictions and draconian prison sentences for opponents of the war whose only crime was to speak out against it. In the 1920s, overwhelming hostility to communism and other left-wing movements translated into Supreme Court decisions affirming the convictions of so-called "criminal anarchists," guilty of nothing more than espousing radical political views. In the 1930s, after Franklin D. Roosevelt won the 1936 presidential election in a landslide, carrying every state except Maine and Vermont, the Supreme Court promptly installed an entirely new braking mechanism in economic regulation cases that was much more to FDR's liking, abandoning many of its earlier precedents along the way. In the 1940s, a lethal combination of racism and jingoistic World War II patriotic fervor stampeded the Democratic Supreme Court into a 6–3 decision upholding the internment of 120,000 Japanese Americans residing on the West Coast. In the 1950s, a spate of national hysteria fueled by fear of communism translated into Supreme Court affirmances of the conviction and imprisonment of the leadership of the American Communist Party for the crime of being the leadership of the American Communist Party. In the 1960s, faced with initial public support for the war in Vietnam, the Supreme Court upheld long prison sentences for draft card burners. The Warren Court couldn't summon up a single vote for the First Amendment, even though the government conceded that the only reason for enacting a ban on draft card burning was to suppress an effective form of protest. In fact, throughout the decade-long war in Vietnam, the justices never summoned up the will to review the legality of an unconstitutional presidential war in which sixty thousand Americans and upward of two million Asians lost their lives.

In my experience, the Supreme Court is best at enforcing consensus national political and social norms against local outposts of resistance that are out of step with the rest of the nation. It's no coincidence that the Court didn't end state-imposed racial segregation until 1954, after the concept had already been rejected by more than three-quarters of the states. And it wasn't until free speech became a source of national pride in the 1960s that the Court got around to building powerful, maybe too powerful, First Amendment doctrine. The history of the Supreme Court's women's rights jurisprudence looks more like a barometer of national public opinion than a principled exercise in law enforcement. Likewise, the Court's welcome protection of gay rights reflects a dramatic generational change in the nation's response to sexual orientation.

Don't despair, though. The Supreme Court's warranty is neither worthless nor fraudulent. It's just misleadingly broad. In the relatively rare settings where the constitutional text is clear; the much more numerous settings where well-reasoned judicial precedent commands the justices' professional respect; and the occasional settings where the prime constitutional values of autonomy and equality point in the same direction, as they often do in cases involving free speech, religious freedom, the ban on racial apartheid, women's equality, and the protection of gay marriage, I am confident that the Supreme Court will continue to provide a reliable, nonpolitical check on majoritarian excess. In those important settings the brakes will work as advertised, at least in the foreseeable future. So please don't kill all the lawyers—yet.

If, however, our forty-fifth president, craven Republican legislators, and a tame Supreme Court combine to impose the will of the

strong on the backs of the weak, only sustained political involve-
ment on behalf of traditional American values can put the democratic train back on track. It will be a tough job, because, as we've
seen, the democratic deck is stacked against us. But it is far from
impossible if only we use the available tools.

Somehow, we must find the will to act as a re-founding generation. After all, we're not being asked to live up to past generations
who risked their lives by fighting a Revolutionary War to create a
nation, waging a bloody Civil War to end slavery, and enduring
fifty years of hot and cold war to protect the nation against Hitler
and Stalin.

All we have to do is fix the damn brakes.

2

Why the Sudden Concern About Fixing the Brakes?

Most experienced lawyers know that the outcome of hard constitutional cases often turns on who the judge is. I've litigated hundreds of constitutional cases. The defining event in many of them—the tough ones where the constitutional text could be read more than one way, the precedents were murky or nonexistent, and important values such as autonomy and equality pulled in different directions—was the moment when I learned the name of the judge.

Once I knew the judge, I had a pretty good idea of the case's outcome. Not every time. Not every judge. But enough times and enough judges to convince me that a judge's honest assessment of the persuasive power of closely balanced legal arguments is shaped as much by her values as by the inherently persuasive power of the legal arguments.

I never publicly admitted it. No active constitutional litigator dares to blow that whistle if he wants to keep on litigating. Behaving as if the judge is a politically neutral arbiter in search of a single correct legal answer is the price of being taken seriously in the courtroom. So I kept my mouth shut and labored mightily over my legal arguments as if the outcome of every case depended on each turn of phrase and each asserted precedent.

Sometimes it did. Often, raw material for persuasive legal arguments existed that guided a principled judge to a clearly preferable legal result, rendering the judge's values irrelevant. Occasionally, I was surprised at the outcome, when principled judges ruled counter to their values. Most of the time, though, the result was predictable and, tolerably often, admirable. The burst of egalitarian precedents that emerged from the Democratic Supreme Court, especially during the years (1954–68) when Earl Warren, a nominal Republican, was chief justice, has salted the legal system with plenty of powerful legal precedents for protecting the weak. And a steady stream of autonomy-protective precedents decided under both Republican and Democratic courts was always available to keep the government at bay.

But then there was Donald Trump, the only president in recent American history to openly despise the twin ideals—individual dignity and fundamental equality—upon which the contemporary United States is built. When you confront the reality of a president like Trump, the state of both sets of brakes—internal and external—become hugely important because Donald Trump's political train runs on the most potent and dangerous fuel of all: a steady diet of fear, greed, loathing, lies, and envy. It's a toxic mixture that has destroyed democracies before, and can do so again.

It shouldn't come as a surprise that Trump is so adept at exploiting fear and inventing scapegoats. He studied at the feet of the master. We know from Ivana Trump's now sealed testimony at Trump's first divorce trial, backed up by her lawyer, Michael Kennedy, and from the president himself, that for years a younger Donald Trump slept with a book of Adolf Hitler's collected political speeches, published in 1941 as *My New Order*, in a locked cabinet at his bedside. Ugly and appalling as they are, those speeches are masterpieces of demagogic manipulation.

Give Trump credit. He did his homework well and became the twenty-first-century master of divisive rhetoric. We're used to thinking of Hitler's Third Reich as the incomparably evil tyranny that it undoubtedly was. But Hitler didn't take power by force. He used a set of rhetorical tropes codified in Trump's bedside reading that persuaded enough Germans to welcome Hitler as a populist leader. The Nazis did not overthrow the Weimar Republic. It fell into their hands as the fruit of Hitler's satanic ability to mesmerize enough Germans to trade their democratic birthright for a pottage of scapegoating, short-term economic gain, xenophobia, and racism. It could happen here.

I lived through McCarthyism. I passionately opposed the undeclared war in Vietnam. I was on Nixon's enemies list. I served as national legal director of the ACLU during the presidency of Ronald Reagan. Edwin Meese, Ronald Reagan's attorney general, once described the ACLU under my leadership as "the criminals' lobby." But I have never experienced the sense of dread that Trump's behavior as president has unleashed in my mind and heart.

Why does an ignorant, narcissistic buffoon like Trump trigger such anxiety? Why do so many Americans feel it existentially (not just politically) important to resist our forty-fifth president? Partly it's just aesthetics. Trump is such a coarse and appalling man that it's hard to stomach his presence in Abraham Lincoln's house. But that's not enough to explain the intensity of my dread. LBJ was coarse. Gerald Ford and George W. Bush were dumb as rocks. Richard Nixon was an anti-Semite. Bill Clinton's mistreatment of women dishonored his office. Ronald Reagan was a dangerous ideologue. I opposed each of them when they appeared to exceed their constitutional powers. But I never felt a sense of existential dread. I never sensed that the very existence of a tolerant democracy was in play.

Partly it's politics. Most of my career has been devoted to construing the Constitution to protect the most vulnerable among us: racial minorities, religious iconoclasts, political radicals, women, gays, trans people, the poor. Many of Trump's policies threaten to unravel the safety net for the weak that the country has painstakingly woven over the past half century. But Trump's signature political positions, whether taxation, immigration, market deregulation, the environment, or civil rights, are not fundamentally different from the right-wing policies I've struggled against for most of my career. I've always viewed winning and losing on policy—even constitutional policy—as part of a long-term democratic process that would continue no matter how a given skirmish turned out.

Watching Trump work his crowds, though, I see a dangerously manipulative narcissist unleashing the demagogic spells that he learned from studying Hitler's speeches—spells that he cannot control and that are capable of eroding the fabric of American democracy. You see, we've seen what these rhetorical techniques can do. Much of Trump's rhetoric—as a candidate and in office—mirrors the strategies, even the language, used by Adolf Hitler in the early 1930s to erode German democracy.

Please don't misunderstand me. I am not equating Donald Trump with Adolf Hitler. In fact, I'm reluctant to use the names Hitler and Trump in the same sentence. It trivializes Hitler's obscene crimes to compare them with Donald Trump's often pathetic foibles. It is also unfair to Trump to cast him as the epitome of evil rather than as the shallow blowhard he is. While our forty-fifth president loves to play at being the boss, I do not believe that Trump hopes or intends to morph into a dictator with an agenda of evil. What Trump does not appear to understand, though, is that the very act of letting Hitler's genies out of the bottle is playing with the fate of the nation.

Donald Trump's channeling of Adolf Hitler's rhetorical techniques is profoundly dangerous to American democracy not because of Trump's ideas (wrongheaded as many may be), his ignorance (profound as it is), or his disdain for people who do not look or sound just like him (ugly as he makes it appear). It is dangerous because the forty-fifth president, by following Hitler's playbook, risks unleashing forces of ignorance, anger, misogyny, racism, xenophobia, selfishness, bigotry, fear, and greed that, once set free, can unravel the social fabric of a nation.

In January 1933, most Germans were sure that Hitler, an ignorant, loudmouthed, widely derided minority chancellor of the Weimar Republic, either would blow over or could be harnessed as a tool to advance their own self-interested policies. Today, too many Americans also dismiss Trump as an ignorant buffoon who will eventually self-destruct and disappear. Too many others, especially the congressional leadership of the Republican Party, are following the disastrous path set by the German center-right political establishment in its treatment of Hitler, disdaining Trump as an appalling man but viewing him as a useful path to power who can be controlled and then discarded. By the time the German political establishment woke up, Hitler had spread enough rhetorical poison to doom German democracy.

Like Trump, Hitler never won a majority in a free and open election. Despite massive and unprecedented support from Vladimir Putin's Russia, Trump lost the 2016 popular election by approximately three million votes. Trump became president with only 46 percent of the vote, compared to the 48.2 percent share won by Hillary Clinton. He became legally entitled to the presidency only because a total of 77,774 voters spread over three crucial states—Wisconsin, Pennsylvania, and Michigan—enabled him to assemble a majority in the Electoral College.

Since the turnout in the 2016 presidential election was just under 55 percent of the eligible electorate, and since Trump received 46 percent of that vote, only about a quarter of eligible voters actually cast their ballots for Donald Trump (55 percent × 0.46 = 25.3 percent).

That's just a little less than the percentage of the German electorate that turned to the Nazi Party in 1932–33. Unlike the low turnouts in the United States, turnout in Weimar Germany averaged just over 80 percent of eligible voters. Thus, excluding the March 1933 elections, which were administered by the Nazis and badly marred by violence and fraud, in the last free Weimar election in July 1932 that brought the Nazis to power, only about 30 percent of the German electorate actually voted for Hitler (80 percent × 0.37 = 29.6 percent).

Once installed as a minority chancellor in January 1933, Hitler set about demonizing his political opponents, and no one—not the vaunted, intellectually brilliant German judiciary; not the respected, well-trained German police; not the revered, aristocratic German military; not the widely admired, efficient German government bureaucracy; not the wealthy, immensely powerful leaders of German industry; and not the powerful center-right political leaders of the Reichstag—mounted a serious effort to stop him. By the time the Summer Olympics were held in Berlin in 1936, German democracy had been destroyed by a buffoonish laughingstock who had never commanded support from more than 30 percent of the electorate.

How on earth did Hitler pull it off? What satanic magic did Trump find in Hitler's speeches?

An important part of the answer is on display at Yad Vashem, the Israeli Holocaust Memorial in Jerusalem, where two small green plastic cubes sit almost unnoticed on modest display tables, surviving examples of the many thousands of radios distributed by the Nazi Party during the early 1930s. The radios were free, but there was one catch: they could receive only a single frequency. And that frequency carried the undiluted voice of Adolf Hitler, speaking directly to the 30–40 percent of the German population frightened enough, angry enough, disaffected enough, and—let's say it—bigoted enough to embrace the Nazi Party's witches' brew of falsehoods, half-truths, personal invective, threats, xenophobia, anti-Semitism, national security scares, religious bigotry, white racism, exploitation of economic insecurity, and a never-ending search for scapegoats.

In the end, it was Hitler's uncanny ability to exploit those cheap plastic radios to manipulate an adoring and disaffected base, never exceeding 30–40 percent of the population, that destroyed the Weimar Republic and eventually plunged the world into catastrophic war.

Donald Trump's tweets, often delivered between midnight and dawn, are the twenty-first century's technological embodiment of Hitler's free plastic radios. Trump's Twitter account, like Hitler's radios, enables a charismatic leader to establish and maintain a personal, unfiltered line of communication with an adoring political base of about 30–40 percent of the population, many (but not all) of whom are only too willing, even anxious, to swallow Trump's witches' brew of falsehoods, half-truths, personal invective, threats, xenophobia, national security scares, religious bigotry, white racism, exploitation of economic insecurity, and a never-ending search for scapegoats.

The social and economic composition of Trump's core political base eerily mirrors Hitler's: both were (and are) relatively poorly educated; patronized, even disdained by smug, better-educated elites; taken for granted, ignored, or worse by the mainstream political parties; and threatened economically and socially by newcomers who do not look, speak, or believe as they do.

By itself, of course, the fact that the social and economic characteristics of core supporters of both Trump and Hitler resemble each other doesn't mean much. A substantial base of disaffected, insecure, relatively poorly educated citizens, angry at what they perceive as political betrayal and economic injustice, and fearful of losing what's left of their political power, economic privilege, and social status to "others," is a longtime staple of right-wing populist politics. But think of those cheap plastic radios broadcasting the unfiltered, deeply personal voice of an ego-driven, power-obsessed leader, spewing an uninterrupted stream of lies, half-truths, insults, vituperation, and innuendo designed to marginalize, demonize, and eventually destroy opponents. Then think of Donald Trump's odd-hours tweets rattling around inside the heads of millions of his core supporters, spewing an unfiltered stream of racist dog whistles, xenophobic lies, political innuendos, and economic half-truths.

That's not just populist politics. That's a proven recipe for the cult of personality and the specter of mobocracy that consumed German democracy.

Hitler used his single-frequency radios to wax hysterical to his adoring base about his pathological racial and religious fantasies glorifying Aryans and demonizing Jews, blaming Jews (among other racial and religious scapegoats) for German society's ills.

Trump's tweets and public statements, whether dealing with black-led demonstrations against police violence, white-led racist mob violence, threats posed by undocumented aliens, immigration policy generally, protests by black and white professional athletes, college admission policies, hate speech, even response to hurricane damage in Puerto Rico, also repeatedly carry racially tinged messages calculated to divide whites from people of color.

Hitler's radio rants blamed most of Germany's problems on a worldwide conspiracy. He pledged to restore Germany's greatness by redressing the claimed economic and territorial injustices imposed on Germany by the Treaty of Versailles, which ended World War I. Trump uses his tweets to mimic Hitler, promising to "make America great again" and conjuring a dark, conspiratorial world order where a naive, weakened America is being systematically victimized at every turn by shadowy international forces.

Hitler unleashed, and Trump stridently echoes, warnings of an impending cultural Armageddon, in which the values of the (white) West will battle for survival against an onslaught of inferior, alien races from the (nonwhite) East.

Hitler's radio harangues demonized his domestic political opponents, calling them parasites, criminals, cockroaches, and various categories of leftist scum. Trump's tweets and speeches similarly demonize his political opponents. Trump talks about the country being "infested" with dangerous aliens of color. He fantasizes about jailing Hillary Clinton, calls Mexicans rapists, refers to "shithole countries," degrades anyone who disagrees with him, and dreams of uprooting thousands of allegedly disloyal bureaucrats in the State Department, the Environmental Protection Agency, the FBI, and the CIA, who he calls "the deep state" and who, he claims, are sabotaging American greatness.

Both Trump and Hitler maintained a relentless assault on the very idea of objective truth. Each began the assault by seeking to delegitimize the mainstream press. Hitler quickly coined the epithet *Lügenpresse* (literally "lying press") to denigrate the mainstream press. Trump uses a paraphrase of Hitler's lying press epithet—"fake news"—cribbed, no doubt, from one of Hitler's speeches. For Trump, the mainstream press is a "lying press" that publishes "fake news."

Hitler labeled his press opponents as socialist, Jewish, or internationalist, bent on spreading false information to undercut Hitler's positions. Trump's tweets fulminate about an allegedly fraudulent mainstream press in the service of the "elites," a press bent on disseminating "fake news" about him, especially his possible links to the Kremlin.

Trump repeatedly attacks the "failing *New York Times*," leads

crowds in chanting "CNN sucks," is personally hostile to most reporters (he initially refused to fly the White House flag at half-mast
to mourn the murder of five journalists in Annapolis, Maryland,
in late June 2018), and may even have sought to punish CNN by
trying to block a merger between AT&T and Time Warner, CNN's
parent. Trump's hatred of the *Washington Post* translates into ful-
minations against Amazon (owned by Jeff Bezos, who also owns
the *Post*) and efforts to undermine Amazon's use of the U.S. Postal
Service to deliver packages.

Both Trump and Hitler intensified their assault on objective
truth by deriding scientific experts, especially academics who questioned Hitler's views on race or Trump's views on climate change,
immigration, or economics. For both Trump and Hitler, the goal
is (and was) to eviscerate the very idea of objective truth, turning
everything into grist for a populist jury subject to manipulation by
a master puppeteer. In both Trump's and Hitler's worlds, public
opinion ultimately defines what is true and what is false. Trump's
pathological penchant for repeatedly lying about his behavior can
succeed only in a world where his supporters feel free to embrace
Trump's "alternative facts" and treat his hyperbolic exaggerations
as the gospel truth.

Once Hitler had delegitimized the mainstream media by a series of systematic attacks on its integrity, he constructed a fawning
alternative mass media designed to reinforce his direct radio messages and enhance his personal power. Trump is following the same
path, simultaneously launching bitter attacks on the mainstream
press while embracing the so-called alt-right media, co-opting both
Sinclair Broadcasting and the Rupert Murdoch–owned Fox Broadcasting Company as, essentially, a Trump Broadcasting Network.

Once Hitler had cemented his personal communications link
with his base via free radios and a fawning media and had badly
eroded the idea of objective truth, he reinforced his emotional
bond with his base by holding a series of carefully orchestrated mass
meetings dedicated to cementing his status as a charismatic leader,
or *Führer*. The powerful personal bond nurtured by Trump's tweets

and Fox's fawning is also systematically reinforced by periodic, carefully orchestrated mass rallies (even going so far as to co-opt a Boy Scout Jamboree in 2017), reinforcing Trump's insatiable narcissism and his status as a charismatic leader.

Hitler's strident appeals to the base invoked an extreme version of German nationalism, extolling a brilliant Germanic past and promising to restore Germany to its rightful place as a preeminent nation. Trump echoes Hitler's jingoistic appeal to ultranationalist fervor, extolling American exceptionalism right down to the slogan "Make America Great Again," a paraphrase of Hitler's promise to restore German greatness

Hitler all but closed Germany's borders, freezing non-Aryan migration into the country and rendering it impossible for Germans to escape without official permission. Like Hitler, Trump has also made closed borders a centerpiece of his administration. Hitler barred Jews. Trump bars Muslims and seekers of sanctuary from Central America. When the lower courts blocked Trump's Muslim travel ban, he unilaterally issued executive orders replacing it with a thinly disguised substitute that ultimately narrowly won Supreme Court approval under a theory of extreme deference to the president.

Like Hitler, Trump has presided over mass deportations, promising to rid the nation of millions of undocumented aliens who "infest" the country, most of whom are nonwhite. He promises to build a wall on the border with Mexico to stop Latino migration; has reversed decades of immigration policy aimed at reuniting families; sought to end protection of the "Dreamers," young people brought unlawfully into the country as small children by their parents; objected to allowing immigration from Haiti and African countries; and, until forced to change course, stooped to tearing children from their parents to punish desperate efforts by migrants to find a better life in the United States. Thousands of children taken from their parents remain missing today.

Hitler promised to make Germany free from Jews and Slavs. Trump promises to slow, stop, and even reverse the flow of nonwhite immigrants, substituting Muslims, Africans, Mexicans, and

Central Americans of color for Jews and Slavs as scapegoats for the nation's ills. Trump's efforts to cast dragnets to arrest undocumented aliens where they work, live, and worship, followed by mass deportation to rid the country of alleged "Mexican rapists" and other nonwhite immigrants whom Trump characterizes as "thieves and murderers" who bring "death and destruction," echo Hitler's promise to defend Germany's racial identity.

Like Hitler, Trump seeks to use national borders to protect his favored national industrial interests, threatening to ignite protectionist trade wars with Europe, China, and Japan similar to the trade wars that, in earlier incarnations, helped to ignite World War I and World War II.

Like Hitler, Trump aggressively uses our nation's political and economic power to favor selected American corporate interests at the expense of foreign competitors and the environment, even at the price of international conflict, massive inefficiency, and irreversible pollution.

Hitler seized the coal-producing Ruhr. Trump has showered benefits on the nation's carbon-based-energy producers, vitiating years of careful protection of the environment, opening the coastline to energy drilling, and eliminating protection of huge swaths of public land from commercial exploitation.

Hitler's version of fascism shifted immense power—both political and financial—to the leaders of German industry. In fact, Hitler governed Germany largely through corporate executives. Trump has also presided over a massive empowerment—and enrichment—of corporate America. Under Trump, large corporations exercise immense political power while receiving huge economic windfalls and freedom from regulations designed to protect consumers and the labor force.

Hitler despised the German labor movement, eventually destroying it and imprisoning its leaders. Trump also detests strong unions, seeking to undermine any effort to interfere with the prerogatives of management.

Hitler's foreign policy rejected international cooperation in favor of military and economic coercion, culminating in the annexation of the Sudetenland, the phony Hitler-Stalin nonaggression pact, the invasion of Czechoslovakia, and the horrors of global war. Like Hitler, Trump is deeply hostile to multinational cooperation, withdrawing from the Trans-Pacific Partnership, the Paris Agreement on climate change, and the nuclear agreement with Iran, threatening to withdraw from the North American Free Trade Agreement, abandoning our Kurdish allies in Syria, and even going so far as to question the value of NATO, our post–World War II military alliance with European democracies against Soviet expansionism.

Instead, Trump has abused his national security powers to impose tariffs on goods from China, Japan, Europe, Canada, and Mexico. Predictably, each nation has retaliated by imposing reciprocal tariffs on goods produced in the United States, creating massive dislocations in affected industries.

Hitler attacked the legitimacy of democracy itself, purging the voting rolls, challenging the integrity of the electoral process, and questioning the ability of democratic government to solve Germany's problems. He sabotaged the March 1933 legislative elections, barring opposition candidates and unleashing mob violence in the streets, a tactic he repeatedly used to eliminate political opposition. In the end, Hitler turned Germany into a mobocracy, governed by fear and violence.

Trump has also attacked the democratic process, declining to agree to be bound by the outcome of the 2016 elections when he thought he might lose, supporting a massive purge of the voting rolls allegedly designed to avoid (nonexistent) fraud, championing measures that make it harder to vote, tolerating—if not fomenting—massive Russian interference in the 2016 presidential election, encouraging mob violence at rallies, darkly hinting at violence if Democrats hold power, and constantly casting doubt on the legitimacy of elections unless he wins.

Trump may even have mimicked Hitler in attacking democracy frontally by criminally colluding with Russia in influencing the outcome of the 2016 presidential election and then committing felonies by seeking to cover up his crimes.

Hitler politicized and eventually destroyed the vaunted German justice system. Trump also seeks to turn the American justice system into his personal playground. He fired James Comey, a Republican appointed in 2013 as FBI director by President Obama, for refusing to swear an oath of personal loyalty to the president; excoriated and then sacked Jeff Sessions, his handpicked attorney general, for failing to suppress the criminal investigation into the Trump's possible collusion with Russia in influencing the 2016 elections; repeatedly threatened to dismiss Robert Mueller, the special counsel carrying out the investigation; and called again and again for the jailing of Hillary Clinton, his 2016 opponent, leading crowds in chants of "lock her up."

Like Hitler, Trump threatens the judicially enforced rule of law, bitterly attacking American judges who rule against him, slyly praising Andrew Jackson for defying the Supreme Court, and abusing the pardon power by pardoning an Arizona sheriff found guilty of criminal contempt of court for disobeying federal court orders to cease violating the Constitution.

Hitler imposed an oath of personal loyalty on all German judges. Many of Trump's judicial nominees similarly appear to have been selected not for their legal acumen, but for their strongly pro-Trump political views.

Hitler demanded—and was granted—deference from his judges. Trump's already gotten enough deference from five Republican justices to uphold a largely Muslim travel ban that is the epitome of racial and religious bigotry.

Like Hitler, Trump glorifies the military, staffing his administration with layers of retired generals (who eventually were fired or resigned), relaxing control over the use of lethal force by the military and the police, and demanding a massive increase in military spending. But there is one difference. At least Hitler served with some distinction in World War I. Trump, a cowardly phony, parlayed questionable medical claims about alleged bone spurs in his heel into five consecutive medical exemptions from the Vietnam-era draft, forcing some poor kid to fight and maybe even die in his place. Isn't it lucky that Trump's chronic bone spurs miraculously healed once the draft ended, just in time for him to take up golf and tennis?

Like Hitler, Trump openly derides the nation's great cities, especially the people of color and immigrants who make up a significant portion of urban America, repeatedly targeting his racist message to his predominantly white political base in the overrepresented rural "heartland."

Like Hitler, Trump has intensified a disturbing trend that predated his administration of governing unilaterally, largely through executive orders or proclamations. Trump imposed his predominantly Muslim travel ban unilaterally, without legislative cooperation or discussion with immigration officials. Trump's tariffs almost all flow from unilateral decisions that go far beyond any statutory authorization. He announced his ban on transgender participation in the military in a tweet, not even bothering with an executive order. He has aggressively unraveled environmental and health care safety nets by unilateral executive action. Until blocked by two lower federal courts, he tried to unilaterally end the protection for Dreamers, incorrectly branding President Obama's unilateral efforts to shield them from deportation as unlawful.

Like Hitler, Trump claims the power to overrule Congress and govern all by himself. In 1933, Hitler used the pretext of the Reichstag fire to declare a national emergency and seize the power to govern unilaterally. The German judiciary did nothing to stop him. German democracy never recovered. When Congress refused to give Trump funds for his border wall even after he threw a tantrum and shut down the government, Trump, like Hitler, declared a phony national emergency and claimed the power to ignore Congress.

Don't count on the Supreme Court to stop him. Five justices gave the game away on the President's unilateral travel ban. They just might do the same thing on the border wall.

Hitler disdained clear lines of political authority, preferring to set power centers against each other, with Hitler eventually intervening to resolve disputes. Trump also resists orderly lines of governing authority, fostering a chaotic set of competing institutional and personal power centers vying for Trump's approval.

Finally, Hitler propounded a misogynistic, stereotypical view of women, valuing them exclusively as wives and mothers while excluding them from full participation in German political and economic life. Trump may be the most openly misogynist figure ever to hold high political office in the United States, crassly treating women as sexual objects, using nondisclosure agreements and violating campaign finance laws to shield his sexual misbehavior from public knowledge, attacking women who come forward to accuse men of abusive behavior, undermining reproductive freedom, and opposing efforts by women to achieve economic equality.

What are we to make of such parallels? Possibly very little.

As I've suggested, they may simply reflect the inherent nature of populist politics. When you scratch a successful populist movement, like Mussolini's Italy, Perón's Argentina, or Huey Long's Louisiana, there's always a charismatic leader, a disaffected mass, an adroit use of communications media, economic insecurity, racial or religious fault lines, xenophobia, a turn to violence, and a search for scapegoats.

Even if all that Trump is doing is marching to that populist drum, he is unleashing forces that imperil the fragile fabric of a multicultural democracy. But I think there's more. The parallels—especially the links between *Lügenpresse* and "fake news," and promises to restore German greatness and "Make America Great Again"—are just too close to be coincidental. I'm pretty sure that Trump's bedside study of Hitler's speeches—especially the use of personal invective, white racism, and xenophobia—has shaped the way Trump seeks to gain political power in our time. I don't for a moment believe that Trump admires what Hitler eventually did with his power, but he damn well admires—and is successfully copying—the way that Hitler got it.

And that's the problem. Hitler wasn't Hitler until he succeeded in talking enough Germans into giving him unchecked power.

Then it was too late. That's why Trump is so dangerous. If he talks enough Americans into trading the values of toleration and democracy for a Trumpist potion of white supremacy, misogyny, militarism, and xenophobia, it's impossible to predict what might happen next. That's why repair of both sets of constitutional brakes is so important.

The brakes may have to withstand a runaway train the likes of which this country has never seen.

3

Would You Buy This House?

Repairing the Cracks in Democracy's Foundation

On November 9, 1989, when the Berlin Wall finally came down and the Soviet empire imploded, democracy emerged as the victor in a bitter, three-cornered struggle for worldwide supremacy with Nazi fascism and Soviet communism. At that luminous moment, savoring victory in the Cold War and watching jubilant German crowds dismantling the hated wall, democracy seemed the best of all possible political systems in the best of all possible worlds.

Worldwide, the number of countries aspiring to democratic rule peaked at historic levels. In the United States, academics and politicians across the political spectrum competed in delivering smug, self-congratulatory orations celebrating the merits of American democracy. I confess that I delivered more than my share.

After the well-earned burst of democratic triumphalism, reality should have set in. Many of us realized that the task of defending democracy against totalitarianisms of the left or right had been the easy part of the job, precisely because the worst version of democratic governance was—and is—clearly preferable to the best version of government that the Nazis or the Soviets could provide. Understandably, in our zeal to defend democracy against totalitarian challenges from the left and right, we had tended to downplay and even ignore democracy's warts. Once democracy became the only plausible game in town, though, the really hard work should have begun—the job of building and operating versions of democracy that would earn the confidence and commitment of a free people.

Sadly, the United States—indeed, the entire democratic

world—has not done a good job of it. Wherever you look, there is an uneasy feeling that democracy is struggling, failing to fulfill its promise of providing governance that is responsive to the people, supportive of human dignity, and both fair and effective in dealing with society's needs. Instead, throughout the democratic world, including the United States, many millions of voters are disillusioned with a political system that appears to cater to the rich and powerful, responds primarily to organized special interests, ignores the common good, and routinely generates seemingly unbridgeable partisan divides.

I suspect that at the core of the decision by millions of Americans to elect a deeply flawed man as distrusted and disliked as Donald Trump to be our forty-fifth president was a misguided hope that he would sweep away the detritus of what many perceived as a floundering democracy and replace it with something better. However foolish it was to view a snake-oil salesman as a quick fix for a flawed democracy, when millions of ordinary folks begin to lose confidence in their democracy's ability to cope fairly and effectively with the nation's difficult problems, it's all too easy for a charismatic phony to persuade them to give up and to start over with him.

Don't get me wrong. I remain convinced that even a flawed democracy is preferable to totalitarianisms of the left or right, or to currently trendy alternatives like (1) Putin's version of populist authoritarianism (which may well be Trump's preferred mode as well), where a popular, powerful autocrat rules for extended periods of time pursuant to a series of rigged elections until being overthrown; (2) Adam Smith's free-market anarchy (often favored by the rich and powerful), where government, even when fairly elected, is rendered so weak that, to quote Thucydides, the rich "do what they will" and the poor "suffer what they must"; or (3) self-appointed deliberative assemblies (often favored by leftist elites), where self-selected so-called experts (like the vanguard of the proletariat) purport to speak for everyone else.

We cannot, however, continue to close our eyes and ignore American democracy's very real shortcomings. By failing to confront the weaknesses in our democratic system, we sentence ourselves to a parade of demagogic charlatans who will feast on our political discontent. In the end, the only enduring way to resist once and future Trumps of the left or right is to confront the unsightly cracks in the foundation of American democracy and be willing to get our hands dirty in repairing them. Especially the widening cracks in the Founders' self-regulating electoral braking system.

Some stuff probably can't be fixed, at least not without an entirely new Constitution. As I've lamented, not even a constitutional amendment can cure the radically unrepresentative United States Senate, where Wyoming has a sixty-five-to-one apportionment advantage over California. I have two long-shot solutions for the Senate, but don't bet your house on either one. First, the Senate rules could be amended to provide for weighted voting, giving each state an equal number of senators, but weighting the impact of their respective votes to reflect the number of people they represent. So, Wyoming's two senators would cast votes worth 600,000 units and California's two senators would cast votes worth 40 million units. It would take votes representing a majority of the population to enact legislation or confirm Supreme Court justices.

Changing the Senate voting rules would be relatively easy. It would take a simple majority of the Senate. In 2016, Republicans changed the Senate rules governing the confirmation of Supreme Court justices by a simple majority vote, just as the Democrats had earlier changed the filibuster rules governing Senate confirmation of Presidential appointments to executive positions and the lower federal courts. The real problem is whether such a change, which would leave California with much more actual voting power in the Senate than Wyoming, would violate the constitutional mandate to give each state "equal suffrage" in the Senate.

The strongest legal argument in favor of such a change is the longtime existence of supermajority rules, such as the filibuster, that give forty-one senators voting against something a greater proportional vote than fifty-nine senators voting in favor. If, so the argument goes, filibusters do not violate "equal suffrage," neither would weighted voting. The problem is that filibusters don't permanently alter voting power on a state-by-state basis. A senator from the same state can be both helped or hurt by a filibuster. My weighted voting proposal is a one-way street. I award it an A for academic ingenuity, and a D for practical significance.

A more defensible long shot would be the enactment of a congressional statute providing that when the population of an extremely populous state reaches a multiple of the population of the least populous state (let's say twenty to one), the larger state is automatically given the option, exercisable by the state legislature, to divide into two or more states, with the boundary between the two new states to be drawn by the state legislature.

Under current population figures, that would give California, Florida, Texas, New York, Pennsylvania, and Illinois, each with a population exceeding twelve million (twenty times the current population of Wyoming), the option of doubling the number of senators representing their radically underrepresented populations. If the ratio was set at ten to one, nineteen states would qualify for division. As I've noted, the ratio at the Founding between Delaware, the least populous state, and Virginia, the most populous, was approximately six and a half to one if you exclude non-voting enslaved people, or twelve to one if you include them. So all such a statute would do is bring us closer to the Founders' understanding of the malapportioned Senate.

Unlike my weighted voting scheme, there is no constitutional objection to congressional consent to granting states an option to go forth and multiply. Vermont, Kentucky, Tennessee, Maine, and West Virginia were all formed from the territory of an existing state. All that is needed is state permission and congressional assent. Nothing prevents Congress from granting a blanket permission designed to enhance the democratic legitimacy of the Senate. That would leave it up to the state legislatures. Why would they turn down two more Senate seats?

Once a state was divided, the resulting two new states could agree to enter into regional compacts maintaining uniform bi-state programs, so the only thing that would change would be a doubling of the residents' voting power in the Senate. If the Democrats win the presidency and control of both houses of Congress in 2020, the enabling legislation could be enacted on January 21, 2020— turning the United States Senate into something roughly resembling a representative organ again.

Finally, the simple, long-overdue act of admitting the District of Columbia and the Commonwealth of Puerto Rico to statehood would provide enhanced Senate representation to populations of color, mitigating (though not eliminating) the current radical over-representation of white voters in the Senate.

The second unfixable problem is, as we've seen, the malapportioned Electoral College, where smaller rural states have the power to swing the presidential election to the loser of the popular vote. Unlike the malapportioned Senate, the Electoral College can be fixed by a constitutional amendment. In fact, it can be fixed without one, by the simple expedient of a promise, in the form of an interstate compact among states casting a total of 270 electoral votes or more, to cast their electoral votes for the winner of the national popular vote. As with my nonconstitutional fix for the Senate, though, it won't happen. Not enough states would join the compact. I don't see reform of the Senate or the Electoral College succeeding any time soon.

But there is still plenty that can be achieved, even within the confines of the currently stacked system.

WHY DON'T MORE PEOPLE VOTE?

Whether or not the Senate or the Electoral College can be fixed, we start any effort at democratic reform with an unpleasant fact: in most elections in the United States, considerably more than half the eligible voters do not cast a ballot. If you view the act of voting as a referendum on democracy, when you compare the "yes" votes of folks who express confidence in democracy by choosing to cast a ballot with the "no" votes of folks who vote with their feet, American democracy hardly ever wins.

In presidential years, a great turnout barely hits the 60 percent mark. Since the advent of voter registration in the early 1900s, presidential turnout has never exceeded the low sixties. Most of the time it's been considerably lower, often falling below 50 percent.

In 2016, as I've noted, Donald Trump was elected president by 46 percent of the 55 percent of eligible folks who bothered to vote—a "mandate" of 25 percent of the total number of eligible voters. Bill Clinton's "mandate" was even lower. He was elected in 1992 with 44 percent of the 48 percent of the eligible population who bothered to vote—or an anemic 22 percent.

Turnout in congressional elections, especially off-year elections when the president is not on the ballot, is much lower, routinely dropping well below 50 percent and often hovering in the 30s or lower. We celebrated the increased turnout for the 2018 midterms, but only 48 percent of the eligible population actually voted. Only 34 percent of the eligible electorate voted in the crucial 2014 congressional elections when the Democrats lost the Senate, a loss that, two years later, would cost them control of the Supreme Court.

In many state and local legislative elections, the turnout is even lower, occasionally dipping into the twenties and teens, especially if political bosses have gerrymandered the election's outcome by rigging the district lines to make it almost impossible for their favored candidate to lose. Governors routinely are elected in statewide contests where fewer than 40 percent of the voters turn out, allowing under 20 percent of the voters to claim the power of "majority rule."

Participation in most party primaries is scandalously low, sometimes falling below 10 percent of the eligible voters, enabling the extreme 5 percent wings of each major party to dominate a nominating process that is tantamount to election in many gerrymandered districts, or in districts where only one party has a real chance to win.

When you remember that the internal brakes on the Founders' democracy train rely on multiple competing interest groups with relatively equal electoral power checking each other, you see that large-scale failure to vote pours acid on the Founders' brakes. If some folks routinely don't vote, important interest groups are left out of the electoral mix. If enough people don't vote, one relatively small interest group is able to capture the government and use it to impose its will on everyone else, with no internal correction possible. Thus, large-scale nonvoting not only harms the nonvoters but also strikes at the core of the Founders' blueprint for American democracy.

Electoral turnout in today's United States compares very badly with turnout in other countries—Australia, where voting is mandatory, routinely hits 95 percent. Our nineteenth-century presidential elections averaged 75 percent participation, only to plunge after the introduction of voter registration at the beginning of the twentieth century, falling to 44 percent in 1924 before slowly rising to the current 55–60 percent plateau.

The disturbing truth is that such large-scale, serial nonvoting endangers democracy itself. Like health insurance, democracy works best when everyone joins the pool; it works badly, if at all, when too many decide to drop out. When, as in many federal and most state and local elections, more than half the eligible population doesn't vote, the outcome of an election can be controlled by less than 25 percent of the eligible electorate. When, as in many off-year House elections and too many state and local elections, turnout is less than 30 percent, the winner can be chosen by 15 percent of the population. Take the turnout number down to 10 percent in a typical primary, and 5 percent of the voters choose the winner. When the primary is in a one-party area where the general election is a foregone conclusion, the winner of the general election is chosen by 5 percent of the people. When you increase the turnout to 60 percent in a presidential election, it still takes only a shade over 30 percent of the eligible voting population to win, and less if you factor in the undemocratic nature of the Electoral College, which allows someone to become president with a smaller share of the popular vote than her opponent.

A democracy routinely built on an electoral "mandate" that rarely exceeds 25 to 30 percent of the eligible voters, and often plunges to between 5 and 15 percent in legislative elections, simply will not work well. Special interests can too easily capture or dominate the shrunken electorate. Small, transient ideological movements can much more easily entrench themselves through unfair manipulation of the voting rules. The complex discussions and trade-offs needed to craft wise, enduring legislation become more difficult, perhaps impossible, when only a handful of the stakeholders are in the room. Most important, the representative mandate that underlies democracy's moral legitimacy is threatened when elected officials "speak" for between 5 and 25 percent of the electorate.

It would be bad enough if a random 50 percent of the country — or even 75 percent of the country — just didn't pay attention to democracy. At least the 25 to 50 percent of people who were paying attention could be counted on statistically to reflect the needs and concerns of their nonparticipating neighbors. But failing to vote isn't random. Nonvoters are disproportionately young, poor, and people of color, clustered at the low end of the educational and economic scale.

The sad truth is that the American voting electorate today looks disturbingly like the eligible electorate of a bygone era, when formal impediments to voting skewed the electorate toward the better-educated, wealthier slice of the population. Now that we've finally eliminated most of the historic formal barriers to voting, why on earth don't more people go to the polls?

The standard progressive response is to blame the government for cynically erecting hurdles designed to disenfranchise the weak and the poor. The standard right-wing response is to condemn serial nonvoters as not interested or committed enough to take the trouble to vote. Both sides have a point. Given the stakes for democracy, I confess that I find myself annoyed at people who routinely don't bother to vote, especially the nonvoters who saddled us with the Trump presidency. Frankly, if I could figure out who those slackers were, I'd make them wear dunce caps and Trump masks. I know it sounds corny, but too many men and women have died on battlefields defending American democracy, or have been killed by lynch mobs, or have suffered through hunger strikes and endured prison terms and beatings for seeking the right to vote, for the modern beneficiaries of their sacrifices to simply walk away from the legacy—and responsibility—of self-government.

We don't let would-be free riders walk away from their duty to pay taxes, serve on juries, go to school, register for the draft, get vaccinations, buy health insurance, and wear motorcycle helmets. Why do we shrug and let at least half the population walk away—or be pushed away—from its right—and its duty—to vote?

It does not have to be this way. But any serious effort to boost electoral participation cannot concentrate solely on lowering the costs of voting without worrying about the vote's real and perceived value. Focusing solely on the important task of removing or minimizing barriers to voting without also worrying about why so many disaffected nonvoters are unwilling or unable to step over very low thresholds to cast a ballot may lead to formal changes in the voting rules but will not, I fear, trigger significant additional voting. On the other hand, making voting more attractive without also worrying about removing barriers erected to disenfranchise the poor will intensify alienation and further erode democracy's moral legitimacy.

Fortunately, an attainable reform agenda exists that could give American democracy a badly needed shot of adrenaline. And you don't need lawyers or judges to implement much of the plan. An easy place to start would be to shift Election Day from the traditional first Tuesday in November to Veterans Day, already a national holiday that is celebrated a few days later on November 11. What better way to honor those who have suffered to preserve democracy than by turning Election Day into a practical celebration of their sacrifice? Since nothing in the Constitution forces us to vote on any particular day, Congress could change the date for national elections tomorrow. State and local officials don't even have to wait for Congress: state legislatures even have the constitutional power to set "the time, place, or manner" of federal elections unless Congress objects.

Moving Election Day to an already existing holiday such as Veterans Day would make it much easier for working people and folks with child care responsibilities to vote without imposing any new costs on employers. I estimate that shifting Election Day to

Veterans Day would immediately boost turnout by as much as 10 percent, especially if we added significant ceremonies celebrating our veterans' battlefield defense of democracy, honoring the mostly black victims of domestic terrorism who died trying to vote, and the heroic American women who endured violence, hunger strikes, and jail in their century-long struggle for suffrage.

Trump wants to celebrate Veterans Day with a childish military parade costing more than $20 million. The grown-up way to celebrate Veterans Day would be to turn it into a full-scale, working celebration of democracy.

While moving Election Day to Veterans Day would almost certainly boost turnout without costing a dime, it would, I fear, not cure the problem of large-scale, serial nonvoting. Once upon a time, large-scale nonvoting could be explained by a patchwork of laws and practices designed to disenfranchise voters of color, women, newcomers, the uneducated, and the poor. Once upon a time, a combination of racial and gender bars, poll taxes, literacy tests, property qualifications, durational residence requirements, and physical intimidation delivered a white, male, prosperous electorate. But not anymore. Although a new generation of cynical, thinly disguised disenfranchisement techniques—including requiring voter IDs and purging the voting rolls—has evolved in several Republican-dominated states, and while voter registration and the act of voting itself often remain unnecessarily inconvenient, there really is no legal or practical excuse today for the widespread failure to vote. A half-century of sustained Supreme Court precedent has swept away almost all the historic legal barriers to voting, leaving three pieces of unfinished business in the movement for universal suffrage—the continuing political powerlessness of children and the mentally ill, felon disenfranchisement in a few key states, and the anomalous electoral status of permanent resident aliens.

Children first. In allocating political power, we've assumed that children under eighteen, who make up about 25 percent of the population but lack the right to vote, would be virtually (and fairly) represented by their parents and by the community's assumed interest in protecting its young. Sadly, that's just not the way it has worked in practice. The young are perennially short-changed in the American democratic process, precisely because they can't vote. Billie Holiday was right: "Mama may have, and Papa may have, but God bless the child who's got his own." I'd love to have had a chance to talk Madison into creating a political power base for children. Perhaps then we'd treat children's health and education issues as seriously as we treat social security, 401(k)s, and estate taxes.

I don't argue for enfranchising twelve-year-olds, but perhaps we should think about artificially increasing the political power of children by designating specially elected individuals pledged to view them as their constituency—a legislative analogy to the use of special guardians in court.

Ending felon disenfranchisement is the next piece of unfinished democratic business. For too many years, felon disenfranchisement has functioned as a covert way to deny the vote disproportionately to millions of black males caught up in the racially discriminatory criminal justice systems of many states. The practice was imposed as a way to keep formerly enslaved persons from voting. In Florida, for example, felon disenfranchisement was added by racists to the 1868 state constitution to subvert the effort to enfranchise black men. Over the years, the practice operated to assure that 25 percent of otherwise eligible black males were locked out of the democratic process because of brushes with Florida's notoriously racist criminal justice system. Virginia and Kentucky weren't much better. The Supreme Court actually invalidated the practice in Mississippi because it was so clearly racially motivated, but refused to knock it out everywhere.

Thankfully, with no help from the Supreme Court, denying the vote to folks with criminal convictions looks like it's on the way out. Kentucky is the last major holdout. Virginia's Democratic governor ended the practice in 2017. Sixty-four percent of Florida voters overwhelmingly rejected it in 2018. But the struggle is not over. Too many states impose a backdoor disenfranchisement on convicted criminals by denying them the ballot until they pay court costs that can routinely exceed $10,000. A number of states require a complex bureaucratic process before restoring the vote on an individualized basis. Many states deny the vote while on probation or parole. Only Maine and New Hampshire allow voting while incarcerated. And, even when the right to vote is restored, how will folks be put back on the voting rolls? Until now, legal challenges to the racially discriminatory aspects of felon disenfranchisement have failed, whether brought under the Fourteenth Amendment or the Voting Rights Act of 1965. As we'll see, the First Amendment may provide an alternative path to reform, even before the current Republican Supreme Court. It's more likely, though, that ending felon disenfranchisement may turn out to be an important example of how democracy can be repaired by the people with no help from the courts.

Finally, to what extent, if any, should noncitizens, especially permanent resident aliens, play a role in American democracy? Some communities invite permanent resident aliens to vote in local elections of particular importance to them, such as school board contests. But the numbers are small. The European Union provides an interesting model for local participation by resident aliens by permitting all citizens of member countries to vote in many local elections.

Even if they can't vote, should resident aliens be excluded from participating in the electoral process? While resident aliens almost certainly have a right to express themselves in the debate, the Supreme Court has upheld a ban on small campaign contributions in connection with federal elections by aliens residing here on long-term visas.

Should aliens—both documented and undocumented—residing in a community be counted for the purposes of allocating political representation? We have always allocated political representation on the basis of residency, not citizenship. Beware, though. The Trump administration is seeking to add questions about citizenship to the 2020 census, indicating that Republican politicians in states such as Texas, Florida, and Virginia plan to push for excluding aliens from the apportionment process. With so much discrimination against urban America already built into our electoral system, removing political representation for the millions of noncitizens residing in the nation's great cities would doom urban America to the status of permanent colonies governed by rural states.

What role, if any, may or should foreigners living abroad, or foreign governments themselves, play in our electoral process? Under a 1965 Supreme Court precedent, *Lamont v. Postmaster General*, Americans enjoy a First Amendment right to hear political or electoral speech from abroad, even when it is sponsored by a foreign government. But, under a 1987 Supreme Court precedent, *Meese v. Keene*, Americans also have a First Amendment right to know the origin and source of political or electoral speech from abroad.

During the 2016 presidential elections, Russians intelligence agents appear to have engaged in a massive covert effort to support the candidacy of Donald Trump, mounting an extensive social media campaign replete with troll farms and phony posts designed to inflame Trump's base and discourage potential supporters of Hillary Clinton from turning out to vote. The Russians lied about their identities, making the legal issue easy. It's clearly a felony for a foreign speaker—whether an individual or a government agent—to deceive his American audience about the true source of electoral speech. The only real legal question is whether the Trump campaign, including the president, knew of, and/or cooperated with, the Russian disinformation operation. That's what the Mueller investigation is all about. We'll look more closely in chapter 7 at President Trump's possible criminal vulnerability for playing footsie with the Russians during the 2016 presidential campaign and then, once he had been elected, obstructing the grand jury's investigation.

Finally, while getting rid of cynical impediments to voting—such as statutes that require voter ID cards under the phony pretext of preventing fraud, and statutes mandating the purging of voter rolls—must be a priority, I've become convinced that the problem of large-scale failure to vote lies much deeper. Unless we insert a chip that responds to a voter's thoughts, the act of voting will always require some effort. The sad truth is that many people just won't vote if they believe that the value of their vote is lower than the cost of casting it. Here are a couple of modest proposals for increasing the perceived value of voting (a few of which may be worthy of Jonathan Swift).

American elections are awash in cash. Candidates can't wait to peddle themselves to the top 1 percent. The top 1 percent can't wait to buy influence. Why not cut poor voters in on the game in a way that puts a little cash in their pockets? Maybe we should just let voters, especially low-income voters, sell their votes to the highest bidder. Since we already operate an electoral bazaar that invites wealthy individuals and business corporations to buy influence and outcomes, and encourages, even forces, candidates to put themselves on the auction block, a free market in votes would simply make our corrupt election process just a little less hypocritical, while funneling some of the cash to folks who need it.

Why not think of an election as an income-redistribution program that funnels money from the rich to the poor, instead of the current political system devoted to transferring money from the poor to the rich? Imagine what a vote would bring in a swing state in a presidential year. How much would you arrange to pay to assemble the 77,800-odd votes that gave Trump the presidency?

If openly buying and selling votes is a bit too crass for you, at least let folks freely assign their votes to authorized, fully revocable proxies—individuals or organizations—that would compete in promising to cast the votes wisely and in the voter's best interest. Corporate shareholder elections routinely permit carefully regulated proxy solicitors to assemble the right to cast the votes of most shareholders. Why not allow competing proxy solicitors to assemble the right to cast votes in a political election, especially in primary elections, where low turnouts of between 5 and 10 percent are so destructive and such a disgrace?

While such a fully revocable proxy solicitation process would, of course, risk increasing the already disproportionate role played by money in our elections, to say nothing of risking fraud, at least poor people, who are currently left out of the democratic process, would either get something tangible for their votes; or, at a minimum, be assured that their votes were being assembled and cast in their best interest.

Maybe we should resort to a little bribery. Why not reward voters for their civic engagement by allowing them to go to the head of lines in government offices, airports, the DMV, and post offices? How about voter discounts at national parks? Maybe voters should get their tax refunds first? Why not accelerate passport issuance for voters? How about conditioning access to highway HOV lanes on voting? Maybe we should link voting to a modest tax credit, provide for lower bridge and tunnel tolls, or arrange for small public utility discounts?

Maybe American Express or Chase should create a voting-linked perk on your credit card? How about a premium internet subscription from Facebook or Google, or cheaper cellphone use? How about a year of Amazon Prime? Perhaps the private sector should reward voters by holding post–Election Day sales that provide special discounts for voters? Maybe early boarding or airline upgrades should be a reward for voting?

Or maybe we should just get over it and compel voting, as in Australia, where voter turnout routinely exceeds 95 percent. We could easily shift our voting system from the current opt-in version, which requires a voter to perform a series of mildly annoying tasks in order to register prior to the election, to an opt-out system, which requires voting unless the voter performs the mildly annoying task of "unregistering" for reasons of conscience.

We use the opt-out process for jury service, registration for the military draft, vaccinations, and compulsory public education. Why not voting?

Short of compulsory voting with the ability to opt out, why shouldn't the government at least have the duty to assemble the rolls of eligible voters without requiring the extra step of voter registration? That's the way things were done in the nineteenth century, before the advent of voter registration. That's the way it's done in virtually every other serious democracy. There wouldn't be too much of a burden on the government. Just build into every contact between the individual and the government, including high school graduation, getting or renewing a driver's license, getting a social security card, a Medicare document, or a passport, filing a tax return, reporting for jury duty, registering for the draft, or visiting a national park, the automatic transfer of registration information to appropriate election authorities.

At a minimum, why not allow voter registration to occur simultaneously with voting (often called same-day voter registration)? There's no risk of fraud, since the first vote you cast under same-day registration can be deemed a provisional ballot subject to post-election verification. States such as Oregon and Minnesota that have shifted to same-day voter registration routinely enjoy a significant spike in voter turnout, especially by poor voters. The cynic in me believes that's probably the reason so few states have adopted same-day registration. The last thing that many pols want is a destabilizing influx of large numbers of new, unpredictable voters.

Finally, it's an embarrassment that the richest nation in the world won't spend enough money to assure competent administration of our elections and has failed to develop voting machinery capable of counting our votes safely and accurately. Even something as mundane as allowing early voting, voting by mail, and/or convenient absentee balloting gets caught up in political controversy and administrative incompetence.

If we are not prepared to offer financial sweeteners to induce folks to vote, turn voting from a right into a duty, or tinker with the voter registration and electoral systems, we can increase the perceived value of voting by making voting intrinsically more important. Not only would that induce folks to vote, but it would rejuvenate democracy for everyone else.

Given the diminished practical importance of a single individual's vote in too many current elections, especially in elections where the outcomes have been rigged in advance by political bosses, the real question is not why so many Americans don't vote; it's why so many of us *do*. Don't be fooled by the large number of very close elections in genuinely contestable districts. Genuinely contestable districts are a rarity. In more than 90 percent of the elections for

Congress, most of the elections to the fifty state legislatures, and most local elections, the almost certain winner of the general election is known well in advance. Sometimes the outcome is rigged by the adroit manipulation of district lines. Sometimes the winner is predetermined by the tendency of like-minded voters to live close together. But rarely is the winner dictated by the voters themselves in a genuinely contestable election. The best that most voters can do is to ratify a choice made for them by the pols.

Voting in such a rigged election is not meaningless. Exercising the right to vote, even when it's been reduced to a formality, is an assertion of individual dignity and an expression of confidence in democracy. It also keeps the pols honest by forcing them to subject their decisions to public scrutiny. Most important, though, the act of voting even though you already know who will win is a tribute to how deeply many Americans revere democracy. It is, frankly, heartening that so many Americans care enough about democracy to continue to participate in its rituals in rigged legislative elections and uncontestable Electoral College contests long after voting in those elections has been drained of practical importance.

I believe, though, that the perceived diminished value of a vote is why it is so difficult to marshal real enthusiasm for voting among those who historically have not voted. In my experience, serial nonvoters will not vote in large numbers, no matter how low the costs, if they view voting as simply a ritual, not an exercise of real power. Thus, while keeping the perceived costs of voting as low as possible is very important, the real key to the problem of widespread nonvoting is increasing the actual and apparent worth of the vote by making votes count again in genuinely contestable elections.

Non-contestable legislative elections come in two flavors—natural and artificial. A substantial number of non-contestable elections are "naturally" baked into the geography of places where large numbers of politically like-minded people live close together. In the inner-city electoral districts of many urban areas, for example, it is often impossible to find enough likely Republican voters to generate genuinely contestable two-party elections. Similarly, in many rural or extremely wealthy enclaves, there are often not enough Democrats to hold a genuinely contestable two-party legislative election.

While it's true, of course, that what looks like "natural" sorting of politically like-minded people into dense population pockets is often the result of generations of housing discrimination, manipulation of zoning laws, mortgage redlining, poor public transportation, and economic inequality, once single-party inner-city or gated suburban communities have become established, for whatever reasons, it's often impossible to draw electoral lines that will deliver genuinely competitive general elections.

But that does not mean that the residents of inner cities, rural farming towns, or gated communities are doomed to a steady diet of meaningless, noncompetitive elections. Voting systems exist capable of transcending geographical sorting. The two that are best known are proportional representation (allocating elected positions in accordance with the percentage of the vote that each party obtains) and multi-member districting (where a large geographical unit elects multiple representatives).

Every vote counts in a system of proportional representation. Almost every vote can be made to count in a multi-member district. Let's assume that New York City elects ten members of Congress and that New York State elects twenty-seven. If we adopted proportional representation in New York City and the popular vote there was 90 percent Democratic to 10 percent Republican, the city's congressional delegation would be nine Democrats and one Republican, but every vote would count. If the Republicans mounted a particularly strong showing, they could pick up one or two additional seats. If the Democrats surged, they could shut out the Republicans altogether.

Statewide, the impact would be even more dramatic. Let's assume a 60 percent to 40 percent Democratic-Republican split, with a twenty-seven-member congressional statewide delegation that included fifteen Democrats and twelve Republicans. It wouldn't take too many statewide votes to shift the allocation in one direction or another, putting an obvious premium on going to the polls, and an obvious penalty for staying home.

If proportional representation is too radical for your taste (though before you condemn it as too radical, you should know that Germany, France, Italy, and Israel use it), geographical sorting could also be made democratically contestable by expanding the boundaries of existing single-member districts, creating multi-member districts, and allowing each voter to cast as many votes as there are vacancies. Voters can choose to spread their votes among the candidates or to give additional votes (or even all their votes) to a single candidate. This system, called "bullet voting," is already in use in many state and local settings.

A third alternative, preferential voting, is made possible by the computerization of vote counting. Under a system of preferential voting, numerous candidates run in a large, often multi-member constituency. Voters are encouraged to rank the candidates in order of preference. Candidates receiving a majority of first-place votes are immediately elected. If no candidate receives more than 50 percent of the first-place votes, the candidate with the fewest first-place votes is eliminated, and her second-place votes are allocated among the remaining candidates. The process is repeated until one candidate receives more than 50 percent of the votes. It's the process that Maine uses to elect members of Congress.

Unlike our present winner-take-all system, which tilts toward the most extreme candidates, the various versions of preferential voting tend to benefit moderate candidates.

Unfortunately, Congress has needlessly limited the states' power to experiment with at-large or multi-member congressional districting. In 1967, in a commendable effort to protect newly enfranchised black and Latino voters, Congress required that all its members be elected from single-member districts. Congress was probably trying to stop racists from taking pockets of minority voters and submerging them in at-large or multi-member districts where whites voters would outnumber them. But a technique—known as cumulative or "bullet" voting—can protect minority voters in a multimember or at-large district by allowing each voter to cast as many votes as there are vacancies to fill, and then allowing them to cast all their votes for a single candidate. Do the math. It would allow minority voters to self-organize and elect a candidate of their choice. It's time to repeal the 1967 statute and give the power to experiment back to the states, with a proviso that all multi-member or at-large congressional districts must adopt bullet voting. Fortunately, the 1967 ban does not stop the states from experimenting with preferential voting. Maine uses it today and makes every vote matter.

The irony is that the Founders used multi-member districts as a common way of electing the members of Congress. It was routine in the early 1800s for the representatives from a state to be elected in a single, at-large election. It wasn't until after the Civil War that at-large or multi-member congressional districts became rare, largely because we had not yet invented bullet voting. Maybe it's time to bring multi-member congressional districts back. Congress could do it tomorrow.

Although I would consider it a long shot, it's even possible that a state could insist on experimenting with at-large or multi-member congressional districting allowing bullet voting, even in the teeth of the 1967 congressional statute banning it. But that's a question for the federalism issues discussed in chapter 9.

Even under a single-member, winner-take-all system, it's possible to inject genuine choice into an election district that is overwhelmingly controlled by one or another political party by making sure that the nominating process is genuinely contestable. The major-party nominating process was once run by political bosses. That wasn't all bad. Professional politicians tended to choose moderate candidates with the best chance of winning the general election. As fewer and fewer general elections became genuinely contestable, however, the pols' incentive to choose moderate, balanced tickets decreased. Once they didn't have to worry about fielding the strongest candidate in order to win a contestable general election, the smoke-filled-room candidate selection process became deeply corrupt and wholly unmoored from voter choice. That's the point where wealthy special interests were able to exercise almost uncontrollable leverage: buying candidates who promised to advance their interests, with those candidates then guaranteed to win the noncompetitive election.

Faced with such a corrupt process, most states have done away with the old boss-controlled nominating process, opting for primary elections that place the power to choose candidates with the voters, not the party bosses. The results have been mixed. As we've seen, voter turnout in primary elections is notoriously low, often falling below 10 percent of the eligible electorate, allowing small blocs of ideologically driven voters to drive both parties further apart by selecting candidates at the extreme left or right, and punishing moderates in the center. In today's political world, the threat of a bruising, expensive primary dominated by a small ideological bloc can drive sitting legislators in both major parties to the extremes, even if they long to move to the center. It's why no Republican officeholder dares to cross or even criticize President Trump. It's why so many moderate Republican legislators have chosen to retire. When, as now, members of Congress fail to perform their checking role because they fear retaliation from the president in the form of a primary contest dominated by a small ideological minority, a dangerous concentration of power is created in the hands of a president.

Since moving nominations back to the corrupt bosses is, for me, a democratic nonstarter, we should concentrate on breaking the existing ideological stranglehold on the primary process. The best way to do it is by increasing voter participation in primary elections so that 5 to 10 percent of the eligible electorate can't dominate the process. My not-so-facetious suggestion is that we use proxy solicitors, perhaps armed with a little cash, to drive up the value of primary voting.

If you don't want to experiment with proxies in the general election, how about using proxy solicitors in primaries, to make sure the political center is heard? A political party choosing a candidate isn't all that different from shareholders electing a board of directors. Proxies and proxy solicitors have been used successfully in corporate elections for many years. Why not give them a try in primary elections?

If that's too radical for your taste, there is a more traditional way to rescue primaries from the ideological extremes: by opening them to as many voters as possible. The more primary voters there are, the harder it is for the extreme wing to dominate the outcome. When primaries were imposed on them, many powerful political leaders sought to retain control of the nomination process by adopting "closed" primaries, open only to enrolled members of the party. New York and Illinois, states with powerful political machines, took the closed primary process even further by requiring an extensive waiting period before a newly enrolled party member could vote in a primary. New York snuck an eleven-month waiting period past a divided Supreme Court. I know. I lost the case 5–4. Illinois set the waiting period at twenty-three months, effectively freezing out new voters and making it almost impossible to mount a successful primary challenge. That was too much even for the Supreme Court.

Check your state's rules about who can participate in primaries. If independents, new voters, and members of other parties are frozen out, the outcomes of primary elections in your state will either drift to the extremes or mirror what the bosses want. Either way, the primary will have failed to enhance voter choice.

One antidote is a move to "open" primaries—full or partial. Many states have adopted partially open primaries, allowing independents and first-time voters to participate even if they are not formal members of the party. A larger number of states have adopted fully open primaries, where any registered voter can participate. California even sought to allow all voters to skip back and forth, candidate by candidate, from one major party to another in a single "blanket" primary, designating one preferred candidate for each office regardless of party affiliation.

It worked: California turnout spiked, candidates became more moderate, and the public's faith in democracy ticked up. Alas, the Supreme Court shut down the blanket primary because, according to five Republican justices, it violated freedom of association by permitting non–party members too much influence in selecting a party nominee. That leaves the Washington State primary, where all candidates regardless of party membership run in a single non-partisan primary with no party labels, with the top two vote-get-ters qualifying for the general election ballot, as the best available option for increasing voter participation in the nominating process.

The Supreme Court has upheld the top-two Washington State process, as long as there is no confusion about the party affilia-tion of the candidates. The top-two single primary system—or, at a minimum, genuinely open primary elections held by each major party—is our best bet for bringing democracy and voter choice into "naturally" uncontestable single-member, winner-take-all districts.

The second flavor of uncontestable election is "artificial." At least half, probably more, of the country's uncontestable legisla-tive districts are "artificial," the result of partisan gerrymandering— careful manipulation of district lines to create rigged election districts where, based on voter registration and past electoral pat-terns, the candidate of one major party starts out at least 10 percent-age points ahead of any potential opponent. While it's theoretically possible for the handicapped candidate to make up the 10 percent difference, it's also theoretically possible for pigs to fly.

When a gerrymandered district starts out 60–40 percent in fa-vor of one of the major party candidates, political scientists label it as a "landslide" district. When the spread is 55–45 percent, they call the district "safe." The few districts that come in at 53–47 or 54–46 percent are labeled "contestable," while a 52–48 percent spread is called a "swing" district.

Take a good look at the party registration numbers in the con-gressional districts and state legislative districts in your state. See how many are close enough to fit into the "swing" or "contestable" slots. You'll be both astonished and disheartened to see how rare it is for you to have a genuinely contestable legislative election, one in which voters, not political bosses, decide the outcome. The usual game these days is for the dominant political party in a state to engage in "pack and crack"—taking advantage of modern tech-nology and data collection to draw lines that pack as many of their opponents as they can into a relatively few landslide districts, while cracking the rest into "safe" districts dominated by the current majority. That allows the dominant party to skew the outcomes of enough legislative elections to entrench its majority for the foreseeable future, even if the political winds change.

As we've seen, only an electoral hurricane can upset a well-done partisan political gerrymander. In 2018, in Republican-gerrymandered North Carolina, 53 percent of the eligible voters turned out, with Democrats winning four statewide races (one state Supreme Court seat, giving Democrats a 5–2 majority; and three intermediate appeals court seats), polling about 50 percent of the statewide vote. But the state's Republican-gerrymandered congressional districts performed exactly as expected—three overwhelming Democratic wins; and ten relatively close Republican victories. So in a state tilting Democratic statewide, voters elected ten Republicans to the House from thirteen districts.

Nowadays, such gerrymanders are primarily a Republican game, but the Democrats did it for years. The single most important step in increasing the worth of the vote in American democracy would be to outlaw excessive partisan gerrymandering. And to do that you don't need lawyers or the Supreme Court's permission.

One approach, which has worked in California, Colorado, and Arizona, is to use nonpartisan (or, sometimes, bipartisan) districting commissions to draw fair district lines that seek to enhance contestability and produce a legislature that roughly reflects the political complexion of the state. The problem, of course, is that political bosses don't want to let go of their stranglehold on the electoral process. One way of going around them is by referendum or initiative. Check to see whether in your state it would be possible to leapfrog the boss-controlled state legislature to place a nonpartisan districting commission before the voters. Arizona voters did exactly that, and the idea was overwhelmingly embraced by the electorate. The Supreme Court upheld it.

If it's impossible or too expensive to follow the referendum route, the issue can be projected into political debate by having a sympathetic legislator introduce a bill establishing the nonpartisan commission, forcing each member of the legislature to take a stand one way or the other. The problem is getting the issue to an up-or-down vote in the teeth of opposition from the pols, who don't want to create a clear issue for the voters. If an up-or-down vote is blocked, once the nonpartisan reapportionment issue is on the state's political radar, it should be possible to launch a slate of highly prominent state legislative candidates who would pledge to enact a fair, nonpartisan districting process and then resign and return to private life, forcing a new election under the new, fair system. Imagine the power of such a single-issue citizen-powered reform slate.

Finally, there's the courts. Thus far, the Supreme Court has declined to intervene in political gerrymandering cases. Four Republican Supreme Court justices have consistently ruled that partisan gerrymandering can't be dealt with judicially because it is impossible for judges to decide whether a partisan gerrymander is too "unfair" or too "unequal." Four Democratic justices have consistently argued that judicially manageable criteria exist that identify when a political gerrymander has gone too far. One justice—Justice Anthony Kennedy—agreed that while political equality doesn't provide an adequate standard because it's too subjective, the First Amendment might provide adequate guidance.

Hopes were high in the 2017 term of the Supreme Court that Justice Kennedy would use his power as the swing justice to provide a way out of the partisan gerrymandering swamp. Instead, he joined his four Republican colleagues in ducking the issue yet again, voting to dismiss partisan gerrymandering cases from Wisconsin and Maryland on technicalities and then stepping down from the Court at eighty-two years of age.

President Trump's nominee to replace him, Judge Brett Kavanaugh, is a Republican stalwart who is likely to join his four Republican colleagues in continuing to reject equality-based challenges to partisan gerrymandering. It's a long shot, but my sense is that the only chance at persuading a Republican-dominated Court to outlaw excessive partisan gerrymandering is to follow Justice Kennedy's advice and to couch it as a First Amendment issue. I have long believed that excessive political gerrymandering (indeed, any interference with the right to vote) violates the First Amendment.

To my mind, voting is the quintessential act of political expression and association. As such, it deserves intense First Amendment–based judicial protection.

The Founders' Constitution, drafted in 1787, has at least two embarrassing holes in it. For starters, unlike the roughly contemporaneous French Declaration of the Rights of Man, it says absolutely nothing about equality. Not a word. How could it, when the very creation of the new American nation depended on a bargain with the devil about the perpetuation of slavery?

Nor did "equality" get mentioned in the first Bill of Rights, ratified in 1791, which brilliantly protects the individual's right to be let alone (individual autonomy) but continues to ignore the right of all persons to be treated by the government as an equal. The concept of equality does not make its way into the Constitution until after the Civil War with the adoption of the Thirteenth Amendment in 1865 (barring slavery), the Fourteenth Amendment in 1868 (guaranteeing equal protection of the laws to all persons), and the Fifteenth Amendment in 1870 (barring racial discrimination in access to the ballot). In chapter 4, we'll look at the doctrinal consequences of giving autonomy a seventy-five-year constitutional head start over equality.

The second embarrassing hole in the Founders' Constitution directly impacts democracy. The 1787 Constitution, the world's oldest continuous charter of democratic governance, doesn't say a word about the right to vote. Neither does the 1791 Bill of Rights.

I like to think that the Founders punted on the voting issue, the way they punted on equality, because they couldn't bring themselves to codify the then-prevailing, extremely narrow idea of the franchise that excluded women, Jews, Muslims, Native Americans, free people of color, and the poor. I choose to believe that, faced with such an unappealing political reality, the Founders opted to remain silent about voting, leaving the constitutional power to expand the franchise to the future. All in all, the future responded well. Eleven of the seventeen constitutional amendments since 1791 have tried the fill the hole in the Constitution where the right to vote should be. The Twelfth Amendment, adopted in 1804, requires separate Electoral College ballots for president and vice president to prevent a recurrence of the Electoral College tie between Thomas Jefferson and his running mate, Aaron Burr, that almost capsized the election of 1800.

Section 2 of the Fourteenth Amendment experimented with a congressional apportionment formula designed to pressure southern states into allowing recently freed people of color to vote. The experimental formula was never tested because it was superseded two years later by the Fifteenth Amendment, outlawing racial discrimination in access to the ballot. Ironically, the only impact of Section 2 of the Fourteenth Amendment has been to provide a tortured constitutional fig leaf for continuing felon disenfranchisement, a principal technique for preventing black men from voting.

The Seventeenth Amendment (1913) provided for the direct election of senators, taking the power away from deeply corrupt state legislatures. The Nineteenth Amendment (1920) outlawed gender discrimination in access to the ballot. The Twentieth Amendment (1933) shortened the "lame-duck" period that elapses between the November election and the entry into office of newly elected presidents and members of Congress. Originally, the old lame ducks served until March. The Twentieth Amendment seats the new Congress on January 1 and the newly elected president in mid-January. The Twenty-Second Amendment (1951) imposed a two-term limit on the president. The Twenty-Third Amendment (1961) allowed residents of the District of Columbia to vote in presidential but not congressional elections. The Twenty-Fourth Amendment (1964) outlawed the poll tax, which had required voters to pay a fee to vote. The Twenty-Fifth Amendment (1967) clarified presidential succession if a president becomes unable to discharge his or her duties. The Twenty-Sixth Amendment (1971) protected persons eighteen years or older from age discrimination in access to the ballot.

But no constitutional amendment talks about a general right to vote or run for office.

Given the textual hole where the right to vote should be, for most of its existence the Supreme Court said little or nothing about a constitutional right to vote. Apart from a series of important cases seeking to prevent discrimination against voters of color in violation of the Fourteenth and Fifteenth Amendments, the Court for more than 150 years made no serious attempt to protect the rights to vote, run for office, and/or enjoy fair political representation, leaving vulnerable members of the electorate to the tender mercies of local politicians. The result of the Supreme Court's initial inaction was massive denial of voting rights, especially to voters of color, the hobbling of third parties, rampant malapportionment in favor of rural America, and widespread political gerrymandering by both parties.

The constitutional ground rules changed in 1962, with the Supreme Court's decisions in *Baker v. Carr* and *Reynolds v. Sims*, the famous "one person, one vote" cases, requiring all elected legislators (except United States senators) to represent a roughly equal number of constituents, currently between 700,000 and 750,000 for each House district.

Important as the doctrine of "one person, one vote" is, the unmistakable, if implied, message sent by the justices' opinions in *Baker* and *Reynolds* was even more important—the Court's acceptance of responsibility for the care and feeding of equal participation in the American democratic process. In the more than fifty years since the Supreme Court's seminal decision in *Baker*, the Court has invoked the concept of equality embedded in the Fourteenth Amendment as a backdoor way to protect the general right to participate in the democratic process. The Court's equality-based reasoning is deceptively simple. If, a majority of the justices reasoned, some people are allowed to vote, run for office, or be represented in the legislature, everyone else must, as a matter of constitutional equality, be allowed to exercise a similar fundamental right, unless the government produces an overwhelmingly persuasive explanation for any unequal political treatment.

Since, as a practical matter, at least one person is almost always going to be allowed to vote, the Court's equality reasoning functions usefully as a de facto equality-based guarantee of everyone's right to vote, as long as the Court insists upon a highly persuasive explanation for denying someone the equal enjoyment of the fundamental right to participate in the democratic process. In the decade following *Baker v. Carr*, the Court did just that, requiring government to prove that any law denying someone an equal opportunity to participate in the democratic process was genuinely necessary to advance a "compelling" governmental interest that could not be advanced by "less drastic means," a carbon copy of the so-called strict scrutiny test used in many First Amendment cases.

Strict scrutiny is almost always lethal. Whether the context is First Amendment protection of autonomy or Fourteenth Amendment protection of equality, it's been virtually impossible for a government regulation to survive strict scrutiny. During the 1960s and early 1970s, the Supreme Court, brandishing strict scrutiny, unleashed a remarkable burst of democratic reform, sweeping away most of the barriers that had unfairly hampered participation in the democratic process, especially by the weak and poor. In *Reynolds v. Sims*, in the name of equal participation in democracy, the Court insisted that all legislative election districts in a state, eventually including both houses of the state's legislature, must represent approximately the same number of people. In *Carrington v. Rash*, the Court ruled that soldiers temporarily stationed in Texas were entitled to vote in state and local as well as federal elections as long as the soldiers, who were often black, viewed their military base as their principal place of residence. In *Harper v. Virginia Board of Elections*, the Court invalidated the poll tax, dooming almost all property qualifications for voting and holding office. In *Williams v. Rhodes*, the Court recognized an equality-based constitutional right to run for office as a third-party candidate. In *Kramer v. Union School District*, the Court ruled that all residents affected by an election must enjoy an equal right to vote in it. In *Cipriano v. Houma*, the Court invalidated a statute limiting the franchise in municipal utility bond elections to property owners and in *Phoenix v. Kolodziejski*, the Court struck down a property ownership requirement for voting in a local general obligation bond election.

In *Dunn v. Blumstein*, the Court capped a remarkable decade by ending all durational residence requirements for voting.

Brilliantly successful as the Court was in sweeping away most formal restrictions on the franchise in the name of equality, the Court's equality-based protection of the vote ran out of gas before the job was done. As the Court's personnel changed, beginning in 1973, the new Republican majority made it much easier for the government to justify rules blocking access to the ballot for some but not others. Instead of strict scrutiny, the Republican justices asked whether a regulation blocking voting or access to the ballot was supported by a "substantial" (as opposed to a "compelling") government interest, whether it was "narrowly tailored" (not whether it was the "least drastic means" of dealing with the issue), and whether it was a reasonable, good-faith effort to advance the government's interests.

Unlike strict scrutiny, government wins most of the cases under such a watered-down test, which parallels the watered-down First Amendment standard used to review—and uphold—the government's ban on burning one's draft card to protest the war in Vietnam. Most important, the Supreme Court ruled in 1976 that proof of bad motive was necessary before the justices would unlimber Fifth and Fourteenth Amendment strict scrutiny artillery, empowering cynical politicians seeking to disenfranchise certain classes of voters to sneak under the Court's radar by pretending to be doing something legitimate.

Under the Court's current equality-based defense of democracy, state and local politicians can purge the registration rolls, force folks to show state-issued IDs, and make the act of voting less convenient, even when it's clear that such harsh behavior isn't really necessary and even when the new rules disproportionately disenfranchise poor voters of color. The sad truth is that, today, cynical politicians can often get around equality-based protections of democracy by lying about why they are making it harder for certain people—usually poor voters, often of color—to vote.

Equality-based protection of democracy also fails to protect against the widespread practice of political gerrymandering. While the Court has repeatedly confronted race-based gerrymandering, it has refused to intervene in partisan gerrymandering disputes, claiming that an equality-based challenge must provide the justices with an objective way to measure whether a gerrymander flunks the test of political fairness. Reformers have tried five times in the Supreme Court in recent years to come up with such a baseline. The five Republican justices keep saying "not objective enough."

Hope springs eternal, though. Courts throughout the country, including state courts operating under state constitutions—most recently Pennsylvania—appear to be waking up to the irreparable damage that excessive partisan gerrymandering is inflicting on American democracy. And, although the Supreme Court once again ducked the issue during the 2017 term, the matter continues to percolate through the lower courts. North Carolina's blatant state-wide congressional gerrymander, which reliably delivers ten safe Republican congressional seats, leaving three seats for Democrats, even when the Democrats win the statewide election, has been invalidated by a federal trial court, while Pennsylvania's equally egregious congressional gerrymander has been struck down under the state constitution by the Pennsylvania Supreme Court. Maybe in the North Carolina case five members of the Court will bite on a fancy new mathematical formula for measuring unfair electoral inequality that measures the number of wasted votes caused by an excessively partisan gerrymander. But I doubt it. Maybe North Carolina's own Supreme Court will clean up the mess.

Time has taught me, at least, that the time has come to tie the law of democracy much more closely to the First Amendment. Using equality to protect the right to vote is fine as far as it goes. But it doesn't go far enough. For one thing, the Supreme Court requires proof of a bad motive. For another, it insists on an objective ideal baseline to measure whether the challenged practice deviates too far from the ideal.

Phony voter ID requirements sneak under the radar because challengers can't prove a bad motive. Everyone in the country, except a narrow majority of the Supreme Court, knows that the rash of voter ID requirements are aimed at knocking out poor voters. Extreme partisan gerrymandering thrives because, until now, five justices have insisted on an objective definition of fair representation—an impossible task—before deciding when a partisan gerrymander crosses the line and becomes so unfair as to be unconstitutional.

I believe that casting a vote in a competitive election is the quintessential exercise of free speech and association. If, as the Supreme Court has already held, campaign spending is "pure" speech, entitled to the highest level of free speech protection, how can voting be granted no First Amendment constitutional protection at all? Listening to the candidates, assessing their ideas, and casting a ballot for your favorite is at the core of what it means to be an autonomous citizen, free to speak and associate. It seems crystal clear (at least to me) that the right to vote is baked into the idea of individual autonomy and human dignity that is at the heart of the First Amendment.

If, for example, the state permitted a speaker to talk but eliminated the audience, the existential, self-affirming act of speech would not be meaningless (think Prometheus raging at the gods), but it would fall far short of the First Amendment's protection of the right to chart your own destiny. Similarly, carrying out the democratic ritual of voting in a rigged election, knowing that the outcome of the election has already been fixed by political bosses, is not wholly meaningless. It is an existential act of faith in democracy and an important assertion of individual dignity. But it falls far short of the right to self-government and the individual and collective intensity that infuses genuine First Amendment activity when a speaker or voter believes that her speech or her vote actually matters in shaping her destiny.

More than twenty-five years ago, in *Burdick v. Takushi*, a majority of the Supreme Court held (wrongly, I believe) that voting is merely a technical way to cumulate preferences, not an exercise in speech or association. Accordingly, the majority ruled that there is no First Amendment right to cast a write-in ballot. But as Justice Kennedy recognized in his dissent, the act of voting, as the culmination of an election campaign, is far more than a mere technicality designed to identify a winner. Parents do not take their children to the polls to celebrate technicalities. Newly enfranchised citizens voting for the first time do not weep because they are engaging in a technical exercise. Millions of Americans did not fight, and too many die, to preserve a mere technical device. Blacks and women did not suffer for centuries in quest of a technicality. Justice White notwithstanding, the act of voting, even if not treated as a form of "pure" speech, should be imbued with First Amendment protection as the communicative act by which a voter expresses his or her preference for self-government. Justice Kennedy was correct in arguing twenty-five years ago that banning write-in votes was unconstitutional because it imposed a significant burden on voter choice, which is protected under the First Amendment.

The excessive gerrymandering cases from Wisconsin and Maryland before the Supreme Court during the 2017 term were Justice Kennedy's great opportunity to use his *Burdick* dissent to rejuvenate the democratic process. Sadly, at eighty-two years of age, Justice Kennedy seemed unable to muster the intellectual force needed to stand against his four Republican colleagues. Instead, with history in his grasp, Justice Kennedy slipped away into a well-earned retirement without putting his 1992 dissent into law. It was a tragedy for American democracy. Partisan gerrymandering, unnecessary voter ID requirements, and unfair voter purge statutes could not have survived a renewed recognition by Justice Kennedy that voting is protected by the First Amendment.

Challengers to extreme partisan gerrymandering returned to the Supreme Court in the 2018 term, this time facing Justice Brett Kavanaugh, who succeeded Justice Kennedy. The new case involves the effort by the Republican-dominated North Carolina legislature to gerrymander Congressional lines to give Republicans a 10–3 edge in a 50–50 state. The case is once again paired with a Democratic effort to gerrymander a single safe congressional seat in Maryland. If the five Republican justices continue to refuse to invalidate partisan gerrymandering this time around, I fear that the issue will be all but dead in the federal courts until the Court's personnel changes—by the ordinary processes of retirement, or the extraordinary process of court-packing.

Nothing in the Constitution requires a nine-person Supreme Court. The Court began in 1788 with six members, then went down to five in 1800, then back to six in 1801, then seven, eight, and nine, even reaching ten before the number slipped back to the present nine. Franklin D. Roosevelt, frustrated by the Court's refusal to approve the New Deal, threatened to add six additional justices, one for each justice over seventy. Roosevelt's effort failed as a formal matter, but it probably bluffed several justices into changing course and upholding the National Labor Relations Act. Contemporary observers called it "the switch in time that saved nine."

If one issue could justify a modern effort to pack the Court, it would be the need to protect the right to vote and the right to fair representation from a Court that refuses to lift a finger to protect American democracy.

But the fight is not over. The Wisconsin and Maryland cases are before the Supreme Court once again, albeit a Court without Justice Kennedy. Maybe the justices will honor Kennedy's thirty years of service on the Court by finally accepting his dissent in *Burdick*. Partisan gerrymandering can also be attacked in the state legislatures, in state courts under state constitutions, and in federal courts under the First Amendment. Viewing the vote as an exercise in communication is deeply rooted in our national heritage. Indeed, for much of the nation's early history, voting was a public act by which an adherent openly declared himself as a supporter of one or another of the candidates. We called it *viva voce* voting. George Washington, Thomas Jefferson, James Madison, Benjamin Franklin, John Adams, John Jay, and Alexander Hamilton—the Founders who built our nation—all proudly cast their ballots publicly, *viva voce*. It's the way Congress votes today.

The adoption of the secret ballot (a reform imported from Australia) during the late nineteenth century shifted the declaration of support from a public setting to a private voting booth, but the expressive nature of the vote remained unchanged, except that it was now a form of anonymous speech directed toward the government official who counts the votes. Whether public or anonymous, though, the communicative act of voting is the declarative culmination of a quintessential exercise in human dignity that cries out for First Amendment protection.

Surely, a fair opportunity to declare your support for a candidate with a genuine chance to win is as entitled to First Amendment protection against systematic state attack as is unlimited campaign spending, unlimited campaign fund-raising, nude dancing, flag burning, cross burning, hate-mongering, lying, selling violent video games to children, depicting the violent death of small animals, advertising toothpaste, threatening an ex-spouse on the internet, spewing racist epithets, and wearing T-shirts with political slogans to the polls, all of which have been granted First Amendment protection by the current Supreme Court.

It wouldn't take much for the Court to recognize a First Amendment right to vote. On numerous occasions the Court has opined that voting, running for office, participating in electoral campaigns, and interacting with a democratically elected representative are quintessential exercises of free speech, association, and redress of grievances at the core of the First Amendment. Justice Hugo Black said it most eloquently in *Wesberry v. Sanders*, one of the one-person, one-vote cases: "No right is more precious in a free country than that of having a choice in the election of those who make the laws under which, as good citizens, they must live. Other rights, even the most basic, are illusory if the right to vote is undermined."

It is time to convert the Court's often eloquent rhetoric about the intimate relationship between participating in the democratic process and the First Amendment into a First Amendment–based law of democracy.

Deploying the First Amendment to protect the right to vote would mean the end of phony voter ID requirements and excessive partisan gerrymandering. It would also be the end of the slow strangulation of third parties as a serious potential challenge to the duopoly of political power exercised by the two major parties.

During the nineteenth century, American democracy experienced a vibrant multi-party culture, enabling voters to launch repeated challenges to entrenched special interests. The early years of the twentieth century also saw significant third-party movements that forced the major parties to confront difficult issues: Teddy Roosevelt's Bull Moose run for the presidency; Robert La Follette Sr.'s Progressive Party, which urged restrictions on big business; Eugene Debs's Socialist Party challenge to the fundamental postulates of capitalism.

While the third-party challengers ultimately failed to attain power, they provided a significant vehicle for voters unwilling to support the two major parties and forced the major parties to alter their platforms in an effort to win back third-party voters. It didn't take long for the two major parties to cement their duopoly status by freezing third parties out of the game.

Despite the Supreme Court's belated recognition in 1968 of a constitutional right to run as a third-party candidate, the pols in both parties have succeeded in making it as hard as they can for third parties to run candidates, skating as close to the constitutional line as possible. Often, state law requires third-party or independent candidates to gather a substantial number of signatures on a petition in a short period of time long before the election as the price of getting on the ballot. Often, voters who are associated with a major party are blocked from signing a petition to place a third-party candidate on the ballot. Often, the petitions require detailed information such as a signatory's Election District. Many third-party candidates can't satisfy the ballot access requirements. Even when they do, they have been forced to use up most of their limited resources getting on the ballot, leaving them with little or no funding in the general election.

The pols' favorite technique for eliminating third parties as a serious threat to their power is to forbid minor parties from opening their nominating processes to major-party voters, while forbidding members of minor parties from voting in the primaries of major parties. The hope of the major parties is to build a legal wall around minor parties to minimize their ability to play anything more than a protest role in the democratic process. The legal wall reaches its highest point in the forty-one states that forbid minor parties from nominating the candidate of a major party, even when the candidate wishes to accept the cross-endorsement.

Shutting down the ability of minor parties to cross-endorse the candidate of a major party sounded their death knell as serious forces in American politics. During the nineteenth century, third parties routinely nominated one of the major parties' candidates and then assembled enough votes to swing the election. Once a third party demonstrated an ability to swing the election, it could force a major party to bid for its support. The Supreme Court's 1997 decision in *Timmons v. Twin Cities Area New Party* upholding laws banning cross-endorsement ended that issue-bending process. It also made it impossible for the supporter of a third party to play a role in who wins the election. Deprived by the cross-endorsement ban of a chance to vote for a candidate with a real chance to win, today's third-party voter faces the Hobson's choice of defecting from her party in order to cast a meaningful ballot for a candidate with a chance to win or remaining loyal to her party but giving up any chance to affect the outcome of an election. It even sets up a sophisticated form of election fraud by encouraging major party officials (or others) to support (even create) phony third-party candidates designed to draw support away from the other major party candidate. That's just what the Russians did in 2016 in a successful effort to induce potential supporters of Hillary Clinton to defect to Green Party candidate Jill Stein.

If we were to recognize that voting is a First Amendment right, it would become impossible to turn the act of casting a ballot into such a manipulated non-event. The obvious solution to the third-party problem is the adoption of the Maine preferential voting system that swung the 2018 congressional election in the Maine 2nd District. As we've seen, under the Maine system, voters could cast a first-choice vote for a third party, and a backup vote for a major party candidate to support when the third-party candidate drops out.

DEALING WITH BIG MONEY IN U.S. ELECTIONS

That brings us to the final but absolutely necessary effort to increase the perceived value of voting—limiting the power of big money to dominate American elections.

Even in the rare contestable legislative election, or in statewide races for presidential electors, the Senate, and statewide office, where you can't gerrymander state lines, many eligible voters do not participate because they believe that when big money talks, genuine democracy walks. Too often they are right.

While the closeness of many national and state elections should make it clear how important each vote can be, many Americans continue to believe that a single vote can't do much against the tide of massive wealth and organized special interests that appear to dominate our electoral process. As long as American elections resemble auctions, with political power for sale to the highest bidders, millions of eligible voters will not think it worth the trouble to cast a ballot.

Sadly, the alienation of millions of Americans from an electoral process awash in big money is a self-inflicted legal wound imposed by the Supreme Court's confusion of free speech with unlimited campaign spending. More than a half century ago, Justice Felix Frankfurter warned that the nation would rue the day that judges, functioning as amateur political scientists—or, worse, as disguised political partisans—were given the power to shape American democracy. Most of the time I'm confident that Justice Frankfurter was wrong about trusting judges to defend democracy. On balance, the courts have been a positive force in protecting the democratic process, especially if the justices can finally find a way to deal with runaway partisan gerrymandering. But Justice Frankfurter was surely right in warning that judges would make a mess of campaign financing. No rational legislator would vote for the campaign finance system currently imposed on the United States by the Supreme Court.

By upholding the power to limit the size and source of campaign contributions from both supporters and political parties but striking down all efforts to limit the amounts a candidate or an independent supporter can expend in connection with an election, the justices badly weakened our political parties, but empowered extremely wealthy individuals, huge corporations, and shadowy independent groups to dominate our electoral process. Can you imagine what a competent economist would say about a system that limits supply but refuses to permit limits on demand? It's Felix Frankfurter's revenge.

Our dysfunctional, deeply unfair campaign finance process is traceable to six mistakes made by the United States Supreme Court.

Mistake One

In 1976, the justices ruled in *Buckley v. Valeo* that campaign spending is a form of "pure speech," entitled to First Amendment strict scrutiny, which requires the government to demonstrate a "compelling state interest" in regulation that cannot be advanced by "less drastic means." Only one government regulation has ever survived full-scale First Amendment strict scrutiny—the ban on electioneering too close to the polls.

Correction One

Campaign spending is not "pure speech." Sure, it's connected to speech. But so are things like burning a draft card, holding a demonstration, and creating a picket line, each of which is treated by the Court as a form of "communicative conduct" entitled to a lesser degree of First Amendment protection, labeled "intermediate scrutiny" by the justices, under which the government often wins.

At most, government efforts to regulate campaign spending should be tested by the more relaxed level of First Amendment protection available to communicative conduct, requiring the government to demonstrate a "substantial interest" in good-faith regulation that is "narrowly tailored" to achieve its goals. What sounds like a lawyer's technical distinction is enormously important. As a practical matter, almost all efforts at campaign finance reform will flunk strict scrutiny but many will satisfy intermediate scrutiny.

Mistake Two

In *Buckley*, justices ruled that efforts to place limits on campaign spending by a candidate or a campaign designed to preserve a degree of political equality flunk First Amendment strict scrutiny because, even if the advancement of political equality is deemed a "compelling state interest," it can be advanced by the "less drastic means" of subsidizing weak political voices, rather than limiting excessively strong ones.

Correction Two

Even if the Supreme Court was right in imposing strict scrutiny on efforts to limit campaign spending by the superrich, the preservation of political equality is unquestionably a compelling governmental interest. The Court's assumption in 1976 that public financing would provide a less drastic means to preserve equality has been proven wrong, in large part because the Supreme Court has undermined efforts to enact feasible public campaign financing programs.

The hobbled system of campaign subsidies permitted by the Court since 2011 is unable to function as an effective, less drastic means of protecting equality. Most dramatically, after holding public subsidies out in *Buckley* as a viable alternative to regulation, in *Arizona Free Enterprise v. Bennett*, five Republican justices invalidated the most effective version of public financing—the granting of matching funds to enable a publicly funded candidate to stay competitive with her privately funded opponent. The five justices reasoned, with absolutely no empirical support, that the prospect of a public match would deter privately funded candidates from raising private funds. In effect, the Court established the First Amendment right of a well-funded candidate to speak without fear of being contradicted. *Arizona Free Enterprise Club* should be overruled.

Mistake Three

Preventing the appearance or reality of excessive political influence linked to massive aggregate campaign contributions to numerous candidates is not a compelling governmental interest, as long as no single candidate receives a contribution large enough to risk corrupting that candidate. Therefore, the generous six-figure limit on the aggregate amount that a single wealthy individual can contribute to all federal candidates in a given election cycle violates the First Amendment.

Correction Three

Ending the systemic corruption of democracy caused by unequal political access and influence linked solely to wealth should be viewed as a compelling governmental interest. No basis can be found in the Constitution for treating the risk of corrupting a single member of Congress as a greater evil than the risk of corrupting the entire political system by making unlimited aggregate contributions to many candidates.

Mistake Four

Independent electoral expenditures by supporters of a candidate, as first-person speech, are entitled to a higher level of First Amendment protection than campaign contributions to the candidate, which merely empower a third person—the candidate—to speak.

Correction Four

In fact, no legally significant First Amendment difference exists between campaign contributions and independent political expenditures. Campaign contributions are exercises in political association. Independent expenditures are exercises in communicative conduct. Both may be regulated to advance political quality and prevent corruption, or neither may be regulated. But it makes no sense to privilege one over the other.

Mistake Five

While large campaign contributions to a candidate may be regulated because they risk creating the appearance or reality of *quid pro quo* corruption, independent expenditures by supporters pose no such threat and are therefore immune from regulation.

Correction Five

Both large campaign contributions to a candidate and massive independent expenditures on behalf of a candidate pose significant risks of generating the appearance or reality of corruption, rendering both subject to substantial regulation. It is naive to believe that office holders remain immune to the temptation to reward an independent supporter who spent massive sums to elect the office holder and may do so again in the future.

Mistake Six

No legally significant First Amendment difference exists between the independent campaign spending of individuals and the independent campaign spending of large, for-profit corporations. Therefore, efforts to limit the campaign expenditures of large corporations violate the First Amendment.

Correction Six

For-profit corporations lack First Amendment rights because they lack the dignitary traits of human beings that underlie the very existence of First Amendment freedoms. Nor may corporations rely on the First Amendment rights of potential hearers, because the vast majority of Americans do not wish to be bombarded by corporate political propaganda. *Citizens United* should be overruled.

Unfortunately, the Supreme Court, as currently constituted, is unlikely to correct any of the six mistakes. Despite such a poor prognosis for short-term success in the current Court, it's important to continue to remind judges and legislators alike that *Buckley* and its 2010 offspring *Citizens United* rest on a series of false premises.

Eventually the Supreme Court will come to its senses and

correct one or all of the mistakes. To hasten that day, it is important to keep pressing for judicial change, even when the prospects of success are slim. We cannot allow the existing law mistakenly hobbling campaign finance reform to harden into concrete without constant challenge.

In the short run, though, if we are to rescue American democracy from the monied swamp it currently inhabits, the lifeline will have to come in the form of imaginative ways to fund democracy without selling out to the superrich or to special interests. One way, of course, is to continue to develop the internet as a means of raising significant campaign funds through small contributions. A second is to explore a modest tax credit for political contributions. Arkansas tried a $50 state credit, and it works in encouraging thousands of small contributions without the need for a bureaucracy to distribute the funds. A third imaginative approach, adopted by Seattle and South Dakota for local and state elections, calls for the issuance of Democracy Vouchers or Democracy Credit Cards with balances varying from $50 to $100, allowing all eligible voters to spend modest sums at no cost to themselves to advance a favored candidate. Republicans have engineered repeal of the South Dakota program, but it remains a model for reform.

Finally, several jurisdictions use an enriched matching system, where small private contributions to a candidate are publicly matched in multiples of up to eight to one. New York City has successfully used such a system, which matches at six to one, since 2006.

There is no need to wait for the Supreme Court's permission to adopt any of these techniques for lessening the influence of the rich on American political life.

Finally, this is the place where I'm supposed to deplore the rabid nature of our political discourse, the profusion of extreme, often fraudulent voices on the internet, the degeneration of cable TV into competing propaganda machines, and the threat posed by Russian meddling in our election campaigns. I dearly wish that we were more civil to one another, that the internet wasn't such a scary place, that someday cable TV will return to journalism, and that the Russians can be forced to keep their hands to themselves. We should, of course, do all we can to preserve the free press from Trumpist attacks. We should do all we can to police the internet for falsity and dangerousness. We should follow the Russian bread crumbs to the end—and then take steps to stop the meddling once and for all.

I fear, though, that none of those desirable actions will cure our democratic ills. If a nation is unable to cope with irresponsible political speech—by refraining from it, rejecting it, or learning to discount it—even well-functioning democratic institutions will not rescue that nation from political instability and dysfunctional government. If Americans are not fit for self-government because we are incapable of dealing with ugly appeals to bias or systematic dissemination of lies and half-truths, neither government paternalism, nor democratic reforms will save us.

A well-functioning democracy mirrors a society. It does not cure it. That we must do ourselves.

4

Do the External Judicial Brakes Work Anymore?

We've just seen that the internal electoral brakes designed by the Founders to slow a runaway democratic train just don't work anymore. The truth is that if another country operated an electoral system as dysfunctional as ours—with its radically malapportioned Senate, its politically rigged House, an Electoral College that has thwarted majority will twice in the last five presidential elections, systematic disenfranchisement of the poor, and outdated election machinery that can't count the votes accurately—we'd probably laugh them out of the democracy club.

So it's a good thing that the Founders didn't stop with the internal brakes. Somewhat reluctantly—perhaps even accidentally—they granted an unelected, life-tenured federal judiciary, headed by the Supreme Court, the power to defend our fundamental constitutional rights against runaway congressional majorities, state legislatures, local cops, and especially the president. They called it the power of judicial review and envisioned it as a fail-safe external braking mechanism capable of stopping a runaway democratic train.

The justices of the Supreme Court—and the Supreme Court's vast echo chamber of lawyers and academics—are not shy about celebrating judicial review as a wise and necessary check on the potential "tyranny of the majority." Faced as we are today with a volatile, impetuous, authoritarian, and deeply ignorant minority president who excels at manipulating mobs and exudes contempt for the very ideas of political toleration and respect for human rights, many Americans, including me, look to the nine life-tenured Supreme Court justices and the nine hundred or so lower federal court judges as the ultimate guarantors of our basic freedoms in a dark time. "It can't happen here," we tell ourselves, because an independent, apolitical Supreme Court can be counted on to protect us by enforcing the rights codified in the Constitution.

Two years into the Trump presidency, in the lower federal courts, at least, where good lawyers can cherry-pick reliable Democratic judges by deciding where and when to file their cases, judicial review has functioned exactly as advertised. In case after case, lower federal courts have rebuffed the forty-fifth president, striking down his travel ban, rejecting his refusal to permit transgender people to serve in the military, enjoining his decision to end the Dreamers program, blocking his attempt to punish "sanctuary cities" for refusing to cooperate in the mass deportation of undocumented aliens, stopping his heartless policy of ripping immigrant children away from their parents in an Orwellian effort to frighten desperate people away from seeking asylum in the United States, blocking him from ignoring congressional rules governing asylum, limiting his attempt to roll back environmental protections, blocking his effort to prevent immigrants in federal custody from exercising the right to choose whether to bear a child, and reversing his efforts to muzzle the press by denying disfavored reporters access to the White House.

I very much wish I could believe that such a soothing story of constitutional stability and judicial resistance will continue when the challenges reach the Republican-controlled Supreme Court. I fear, though, that excessive reliance on the Supreme Court to protect the fundamental rights of the politically and economically weak in the time of Trump is doomed to disappointment on two levels.

First, history warns that, apart from an uncharacteristic burst of egalitarianism from 1937 to 1972 (the only time since the Civil War that the Supreme Court has been controlled by the Democrats), a Republican-controlled high court has usually been a bad bet to protect the weak. Far more often than we like to admit, when the autonomy-based interests of the strong to "do what they will" have collided in the Supreme Court with the equality-based interests of the weak, Republican justices have tended to break legal ties in favor of the strong, forcing the weak to "suffer what they must."

Even before there were Republicans and Democrats as we know them today, during the more than seventy-five years from the Founding to the Civil War, in the absence of any formal protection of equality in the 1787 Constitution or the 1791 Bill of Rights, the justices repeatedly broke legal ties in favor of the autonomy-based rights of the powerful, whether slave owners or budding industrialists, at the expense of equally plausible legal arguments protective of the weak. In *Dred Scott v. Sandford*, a consensus pick for the Supreme Court's worst opinion, the Supreme Court enshrined slave ownership as a constitutional property right, denying free blacks any hope of citizenship. The appallingly racist decision in *Dred Scott* was neither an accident nor, as we like to view it today, an inexplicable exercise in pure evil. Viewed strictly as a formal legal matter, the 1857 decision wasn't even clearly wrong. It's what inevitably happens when judges are asked to enforce a Constitution saturated with concern for the rights of powerful individuals to be left alone, but utterly devoid of anything about a countervailing right of equality.

Under such a one-way autonomy-protective Constitution, judges, with no formal equality handholds to grasp, will almost always be persuaded by legal arguments granting the strong a constitutional right to crush the weak. It should come as no surprise that the first state statute declared unconstitutional by the Supreme Court in 1841 was a Pennsylvania anti-kidnapping law designed to protect blacks from being plucked from the streets of Philadelphia as alleged runaway slaves. Faced with a Constitution that protected the right of slave owners to recover escaped slaves but was utterly silent about the existence of any countervailing equality rights, the Supreme Court dutifully read the document as protecting the constitutional right of an autonomous slave owner to use self-help in recovering an alleged runaway slave, with any legal proceedings delayed until the alleged runaway was carried South.

The outcomes and reasoning in *Dred Scott* and *Prigg v. Pennsylvania* go a long way to explain why many conservative, autonomy-protective Republican justices such as the late Antonin Scalia and his replacement, Neil Gorsuch, are so besotted with the idea of an "originalist" reading of the constitutional text. As *Dred Scott* demonstrates, originalism asks modern justices seeking to interpret the current Constitution, which protects both equality and autonomy, to ask what the members of the Founders' generation would have understood the constitutional text meant. Asking that question enables—indeed, it commands—a justice to ignore the constitutionalization of equality in the post–Civil War amendments. Liberated from the complexity of interpreting the current Constitution protective of both autonomy and equality, originalist justices—like the justices who decided *Dred Scott* and *Prigg*—are free to pursue a single-minded defense of individual autonomy in the text of an outdated document that says nothing about equality.

Sadly, the post–Civil War Supreme Court—both Republican and Democratic justices—tended to ignore the newly minted equality rights inserted into the Constitution by the Thirteenth, Fourteenth, and Fifteenth Amendments. Whether the issue was the power of the federal government to protect the rights of freed slaves against local racists, the effort to regulate emerging monopolies, the power to set railroad or utility rates, or the attempt to form labor unions, the late nineteenth-century Supreme Court repeatedly accepted plausible legal arguments designed to protect the autonomy-based right of the strong to be free from regulatory interference (the Court even extended the protection of individual autonomy to corporations), at the expense of equally persuasive equality-friendly legal arguments that would have protected the weak.

During the first third of the twentieth century, in the name of protecting individual autonomy, the Republican-dominated Supreme Court repeatedly vetoed equality-enhancing legislation aimed at protecting vulnerable employees and consumers against the tyranny of an unregulated market and continued to block equality-based efforts to aid racial minorities in the South. The landmark 1905 case of *Lochner v. New York*, where the Supreme Court struck down minimum-wage and maximum-hour protections, was the twentieth-century economic analogue of *Dred Scott*. Instead of the autonomy-enhancing constitutional right of the strong to own enslaved people in *Dred Scott*, the *Lochner* Court protected the autonomy-enhancing constitutional right of the strong to impose contracts on "wage slaves" free from regulatory interference.

Lochner and the numerous other early twentieth-century cases striking down minimum wage, maximum hours, and safety regulations are examples of what happens when judges decide constitutional cases by unthinkingly glorifying autonomy over equality. It's important to recognize, though, that aggressive judicial protection of individual autonomy can help the weak, as well as reinforce the strong. The two Supreme Court cases that launched the modern protection of individual human rights—*Pierce v. Society of Sisters* (1923) and *Myers v. Nebraska* (1925)—were pure autonomy cases decided under the same substantive due process clause that drove the result in *Lochner*.

In *Pierce*, the state of Oregon lashed out at Catholics by forbidding parents from sending their children to private elementary schools. In *Myers*, post–World War I anti-German feeling caused Nebraska to ban the study of the German language. In both cases, the justices—both Democrats and Republicans—lined up to protect the individual autonomy of the weak against the tyranny of the transient electoral majority. That's an important lesson for today's world, where a Republican-controlled Supreme Court is likely to favor legal arguments advancing autonomy for the foreseeable future. It's one reason not to kill all the lawyers—yet.

As a purely legal matter, things improved considerably for the weak in the Supreme Court from 1937 to 1972, when the only Democratic-controlled Supreme Court since the Civil War conducted a master class in how to read the Constitution from the bottom up instead of from the top down, giving us FDR's New Deal, *Brown v. Board of Education*, "one person, one vote," broad protection for people of color, and the beginning of women's rights as part of a flood of equality-driven Warren Court constitutional cases that rewrote much of the Constitution.

(Even the Democratic Supreme Court buckled, though, when things really got tough, upholding the confinement of Japanese Americans in concentration camps during World War II, upholding the jailing of the leaders of the American Communist Party during the Cold War, and upholding the jailing of anti–Vietnam War draft card burners in the late 1960s.)

When Republicans regained control of the Court in 1972, the Supreme Court quickly reverted to autonomy-driven top-down form, tilting toward the strong in a series of closely divided cases favoring autonomy over equality that shaped the nation's approach to, among other things, funding public education, racial justice, violence against women, reform of the democratic process, access to the courts, and criminal procedure.

There's no reason to expect the current five Republican justices to be more enthusiastic about regulating the strong in order to protect the weak than were the Republican-controlled Supreme Courts of the past. If anything, with the resignation of Justice Anthony Kennedy, a maverick Republican justice who occasionally championed equality rights, things will only get worse as Trump repopulates the Court with handpicked justices, such as Neil Gorsuch and Brett Kavanaugh, likely to further shrink the Supreme Court's already relatively shallow commitment to equality. Get ready for an effort to push the constitutional balance between autonomy and equality back to where it was before FDR's New Deal.

That is cause for alarm, but perhaps not complete panic. Remember, the pre–New Deal legal world included the protection of individual autonomy in *Pierce* and *Myers*. And, as we'll see in chapter 6, it's not so easy to overturn generations of equality-protective Supreme Court precedent.

Let me be clear: I do not claim that Republican justices—past or present—were or are hostile to basic equality. Were the mob to reintroduce racial apartheid or engage in intentional racial discrimination, I am confident that Republican justices would join with their Democratic colleagues in declaring overtly racist behavior unconstitutional. Nor do we face a wholesale repudiation of most existing equality-based precedents. But in areas such as the right to choose, affirmative action, voting rights, campaign finance reform, police abuse, and religion-based exemptions from the legal duty to treat women and gays equally, where a delicate balance must be struck between powerful legal arguments favoring either the autonomy of the strong or the equality of the weak, Republican justices will tend to find plausible legal arguments advancing autonomy more persuasive than equally plausible legal arguments advancing the equality rights of the weak. Democratic justices will dissent. And all nine justices will continue to tell themselves—and everyone else—that they are just applying the law, not making it.

The bottom line is that Supreme Court protection of autonomy-based rights, like free speech and free exercise of religion, is likely to flourish, while protection of equality-based rights is likely to continue to atrophy. That's good news for the folks riding in first class, but not so good for the rest of us. Perhaps more important, expecting a *deus ex machina* called the Bill of Rights or the Supreme Court to drop down from democracy heaven and rescue us from Donald Trump at the head of a populist mob is not merely wishful thinking; it's downright dangerous because it encourages Americans to rely on someone other than themselves—and something other than the vote—to resist a Trumpist drift toward intolerance, authoritarianism, misogyny, and scapegoating. While judicial review can (and, I hope, will) play a significant short-term role in curbing Trump's worst impulses, in the end the American people will get the Constitution they want—and deserve. Unless Trump is defeated at the polls, he will remake the Supreme Court in his image, altering the meaning of much of the United States Constitution. FDR did it in 1937. Richard Nixon did it in 1972. Trump could do it in 2020. It turns out that the myth of a timeless, apolitical Constitution that embeds our rights in concrete is just about as accurate as one of Donald Trump's tweets.

Here's why: Judicial review is, at its core, anti-majoritarian. It licenses unelected, life-tenured mandarins called Supreme Court justices to veto the acts of democratically elected officials. Living with democracy-challenged institutions such as the Electoral College, the malapportioned Senate, and the gerrymandered House is bad enough, but how can anyone who genuinely believes in democracy sit still for nine Platonic guardians telling duly elected officials what they are allowed to do?

To help the anti-democratic medicine go down, we've invented a bedtime story. We try to defuse the tension between judicial review and respect for democracy by insisting that when the Supreme Court says no to Congress, elected state officials, or the president, the justices are merely obeying a superior, democratically legitimate command from the Founders. The trouble is that nobody believes that bedtime story anymore. The justices, especially the Republican "originalist" justices, cling to it because it legitimates their power. But the idea that Supreme Court justices engaged in deciding constitutional cases are merely talented archaeologists discovering and enforcing commands from long-dead white men was a self-serving fiction on the day in 1803 that John Marshall invented it in *Marbury v. Madison.*

The closest thing we have in the United States to a theater of the absurd is a Supreme Court Senate confirmation hearing, where senators and Supreme Court nominees from both parties fall all over each other pledging allegiance to a cartoon version of judicial review where the justices merely apply law made by the Founders but never make it themselves. It's a wonder that the Supreme Court nominees' noses don't get appreciably longer as the Senate hearing drones on. Every one of them knows better but dares not speak the truth. The raw passions on display during the bitterly contested confirmation hearing on the nomination of Brett Kavanaugh to the Supreme Court raised the curtain a bit on the real stakes of who gets to control the Court, but even then, Justice Kavanaugh insisted—and fifty senators took him at his word—that he would serve as a nonpartisan justice dedicated to applying law, not making it.

The actual relationship between judicial review and democracy is much more complex than a false dichotomy between making law and applying it. When, as it is in many important cases, the constitutional text is ambiguous and precedent confused, I believe that the justices' values—especially their relative ranking of the values of autonomy and equality—drive the outcome whether or not the justices admit it, even to themselves. Once such a values-driven Supreme Court case is decided, however, pursuant to a kind of legal alchemy known only to British and American lawyers, the Supreme Court's initial value-driven decision enters the pantheon of binding judicial precedent, creating the raw material for future apolitical judicial defense of the rights it announces and protects. It's like weaving nonpolitical gold from value-driven straw.

In the relatively few cases where the constitutional text is crystal clear, or in the many, many cases where powerful Supreme Court precedent exists, judicial review can—and often does—act as a significant, nonpolitical brake on the ability of the winner of an election to beat up on the losers. The value-driven, partisan heavy lifting in the Supreme Court takes place in the many important cases where the raw material for apolitical judging does not exist. While the Founders did indeed codify our basic individual rights in the 1787 Constitution, the 1791 Bill of Rights, and the post–Civil War equality amendments, the naked constitutional text is almost always maddeningly ambiguous. The hard work of deciphering the precise meaning of a constitutional text in specific settings— "saying what the law is"—falls to fallible human beings who dress in black robes and call themselves judges.

When the raw material for nonpolitical judging—clear text and binding judicial precedent—just isn't there, Supreme Court justices must use their values to break constitutional ties. There's no other way to get the job done. Moreover, because Republicans and Democrats tend to embrace characteristically different value hierarchies, Republican and Democratic justices tend to break constitutional ties in characteristically partisan ways. As I've argued, Republican justices tend to be persuaded by plausible legal arguments favoring autonomy over equally plausible legal arguments favoring equality. Democratic justices tend to be more receptive to legal arguments favoring equality. Not every justice. Not every time. But enough times to generate a partisan difference that results in two Constitutions—one red, one blue.

I acknowledge that characterizing constitutional judgments as Republican or Democratic borders on heresy. It comes dangerously close to erasing the important distinction between law and politics. But I have no choice. An honest analysis of the constitutional decision-making process makes it clear (to me, at least, after fifty-five years of immersion in the process) that a justice's hierarchy of values often plays a determinative role in resolving many constitutional cases. The standard defense of judicial review argues that since all that judges do when they exercise judicial review is carry out commands issued by the Founders, judicial review is perfectly compatible with democracy, even when it sets aside the actions of the electoral majority. That defense of judicial review—endorsed by Justice Scalia, Justice Gorsuch, and now Justice Kavanaugh—turns on an indefensible assumption that the constitutional text conveys a single correct command to a faithful judicial reader, rather than a series of plausible choices.

The moment that judicial choice enters Supreme Court Eden, it destroys the fiction that the Founders are doing all the work. If, after all, it's the justices who ultimately get to choose what the constitutional text means, the political heavy lifting is really being done by a non-elected, life-tenured mandarin, not a democratically privileged mythic Founder.

So the crucial question becomes: "Does the constitutional text convey a command or pose a choice?" In order to harmonize judicial review with democracy, American judges and most academics turn themselves inside out trying to persuade themselves—and everyone else—that the constitutional text conveys a single command from the Founders. But thus far their efforts have all failed. One group of constitutional experts, calling themselves "literalists," insist that the Constitution's commands are hiding in plain sight in its 4,543 words. All you really need, they claim, to decipher the Constitution's one true meaning is a good dictionary (preferably about two hundred years old) and the courage to read the text literally.

Sometimes the literalists are right. When you want to know how many witnesses are needed to convict someone for treason (two), how old the president must be (at least thirty-five), the president's required citizenship status (native-born, not naturalized), how many votes each state gets in the Electoral College (one for each of the state's two senators and one for each representative in the House), or how many electoral votes it takes to elect a president (currently 270), the Constitution's literal words deliver a single, definitive answer.

But useful as literalism is in some settings, everyone agrees that the dictionary has its limits. Many of the Constitution's words and phrases plausibly carry multiple literal meanings, especially the words and phrases used in the Constitution's rights-bearing provisions. Consider the free speech clause of the First Amendment: "Congress shall make no law . . . abridging the freedom of speech." Even if we wanted to, we couldn't read the free speech clause literally. First, there is the difficulty of reading the phrase "*Congress* shall make no law" to apply to the president, the military, and every level of state and local government. Second, the seemingly absolute phrase "*no law*" turns out to be a semantic dead end. The text does not say "no law abridging speech." That would be easy enough to apply literally, but the text would also protect threats, extortion, and blackmail. Instead, the text says "no law abridging *the freedom of speech.*" But what exactly is "the freedom of speech"? Like the term "witnesses" in the treason clause, or "native-born" in the presidential qualifications clause, "the freedom of speech" is a legal concept that must be filled in by human readers of the text. There is no definitive dictionary-based road map for the job.

It only gets harder to impose a single literal meaning on phrases such as the ban on "establishing" religion and the guarantee of "free exercise" of religion in the First Amendment, the prohibition on "unreasonable searches and seizures" in the Fourth Amendment, the guarantee of "due process of law" in the Fifth Amendment, and the prohibition on "cruel and unusual punishment" in the Eighth Amendment. When you add the right to the "equal protection of the laws" in the Fourteenth Amendment and the implied guarantee of equality latent in the Fifth Amendment phrase "due process of law," to say nothing of the nontextual doctrines of separation of powers and federalism, the idea of a single, literal constitutional command loses all meaning in most important constitutional settings.

Sophisticated textualists such as Justice Scalia and Justice Gorsuch have conceded that most important constitutional provisions can plausibly be read to mean more than one thing. They argue, though, that constitutional ambiguities can be reduced to a single correct meaning by asking what the Founders originally intended the words to mean. They call their approach "originalism" and claim that it resolves the tension between democracy and judicial review by turning the seemingly ambiguous text into a precise command from the Founders.

I have real sympathy for Justice Scalia's lifelong originalist effort to domesticate the Constitution by turning it into a series of externally imposed commands. If he had been able to pull it off, he would have turned judicial review into nothing more than a politically neutral, democratically legitimate enforcement of the Founders' commands. But, despite a lifetime of intellectually powerful effort, he couldn't pull it off. First, it's unclear why we would want to adopt a method of reading the Constitution in the twenty-first century that refers us back to the mind-set of an earlier era in human history when equality had not yet entered the Constitution, slavery was legal, women were excluded from the polity, the franchise was confined to the rich, and the idea of freedoms of speech, press, and political association was so weak that President John Adams locked up many of the newspaper editors who opposed him in the election of 1800.

Many originalists acknowledge the dangers of looking backward to a constitution bereft of equality but claim that we have no choice if we are to reconcile judicial review and democracy. The democratic legitimacy of the power of an unelected judge to invalidate a congressional or presidential act, they claim, depends upon the existence of a single definitive constitutional command from the Founders capable of binding a reviewing judge. When literalism can't deliver such a binding command, originalism becomes the textualists' safety net.

As we've seen, though, it's not clear that originalists are right in claiming that a constitution with a single command is necessary to the democratic legitimacy of judicial review. I have argued that, as a matter of deferred democracy, not only is the exercise of value-laden legal tiebreaking a necessity in deciding many constitutional cases, it is the most desirable way to harmonize judicial review and democracy because it leaves the ultimate choice of the Constitution's meaning to the people.

Nor are originalists necessarily right in arguing that such a backward-looking exercise in legitimation is worth the price of locking the Constitution into an eighteenth-century mind-set. To my mind, the moral disgrace of *Dred Scott* just wasn't—and isn't—worth it.

Even if you concede both points, though, it turns out that an honest exercise in originalism almost never delivers on its promise to turn the Constitution into a document that can be read only one way. In the first place, it's a matter of controversy which Founders' original intent counts—the principal drafters like Madison, the back-bench members of the Philadelphia Constitutional Convention, the 1791 Congress that adopted the Bill of Rights, the members of the various state ratifying conventions, the voters who selected the members of the ratifying conventions, or the late eighteenth-century "general public" (whatever and whoever that means)?

Over the years, originalists have dallied with each category of definitive reader, abandoning each when the proposed reader became intellectually untenable. Current originalists such as Justice Gorsuch ask what an ill-defined slice of the Founders' generation called the "general public" would have understood the text to mean, without specifying whether the "general public" included women, free blacks, enslaved people, Native Americans, and non-Christians.

Thus, after more than twenty years of trying to define who the originalist readers are, confusion still reigns. If you don't know for sure whose original understanding you are looking for, it is virtually impossible to deliver a single right answer about the meaning of the constitutional text.

Even more troubling, whichever category of Founders you choose to be the definitive originalist readers, it turns out that if you are intellectually honest, it's clear they were as confused and divided over the meaning of the Constitution's ambiguous text as we are today.

You can't get a more privileged set of Founding insiders than Thomas Jefferson and Alexander Hamilton. Yet they spent most of their time in President Washington's first cabinet squabbling over how the necessary-and-proper clause affects the scope of Congress's power to regulate interstate commerce. If Jefferson and Hamilton couldn't agree on a single correct meaning of the constitutional text even though they participated in the drafting and ratification process and had personal access to the principal drafters, including Madison and John Jay, how can we expect to generate a single, definitive answer to the meaning of the commerce clause more than two hundred years after its adoption?

The repeated failure of originalism to generate single right answers to the meaning of an ambiguous constitutional text is demonstrated by the sheer volume of Supreme Court opinions, such as the Affordable Care Act case, where the justices divide 5–4 over what the Founding generation intended the Constitution's text to mean. The Court's tragicomic performance in *District of Columbia v. Heller* in 2008 is a particularly revealing example of the failure of history to generate clear answers.

Heller dealt with the meaning of the Second Amendment, which reads: "A well-regulated militia, being necessary to the security of a free state, the right of the people to keep and bear arms, shall not be infringed." Over the years, two plausible competing readings of the constitutional text emerged, one blue and one red. The blue reading construed the right of the people to keep and bear arms as a way to ensure the ready availability of a pool of armed citizens needed to staff the "well-regulated" citizens' militia as a protection against military overthrow of the government. The competing red reading argued that the clause about the right to keep and bear arms should be read in isolation from the militia clause because discussion of militias was merely an explanatory preface, not a legal restriction. Under the red reading, the right to bear arms becomes a deep protection of individual autonomy, not an engine of community.

Literalism fails to break the tie between the two competing readings. No matter how many dictionaries you consult, the riddle of which clause should predominate remains unanswered. Stymied literally, all nine justices in *Heller* embarked on an originalist quest for the true meaning of the Second Amendment, virtually cornering the market on historical texts. When the history smoke cleared, five Republican justices were sure that the Founders had intended the autonomy-protective "bear arms" clause to trump the equality-protective "militia" clause. Four justices—two Democrats and two maverick Republicans, John Paul Stevens and David Souter—after communing with the same historical materials, were equally sure that the "militia" clause trumped the "bear arms" clause.

You can agree or disagree with the result in *Heller*, but it is simply impossible to claim that the justices' intensive historical investigation into the Founders' intentions and understandings about the meaning of the Second Amendment delivered a single right answer to the text's meaning. The justices' values broke that legal and historical tie.

If originalism cannot produce a single right answer in a case like *Heller*, it's fair to ask why we should look to the eighteenth century, with its quaint world of muskets and rural farmers, for guidance about constitutional law governing gun ownership in a twenty-first-century world of massive firepower in densely populated urban settings. Justice Scalia, a dedicated originalist, answered that even if historical research into original meaning results in more than one plausible answer, it is better for the justices to disagree over history than to disagree over values and politics.

Such a last-ditch defense of originalism might seem more persuasive if, as an empirical matter, a justice's view of history didn't almost always reflect the justice's values. It's simply amazing how often the members of the eighteenth-century "general public" share the values of the justice who is asking them about the original meaning of an ambiguous constitutional phrase. In *Heller*, the Founding rascals told one thing to Justice Scalia and another to Justice Stevens.

In fact, experience and common sense teach that whenever uncertainty and legitimate disagreement emerge about the historical meaning of an ambiguous text, originalism becomes a replay of the scene in *Guys and Dolls* where Big Julie is losing at craps and wants to substitute his own dice. "But Big Julie," objects Nathan Detroit, "there are no spots on your dice." Big Julie responds: "I remember where the spots were." Antonin Scalia couldn't have put it better.

Constitutional experts and judges spend a great deal of time doubling down on their claims that their particular approach is the Rosetta Stone decoding the Constitution's one true meaning. If decibels equaled truth, the originalists, who tend to shout the loudest and pound the table, would prevail. But simply shouting louder can't turn originalism into a way to decipher the Constitution's one true meaning. In the end, originalism merely licenses justices to maximize autonomy without worrying about equality—and to pretend that Madison made them do it.

While you'll never find a Democratic justice who embraces Justice Scalia's brand of originalism, it is possible to generate a Democratic version of originalism that would treat the drafters of the Thirteenth, Fourteenth, and Fifteenth Amendments as a second set of Founders on a par with the first set of Founders in Philadelphia. A Democratic (or principled Republican) originalist judge would then feel bound to insert the idea of equality into the ethos of the Founding and imagine how equality would have interacted with the Founders' commitment to autonomy. Maybe that's what justices like Ruth Bader Ginsburg, Sonia Sotomayor, and Elena Kagan actually do.

In fairness, no one else makes a more persuasive case for their recipe for teasing a single correct meaning from the constitutional text. Justice William Brennan Jr., the great liberal icon and my personal hero, called his approach "constructive originalism." He also claimed to talk to Founders. Unlike Justice Scalia, though, Justice Brennan didn't pretend that he was talking to a real Founder and discovering an actual historical fact. Instead, he invented a "reasonable Founder," rotated the reasonable Founder forward two hundred years and asked him (it was always a him) what the text should mean today. He called it a search for "the living Constitution."

While Justice Brennan's "living Constitution" approach frees us from the prejudices of the eighteenth century, allows us to factor equality into the text, and, in my opinion, delivered magnificent constitutional law, it hardly qualifies as a serious method of finding a single right answer in the constitutional text. As with Justice Scalia's real Founders, I wonder whether any of Justice Brennan's fictive Founders ever disagreed with him. As an effort to derive a single correct objective meaning from the constitutional text, Justice Brennan's nocturnal conversations with fictive Founders were even worse than Justice Scalia's scene from *Guys and Dolls*. It's closer to Monty Python. Communing with fictive Founders may have assured Justice Brennan that those Founders would wish the Constitution to enshrine the "one person, one vote" principle in *Baker v. Carr* and the First Amendment "marketplace of ideas" in *New York Times v. Sullivan*, but the rest of us were just not in on the conversation.

A third approach, often called "purposivism," championed by, among others, Justice David Souter during his underappreciated nineteen years on the Supreme Court, does not pretend to talk to long-dead Founders, real or imagined. Instead, it seeks to ascertain the underlying "purpose" of a constitutional phrase, using text, precedent, history, values, and the structure of the Constitution as a guide, and to construe doubtful constitutional phrases in a way that advances their underlying purpose. In effect, it's the Brennan approach without the nocturnal theatrics.

Most American judges, including a majority of the current Supreme Court, use the Souter method today as their preferred way of deciphering the constitutional text. But while constitutional purposivism is capable of producing excellent constitutional law, it too fails to produce single right answers about the Constitution's true meaning. The twin judicial tasks of ascertaining the dominant purpose of an ambiguous constitutional provision and deciding how best to advance that purpose in the modern era require repeated value-laden judgment calls.

Justice Stephen Breyer's spin on purposivism takes it to an even higher level of generality. He finds a dominant general purpose to enhance equal participation in democratic self-governance in the Constitution's deep structure and professes to break legal ties in hard constitutional cases in a way that advances such a laudable ideal. There is, of course, nothing wrong with such a characteristically Democratic, equality-friendly approach. It usually leads to excellent blue outcomes. But it hardly qualifies as a blueprint for single right answers. Why not, for example, treat the characteristically Republican vision of robust individual autonomy as the overarching purpose of the Founders? That would lead to red outcomes.

Finally, a few intrepid souls calling themselves "pragmatists," led by former judge Richard Posner, acknowledge that the constitutional text is usually too ambiguous to generate single right answers, and that the variants of originalism and purposivism fail to deliver an objectively correct reading of the text. Judge Posner, during his distinguished service on the Court of Appeals for the Seventh Circuit, argued that the Founders' use of ambiguous constitutional phrases at a high level of generality operated as a grant of power to future generations to interpret the constitutional text pragmatically. That is just what the Supreme Court did in *Brown v. Board of Education* when, in 1954, it rejected ninety years of contrary precedent to begin the process of ending racial apartheid in the United States. But such a process, wholly dependent on a judge's personal assessment of what the times require, cannot possibly generate a *single* right answer.

So the dirty little secret of American constitutional law is that, except for literalism in a few trivial settings, none of the approaches to reading the constitutional text delivers a single constitutional meaning. Like it or not, Supreme Court justices must make choices about the text's meaning in deciding many constitutional cases. That's where values come in.

Dirty secrets about judicial role also generate guilt. American judges, trapped between democratic political theory that asks skeptically where the power of value-driven judicial review comes from and a constitutional text that stubbornly resists yielding clear constitutional commands, often harbor guilt complexes about exercising judicial review. It's what drives many judges into embracing originalism, even though they know it doesn't work. I wish American judges would get over their guilt complexes and confront the inevitability of judicial choice about what the Constitution means. They have nothing to be ashamed of when their values operate to break legal ties in hard constitutional cases. To the contrary, I believe that American judges should proudly acknowledge that when text, precedent, and consensus values fail to provide a single right legal answer, a justice's value choices often underlie the act of reading the constitutional text—not merely because such value choices are inevitable in many cases but also because using a justice's value choices to break textual ties in hard constitutional cases is at the core of the deferred democratic process that harmonizes judicial review with our deep commitment to government by the people.

As I've argued, although it markets itself as an apolitical institution operating outside of politics, the Supreme Court often functions politically as a forum of indirect, deferred democracy. Viewed as an institution of deferred democracy, the Supreme Court has been a remarkably stable partisan institution. As we've seen, partisan political control of the Court has changed hands only three times since the Civil War. Republicans controlled the Supreme Court from 1865 to 1937. Twenty-one Supreme Court vacancies were filled between 1900 and 1932. Republican presidents filled eighteen, appointing a Republican-dominated Supreme Court that generated a series of autonomy-driven, characteristically Republican constitutional precedents favoring legal arguments protective of autonomy in cases such as *Lochner v. New York* striking down wage and hours protections for workers and *Hammer v. Dagenhart*, invalidating child labor laws.

Democrats have controlled the post–Civil War Supreme Court only once, from 1937 to 1972. Twenty-two Supreme Court vacancies were filled between 1932 and 1968. Democratic presidents appointed seventeen (not counting President Eisenhower's

nomination in 1954 of maverick California Republican governor Earl Warren as chief justice), ushering in the nation's only
Democratic-dominated Supreme Court, which repeatedly
broke legal ties in favor of the weak, sweeping away two layers of
Republican-era blocking precedents and enabling progressive reforms in both the economic and social arenas.

The first layer of dead Republican precedents was swept away
by "the switch in time that saved nine"—the about-face by one
Republican justice, Owen Roberts, who apparently changed his
voting pattern to uphold the National Labor Relations Act in response to President Roosevelt's threat to pack the Court with six
additional Democratic justices—and by FDR's ability to appoint
four new justices between 1937 and 1941. The newly Democratic
Supreme Court dramatically expanded the power of Congress
(under the commerce clause) and states (under the due process
clause) to regulate the economy in order to protect the vulnerable,
ushering in the constitutional foundation for the modern regulatory state.

The second layer of dead Republican precedents (such as *Plessy
v. Ferguson*, upholding racial segregation), which had favored the
autonomy interests of southern racists over racial equality interests,
was swept away by an avalanche of equality-driven cases (such as
Brown v. Board of Education) that established the constitutional
foundation for mass movements seeking equality for people of
color, women, and gays.

Republicans regained majority control of the Supreme Court
in 1972 and have held it ever since. In the early 1970s, the newly
Republican-controlled Supreme Court quickly reverted to form,
announcing a series of constitutional decisions favoring autonomy
over equality. The newly minted Republican precedents froze the
progressive reform agenda in areas ranging from educational equity
to racial fairness, gender equity, access to the courts, democratic
fairness, and regulatory authority.

The heightened Republican focus on autonomy provided a
welcome boost for women's equality. It turns out that abortion is
one of those areas, like free speech, where autonomy and equality

run on parallel tracks. Concern for a woman's autonomy reinforces her right to control her own body. Concern for women's equality reinforces the right of a woman to plan her life. In 1973, under a newly Republican Supreme Court, a signature gender-equality precedent, *Roe v. Wade's* protection of a woman's right to control her reproductive life, was established. The majority opinion was written by Harry Blackmun, a Republican justice, and the case was decided 7–2 by a Republican-controlled Court. But recall that *Roe* was initially viewed as a pure autonomy case, protecting a woman's right, in consultation with her doctor, to decide what is best for her health, both physical and mental.

Viewed as a case about the right to be left alone, *Roe* fit neatly into the value system of the Republican justices as a logical extension of the well-established autonomy-driven precedents protecting the right to use contraception. It was not until sustained, religiously motivated insistence that the fetus also deserved autonomy-based protection had eroded the autonomy underpinnings of *Roe* that Justice Ruth Bader Ginsburg—the "Notorious RBG"—reconceptualized the case in gender equality terms.

As *Roe* demonstrates, shifting the Supreme Court from Democratic to Republican control does not endanger autonomy-based rights. Indeed, it usually strengthens them. Thus, the development of a Supreme Court jurisprudence deeply protective of free speech, begun in the 1960s under a Democratic Court that viewed free speech as protective of both autonomy and equality, continued with the post-1972 Republican-controlled Supreme Court, in which Republican justices were enthusiastically joined by the Democratic minority to double down on powerful free speech protections.

The Republican justices saw themselves as protecting autonomy. The Democrats extolled the equality-enhancing power of free speech to alter the status quo to protect the weak. Only when the autonomy rationale ran headlong into the equality rationale, as it did in cases involving campaign finance reform, hate speech, and privacy, did the Court fragment into Republican and Democratic First Amendment voting blocs.

Not surprisingly, the post-1972 Republican majority eviscerated many Democratic precedents designed to advance equality, especially the Warren Court's criminal procedure cases, which were indirect efforts to deal with rampant racial discrimination at every level of the criminal process. And as *Roe* increasingly became understood as an equality case, it too became the target of a Republican majority bent on eroding it.

With Justice Scalia's unexpected death in February 2016, the Court reverted to a 4–4 partisan tie. President Obama's nomination of Chief Judge Merrick Garland, a moderate Democrat, to fill the ninth seat moved the Court to the cusp of a shift to the nation's second post–Civil War Democratic majority. The Republican Senate's adamant, unconstitutional refusal even to consider the Garland nomination, followed by President Trump's unexpected minority victory in the 2016 presidential election and the confirmation of his nominees, Neil Gorsuch and Brett Kavanaugh, by a radically malapportioned Senate narrowly controlled by the Republican Party, not only maintained the Supreme Court's Republican 5–4 majority but shifted the ideological balance even more firmly in favor of autonomy and against equality.

At best, the current Republican-controlled Supreme Court will value autonomy over equality; at worst, it will permit the erosion of both of those prime constitutional values in the name of deference to the imperial presidency. The process may have already begun in *Trump v. Hawaii*, the challenge to President Trump's travel ban targeting predominantly Muslims, where the Court's five Republican justices subordinated the equality and autonomy-enhancing values of religious toleration to deference to unconstrained presidential authority in national security settings. As the travel ban case illustrates, the greatest risk posed by a Trumpist Supreme Court is not that it will favor autonomy over equality. Republican justices have been doing that for years. As long as we don't revert to a *Dred Scott* world where equality is entirely written out of the Constitution, damage to the weak caused by overvaluing autonomy, while deeply troubling, can eventually be reversed at the polls and by future courts.

The greater risk is that additional Trump appointees may share the president's disdain for *both* autonomy and equality, as well as the very idea of judicial review. That's the formula that gave us *Korematsu v. United States* (upholding the placement of Japanese Americans in concentration camps during World War II), *Dennis v. United States* (upholding the jailing of the leadership of the American Communist Party during the Cold War), and *United States v. O'Brien* (upholding the jailing of draft card burners during the Vietnam War). That's also the formula that upheld the president's travel ban, despite the chief justice's pious assertion that the Court's five-justice majority was rejecting *Korematsu. Trump v. Hawaii* is simply *Korematsu* in modern dress. Imagine the damage a narcissistic authoritarian such as Trump can do if the Supreme Court, like the craven German judges in 1938, routinely defers to the leader's judgment on questions of national security.

In the long run, therefore, the Constitution is not above politics. It is shaped by politics. The meaning of crucial provisions of the Constitution in our time will be decided not in some apolitical legal world by idealized Platonic guardians responding to legal arguments but by whether our presidential and senatorial elections turn the Supreme Court red or blue.

Though that may sound frightening, I believe that's just the way it should be in a legal and political system genuinely committed to government by the people. When an American judge is confronted with a constitutional case where the text is ambiguous, the precedent weak, and the values point in different directions, the judge has four options: (1) refuse to decide the case, claiming a lack of judicial standards for decision; (2) use criteria unconnected with the merits, such as the race of the litigant, partisan politics, friendship with one of the lawyers, or self-interest; (3) use random criteria such as flipping a coin; or (4) consult his or her—or the society's—values to determine what is, in the judge's view, the best way to read the ambiguous text.

The first response—deciding not to decide—is plausible. An entire branch of constitutional law called the "political question doctrine" is devoted to deciding when a judge should decline to exercise judicial review because of a lack of "manageable judicial standards." It's how the Supreme Court has ducked dealing with partisan gerrymandering for two generations. If, however, the option of judicial silence is widely invoked whenever the constitutional text can be read in more than one way, most judge-made constitutional law would cease to exist.

We could, like Great Britain, adopt such a minimalist version of judicial review, but only at the cost of reversing *Marbury v. Madison* and radically altering the American Constitution.

Since the second and third options are clearly unacceptable, that leaves the judge's values as the only game in town. As we've seen, for most of our history, we have lived under a Republican Constitution that privileges autonomy over equality. For one thirty-five-year burst, from 1937 to 1972, we lived under a Democratic Constitution that injected equality into American law as a serious rival to autonomy.

We have lived since 1972 under a Republican Constitution restoring autonomy and security as primary tiebreakers in hard cases, but have continued to enjoy the fruits of the once and future Democratic Constitution in the form of respect for equality-enhancing precedent, and an occasional lurch forward propelled by an alliance between a maverick Republican justice's principled commitment to autonomy and the four Democratic justices' sympathy for legal doctrine protective of equality. That's what brought us constitutional protection of gay marriage.

We are, I believe, about to enter a period of even more intense protection of autonomy and a corresponding weakening of protection for equality. But that won't last forever. The truth is that the federal judiciary, including the Supreme Court, is constantly being remade by an infusion of newly appointed judges. That infusion reflects the sustained political choices of the people who elect both the appointing and confirming authorities. Over time, therefore, the constitutional balance between autonomy and equality will be decided in the voting booth.

5

The Fortas Fiasco

How Not to Maintain the Brakes

My candidate for the worst political fiasco of the twentieth century is President Lyndon Johnson's almost inexplicable failure in 1968 to name a Democratic successor to Chief Justice Earl Warren. Johnson's blunder cost the Democrats control of the Supreme Court for the next fifty years and changed the course of constitutional history.

There was no obvious political excuse for the failure. In 1968, Democrats enjoyed a comfortable 6–3 Supreme Court majority, with Earl Warren, a Republican in name only who had been cross-endorsed by the Democrats when he ran for Governor of California, counted as a Republican. Democrats also enjoyed an overwhelming 66–34 majority in the Senate, even after losing three seats in the 1966 election. LBJ, who had been elected president in a landslide in 1964, was a master legislative tactician who had successfully shepherded more than a hundred administration-supported bills through Congress, including Title VII, barring race and gender discrimination in employment; Title VIII, banning housing discrimination; and the Voting Rights Act of 1965, barring racial discrimination in access to the ballot.

By 1968, though, President Johnson had been weakened politically: his lame-duck status, liberal opposition to the Vietnam War, southern opposition to the 1960s civil rights statutes, and intense Republican-led opposition to the Warren Court's equality-friendly rulings—triggering a backlash that presaged the ultimate collapse of the Democratic Party in the states of the old Confederacy.

On the other hand, back in 1968, the Supreme Court nomination process had not yet degenerated into its current toxic, hyperpartisan state. The consensus belief in 1968 was that presidents were entitled to appoint Supreme Court nominees of their choice as long as the Senate reviewed and certified the nominee's ethical and intellectual qualifications. As recently as 1956, President Dwight Eisenhower had used a recess appointment, without the objection of a single senator, to place Justice William Brennan Jr. on the Court.

Although Supreme Court confirmation controversies had broken out regularly in the eighteenth and nineteenth centuries, the first formal Senate committee hearing on a Supreme Court nominee did not take place until 1916, driven by opposition to Justice Louis Brandeis's nomination to be the first Jewish justice. Even then, Brandeis was not called to testify. In fact, prior to 1968, no Supreme Court nominee had been called to testify before the Senate.

To make things easier for LBJ, Earl Warren, who despised Richard Nixon, tried to ease the transition by giving the president a year's notice of his intention to resign, and by making his resignation conditional, effective only on the confirmation of a successor. A bulletproof successor was waiting in the wings: Arthur Goldberg, appointed to the Court by President Kennedy in 1962, Goldberg had resigned in 1965 at LBJ's request to represent the United States at the United Nations. Goldberg would have been a shoo-in the second time around. But LBJ was reportedly reluctant to place a second Jew (and a Kennedy loyalist at that) on the Court.

Instead, he sought to elevate his crony and longtime legal advisor, Associate Justice Abe Fortas, to the chief justiceship. Not only would elevating Fortas reward a political ally, but it would also open a second vacancy, allowing Johnson to appoint another close political ally, Homer Thornberry, formerly a Texas congressman, who was then serving on the Fifth Circuit Court of Appeals.

Then the wheels fell off. Fortas, who prior to Johnson's nomination as vice president had successfully defended LBJ in litigation arising out of highly plausible allegations of corruption in Texas

House and Senate primary elections, had raised eyebrows by continuing to provide informal legal advice to the White House, even after his confirmation in 1965 as an associate justice.

LBJ then alienated the leader of the southern bloc, Senator Richard Russell of Georgia, by stalling on approving Russell's allegedly racist choice for a Georgia district court nomination. When Fortas was finally forced to testify under oath before the Senate Judiciary Committee, he revealed his ethically doubtful post-appointment legal ties with the White House. Fortas also disclosed a questionable financial relationship with American University under which he received a substantial payment, equal to almost 40 percent of his Supreme Court salary, for teaching a single course at the law school.

The twin admissions allowed senators to claim to be opposing Fortas's nomination on grounds of ethics and judgment, not because of his legal views. Although a majority of the Senate Judiciary Committee recommended confirmation, the Fortas nomination was in trouble from day one on the Senate floor, where Republicans launched the first filibuster in the Senate's history against a Supreme Court nomination. In those days, it took as many as sixty-seven votes to break a filibuster. The Fortas nomination never had a chance. President Johnson stubbornly forced a floor vote on breaking the filibuster, hoping to save face by securing a comfortable majority, but the final vote was a bare 45–43 for advancing the Fortas nomination, far less than the two-thirds present and voting needed to break the 1968 version of the filibuster.

It's ironic that under today's fiercely politicized rules, a simple 45–43 majority would have been enough to confirm Abe Fortas as chief justice, changing the course of twentieth-century constitutional history. Brett Kavanaugh was confirmed by a vote of 50–48.

In 1968, though, the Fortas nomination, needing a supermajority, was dead in the water. Fortas withdrew his candidacy that afternoon. Since Earl Warren's resignation was conditional on the confirmation of a successor, Warren remained on the Court as chief justice, along with Fortas. The Court's 6–3 Democratic majority remained intact through the 1968 presidential election, in which Richard Nixon successfully campaigned against the Warren Court, especially in the South.

Things got much worse in the new year. In February 1969, shortly after Nixon's inauguration, Fortas admitted to receiving post-appointment legal payments of $20,000 per year (more than $120,000 in today's dollars) from a shady Wall Street financier, Louis Wolfson, in return for undefined legal advice. When Earl Warren learned of this outrageously unethical arrangement, he demanded Fortas's resignation to head off impeachment. Fortas resigned in disgrace in May 1969, closely followed by Warren in late June for health reasons at the close of the Supreme Court's term.

The resignations of Fortas and Warren handed Richard Nixon two unexpected Court vacancies during his first term, which he filled with two Republicans—Warren Burger and, after two failed nomination attempts, Harry Blackmun. When the illness of Justice Hugo Black (a Democrat) and the resignation of Justice John Marshall Harlan II (a Republican) opened two additional vacancies, Nixon filled them with two more Republicans, Lewis Powell and William Rehnquist—shifting the political makeup of the Supreme Court to 5–4 Republican from the 1968 lineup of 6–3 Democratic, with Earl Warren being counted as a Republican.

Had the Warren succession not been bungled, Democrats would almost certainly have maintained no worse than a 5–4 Supreme Court majority, and the constitutional landscape would look very different today. Once they lost their Supreme Court majority on January 7, 1972, the Democrats never regained control of the Supreme Court. Instead, the new Republican Supreme Court majority flipped the switch from equality to autonomy and, with the anomalous exception of *Roe v. Wade*'s autonomy blip in 1973, stopped the progressive legal movement toward racial, gender, and economic equity dead in its tracks.

It's hard enough to score in the game of Supreme Court deferred democracy. It's heartbreaking to have won the game in 1968, only to be undone by the greed and arrogance of a single Democratic nominee and the overweening pride and ambition of a Democratic president. It's almost as bad as having won the game in 2016, only to have President Obama's nomination of Merrick Garland unconstitutionally sabotaged by a malapportioned Republican Senate.

Here's just a sample of the cost of Abe Fortas's greed, arrogance, and ethical insensitivity, providing a tangible measure of how important it is for progressives to use deferred democracy to regain control of the Supreme Court.

EDUCATIONAL EQUITY

The Warren Court began in 1954 with the Supreme Court's unanimous rejection of "separate but equal" racially segregated public education, followed by a ferocious, largely successful assault on government-imposed racial apartheid. The Warren Court ended in 1973 with the newly minted Republican Supreme Court's 5–4 decision in *San Antonio v. Rodriguez*, upholding separate but *unequal*, racially polarized public education.

Invoking the right to equal protection of the laws guaranteed by the Fourteenth Amendment, advocates for Hispanic children attending poorly funded public schools in San Antonio, Texas, attacked the constitutionality of Texas's decision to fund its public education system almost exclusively through local property taxes, resulting in very significant, wholly predictable differences in per capita educational spending depending on whether a child lived in a wealthy white neighborhood with lots of valuable real estate to tax or in a poor black or Latino neighborhood with a minimal tax base. Under the Texas school financing plan, rich white suburbs such as Plano (a wealthy suburb of Dallas) boasted fine, well-funded public schools, while public schools in poor black or Latino neighborhoods in San Antonio were woefully underfunded.

The Supreme Court's five Republican justices rejected the argument that the Constitution's promise of the equal protection of the laws forbade Texas from knowingly adopting a school funding program that would spend far more government money per capita on rich white children than on poor black or Latino children. The four Democratic justices dissented, stressing the fundamental nature of education and the social consequences of funding rich white schools more generously than poor black ones.

Viewed from a purely legal perspective, the constitutional arguments in *Rodriguez* were in rough equipoise. The challengers' invocation of the Fourteenth Amendment to forbid predictable but unintentional racial discrimination in per capita educational funding was certainly plausible. In 1973, when I directed the ACLU's Supreme Court docket, I found it overwhelming. It built on *Brown* and on the Democratic Supreme Court's refusal to countenance unequal allocation of the right to vote in the absence of a showing of overwhelming need.

But Texas's counterargument that, in the absence of intentional discrimination, the Fourteenth Amendment required not strict equality in educational spending but merely enough spending to reach a minimal baseline of adequacy was not without legal force, especially since no intent to discriminate on the basis of race was alleged or proven.

I believe that the legal tie in *Rodriguez* was broken not by the intrinsic merits of the evenly balanced legal arguments but by the degree to which the five Republican justices subordinated the equality claims of the black and Latino challengers to the autonomy claims of white local residents of Texas to fund and control the education of their children as they saw fit.

I am not saying that the Republican justices were hostile to the claims of the black and Latino children. Rather, I assert merely that the Republican justices' intuitive ranking of the relative importance of the values of autonomy and equality caused them to perceive Texas's autonomy-advancing legal arguments as more persuasive than equally valid equality-enhancing ones advanced by the challengers. The four Democratic justices disagreed about the legal merits, not because they were smarter or morally superior but because the challengers' equality-enhancing legal arguments reinforced the Democratic justices' intuitive sense of the appropriate balance between autonomy and equality. In *Rodriguez*, when it was impossible to find a legal argument that advanced both autonomy and equality, Republican justices chose the legal argument that advanced autonomy; Democratic justices chose the legal argument that advanced equality. And that has made all the difference.

If LBJ and Abe Fortas had not run the Democratic Supreme Court off the cliff, *Rodriguez* would have been decided in favor of the poor Hispanic students, dramatically changing the face of public education in America. When someone tells you that voting doesn't really matter, think about the America that might have been in the last half of the twentieth century if there had been equal funding of public schools in both impoverished inner cities and affluent gated communities.

RACIAL EQUITY

Three years later, in 1976, the same five members of the Republican Supreme Court majority, this time joined by Democratic Justice Byron White (John F. Kennedy's only serving nominee to the Supreme Court), seriously weakened progressive efforts to use the Fourteenth Amendment's promise of equal protection of the laws to advance racial equity by holding in *Washington v. Davis* that the Fourteenth Amendment's equal protection clause provides protection against intentional racial discrimination but no protection at all against the knowing, reckless, negligent, or careless adoption of government policies that disproportionately harm minorities for no good reason. Three Democratic justices dissented.

The challengers in *Washington v. Davis*, black applicants for jobs in Washington, DC, argued that the city's civil service exams were full of questions that unfairly disadvantaged poorly educated black applicants but had little or nothing to do with how well an applicant could perform a particular job. Perfectly competent janitors and bus drivers, the argument went, do not have to know how to multiply and divide complex fractions.

The Democratic Warren Court had already accepted the argument—sometimes called a ban on unjustified "disparate impact"—in connection with the Title VII ban on employment discrimination. Under the Title VII test, once the racially disparate impact of a criterion for employment policy was demonstrated, an employer was obliged to either prove that the criterion was job-related or cease to use it.

In 1976, though, the District of Columbia wasn't covered by Title VII, which at that time applied only to private employers, so the challengers relied on the due process clause of the Fifth Amendment, with its long-recognized implied protection of equality.

In *Washington v. Davis*, five Republican justices, plus Justice White, refused to import the disparate-impact test into the Fourteenth Amendment. Instead, they insisted on a "discriminatory purpose" test that prohibits intentional or purposeful racial discrimination but has nothing at all to do with unintentional discrimination caused by knowing disregard, carelessness, negligence, or lack of concern.

The decision was a disaster for racial equity on two levels. First, the plight of racial minorities is never solely the result of purposeful discrimination. Much of the time, the majority makes policy (or fails to make policy) without thinking—or caring—about its potential impact on weak minorities. From the standpoint of a minority job applicant, though, it doesn't make any difference whether a disqualifying question was included on the test with the purpose of disqualifying black employees or is being asked because no one bothered to think about whether the question would knock out minorities for no good reason. In both settings, the minority applicant is out of a job because of his or her race.

Under *Washington v. Davis*, the Republican Supreme Court ruled that government has no constitutional duty to think about the foreseeable impact of its actions on vulnerable groups. Imagine what our highways would look like if new drivers were told that they were not allowed to injure someone intentionally but were under no duty to avoid negligent or reckless driving. *Washington v. Davis* turns vulnerable minorities into sitting ducks on that toxic highway, just waiting for an "accident" to happen. Worse, once you tell a cynical racist that all he has to do is make up a story about why his foreseeably discriminatory actions "unintentionally" harm blacks, how long do you think it will take him to come up with a pretextual explanation? What else do you think is going on when cynical Republican politicians claim that unnecessary voter ID requirements, stringent voter registration rules, or overly broad voter purge statutes are about preventing nonexistent fraud, not keeping poor blacks and Latinos off the voting rolls?

As in *Rodriguez*, the technical constitutional arguments in *Washington v. Davis* were, at a minimum, in rough equipoise. The Fifth Amendment's implied protection of equality could plausibly be read either way. I have no doubt that a Democratic Supreme Court would have broken the legal tie in favor of racial equity. Five Republicans broke the tie in favor of local autonomy. Subsequent Republican Supreme Court decisions extended the necessity of proving discriminatory intent to the Fifteenth Amendment's protection of voting rights, the Fourteenth Amendment's protection of women, and the protection of Native American religious exercises inherent in the First Amendment clause guaranteeing the free exercise of religion.

The sorry saga of hundreds of unsuccessful efforts by civil rights lawyers to prove "discriminatory purpose," as opposed to "disparate impact," demonstrates the magnitude of the Court's error—and just how much the Fortas fiasco really cost the movement for racial equity.

FELON DISENFRANCHISEMENT: THE ROOTS OF *BUSH V. GORE*

The 2016 presidential election wasn't the first to be hijacked and delivered to a minority president. In 1876, southern racists stole the Hays-Tilden election by disqualifying enough Tilden electors to give Hays a one-vote victory in the Electoral College despite losing the popular vote, in return for Hays's promise to abandon southern blacks by ending the military occupation of the defeated South. Hays kept his promise, and lynch law swept the South.

In 2016, it was the Russian government's disinformation campaign and a presidential candidate named Trump willing to violate the campaign finance laws to cover up evidence of his sexual escapades, and perhaps his willingness to cooperate with the Russians that hijacked the Electoral College for the losing candidate.

In 2000, it was a Republican Supreme Court that executed the heist by refusing to permit Florida to complete a recount of the presidential balloting ordered by the Florida Supreme Court, a recount that the Democratic candidate, Al Gore, plausibly expected to win. Largely because of incompetent administration of the paper ballot voting in Palm Beach and Broward Counties (Democratic strongholds), the Republican candidate, George W. Bush, carried Florida by just over six hundred votes after thousands of paper ballot votes for Gore were disallowed on dubious technical grounds.

The Democratic-controlled Florida Supreme Court ordered a careful manual recount of the disqualified paper ballots to ensure the integrity of the election. A five-justice Republican majority on the Supreme Court first stayed the recount, and eventually blocked it as coming too late (because of the stay). George W. Bush carried Florida and became a minority president.

But it should never have been that close. At the time of the 2000 election controversy, a provision of the 1968 Florida constitution that dated from 1868 barred individuals with a criminal record from voting, even after they had fully served their sentences—a ban that disenfranchised 25 percent of Florida's black male population in that election year. Had even one thousand of the hundreds of thousands of disenfranchised black males been allowed to vote in 2000, Al Gore would probably have been elected president.

Were the 2000 election held under today's rules, the decision in 2018 of 64 percent of Florida's voters to end felon disenfranchisement would probably have delivered the state to Gore. Ending felon disenfranchisement may flip Florida from Republican to Democratic in 2020, but only if a substantial proportion of the hundreds of thousands of re-enfranchised black voters are brought back into the process.

Given the massive racial disparities at work in the criminal justice system, it's no surprise that felon disenfranchisement always falls with discriminatory severity on poor people of color. Imagine two kids arrested for drunk driving in Florida. One's a young black teenager with no money. He'll be lucky to be allowed to plead to a felony and get probation. Depending on the judge, he may even serve time. Either way, as a convicted felon, under the old rules, he'd never vote again in Florida.

The other young drunk driver's name is George W. Bush Jr. He's represented by high-powered lawyers, appropriately supported by his influential family, and placed into an alcohol treatment program in lieu of facing a criminal charge. The drunk driving charges are dropped after he completes a rehabilitation program. To his credit, the young Bush beats his alcohol problem and goes on to become president of the United States.

We have the Fortas fiasco to thank for the legal and moral disaster of *Bush v. Gore* and the persistence of felon disenfranchisement. In 1974, in *Richardson v. Ramirez*, the newly minted five-justice Republican majority made a mockery of the equality-enhancing purpose of the Fourteenth Amendment, reading its Section 2 hypertechnically to permit the continued disenfranchisement of felons, despite the massive disparate impact on black voters. Predictably, the four Democratic justices dissented. A Democratic-controlled Court in 1974 would almost certainly have invalidated the racist practice once and for all, changing the face of American democracy, changing the outcome of the 2000 presidential election, and changing the political composition of the Supreme Court.

At a minimum, no disastrous invasion of Iraq. Perhaps no 2007–8 financial collapse. No Chief Justice John Roberts. No Justice Samuel Alito. No Justice Neil Gorsuch. No Justice Brett Kavanaugh.

In a futile effort to close the barn door after the horses had already escaped, once the 2000 election was over, the Brennan Center challenged the constitutionality of the racially discriminatory impact of Florida's felon disenfranchisement rules. *Washington v. Davis*'s insistence on proving "purposeful" discrimination could not save felon disenfranchisement, we argued, because it was clear that felon disenfranchisement had been adopted by Florida in 1868 in an intentional effort to disenfranchise formerly enslaved persons. Even Republican justices reject felon disenfranchisement when it is purposefully imposed to block blacks from voting. Mississippi's version of felon disenfranchisement was invalidated under the Fifteenth Amendment for just that reason

"Ah," replied the Republican district judge in Miami, "that's true." "But the 1868 Florida constitution is no longer in force. Florida adopted a new constitution in 1968."

"That's also true," we replied, "but the 1968 Florida constitution uses virtually the exact language as the 1868 constitution." At a minimum, we argued, if Florida repeats the exact language that it once used to discriminate on purpose, surely Florida should be required to prove that its motive has changed, especially when the provision continues to discriminate against black voters. No Democratic judge would have rejected such a plausible, equality-enhancing legal argument. No such luck, though, with Republican judges, for whom Florida's autonomy was apparently more important than the equality of its black citizens.

After years of bitter litigation, we lost because, in the twenty-first century, there was no surviving formal evidence of what the white pols in Florida had intended in 1968 when they decided to reenact the exact terms of the racist 1868 felon disenfranchisement provisions. The white pols were too smart to admit why they were copying the 1868 language that just happened to block thousands and thousands of black men from voting.

So George W. Bush beat Al Gore in 2000 because the Fortas fiasco cost the Democrats control of the Supreme Court in 1972. Were it not for the Fortas fiasco, felon disenfranchisement would have been struck down in 1974, Al Gore would have been elected president in 2000, and the Supreme Court would be blue today.

VIOLENCE AGAINST WOMEN

Persistent violence committed by men against women is a public health disaster and an enormous drag on the economy. It is a major cause of female absenteeism from work, and the principal reason women are reluctant to work in certain isolated or high-crime areas and at certain times. Violence against women is, of course, against the law in every state. But two centuries of hostility or indifference from too many male-dominated state judiciaries had barely made a dent in the problem.

In 1994, Congress recognized the economic cost of violence against women by exercising its power under the commerce clause to enact the Violence Against Women Act, opening the elite federal trial courts to women seeking redress for gender-motived violence.

For most of their history, those courts, staffed today by more than nine hundred of the nation's most respected trial judges, had virtually ignored issues of importance to women. The nineteenth-century Supreme Court had rejected a woman's right to vote and upheld the exclusion of women from the legal profession. It wasn't until 1934 that President Franklin Roosevelt appointed the first woman to a federal appeals court. President Harry Truman appointed the first woman to the federal trial bench in 1949. Until the Notorious RBG got her hands on it, a judge-made "domestic relations" exception blocked women from asking federal judges to deal with intrafamily disputes, including allegations of marital rape, child abuse, and domestic violence.

For more than two hundred years, women seeking to cope with state judicial and legislative indifference to gender-motivated violence—especially rape—were routinely shunted out of the elite federal courts and back into the very male-dominated state courts whose hostility and indifference had led to the judicial failure to act effectively to protect women in the first place.

The Violence Against Women Act sought to open the federal courts to women who were victims of gender-motivated violence, allowing our elite trial judges to confront the ongoing epidemic. In 2000, in *United States v. Morrison*, the Republican Supreme Court majority (the same majority that would hijack the presidential election later that year) reached back to pre-FDR Republican precedents limiting Congress's power to use the commerce clause to protect the weak, and invalidated Congress's effort to enhance the equality interests of women.

In *Morrison*, a student at Virginia Polytechnic Institute invoked the Violence Against Women Act to sue the school in federal court for failing to act against an athlete whom she accused of rape. The Republican majority invalidated the federal law, claiming that Congress had not sufficiently linked the statute to the adverse economic effects of gender-motivated violence. It was not enough, held the Republican majority, to demonstrate the economic link after the fact. Congress had to have been actually motivated by the link when it passed the law.

The four Democratic justices dissented, arguing that the issue was not the subjective intention of Congress (whatever that means, since Congress is made up of 535 different people with 535 different motives), but whether gender-motivated violence in fact affects the national economy. If it does, argued the Democratic dissenters, Congress has power to move against it to protect interstate commerce.

A Democratic-controlled Supreme Court would almost certainly have upheld the statute, providing women with a potent new legal remedy for failure to act vigorously against gender-motivated violence. At a minimum, a Democratic majority would have recognized that the equality-enhancing provisions of the Fourteenth Amendment authorize Congress to act to protect women against the indifference of the state courts. In later cases, the Notorious RBG rescued women from part of the problem by persuading a Republican Court to respect the right of a woman trapped in an intrafamily cycle of violence to seek relief in a federal court free from the nineteenth-century domestic relations exception. That's something, of course. But it's only a pale shadow of the equality-enhancing right to seek relief in federal court that women would have exercised if a Democratic Court had upheld the Violence Against Women Act.

REPRODUCTIVE FREEDOM

Roe v. Wade, decided in 1973 by a newly minted 5–4 Republican Court, protects a woman's right to choose whether to bear a child. It's hard to believe today, but both Republican and Democratic justices initially viewed the constitutional right to choose as an easy

legal (if emotionally wrenching moral) case advancing the autonomy interests of the woman and her doctor. Roe was decided by a
7–2 bipartisan vote.

Over the years, though, passionate, often religiously driven opposition to abortion persuaded several Republican justices (who
happened to be Catholic) that Roe had underestimated the potential autonomy interest of the fetus. If, the dissenting justices argued,
a genuine dispute exists over whose autonomy right to favor, the
dispute should be resolved by the democratic process, not by constitutional judges.

Once the autonomy issue became complicated by rival claim-
ants, Ruth Bader Ginsburg, then a judge serving on the District of
Columbia Court of Appeals, sought to alter the terms of the debate,
arguing that the right to choose was not solely a question of autonomy; rather, she argued, it was central to the attainment of equality
for women. No woman, RBG argued, could hope to participate
equally in the economic, political, and social life of the nation if
she was required by her reproductive organs to involuntarily spend
considerable time bearing and then raising children. No society,
she observed, had ever attained equality for women without permitting them to control their reproductive lives.

The real legal issue posed by the abortion cases, Justice Ginsburg
argued, is whether the unquestionable equality interests of women
outweigh the deeply contested alleged autonomy interest of a fetus.
Viewed as a collision between conflicting claims to autonomy and
the clear equality interests of women, the minority Democratic justices dug in and supported Roe. Republican justices (in particular
the male Republican justices), less moved by the equality interests of
women, have chipped away at Roe, especially at protections for poor
women. Troubled by the implications of overruling a rights-bearing
precedent, however, they have stopped short of overruling it.

In 1992, in Planned Parenthood v. Casey, a Republican-
controlled Court, this time with a comfortable 8–1 Republican
majority (reflecting the deferred democracy consequences of
twelve consecutive years of Republican presidents), came within
a whisker of overturning Roe v. Wade. At the last minute, cooler

Republican heads, committed to the stability and sense of security that respect for precedent provides, declined to overturn *Roe* but began the process of chipping away at the case—especially when the rights of poor women are at stake.

The watered-down judicial review standard imposed in *Casey*—whether a regulation poses an "undue burden" on the right to choose—has operated as a green light for anti-choice Republican legislators to pile on as many regulations as possible in an effort to undermine the right to choose whether to bear a child. In *Rust v. Sullivan*, for example, a 5–4 decision by the Republican majority upheld a federal gag rule banning federally funded doctors from talking to their patients about abortion. The five Republican justices insisted on viewing federally funded doctors for the poor as shills for the government, instead of as full-fledged providers of medical services. *Rust* should be appalling from both Republican autonomy and Democratic equality perspectives. The case runs roughshod over the autonomy interests of both doctor and patient in service of the government's decision to advance the highly contested alleged autonomy interest of the fetus. The majority opinion entirely ignores both the equality interests of poor women patients, and the autonomy interests of poor women and their doctors. No Democratic Court would have voted that way.

In 2007, in *Gonzales v. Carhart*, a five-justice Republican majority further eroded *Roe*, applying the *Casey* "undue burden" test to uphold a ban on generally accepted medical procedures for late-second-trimester abortions, further elevating the contested autonomy interest of the fetus at the expense of the autonomy and equality interests of women and their doctors. No Democratic Court would have given such short shrift to the equality values bound up in the question of whether women can control their reproductive lives.

In 2016, in *Whole Women's Health Clinic v. Hellerstedt*, in what was Justice Anthony Kennedy's last hurrah before retiring, the four Democratic justices, plus Justice Kennedy, struck down a Texas anti-abortion law that piled so many onerous restrictions on abortion facilities that they were forced to shut down in large areas of rural Texas, leaving women with no opportunity to exercise what is left of the right to choose. But with Justice Kennedy gone, there's no guarantee that Justice Kavanaugh will provide a fifth vote in such a case in the future. In fact, it's quite possible that he'll join with his four Republican colleagues to render *Roe* a dead letter for poor women, without the need to overrule it formally. As far as middle-class women are concerned, though, under a Republican Court with a thin commitment to equality, *Roe* clings to life on the fragile support system of respect for rights-bearing precedents. As we'll see in chapter 6, the Supreme Court has never overruled a rights-bearing precedent.

EGALITARIAN DEMOCRACY

Modern campaign finance law begins in 1976 in *Buckley v. Valeo* before a 5–4 Republican Supreme Court. As in *Roe*, the justices—both Republican and Democratic—initially thought the issue of limiting campaign spending by the rich was an easy autonomy case. The deeply flawed 1974 congressional statute at issue in *Buckley* capped campaign spending at an unreasonably low figure, making it difficult for a challenger to oust an incumbent with a built-in set of advantages, including name recognition and free mailing privileges. The law limited independent expenditures by supporters to just enough money to buy a quarter-page ad in the *New York Times*. The statute also discriminated in favor of the two major parties and made it difficult to run for president as an independent.

The Republican justices predictably recoiled at the assault on speaker autonomy imposed by draconian government-imposed political spending limits and gave predictably short shrift to the asserted equality interests of most Americans in limiting the power of the rich to influence the outcome of elections.

The Democratic justices, confronted by such an extreme statute, shared the Republicans' concern for the autonomy rights of speakers. Since the Democratic justices, led by Justice Brennan, were sure that the equality interests of ordinary voters could be adequately advanced by the prospect of public funding of election campaigns, they did not hesitate to join with Republican colleagues in striking down the 1974 law. The *Buckley* decision was really a grand bargain, where the Republican justices preserved autonomy and the Democratic justices provided a road map for electoral equality.

As with *Roe*, however, it soon became apparent that the autonomy and equality interests of participants in the democratic process could not be so easily reconciled. At that point, the Supreme Court fragmented along familiar partisan lines, with the Republican autonomy-friendly majority repeatedly blocking Democratic efforts to promote a more egalitarian democracy at the expense of even a dollop of autonomy. The Democratic minority consistently dissented on egalitarian grounds.

In the 2011 decision in *Arizona Free Enterprise v. Bennett*, for example, the five-justice Republican majority arguably reneged on the *Buckley* bargain, striking down Arizona's plan to provide public funds to poorly funded candidates that roughly matched the spending of rich, privately funded opponents. The Republican majority—deeply committed to protecting speaker autonomy—reasoned that the Arizona matching scheme would violate the autonomy-friendly First Amendment rights of privately funded candidates by potentially deterring them from raising private money. The Democratic minority argued, unsuccessfully, that the First Amendment does not protect the right of the rich to enjoy unanswered campaign speech.

In *McCutcheon v. Federal Election Commission* (2014), the same five-justice Republican majority struck down generous six-figure limits on the amounts that a single donor could contribute to all candidates for federal office in a single year, rejecting the idea that massive amounts contributed to large numbers of candidates would allow a large donor to exercise excessive, unequal political influence. The five Republican justices reasoned that as long as each contribution was too low to risk influencing a single legislator, no reason existed to interfere with the autonomy interests of someone wishing to contribute unlimited amounts to all legislators. The Democratic minority dissented, unsuccessfully arguing that unlimited contributions to large numbers of candidates was certain to vest the donor with disproportionate political influence with the party's leadership, if not with each legislator.

Four years earlier, in *Citizens United* (2010), the same five-justice Republican majority struck down the ban on corporate campaign spending, taking the extraordinary step of recognizing that large profit-making corporations are endowed with the same autonomy interests as human beings.

Stay tuned for the corporate right to bear arms, or, at least a corporate Fifth Amendment right to resist self-incrimination. The Republican Supreme Court has already recognized a corporation's right to seek religiously based exemptions from the duties of citizenship. If things keep going the way they are in the Supreme Court, soon you'll be able to be adopted by a corporation. Maybe even marry one. Until then, though, you'll just have to get used to being screwed by them.

In all three campaign finance reform cases, the five-justice Republican majority broke a legal tie in favor of arguments advancing the autonomy interests of rich speakers—the red Constitution in action. In all three cases, the four-justice Democratic minority fiercely dissented, arguing that under the blue Constitution, campaign finance regulation was constitutional as an effort to advance an egalitarian democracy, with only minimal costs to autonomy. They lost. And they will continue to lose until Democrats regain control of the Supreme Court.

GUN CONTROL

In *District of Columbia v. Heller*, faced with legal arguments ending in a tie, the Supreme Court split 5–4 on gun control along predictable partisan lines. Five Republican justices embraced legal arguments upholding a pure autonomy-based right to own a gun. A Democratic Court would have upheld equally plausible equality-enhancing legal arguments upholding a ban on gun ownership in the inner cities designed to protect the community against excessively powerful armed thugs.

Chalk up another cost of the Fortas fiasco and the Republican

Supreme Court's hijacking of the 2000 election. The list could go on—gutting criminal procedure protections for the poor, closing the courts to the vulnerable, and the replacement of civil juries with compulsory arbitration. All courtesy of a red Constitution made possible by the Democratic leadership's failure at the game of deferred democracy.

Imagine what American democracy might look like today if LBJ had not blown the Warren succession—the Supreme Court would be blue; inner-city schools would receive equal funding; the Sheldon Adelsons of the world would not be able to buy elections; black men who had served their time would have been able to vote in Florida and elsewhere; the Voting Rights Act would still protect the voting rights of blacks and Latinos; partisan gerrymandering would no longer protect Republican members of Congress against a nationwide Democratic majority; and the right to vote would be protected by the First Amendment.

THE CLINTON SHIPWRECK

With Democrats in the Supreme Court wilderness after 1972, the process of deferred democracy continued to percolate in the background, initially favoring Republicans in 1976, 1980, 1984, and 1988, eventually producing an 8–1 Republican Supreme Court. Democratic success in the 1992, 1996, 2008, and 2012 presidential elections (Democrats also won the popular vote in 2000 and 2016, only to lose in the Electoral College) translated, through the processes of deferred democracy, into increased Democratic representation on the Supreme Court. The appointments of Justices Stephen Breyer, Ruth Bader Ginsburg, Sonia Sotomayor, and Elena Kagan and the unexpected death of Justice Antonin Scalia in February 2016 allowed the Democrats to claw back to 4–4 status, with control of the Court in their grasp.

As I have noted, had the Supreme Court vacancy opened by the death of Justice Scalia in February 2016 been filled with a fifth Democratic justice, Democrats would have controlled the Supreme Court for the first time since 1972 and only the second time since the Civil War. The stage would have been set for the resurgence of the blue Constitution. But it was not to be. Just as the Fortas fiasco cost the Democratic Party control of the Supreme Court during the last third of the twentieth century and the Supreme Court's heist of the presidency in 2000 cost Democrats control in the early twenty-first century, the inexplicably anemic Democratic turnout in the 2014 congressional elections cost the Democrats control of the Senate and, hence, of the Supreme Court in 2016.

To my mind, the appallingly low Democratic turnout in the 2014 congressional elections, in which only 34 percent of eligible voters bothered to vote, rivals both the Fortas fiasco and the hijacking of the 2000 presidential election in the annals of Democratic ineptitude in the deferred democracy game. It's not as though there was some great Republican groundswell in 2014. Republicans won the Senate first, because of the radical malapportionment of Senate seats: Republican senators elected from sparsely populated states that skew white and rural resulted in a Senate majority that represents far less than 40 percent of the population; and second, because only a third of the eligible voters bothered to vote in the 2014 senatorial elections, a sliver of ideologically motivated voters representing no more than 17 percent of the electorate wound up choosing that majority.

Once they gained control, the Republican majority was able to torpedo President Obama's nomination of Merrick Garland by simply refusing to consider it. With the Garland nomination becalmed, Hillary Clinton's unexpected defeat in the Electoral College in the 2016 presidential election cost the Democrats control of the Supreme Court yet again. If just a fragment of the Democratic base had turned out in the 2014 senatorial elections, the Democrats would have retained the Senate and Merrick Garland would have been confirmed as the fifth Democratic justice long before the Clinton shipwreck.

Entire ecosystems will be wiped out in order to generate the pulp needed to publish books analyzing the 2016 election. This book won't be one of them. Who knows why Trump carried Wisconsin, Michigan, and Pennsylvania? Maybe the Russians did it, with or without Trump's cooperation. Maybe it was Trump's willingness to violate the campaign finance laws by paying to suppress stories about his sexual escapades. Maybe it was James Comey's loose lips. Maybe it was the ceaseless infighting within the Clinton campaign. Maybe it was the Wikileaks hack of the Democratic National Committee. Maybe it was the smugness and self-righteousness of the Clinton leadership team, which allowed the campaign to ignore Michigan and to patronize blue-collar voters in the Rust Belt. Maybe it was the presence of Bernie Sanders as the ultimate spoiler. Maybe it was the Green Party's diversion of votes from Clinton. Maybe it was the decent folks who sat on their hands because they just didn't like the Clintons. Maybe it was black voters who punished Hillary for the crime bill that passed in 1994, when her husband was president, and which she supported. Or maybe Hillary was punished for not being Barack Obama. Maybe it was the women who turned on Hillary because she didn't seem to respect or understand their more conventional life choices. Maybe it was Trump's satanic genius at appealing to racism, misogyny, economic insecurity, and xenophobia.

It was probably all those things—and more. Whatever the causes, though, it's important to tally the cost of the lost Supreme Court opportunity, if only to remind folks of the constitutional stakes in every senatorial and presidential election. The major cost of the 2014 electoral swoon and 2016 Clinton shipwreck is the loss of a golden opportunity for Democrats, earned by years of deferred democratic success—including victory in the 2000 and 2016 popular vote—to undo or at least blunt the worst of the Republican Supreme Court precedents unleashed by the Fortas fiasco. Every one of the cases that I've described above, where a Republican majority broke legal ties in favor of autonomy of the strong rather than equality for the weak, would have become a candidate for reversal or erosion under a Democratic Court. It would have taken time, but a Democratic Supreme Court would have recalibrated the constitutional balance between autonomy and equality in a blue Constitution requiring equal funding of public education, rejecting pretextual defenses of government policies that openly discriminate against women and racial minorities, upholding thoughtful efforts to deal with the corrosive effect of big money on egalitarian democracy, authorizing Congress to take action on violence against women, protecting reproductive freedom for poor women, and reopening the federal courts for the weak.

I harbor no illusions that a Supreme Court, remade in a Trumpist image, will meddle with existing Republican precedents that systematically subordinate equality to autonomy. If anything, I fear that it will further entrench them. Get ready for a barrage of religion and free speech cases under the First Amendment allowing true believers to harness government as an engine in their holy wars, while also offering fellow true believers the right to opt out of the duties of citizenship. It will all be done under the red Constitution in the name of autonomy—and at the expense of equality.

But while Republican readings of the First Amendment may usher in an era of deeply mistaken constitutional law that will further prop up the strong and subordinate the weak, it will just be more of the same. We've lived under a red Constitution for the last half century. Wrong as future autonomy-driven decisions will be, they will not further weaken the fabric of our democracy, any more than the Republican decisions described above already have.

My real fear is that Trump will reconstitute the Court in his appalling image as a populist organ that disdains judicial review as anti-democratic. That's how strongmen usually attack judicial checks on their power. The code word they always use is "deference." Under a regime of deference, the courts are left in place. There is no change in formal doctrine. But the constitutional tiebreaker is changed from protection of autonomy or equality to deference to the views of the populist officials whose policies are under judicial review.

We've seen where the deference road takes us. In 1944, a Democratic Supreme Court upheld the internment of Japanese Americans in concentration camps, euphemistically called "detention centers," because iconic Democratic justices Hugo Black and William O. Douglas opted to defer to the wartime military's racist views about the importance of locking up people with "yellow" skin. In 1951, a Democratic Supreme Court upheld the jailing of the leadership of the American Communist Party for the crime of being active communists because iconic justices Robert Jackson and Felix Frankfurter deferred to Congress's paranoid view of the threat to national security posed by the mere existence of a militantly Marxist American Communist Party. In 1969, iconic justices William Brennan and Earl Warren upheld the jailing of young men for symbolically burning their draft cards to express opposition to the war in Vietnam, deferring to the view of the military about the significance of the virtually nonexistent risks resulting from not possessing a draft card during the brief period needed to issue a replacement. And in 2018, the blatantly discriminatory travel ban predominantly targeting Muslims was upheld by a five-justice Republican majority chanting about deference to the president.

If the travel ban decision is a harbinger of a generalized Republican jurisprudence of deference, dark days may lie ahead unless Trump and his like are defeated at the polls. I hope I'm wrong, but don't count on anything except spineless deference from a Trumpist Supreme Court.

6

What's Law Got to Do with It?

Please Don't Kill All the Lawyers—Yet

If the outcome of so many constitutional cases is predetermined by the partisan makeup of the Supreme Court, what exactly do high-powered lawyers add to judicial review? Maybe nothing. Maybe constitutional lawyers are just decorative. They strut and preen in pinstripes and pantsuits, charge large fees, use big words, and communicate in codes largely designed to keep nonlawyers in the dark about what is really going on. I know. I've been one of those constitutional lawyers for more than fifty years.

Maybe fancy constitutional lawyers are just glorified travel agents. When I maneuver to file a case before a friendly judge, I'm really just reserving a table at a fashionable restaurant. If the dinner ultimately tastes good, I'm entitled to credit for excellent taste in judges, but not necessarily for cooking the meal. I can suggest a recipe, but it's the judge who does the cooking.

So, apart from decoration, pontification, and judge-shopping, can good lawyers really affect the outcome of a constitutional case? My highly self-interested answer is a resounding "sometimes," "maybe," and "I think so." But not in the way lawyers often claim. While high-powered lawyers like to tell themselves—and their clients—that skill in crafting an imaginative legal argument can play a crucial role in virtually every case, in the many intensely contested constitutional cases that lack clear textual direction, persuasive binding precedent, and/or a tidy package of values pulling in the same direction, competent constitutional lawyers are likely to fight to a legal tie that will be broken by a judge's values. In such value-driven cases, lawyers are like the oarsmen in Tolstoy's rowboat trying to tow a legal ocean liner on a sea of judicial values.

But don't kill all the lawyers, at least not yet. In the many important constitutional cases where the raw material for value-free persuasive lawyering exists—cases with clear text, persuasive precedents, and consensus values—excellent lawyers can and do play a crucial role in shaping the case's outcome. The important contribution of lawyers to the process of judicial review occurs when a well-crafted legal argument based on a combination of clear text, well-reasoned precedents, and/or the tug of shared values is sufficiently persuasive to guide a thoughtful, principled judge to a single, preferable legal result, regardless of the judge's values.

It is in those cases—the true "rule of law" cases—that the value-driven red and blue Constitutions often merge to form an apolitical, relatively value-free purple Constitution. Given the vast array of rights-affirming precedents decided by both Republican and Democratic Supreme Courts over the years, the prospect of apolitical, lawyer-driven enforcement of fundamental rights embedded by precedent in the purple Constitution's text, provides real hope for a genuine bulwark against a Trumpist drift toward authoritarianism and scapegoating.

But just how strong is the purple Constitution? Can it provide enduring protection in the time of Trump? I wish I could assure you that the core of our constitutional heritage is safely nestled in the purple Constitution, just waiting for apolitical enforcement at the hands of excellent lawyers and principled judges. But I can't make that promise. I can only express a belief—maybe only a hope—that most of the purple Constitution will hold, even in a relentlessly conservative Supreme Court. I'm relatively confident that precedents protective of autonomy—First Amendment protections of religious freedom and free speech, as well as Fourth Amendment protection against unreasonable searches and seizures—will hold. It's the equality precedents that worry me.

To understand why I can't promise, only hope, we need to survey the idea of precedent and the binding rule of law at the heart of the purple Constitution's DNA. That survey must start with the question of whether we ever live under a judicially enforced rule of law. Critics have argued, from both the left and the right, that the very idea of a rule of law is a myth. Given the limitations of language and logic and the power of politics, thoughtful critics argue that judges can almost always decide any case any way they wish, and then disguise the outcome as "compelled" by legal commands from legislatures or past judges.

If that critique is true, we live not under a rule of law but under the rule of judges, where the purple Constitution—and every other legal document—is just an excuse for covert judicial lawmaking. In my experience, though, critics who focus solely on important areas where good lawyering is likely to fail to generate a single clearly preferable legal result seriously underestimate how often good lawyers and principled judges *do* succeed in operating under the apolitical rule of law.

I have found that most of the time, the law speaks relatively clearly to competent lawyers and principled judges. If I took ten excellent lawyers and placed them behind a veil of ignorance, eliminating the usual client-driven or personal incentives for lawyers to seek to twist the law in one direction or another, I would be willing to bet that in cases reaching across the full spectrum of the law, at least eight and perhaps all ten, using the analytic skills they learned in law school, would reach a consensus about what the law expects in a given setting.

Think of the legal system as a huge pyramid. The lawyer's office sits on the bottom rung. It's a place where the law usually sends relatively clear signals that are easy enough to decipher if a skilled, principled lawyer takes the time to study them. When a client consults a competent lawyer before she makes a will, buys a house, or invests money in a business, the lawyer is generally able to provide useful guidance, because the law is speaking relatively clearly to her. Not always, of course. But most of the time.

Don't be confused by that fact that it is almost always possible for an agile lawyer to argue that the law is sending more than one signal. That's just legal smoke, usually aimed at advancing a client's interests or the lawyer's personal interests. A good, self-aware lawyer usually knows, though, when she is acting as the law's oracle and when she's blowing smoke. When a client has already behaved in a certain way by the time he arrives at his lawyer's office, under our adversary system of justice it is the lawyer's duty as a zealous advocate to blow as much legal smoke as possible—to try to twist the law into a pretzel to get the client off. At that point, it's usually a competent judge or skilled opposing counsel who brings a dose of reality to the proceedings by cutting through the implausible legal smoke. That's why competent judges are so important. It's also why ensuring that both sides have competent counsel is so important. Without a competent judge and competent adversary counsel, the rule of law is helpless to defend itself from legal smoke.

When, however, a lawyer is advising a client *before the client acts*, the lawyer plays a vastly different role. Before a client has acted, an ethical lawyer should function as the law's oracle, not the client's mouthpiece. The temporal distinction is crucial. Before the client has acted, an ethical lawyer's function is to educate clients about the behavior that the law expects. After the client has acted, the lawyer's duty is to get the client off by confusing the law's signals, if necessary. In both settings, though, good lawyers usually know what the law is trying to say. Fortunately for the rule of law, so do good judges.

So in the wake of 9/11, when President George W. Bush's lawyers told him, before he acted, that torturing prisoners didn't violate international law, they were confusing their roles as advisors and advocates. If the president had already acted, a good lawyer-advocate would have been duty bound to advance any legal argument that might have shielded the president from legal sanction, even an argument that the advocate would reject if she were the judge. That's what Rudy Giuliani is trying to do for an embattled Donald Trump.

Before President Bush acted, though, the lawyer-advisor's duty was to tell him that international law is relatively clear: torture is unlawful anywhere, anytime. It was not to assure him that some loophole might be found if he ignored the law's relatively clear signals.

Ultimately, of course, it's the client's call. All a lawyer can do is explain what behavior the law appears to expect, assess the client's level of risk if she decides to act differently, and decline to participate in the commission of a crime or a fraud. Make no mistake, though—as I've said, a good lawyer usually knows what the law is trying to say.

Now, move up one level on the legal pyramid from the lawyer's office to the trial court, where opposing parties are in formal disagreement, but not necessarily over what the law says. In fact, most of the time in the trial court, the governing law is relatively clear to a competent judge, despite the legal smoke. The parties' real disagreement is very often over the facts. That's where excellent trial lawyers really earn their keep. Persuading a judge or jury to accept a client's version of the facts is a skill of a high order (worth a book of its own, but not this one). We're focusing on the governing law in the trial courts, which is usually clear enough to an able, intellectually honest trial judge. Not always. But most of the time.

Another layer up the legal pyramid are the intermediate appeals courts. Since appellate courts in our system usually can't challenge the factual findings of lower courts, most appeals center on disputes over what the law is. Even then, I've found that if I can avoid viewing the issue through an advocate's glasses, a combination of persuasive text, well-reasoned precedent, and shared values usually points the way to a legally preferable result. That's why the vast bulk of appeals to three-judge federal appeals panels are resolved by unanimous vote.

Finally, move to the highest appellate court, the apex of the pyramid—the Supreme Court. That's where the rarefied air is richest in legal ties caused by ambiguous text, conflicting values, and nonexistent, ambiguous, or conflicting legal signals. When, as with the United States Supreme Court, the highest court can pick and choose the cases it hears, the percentage of legal ties is at its highest because one criterion for accepting a case is to resolve disagreements in the lower courts over the correct legal outcome. But even then, at the height of potential legal uncertainty, I have found that most of the seventy to eighty cases heard each term in the modern Supreme Court can be resolved on the basis of strong legal signals, without resort to the justices' values. It's why so many Supreme Court decisions are either unanimous or decided by lopsided majorities.

Sometimes, of course, the legal signals just don't work. Incompetent lawyers may do a lousy job of decoding them and presenting them to clients and judges. Shady clients may ignore them. Ambitious lawyers may garble legal signals in the hope of pleasing a powerful client. A judge of limited ability may be unable to understand the legal signals, even when lawyers do a competent job of decoding them. Occasionally a judge's values may be so intensely felt that they blot out the legal signals. Relatively rarely, judges can see the legal signals just fine but, driven by values, self-consciously decide to ignore them.

In a surprisingly high percentage of Supreme Court cases, the signals work just fine, guiding the justices to a legally preferred, value-neutral result. Each term, however, there are at least several important cases in the Supreme Court, usually involving constitutional questions, where conflicting or weak legal signals result in formal legal ties that are broken by characteristically partisan values. As we've seen, in such cases Republican justices have tended to favor legal arguments advancing individual autonomy, while Democratic justices will more often be persuaded by an equality-enhancing legal argument.

Even though such cases are crucially important and deservedly get most of the public and academic attention, value-laden tie cases are black swans, surrounded by the great mass of cases where good judges and good lawyers work together to deliver the apolitical rule of law. It's a mistake to pretend that the black swans do not exist. But it's also a mistake to treat the Supreme Court's black swans as if they were the entire flock.

If all we had were black swans, our entire legal system would be a lie. Killing all the lawyers wouldn't matter much. But please don't—not yet, anyway—because it's the lawyers, with all their posturing and infuriating antics, who provide able, principled judges with the raw material for the purple Constitution's rule of law in

the many, many cases where it is possible to aspire to it. How do
they do it?

In the beginning, there's the purple Constitution's naked text. If all
we had was that text, though, there wouldn't be much of a purple
Constitution. Given the inherent ambiguity of virtually every word
in the Constitution, almost every constitutional case would turn
not on a genuine command from the text but on the judge's values.
Much of the late Justice Antonin Scalia's formidable legal career
was spent trying to increase the number of cases governed by a
genuine command from the purple Constitution's text by deploying his theory of originalism. As we've seen, though, originalism, in
practice, fails to point the way to a single, correct way of reading the
Constitution's necessarily ambiguous text.

The failure of originalism to generate single right answers in
most settings does not, however, render constitutional text wholly
incapable of providing an intellectually honest judge with persuasive apolitical guidance. When guidance can't be found in the naked text, sometimes it can be found in context and structure. Words
in a complex legal document such as the Constitution are rarely
free radicals existing in splendid isolation from one another. When
the entire text is read holistically, relationships between and among
the individual words become visible, potentially infusing a single
word with enriched persuasive meaning. Justice David Souter's
opinions during his nineteen years on the Supreme Court often
used context and respect for structure as a way of giving the naked
text a preferred meaning. Souter's work demonstrates that it is possible to take text seriously without being sucked into the originalist
vortex.

In the past, I've argued that the forty-five words of the First
Amendment when read as a whole reveal the careful organization
of its ideas—starting with freedom of conscience, moving outward
to freedoms of speech, press, and assembly, and culminating in the
right to petition for redress of grievance. Read that way, the First
Amendment describes the half-life of a democratic idea, born in

the conscience of a free citizen and shared with the political community in ever-widening concentric circles of speech, press, and assembly, culminating in formal petition for adoption by the polity. Such a democracy-enhancing document, I've argued, cannot plausibly be read to forbid the campaign financing reform needed to save democracy.

The trouble with such holistic readings and flights of poetic fancy, though, is that they often don't deliver a single right answer, just a plausible one. In my experience, the holistic persuasion meter usually stops at "plausible." All that does is give a judge another potential outcome. Sometimes, of course, that's all a judge wants—a plausible excuse for advancing her values. Every once in a while, though, a really good lawyer with the right raw material can hit the apolitical jackpot by cloaking the naked text in an elegantly persuasive coat of underlying purpose and structural context capable of persuading a principled judge without resort to values.

More often, instead of using the text, skilled lawyers try to persuade a judge to follow an apolitical trail to a preferred legal outcome by invoking the principle of *stare decisis*, the fancy Latin term for respecting judicial precedent. In lawyer-speak, that's the unwritten rule that directs a British or American judge (but not judges in France, Germany, or other civil-law countries) to treat prior judicial decisions concerning the same (or an analogous) legal question as binding, without considering whether the earlier case was correctly decided.

Why on earth, you may ask, would we want to saddle our judges with a duty to recycle used judicial decisions, without even considering whether they are right or wrong? Most European lawyers and judges think we're nuts. In their legal world, judges pay respectful attention to earlier decisions but follow them only when they think those cases have been rightly decided.

Where does our commitment to *stare decisis* come from? How strong is it? And can it really protect us from Trump?

Our deep, if unwritten, commitment to following judicial

precedent is part human nature, part thoughtful attempt to make law predictable, part concern for equal treatment, and part crafty, self-interested judicial behavior. Let's look at each.

There is something in human nature that calls us to respect and repeat what we've already done. Occasionally the urge to respect the past morphs into tradition, habit, even obsession. Often the urge is recycled as superstition. Sometimes it's revered as experiential learning.

Imagine, once upon a time, that our distant ancestors skipped a meal the night before a particularly successful hunt. If I were leader of the pack, I'd associate skipped meals with successful hunts. I'd insist that all future hunters repeat the ritual fast. If the hunt failed, anyone who hadn't followed the ritual would be on the hook.

British and American judges venerate past practice just as intensely, maybe more so. Like fasting before the hunt, respect for precedent can become an obsession. Until 1956, for example, it was the law in Great Britain that once the Law Lords (Britain's highest court) had decided a legal issue, the decision became embedded in precedential concrete for all time. Not even later Law Lords themselves could undo it. Only Parliament could fix a broken precedent.

In our current system, following judicial precedent is merely habitual. British and American judges are expected to defer to past decisions; but, like breaking the smoking habit, if the judge can be persuaded that the past decision was wrong enough and its consequences harmful enough, a binding precedent can be judicially overruled and replaced. The Supreme Court did it in 2018 when it overturned a 1977 case that had permitted public employee unions to charge "agency fees" to nonmembers to cover the cost of providing collective bargaining services. Five Republican justices ruled that requiring dissenting public employees to support unions in any form violates the First Amendment. The four Democratic justices dissented.

Not surprisingly, overruling a past precedent occurs most often in constitutional cases, where it takes the earthquake of a constitutional amendment to correct a judicial mistake. But even then it's rare. Instead, judges tend to erode a disfavored precedent, leaving the formal shell in place but draining it of much of its force. That's what's already happened to *Roe v. Wade* under forty-five years of a Republican Supreme Court.

Roe is an extreme case generating almost unparalleled levels of intensely value-driven disagreement, especially from people (including justices) whose deeply held personal beliefs equate abortion with murder. As we've seen, in 1973, the justices viewed *Roe* as a relatively straightforward autonomy case allowing women to control their bodies. Over time, the autonomy issue became complicated by demands to grant a measure of autonomy protection to the fetus. Repeated efforts to overrule *Roe* have thus far foundered on respect for precedent (no Supreme Court rights-granting precedent has ever been overruled), continuing concern for a woman's autonomy, and the force of Justice Ginsburg's equality-based defense of a woman's right to choose. But *Roe* remains uniquely vulnerable to being overruled or further eroded by a current Supreme Court majority, many of whom are personally committed to recognizing the autonomy interests of a fetus and are unmoved by legal arguments advancing equality.

In the vast bulk of settings, though, since American judges, as a matter of training, social convention, self-interest, and received wisdom, are deeply wedded to respecting past precedent even when they disagree with it, rejecting clear precedent is—and will continue to be—relatively rare in the American legal system.

Such a veneration of the past isn't just an atavistic impulse. Respecting precedent is what makes it possible for British and American law to send reliable signals about how people are expected to behave. As a matter of theory, civil-law countries such as France or Germany don't need binding precedent because they operate under comprehensive statutory codes that are supposed to send clear signals on just about everything. Common-law systems such as ours don't have comprehensive codes. Indeed, until recently, statutes played a relatively minor role in British and American law. Instead, judges, in deciding cases before them, announced judge-made common-law rules derived from logic and custom that filled in the huge gaps in the statutory world.

Think about it for a minute. In the absence of a comprehensive statutory code binding on everyone, unless the common-law rule announced by the first judge is deemed binding on future judges, there would be no way to provide a client with firm guidance about how the law expected her to behave.

"So what?" you might say. "Let the clients believe what they want." But that can't be the answer when you are talking about law. Most of the time we think of law as the punishment we impose—or should impose—on someone who has allegedly acted badly. The second Justice Harlan used to call it the "post-event" function of law. It's what we see on television and in the movies. *Perry Mason, Twelve Angry Men*—that's where all the drama is.

As Justice Harlan reminded us, though, the more important function of law is to act as a great educator *before* the bad conduct takes place—persuading, cajoling, threatening, deterring, and inducing its audience to behave a certain way. But how can law persuade its audience if the audience can't predict what it is? Respect for precedent turns the first judge's decision—right or wrong—into the raw material for an accurate prediction of what the law will be in the future. Thus, respect for binding precedent provides us with a predictable pre-event way to know what the law requires, enabling us stay out of the clutches of post-event law. In our common-law legal system, veneration of past judicial precedent, even when we think it is wrong, is the price we pay for a coherent system of pre-event legal signals.

Respecting past judicial precedent is also a key component of the notion of "equal justice under law." If *stare decisis* didn't exist, judges, bound only by ambiguous naked text and their own values, would routinely decide identical cases differently. It happens in Europe all the time.

Imagine two litigants with the same legal case in the same courthouse on two consecutive days. *Stare decisis* ensures that once the first case is decided, both litigants will receive the same legal result—the essence of equal treatment. Maybe both are being treated wrongly, but at least they are being treated the same. If the order of the two cases were reversed, the first case might have come out differently, and the binding precedent in the second case might be wholly different. It is far from reassuring to realize that decisional equality often comes at such an arbitrary price.

Finally, there's a strong whiff of institutional self-interest in a judge's respect for precedent. *Stare decisis* turns out to be very good for judicial business. You might think that a judge would be resentful of the duty to defer to a dusty precedent, especially if she has doubts about its correctness. But most judges embrace their precedential chains for at least three self-interested reasons. In the first place, it's a relief for a judge to be able to say, "I know this decision may seem unfair. But don't blame me. I'm just following orders from a past judge." Every one of us craves the absolution of duty. Judges are no different.

If, moreover, every case had to be decided anew, the strain on judicial resources would be enormous. It's much easier to buy an existing suit off the rack, even if the color and fit aren't quite right, than to weave, cut, and sew the perfect suit from scratch.

Most important, the loss of individual judicial autonomy that *stare decisis* imposes is more than compensated for by an increase in collective judicial power. Paradoxically, if every judge were free to ignore precedent, each would enjoy greater individual power, but who except for the litigants would care what the judge says? The judiciary would lose its institutional power to command. Everyone except the litigants would be free to ignore the first judge and take their chances with the next one. If, however, the judges all pledge allegiance to the first decision, right or wrong, each judge— and the judiciary as a body—acquires the capacity to issue powerful commands that bind everyone precisely because there is no future wiggle room to avoid them.

So whether it's just human nature, practical wisdom, concern for equality, or judicial self-interest, scratch an American judge and she bleeds *stare decisis*. That means that precedents enforcing substantial autonomy-enhancing aspects of the red Constitution announced by past Republican-controlled Supreme Courts and decisions enforcing substantial equality-enhancing aspects of the blue Constitution announced by past Democratic Supreme Courts unite under *stare decisis* to form a legally congealed body of constitutional norms that bind the lower courts and are binding on future Supreme Courts, whether red or blue—even when one or more of the justices think those cases may have been wrongly decided.

That's the principal raw material for our constitutional rule of law. How stable is it?

Constitutional precedents exist in two dimensions. The most enduring aspect of a precedent is the precise fact pattern or legal issue before the first court. That outcome is locked in stone, not only by *stare decisis* but also by the related doctrines of *res judicata* and *collateral estoppel*, requiring future courts to respect the first court's resolution of the fact pattern or legal issue. If that's all there were to *stare decisis*, though, it would be thin gruel. It wouldn't cover much. If, for example, our ancestors required the ritual fast only when the hunt fell on January 1 or involved a certain kind of prey, the precedent would have a limited scope. We endow our judicial precedents with much greater power to bind. A principled American judge is expected to respect a precedent not only in factually or legally identical settings but in logically indistinguishable ones as well. Thus, judges in the American system must decide how far the analogical tentacles of a past precedent reach. If a case bars racial discrimination in access to public schools, does the precedent cover gender discrimination? Does it cover racial discrimination in public parks? How about private employment? In effect, our judges get to ask: "If the duty to fast applies to hunting, why not to fishing? Why not to harvesting crops? Why not before human births?"

As with imaginative readings of text, therefore, the imaginative analogical use of precedents is a narrative analytical skill of a high order. Good lawyers can use analogy to weave a skein of logically related precedents purporting to bind a judge. The problem is that good lawyers on the other side can seek to unravel the skein by attacking the analogies—in lawyer-talk, "distinguishing" the precedent.

The process is further complicated because judges speak in two voices—"holding" and "*dictum.*" "Holding" is the voice of judicial command, setting forth the legal rule that is entitled to *stare decisis* respect. *Dictum* is the voice of judicial persuasion, explaining and defending the judge's reasoning. The working definition of a holding is the portions of a judicial opinion that are logically necessary to the result. Everything else is *dictum*.

Unfortunately, judges do not use different color ink to separate holding from *dictum*. Later judges are often confronted with conflicting arguments about what the first court actually held—as opposed to what it just said. You can imagine how often lawyers bicker over whether a past precedent is a holding or just a *dictum*. The problem only gets worse as judges—especially Supreme Court justices—complicate judicial opinions with academic articles and political essays, routinely writing extremely long opinions replete with learned asides and elaborate footnotes.

On the other hand, *dictum* is valuable as a window into the judge's mind, helping lawyers and clients to make educated guesses about what the legal world will look like in the future—but only as long as the judge spouting the *dictum* remains on the bench. Newly appointed judges must respect holdings but will be free to reject *dictum*.

Complex as the process of applying *stare decisis* may be, in a surprising number of cases, good lawyers and able judges generate persuasive stories about the scope and binding nature of past precedents, allowing an intellectually honest judge to be persuaded that the legal landscape tilts in favor of one of the parties. Values don't come into play—at least consciously. Often, though, contested questions about the scope of the holding, its analogical force in the current case, and the wisdom of remaining blindly loyal to the past, present a principled judge with a legal tie that must inevitably be broken by resort to values.

The value-laden tiebreakers impacting *stare decisis* are often more complex (and less partisan) than the choice between autonomy under the red Constitution and equality under the blue. In addition to the usual values of autonomy and equality, the judge, in deciding whether to recognize or respect a precedent, must balance the importance of stability in the law against the need for change; the social and economic consequences of uprooting settled expectations created by the old precedent, especially when what is being uprooted is a rights-bearing precedent (that's why the Supreme Court has never formally overturned a constitutional case granting rights, including the notorious *Lochner v. New York*); the social harm being caused by the old precedent; the degree to which the factual or intellectual underpinnings of a precedent have already been eroded; and the effect on law itself of weakening *stare decisis*.

In my experience, those choices are, ultimately, so complex that no two judges approach the issues in the same way. The result is a kaleidoscopic array of possible outcomes depending on the interplay of a judge's raw intellectual ability, the intensity of the judge's commitment to stability, the intellectual power of the arguments in favor of retaining the binding power of a given precedent, and the intensity of the judge's value-laden agreement or disagreement with the original precedent.

Such a complex interplay ordinarily results in the enforcement of a controversial precedent. Occasionally, though, the binding force of precedent will be rejected or circumvented. That's what happened in *Brown v. Board of Education* in 1954 when the Warren Court unanimously overruled precedents upholding government-imposed racial segregation. It's what happened in 2018 when the Supreme Court narrowly overruled forty years of precedents authorizing public employee unions to levy agency fees on dissenting nonmembers. It's what may happen to *Roe v. Wade*.

It turns out that the moving parts of applying the doctrine of *stare decisis* are so complex, so intellectually difficult to operate, and so shot through with discretionary branching points that the act of deciding whether a precedent is binding, to say nothing of whether it should be abandoned or eroded, is often influenced, perhaps unconsciously, by a judge's values. The bottom line is that *stare decisis* will usually, but not always, provide powerful protection for large swaths of the purple Constitution. Change the judges, though, and what looks like stable protection can evaporate overnight.

So don't kill all the lawyers, but don't count on them too much, either. Reliance on precedent can only take you so far. The name of the game is still winning elections and populating the judiciary with judges who care deeply about equality as well as autonomy.

Finally, in addition to text and precedent, the bipartisan purple Constitution thrives when powerful legal arguments exist that advance *both* autonomy and equality. Consider, for example, the strong current bipartisan Supreme Court protection of free speech beginning in the late 1960s and peaking in 1989 when two iconic Democratic justices, William J. Brennan Jr. and Thurgood Marshall, joined three Republican justices—Harry Blackmun, Anthony Kennedy, and Antonin Scalia—to rule that burning the American flag in protest is a protected form of free speech. The Democratic justices saw the case as both respecting a "speaker's" autonomy and as protecting the equal rights of radicals to protest the status quo. The Republicans saw it as a pure protection of individual autonomy. The rest is history.

When, however, as in later First Amendment cases involving campaign finance regulation or hate speech, autonomy and equality tugged in different directions, the purple Constitution's value consensus fell apart, moving the case back into the contested realm of the red and blue Constitutions, where a Republican Supreme Court will break the value tie in favor of autonomy, while a Democratic Supreme Court will break it in favor of equality—with either or both decisions qualifying as a binding precedent for the future.

Progressive lawyers should, therefore, continue to invoke the purple Constitution in defense of both autonomy and equality. The success of their efforts will undoubtedly be significantly affected by their skill and dedication. But, no matter how skilled the lawyers, the project is far more likely to protect autonomy-based rights—such as speech and the free exercise of religion—and already existing equality-based rights that are rooted in powerful precedent, rather than to provide additional equality-based protection for the weak.

7

In Praise of Seventh-Grade Civics

Separation of Powers in the Time of Trump

I've been looking through my seventh-grade civics notes for hints about how to protect the Constitution from Trump. You'll no doubt be relieved to learn that my class notes assure me the twin constitutional doctrines of separation of powers and federalism are designed to prevent the president from assembling a dangerous concentration of power. My notes also assure me that if we defend those two doctrines, the Trump era will eventually disappear in the rearview mirror, reduced to a speed bump on the road to genuine democracy.

I wish that my notes were easier to decipher, though. The doctrines of separation of powers and federalism, like the other parchment barriers in the Constitution, are only as strong as the people's commitment to them. What does it mean for an ordinary American who hasn't suffered through law school to be committed to amorphous concepts such as separation of powers and federalism? How can an ordinary American know what types of power the Constitution is referring to, how they should be separated, and who should exercise them?

Similarly, when we talk about federalism, how does an ordinary American know what issues to leave to the states, what to put into the national pot, and what to share?

Until we free these questions from the political polemic and legal jargon in which they are currently enmeshed, it will be virtually impossible for most Americans to distinguish Trump's painful but ultimately correctible political mistakes from his dangerous, potentially lethal assaults on our constitutional structure. The distinction between mere political error and structural assault is very important. I oppose pretty much everything Trump does and stands for. But there are only twenty-four hours in the day. I reserve my most intense opposition for Trump's assaults on three foundational ideas on which American democracy rests—separation of powers, federalism, and achieving a morally acceptable balance between individual autonomy and collective equality.

As we've seen, finding the constitutional sweet spot between autonomy and equality is the essence of much constitutional judging. It's our way of trying to balance the right of the individual (especially a strong individual) to do whatever he or she wants against the right of everyone (especially the weak) to be treated as an equal. That's what the Supreme Court does when it interprets the First Amendment as a great bulwark of individual autonomy and the Fifth and Fourteenth Amendments as great bulwarks of collective equality.

As we've also seen, over the years, principled disagreement over the proper balance between autonomy and equality is what differentiates most Republican Supreme Court justices from their Democratic colleagues. Ordinary Americans need not attend law school to have strong opinions on whether the justices are getting that balance right. When it comes to separation of powers and federalism, though, how can an ordinary American know which resistance gear to be in? It's one thing to make a personal assessment about whether Trump (or the Supreme Court) is veering dangerously close to allowing the glorification of individual autonomy to erode or even extinguish the protection of equality. It's another to make an informed judgment about whether the president or the Court is eroding structural protections against excessive government power, such as separation of powers and federalism.

I would not put much hope into getting useful guidance on those questions from the electronic media, especially cable TV or the internet. A steady diet of semihysterical political polemic has reduced virtually everything in the electronic media to slogans designed to score points for or against the president. Don't even think of getting thoughtful guidance from politicians. They know less about the Constitution than you do. Even if they knew the answers, they wouldn't tell you unless doing so advanced their short-term political interests. Nor are lawyers and judges likely to give ordinary Americans serviceable answers. They will be quick to tell you that the answers are revealed in the constitutional text. They will also assure you that they know exactly what the text says. Unfortunately, no two of the so-called textual experts agree. The task is made even harder because the words "separation of powers" and "federalism" do not appear in the Constitution. James Madison urged the Founders to insert an explicit protection of separation of powers into the Bill of Rights, but Madison's colleagues didn't think it was necessary.

Despite the lack of textual guideposts and the political sloganeering, though, it is possible for someone who has not suffered through law school to know when Trump crosses a red line. Let's start with separation of powers, which is just a label describing a cautious way to run a government by seeking to identify and catalogue the various tasks (or powers) carried out by government, and then allocating each task to a separate group of officials. It could just as easily be called "separation of tasks," "division of functions," or "allocation of powers."

Separation of powers should be contrasted with a competing way of running a government where complete governing authority is concentrated in a single person or group. One of the crucial branching points in the history of political thought occurred in Europe during the seventeenth and eighteenth centuries in connection with efforts by segments of the landed aristocracy and the newly wealthy merchant classes to limit the "divine right" of kings, a theory of government that concentrated absolute governing authority in the hands of a hereditary monarch.

One revolutionary path, trod by the French, called for the overthrow of the absolute monarch and the substitution of something or somebody more palatable—like an elected legislature or a strong leader—with the complete power to govern. We have learned from painful experience that transferring absolute governing power from a king to somewhere else isn't all that much of an improvement. The potential for royal terror just morphs into a potential tyranny of whoever manages to get their hands on the levers of absolute power, whether his name is Robespierre at the head of the National Assembly; or Adolf Hitler, Joseph Stalin, or Pol Pot, governing at the point of a gun.

Forget about history and political science. If you really want to know why vesting too much governing power in the hands of a single person or group is so dangerous, read Stendhal's great 1839 novel *The Charterhouse of Parma*, which describes the terror of living under arbitrary one-man rule. Lord Acton, the celebrated nineteenth-century British historian, was right when he warned that "absolute power corrupts absolutely."

Fortunately, the Founders did not go down the absolute-power path. A second path, our own, seeks to eliminate the very idea of absolute governmental power vested in a single person by dividing the functions of government among multiple power centers. Unlike the absolute-power approach, which offers a romantic promise of quick justice and ruthless efficiency, separation of powers is self-consciously inefficient. It treats government power like a dangerous bomb capable of exploding in ways that can cause immense harm to individuals and the society.

To limit foolish or dangerous eruptions of government power, the formula for the government bomb is cut into separate pieces (or powers), with each group of officials given access to only one part of the formula. The hope is to make it impossible for a single runaway official (aka Donald Trump) to set the bomb off by himself.

In order to make such a cautious system of government work, the Founders had to complete two important tasks — identifying the functions of government; and deciding how to separate them. Let's start with identifying the functions of government.

In 1787, when the Constitution was written, separation of powers was already a well-traveled idea. The traditional British version of separation of powers, designed to curb the power of the king, divided the idea of government into two functions: the power to make new laws and the power to carry out existing laws. Parliament (divided into a House of Commons, controlled by the emerging wealthy merchant class, and the House of Lords, controlled by the landed aristocracy) was given the exclusive power to make new laws, while the king and his men (they were always men) had exclusive power to carry out the laws.

Judges weren't seen as exercising a separate "power." Rather, the lower court judges were lumped in with the king's men, engaged in carrying out the laws made by Parliament, while the high court judges sat as a committee of the House of Lords.

To this day, British judges lack a separate power-holding status. That's why British judges—even high court judges—still can't challenge acts of parliament, such as press censorship laws, as violations of Britain's unwritten constitution.

Inspired by Montesquieu, the Founders pushed beyond the British model. Instead of stopping at two powers—the power to make new law and the power to enforce the law—the Founders added a third function of government: the power to resolve disputes (the Founders called them "cases or controversies") over exactly how the law applies in a particular setting. The Supreme Court calls it "the judicial power and duty to say what the law is." It's where the power of judicial review comes from.

Once they had identified the three functions or powers of government, the Founders then decided which government officials should be empowered to carry out what power. They used two basic formulas. First, they made sure that no single official or closely connected set of officials could exercise more than one function (or power). They called that the principle of negative separation. Under negative separation, it doesn't matter who gets to exercise the power in question as long as the official doesn't also control another power. You get to exercise only one power.

Then they allocated each function (or power) to the government officials who were likely to carry out the function well. That's called the principle of positive separation. So, as with the British model, the exclusive power to make new law was given to the legislative branch—a large, bicameral, popularly elected national legislature capable of navigating the complex trade-offs and compromises needed to make the law for a disparate, populous nation.

The power to enforce the law was given to the executive branch, headed by the president, a single person indirectly elected by the Electoral College, capable of engaging quickly in robust and efficient action to carry out Congress's will.

Finally, the new power to resolve "cases and controversies" was given to a judicial branch, headed by the chief justice of the Supreme Court, made up of life-tenured judges nominated by the president and confirmed by the Senate, capable of accurately ascertaining and applying the rule of law without fear or favor.

In setting up their version of separation of powers, the Founders were obviously doing three things—negatively treating the power of the national government like a dangerous bomb, much too lethal to be entrusted to a single person or branch; positively allocating each of the three separated powers to officials who were organized to allow them to carry out those powers independently and well; and, finally, providing the politically vulnerable with access to a level playing field in the federal courts through the process of judicial review. It's an elegant, if cumbersome machine.

The Founders' complex separation-of-powers machine works well, though, only if the underlying mechanisms of democracy are also working well. If large numbers of poor voters of color are disenfranchised; if representative democracy breaks down in the Senate because voters in rural, predominantly white states are radically overrepresented compared to voters in urban, more diverse states; if representative democracy breaks down in the House because rampant partisan gerrymandering makes it necessary for Democrats representing urban constituencies to win the national legislative elections by more than 10 percent in order to secure a majority in the House; and if democracy breaks down in the Electoral College because its membership is skewed to favor states with smaller, rural, white populations, resulting in the repeated election of presidents who lost the national election by millions of votes, separation of powers won't work very well, either.

As with everything else that ails American democracy, therefore, the remedy must begin with repairing the cracks in the pillars of democracy. While the democracy repair work is going on, though, it's important to concentrate on making separation of powers function as well as it can, especially in an era with a power-obsessed president who seems to recognize no limits to his overweening ambition. Two recurring problems will arise.

First, what happens when the Founders' negative separation, or the refusal to give an official too much power, conflicts with their positive separation, the allocation of power to officials most likely to perform it well? Deciding who has power to initiate military combat is a classic point of tension between positive separation theorists, who stress the need for immediate, decisive action by the president to avert a national security crisis, and negative separation theorists, who, worried about the ability of a single person to plunge the nation (and the world) into nuclear war, insist on both congressional and presidential cooperation before launching America's military might.

How should the "war power"—the power to use lethal force abroad—be allocated when values of negative and positive separation collide? It's clear that the Founders tried to follow both classic negative and positive separation-of-powers rules in allocating the war power. Article I, Section 8, gives the power to declare war to Congress, while Article II gives the power to act as commander in chief of the armed forces to the president. Thus, Congress decides whether to change the military status quo by authorizing the use of lethal military force, while the president decides how to deploy and use the military force.

But what happens when the president decides on his own to launch missiles against Syria, to send hundreds of thousands of troops to Vietnam, or to wage a never-ending worldwide war against terrorism in Afghanistan, Yemen, and who knows where else, without congressional authorization? And what happens if he decides to up the military ante by using nuclear weapons? Must Congress authorize such use of military force abroad? What form should such an authorization take? Must the authorization precede the use of force? What about defensive emergencies? Who gets to pull the nuclear trigger? And what is the role of the Supreme Court in enforcing the separation of powers against the president's allegedly unconstitutional unilateral use of lethal military force?

The Supreme Court has consistently ducked the war powers issue. The justices never summoned the will to pass on the constitutionality of the undeclared Vietnam War. The Court's timidity has vested virtually uncontrollable de facto power in the president as commander in chief of the armed forces. I believe that it verges on the suicidal to grant the unilateral power to end life on earth to a man as flawed and mentally unstable as Donald Trump. If you do only one thing to defend separation of powers in the time of Trump, contact your senators and congressional representatives and implore them—no, direct them, on pain of being denied reelection—to stiffen congressional limits on unilateral executive power to make war, especially nuclear war.

Another point of tension between negative and positive separation of powers is the modern, post–New Deal administrative state itself. As we've seen, the Founders created a government machine with three parts—legislative, executive, and judicial—and gave each part one (and only one) power. Where do administrative agencies such as the Securities and Exchange Commission, the National Labor Relations Board, or the Federal Communications Commission fit into the Founders' tripartite structure?

The story we tell ourselves is that, as a matter of both negative and positive separation, the administrative agencies are just part of the presidentially supervised executive branch, with the duty to enforce the laws made by Congress, subject to judicial review by the federal courts.

But then we interfere with the president's power to appoint or remove administrative officials, allow Congress to enact a vast body of laws that are so ambiguous that they fail to give administrative official guidance on how to act, and strip the federal courts of the power to exercise judicial review over large aspects of the administrative state. The net result is the slow emergence of a "fourth branch" of government, staffed by unelected administrative officials who make new rules, adjudicate disputes, and enforce regulations free from effective judicial supervision.

Defenders of the administrative state argue that in the modern world, we need the expertise, independence, and sheer bulk of the administrative agencies to govern effectively in an immensely complex world, even though that means vesting administrative officials with more than one power. Opponents argue that vesting unelected officials with the complete power of government is the road to tyranny.

Unlike the war powers debate, which has a single right answer—enforce negative separation against the president—the disagreement over the administrative state requires a more nuanced analysis, though one that is not beyond the capacity of ordinary folks. In the end, it's up to you—not nine Platonic guardians on the Supreme Court—to decide whether negative separation-of-powers principles should be bent in order to permit administrative agencies to function as efficient regulators of big business. That's a hard question, but it's too important to leave the answer solely to judges, lobbyists, and politicians.

The second recurring problem is distinguishing the making of a new law (which must be done by Congress) from simply changing the way an old law is interpreted or enforced (which can be done by the executive). For example, when President Obama announced that he would no longer enforce the immigration laws against the more than one million Dreamers but would instead issue executive regulations regularizing their immigration status, was the president unilaterally making a new law in violation of the separation of powers or simply making executive choices about how existing immigration laws should be implemented and enforced?

Don't feel too bad if you find it hard to answer the question. The Supreme Court split 4–4 on it. Surprise: the Court's four Democratic justices backed President Obama, and the Court's four Republican justices opposed him. (Want to bet what Brett Kavanaugh will do?)

Ideally, the answer should not depend on whether you agree or disagree with the president's policies or whether you happen to support the president who happens to be in the White House. If separation of powers is simply a proxy for a justice's political preferences, we might as well stop pretending that the doctrine does any real work except to license political support for or opposition to a sitting president. I believe there is a more value-neutral way to approach hard separation-of-powers issues like the Dreamers without getting trapped in the definitional or partisan swamp.

Rather than agonizing over the metaphysical question of whether a challenged action is essentially law-making or law-enforcing, I find it helpful to go back to my seventh-grade civics notes about why we adopted separation of powers in the first place. The core value at the heart of separation of powers is keeping any single official from getting dangerous unilateral control of the throttle on the democracy train. For me, therefore, the key to evaluating a separation-of-powers decision is to ask whether, when the smoke clears, a single official or branch is seeking to assemble and exercise two or more of the three separated powers in ways that vest that official or branch with dangerously concentrated power.

If the answer is yes, I would not budge from a finding of unconstitutionality, even if officials argue that it would be much more efficient to vest more than one of the powers in a single person. Under my (perhaps overly) simplified approach, it doesn't matter which branch is trying to exercise more than one power. So back in 1952, when President Truman unilaterally ordered nationalization of the nation's steel mills during the Korean War to head off a steel strike that had potentially disastrous military consequences, his own Supreme Court appointees forced the president to back down because he was asserting the dangerously concentrated power to make a new law about how to deal with disruptive strikes during wartime, as well as the power to enforce the new law by military force.

Similarly, when President George W. Bush's lawyers argued that Congress could strip the federal courts of power to resolve legal challenges (called writs of *habeas corpus*) filed by detainees at the

United States military prison at Guantánamo Bay, Cuba, the Supreme Court refused to allow Congress to exercise both the power to enforce the laws and the power to resolve disputes about the law's meaning and application.

When Congress enacted a campaign finance law granting the power to appoint four of the six members of the Federal Election Commission to ranking members of Congress, the Court struck down the law because Congress was seeking the dangerously concentrated power to make a new law while retaining significant control over its enforcement. And when Congress sought to pass resolutions vetoing administrative regulations with which it disagreed, the Supreme Court struck down the congressional vetoes because, having made a new law, Congress was seeking a dangerously concentrated power to keep a finger on decisions about how to enforce it.

Finally, when federal judges claimed power to create judge-made crimes, or to make new federal common law in noncriminal cases, the Supreme Court correctly said no on both occasions because it would have given federal judges both a dangerously concentrated power to make new laws and the ability to resolve disputes about the laws' meaning and applicability.

That's the classical negative separation model in operation: check to see whether a single official is exercising at least two of the three powers in ways that generate a potentially dangerous concentration of government power in a single group of officials, and if so, blow the whistle and don't back down. And it shouldn't matter whether or not you agree or disagree with what the government is trying to do.

My seventh-grade civics notes end here. Frankly, the law could do worse than end here, too. Unfortunately, though, we can't wrap up where my 1953 notes run out. It's more complicated today because the classical tripartite vision of separation of powers embraced by the Founders over two hundred years ago has suffered more than a few dents over the years.

Most dramatically, as I've noted, since the New Deal of the 1930s, multiple newly minted executive agencies such as the

Securities and Exchange Commission and the National Labor Relations Board routinely promulgate new rules in the form of regulations implementing vague congressional statutes. These agencies also use in-house enforcement agents to enforce the agency's regulations and, initially at least, resolve disputes over the facts and the meaning and applicability of statutes and rules in their own internal courts. By my count, that boils down to one group of executive branch officials under the control of the president with power to exercise all three functions of government—a separation-of-powers nightmare.

The Supreme Court seeks to maintain a modicum of separation-of-powers discipline over the post–New Deal administrative agencies by exercising judicial review over the constitutionality of administrative agency action. To that extent, the Founders' original model has held. But, except in constitutional cases, judicial control over administrative agencies has atrophied. The truth is that Congress has given away much of its lawmaking power to the executive branch by enacting hundreds of ridiculously ambiguous statutes that delegate enormous discretion to the executive officials charged with enforcing them, and the Supreme Court lets Congress get away with it. Then, to make matters worse, the Supreme Court has decided to grant deference (there's that word again) to the views of administrative officials about the scope and exercise of their vague statutory powers. That allows administrative agencies to, in effect, decide the limits of their own power to make new law. Finally, in non-Constitution-related settings, the Supreme Court has granted administrative agencies virtually unreviewable power to find the facts in disputed cases, virtually ousting the jury from the administrative process.

The one-two-three punch of extremely vague congressional authorizations, judicial deference to an administrative agency's interpretations of vague laws, and transfer of much of the judiciary's fact-finding function to agency adjudicators has concentrated vast power in the executive branch, operating under the president's supervisory thumb. The Time of Trump may be an ideal moment to begin rescuing the Founders' vision of separated powers from the slow accretion of dangerously concentrated power in the executive branch.

There's nothing like an unstable president to generate sympathy for negative separation-of-powers doctrines that limit the president's ability to exercise enormous executive power through administrative agencies. Maybe the Supreme Court should force Congress to provide more precise statutory guidance to administrative agencies. Maybe the justices should reassert the power to say what vague delegations of statutory power to administrative agencies really mean, instead of deferring to the agencies. Maybe the Court should subject fact-finding by administrative officials to review by a federal judge, or perhaps even a jury. Maybe it should do all three.

We'd be safer for it—but at a cost. When we weaken the administrative state because we are afraid of its concentration of powers, we strengthen the hand of the powerful private players that the agencies are supposed to regulate. In many ways, the growth of the administrative state into a separation-of-powers nightmare has been the result of Congress's failure to do its job. When Congress doesn't act in settings crying out for government regulation, the president must step in. When Congress acts by passing absurdly ambiguous laws delegating vast discretion to agencies, the agencies have no choice but to do the best they can. Unless voters compel Congress to fulfill its responsibility to be the sole organ to make new law by enacting thoughtful, relatively precise laws for the agencies to enforce, the cure of negative separation may be worse than the disease of concentrated agency power. In the end, it's your call, enforceable through the democratic processes through which Congress and the president are elected, and the deferred democratic process through which Supreme Court justices are placed into office.

My seventh-grade-civics version of classical negative separation of powers is dented—but it is not completely broken. The touchstone is still whether there has been an unduly dangerous concentration of powers in the hands of a single branch. Don't leave it entirely to the lawyers and an opaque process of judicial review to decide how the modern, somewhat dented version of separation of powers should function in the Time of Trump.

8

Applying Separation of Powers
in the Time of Trump

Five Test Cases

We're now at a point where we can assess the thrashings of the current very large presidential bull in the separation-of-powers china shop. This isn't just an academic exercise. As we've seen, we start with a dangerously bloated executive branch far more powerful than the Founders imagined, and a dangerously unstable man wielding that enormous executive power.

Every time Trump crosses the separation-of-powers line and seeks to accumulate yet more unilateral power, he is one step closer to a point of no return where the concentration of power in the hands of an unstable president threatens our constitutional republic. My fear is that craven Republican legislators can't be counted on to exercise an effective separation-of-powers check. That leaves an informed public and the Supreme Court as the only two games in town.

The following five case studies drawn from the first eighteen months of the Trump presidency—the overwhelmingly Muslim travel ban; the Mueller investigation into Russian interference in the 2016 elections; the setting of immigration policy, especially for the Dreamers and asylum seekers; the status of government regulations designed to protect the environment; and the struggle between Congress and the president over whether to build the Great Wall of Trump—allow us to assess the degree to which powers have remained effectively separated. They also offer opportunities to think about how the Supreme Court, Congress, and average citizens can tighten the separation-of-powers brakes on the democracy train.

THE TRAVEL BAN

As one of his first acts as president, Donald Trump delivered on an ugly campaign promise to bar Muslims from entering the United States. Six days after his inauguration, the new president unilaterally issued an executive order preemptively blocking 180 million nationals of six predominantly Muslim nations from entering the United States as immigrants, tourists, students, or employees. As successful challenges to the Muslim travel ban careened through the lower federal courts, the president scrapped the first, hastily prepared, legally indefensible version and issued successive amended executive orders and presidential proclamations barring Muslims, finally settling on a complex executive order blocking entry into the United States indefinitely by some or all of the nationals of six overwhelmingly Muslim nations—Iran, Syria, Yemen, Chad, Somalia, and Libya—as well as two non-Muslim nations, North Korea and Venezuela.

Understandably, given Trump's crude campaign statements appealing to religious bigotry about the necessity of closing the border to Muslims, public discussion and criticism of the travel ban centered on allegations of religious bigotry, with little public discussion of the constitutionality of the president's insistence on acting unilaterally in disregard of limits on presidential lawmaking imposed by the separation of powers.

The president denied that the travel ban was—or is—an act of religious bigotry, insisting that he was seeking to protect the security of the United States by imposing blanket entry bans on travelers from nations deemed at risk of harboring substantial numbers of ISIS, Taliban, or Al Qaeda terrorists, and where reliable information permitting trustworthy individualized screening is difficult or impossible to obtain. Trump's critics scoffed at his attempt to articulate a religiously neutral explanation, pointing to four factors: the ban's dramatic, predictable impact on the ability of as many as 180 million Muslims to visit the United States; a series of openly bigoted anti-Muslim campaign statements made by the president promising to close the border to Muslims; the long-standing existence of an effective pre-entry vetting process capable of screening out potential terrorists; and the utter lack of any evidence indicating that nationality correlates with risk of terrorist behavior.

Given his anti-Muslim tirades, I'm prepared to believe that Donald Trump was motivated by religious bigotry when he issued the travel ban. But what if Trump's motives were an untidy blend of concern over national security, concern over the effectiveness of existing screening procedures, a desire to please his rabidly anti-Muslim base, and a healthy dollop of anti-Muslim bias of his own? As a legal matter, should it be necessary to decide which motive predominated? How can you possibly tell?

In *Trump v. Hawaii*, five Republican Supreme Court justices (including Justice Kennedy and the newly appointed Justice Neil Gorsuch, occupying the seat that should have been filled by President Obama's nominee, Merrick Garland) decided to ignore the apparent religious bias at the core of the travel ban and to defer to the president's other alleged motive—protecting national security. The four Democratic justices dissented.

We've already seen how dangerous it is for the Supreme Court to shirk its responsibility to enforce the Constitution by granting excessive deference to the president, especially in the name of national security. Excessive Supreme Court deference to the president is what allowed the United States to place Japanese Americans in detention camps during World War II, to jail the leaders of the American Communist Party during the Cold War, and to wage an undeclared war in Vietnam that killed 60,000 Americans and more than two million Southeast Asians. For each of those cases, the Supreme Court was paralyzed by the word "deference."

While Chief Justice Roberts, in choosing to ignore the issue of religious bias posed by the travel ban, piously disclaimed reliance on the World War II *Korematsu* decision upholding Japanese American internment—indeed, he claimed to overrule the appalling precedent—he followed the *Korematsu* playbook to a tee, deferring to the president's invocation of national security to uphold a shocking exercise in religious, as opposed to racial, bigotry.

Justice Anthony Kennedy, after casting the swing vote upholding the travel ban 5–4, wrote a valedictory concurrence on the eve of his retirement warning that the Supreme Court must be vigilant in protecting the weak against the religious bias and xenophobic hysteria of the strong. Unfortunately, Justice Kennedy didn't back up his words with the only thing that mattered: his vote to protect them. In the end, he sounded for all the world like Pontius Pilate washing his hands. It was an unworthy end to a Supreme Court career that warrants our gratitude and respect.

Once the five Republican justices had ducked the religious discrimination issue by giving it a deference-based national-security bath, the powerful separation-of-powers objection to the travel ban became the principal legal issue before the Court. In imposing the travel ban unilaterally, without consulting Congress, didn't President Trump make new law by himself—just as President Truman did back in 1952 when, in the midst of the Korean War, he unilaterally seized the nation's steel mills and ordered the strikers back to work?

In *Youngstown Sheet & Tube v. Sawyer*, the Supreme Court made short work of President Truman's unilateral effort to make new law. Why didn't the Court do the same with Trump's?

A platoon of lower-court judges—most of them Democrats—had little difficulty in striking down the unilateral travel bans down on separation-of-powers grounds. In *Trump v. Hawaii*, though, the five Republicans on the Supreme Court reversed the lower court decisions. Can the Supreme Court's reversal be defended on principled grounds, or is it a frightening harbinger of a tame Supreme Court in the mold of the 1938 German judiciary, unwilling to defend separation of powers against the will of the leader?

In trying to answer that question, we start with two clear propositions: the explicit constitutional grant to Congress in Article I,

Section 8, of the sole power to make the laws governing immigration, and the undeniable fact that President Trump consulted with no one outside his narrow circle (not even executive officials in the State Department or the Department of Justice) before unilaterally imposing the first version of the travel ban, and adamantly refused to seek congressional authorization for the next two versions. Does such unilateral executive action in the teeth of a constitutional delegation of exclusive lawmaking power to Congress require a principled court to hold the travel ban illegal?

President Trump's lawyers began his defense in the courts by mounting a separation-of-powers counterattack, challenging the power of courts to question a president's exercise of unilateral power over immigration in settings where national security is at stake. They argued that the president, as chief executive and commander in chief of the armed forces, enjoys inherent, unchallengeable power to seal the nation's borders to protect us from an armed threat from abroad. Trump's lawyers then followed up their inherent-power argument with an assault on the power of the Supreme Court to "say what the law is" in settings where the president claims to be restricting the entry of immigrants into the United States in the name of national security. The duty of the courts in such a national security setting, Trump argued, is to defer (that word again) to the president's judgment about what must be done to protect the nation.

In effect, therefore, in the name of national security, President Trump's lawyers claimed the right of the president to exercise supreme governmental power over immigration into the United States, with unilateral power to make new laws, enforce existing laws, and resolve disputes about the application of the laws to individuals, without consulting anyone else, including the Supreme Court. It's hard to imagine a more chilling rejection of the Founders' commitment to checks and balances.

If the Supreme Court were to accept Trump's grandiose vision of an all-powerful president with unilateral power to control entry into (and out of) the United States, the idea of separation of powers would suffer irreparable harm. Presidents would be licensed, in the name of national security, to wield the very supreme governing power that separation of powers was supposed to eliminate once and for all.

I wish I could report that the Supreme Court rose up and indignantly rejected the president's assertion of imperial power. While the lower courts reacted with incredulity and anger to such a dangerous assertion of excessive power, all five Republican justices ducked the issue by saying that it wasn't necessary to pass judgment on the president's extreme arguments.

Make no mistake about it: the Court's failure to rebuff Trump's assertions of imperial presidential power leaves a ticking time bomb at the heart of the structural Constitution. I have no doubt that Trump will exploit the Court's timidity by insisting on acting as an imperial president whenever he wishes—until the people push back at the polls.

In fact, Trump is already doing just that, invoking national security to impose tariffs unilaterally on a wide range of products; refusing to entertain asylum petitions in the teeth of contrary congressional rules; seeking to impose more stringent work rules on recipients of food subsidies in the teeth of a congressional refusal to do so; and invoking national emergency powers to build his border wall unilaterally in the teeth of congressional opposition. The Supreme Court's spineless response is why Trump believes he can get away with threatening to issue an executive order purporting to abolish birthright citizenship for children of undocumented aliens born in the United States.

Trump seems confident that a tame Supreme Court will continue to roll over in the name of deference to unilateral presidential actions assertedly aimed at protecting national security. The frightening thing is that, based on the five votes failing to reject the idea of imperial presidency in the travel ban case, he may be right.

Trump's fallback separation-of-powers argument in defense of the travel ban was more conventional. The president argued that, in issuing the ban unilaterally, he was not making new law at all, but simply enforcing existing law by implementing Congress's decision in 1952 to pass a law delegating unlimited power to the president to bar entry into the United States of anyone he deems detrimental to the national interest. It is true that Congress made no effort in the 1952 law to define what it meant by "detrimental," leaving Trump free to argue that he has been given a blank check to ban anyone he wishes for any reason.

If the 1952 statute actually authorized the president to exercise such an unfettered discretionary power, the statute itself should be deemed to violate separation of powers because it unconstitutionally delegates Congress's exclusive lawmaking powers over immigration to the president. A Supreme Court that genuinely respected separation of powers would instruct Congress to go back to the drawing board to give the president real policy guidance, not a blank check. Ironically, had he lived, Justice Scalia might well have rejected the president's blank-check argument. Before his death, Scalia had for years campaigned for a renaissance of the so-called delegation doctrine, which once forbade Congress from giving away (delegating) to the president its exclusive power to make new law. I think Scalia was right. The last time the Supreme Court invoked the delegation doctrine was in 1935 to strike down FDR's National Recovery Act.

At a minimum, any president who wished to implement the 1952 statute in a manner consistent with separation of powers should have been required to make specific findings on what he or she meant by "detrimental," and show why the presence of every single one of the 180 million nationals of the six designated Muslim-majority nations would be detrimental to the United States. The lower courts refused to uphold the ban in the absence of such findings. In its rush to deference, the Supreme Court made no effort to narrow the massive grant of discretion to the president in the 1952 statute.

Even more dramatically, in 1965 Congress took away the president's power under the 1952 statute to use a person's "nationality" to decide who gets long-term immigrant visas to settle in the United States. In 1924, Congress had adopted an openly racist immigration system that formally locked the issuance of long-term immigration visas into the racial and ethnic mix of the United States as it existed in 1890. Under the 1924 statute, immigration officials repeatedly saw to it that people from white nations, such as Norway, were awarded lots of immigrant visas. Prospective long-term immigrants from nonwhite nations received few or none.

In 1965, troubled by the use of nationality as a stalking horse for racial and religious bigotry, Congress barred the use of nationality as a criterion for long-term visas. But that's exactly what President Trump did in January 2017, using nationality in a predominantly Muslim nation as a proxy for religious bigotry against Muslims.

I believe that Congress's expression of hostility in the 1965 statute to the president's use of nationality as a criterion for granting long-term immigration visas should have blocked Trump's power to invoke the identical criterion unilaterally in imposing a nationality-based ban on entry into the United States. Just as with President Truman's effort to seize the nation's steel mills in the teeth of a prior congressional refusal to authorize such a remedy for breaking a strike, Congress's 1965 statute should have ended the president's power to act unilaterally to impose an immigration criterion explicitly rejected by Congress. But it didn't. While the Democratic-controlled lower federal courts read the 1965 law as limiting the president's power under the 1952 law, the five Republican justices ignored the 1965 law because, they argued, it dealt with the issuance of immigration visas, not physical entry into the United States.

It borders on the absurd, though, to argue that Congress can prevent the president from using nationality to allocate the issuance of entry visas but then be forced to watch the president unilaterally shred the prohibition by refusing to let the newly protected visa holders into the country. Yet that's just how the five Republican justices made the 1965 statute disappear.

That's not a good sign. Remember the 1938 German judiciary.

THE MUELLER INVESTIGATION

From 2014 to 2016, the Russian government mounted a massive intelligence operation designed to elect Donald Trump as the forty-fifth president of the United States. We don't know exactly why. Some say it was Putin's revenge against Hillary Clinton for her vocal criticism of Russia's rigged 2011 parliamentary elections. Perhaps that's where it started. For whatever reason, once Trump's presidential candidacy surfaced, Russia became hell-bent on installing Donald Trump as the leader of its principal global rival.

When the Trump candidacy burst onto the scene, the Russians could not believe their good fortune. If Vladimir Putin could have handcrafted an American president incapable of responding effectively to Russia's resurgence as a dominant world power, that individual would look just like Donald Trump.

Maybe Putin thought he would literally own Trump. The money that rescued Trump's failing business empire from bankruptcy and collapse in the 1980s was largely Russian, much of it funneled secretly through German banks. Until we see Trump's tax returns, which to this point he has refused to release, we'll never know how deeply in hock Trump still is to Russia.

Maybe the Russians thought Trump was crooked, ready to participate in shady scams that would make billions for Putin and his corrupt Russian oligarchs. Trump had already made an ill-gotten fortune by repeatedly cheating his creditors, exploiting the bankruptcy laws, misleading his customers, and turning a blind eye to Russian money laundering through his real estate ventures. We now know that Trump was negotiating with Putin's henchmen for permission to build an immensely lucrative Trump Tower in Moscow while the presidential campaign was unfolding in the United States.

Maybe the Russians thought Trump was vulnerable to some old-fashioned blackmail. Trump was once the star of a reality TV show, but that would be nothing compared to his alleged starring role on sex tapes Russian intelligence reportedly made during the

2013 Miss Universe Pageant in Moscow. Alert: the tapes may be a hoax. Trump had already paid a small fortune in violation of the campaign finance laws to silence women ready to talk about his raffish sexual escapades; if those tapes or something like them exists, imagine what he'd do to keep them out of the public eye.

Maybe Putin realized that Trump was incapable of sustaining the level of intellectual effort and disciplined attention needed to lead a rival world power wisely. Trump's handpicked secretary of state called him "a moron" before being pushed out. His handpicked chief of staff called him worse before getting the sack. His handpicked secretary of defense quit because he got tired of being the only adult in the room with Trump. Putin probably thought that if you have to play diplomatic poker against someone, it's a good idea to pick the worst card player in the room.

Maybe the Russians thought Trump was so driven by uncontrollable ego and prone to untempered rage that he would plunge the American presidency into chaos and ineffectiveness, weakening our ability to lead the world against Russian expansionism.

Maybe the Russians hoped that Trump would exacerbate the racial, gender, and ethnic fault lines that plague American society, delivering a body blow to Russia's chief rival. Putin knew that an America at each other's throats would be no match for a ruthless foreign power like Russia.

For whatever reasons, we now know that once Trump became the Republican nominee, the Russians mounted a fierce social media disinformation campaign, reinforced by the *National Enquirer's* tabloid empire, aimed at electing him—and defeating Hillary Clinton—that reached vast numbers of American voters and may well have flipped the 77,000 voters in Michigan, Pennsylvania, and Wisconsin that gave Trump the presidency.

What we don't know is whether Americans knew about and cooperated in Russia's apparently successful effort to meddle in the 2016 presidential election. Ordinarily, we would look to Congress to get to the bottom of whether anyone connected to the Trump campaign was playing footsie with the Russians in tilting the 2016 election to Trump. After all, Congress blew the lid off the Nixon

Watergate scandal and forced the president to resign under threat of impeachment.

That's exactly how the Founders assumed separation of powers would work: one branch checks and balances the others. But that's not how things worked in Washington, DC, during Trump's first two years in office, where Republicans controlled both houses of Congress and the Supreme Court.

The initial House "investigation" into Russian meddling was a bad joke—an obvious effort to whitewash any connection between the president and the Russian disinformation campaign. The Senate investigation was earnest but ineffectual, hampered by a lack of expertise, resources, and enthusiasm. That's where the separation-of-powers issues raised by the Mueller investigation come in. When a craven and/or incompetent Republican Congress refuses or fails to investigate alleged criminal wrongdoing by a Republican president, can either of the other two branches—the executive or the judiciary—step in to fill the investigatory vacuum?

The judicial branch doesn't seem like a viable candidate to lead such a backup investigation. Unlike a European examining magistrate, American judges don't have the authority, resources, or expertise to conduct investigations into potential criminal activity. That's a prosecutor's job. In fact, it would probably be a violation of separation of powers to give judges both the power to decide criminal cases and the power to investigate them.

Federal judges can, however, play an important supporting role by protecting the ability of the grand jury, an age-old hybrid investigatory and adjudicatory institution that straddles the borderline between the executive and judicial branches, to conduct an effective investigation. Once upon a time, grand juries, usually consisting of between sixteen and twenty-three randomly selected citizens, were designed to protect individuals against unjustified criminal prosecutions by making sure that the prosecutor had uncovered enough evidence of guilt to warrant a full-scale criminal trial.

Over time, though, grand juries have morphed into a powerful investigative tool used by prosecutors. Guided by a prosecutor, modern grand juries can demand documents and call witnesses to testify under oath about potential criminal activity. If the grand jury investigation generates enough evidence of guilt, the grand jury, still guided by the prosecutor, can formally charge an individual with a crime, leading to a full-scale trial before a twelve-person criminal jury. While a judge does not direct the grand jury, judges play a crucial supporting role in the grand jury process by formally convening the jury, supervising it to ensure that it complies with the rule of law, enforcing its legitimate orders and demands, and protecting it against outside interference. Although it never became necessary, that may have included appointing a backup prosecutor if the president or his lackeys tried to fire Robert Mueller.

Most of the heavy lifting in a grand jury investigation is done by the prosecutor, a member of the executive branch whose job it is to enforce the law. It is the prosecutor who asks a judge to convene a grand jury. It is the prosecutor who urges the grand jury to demand certain documents and to call certain witnesses. It is the prosecutor who questions the witnesses under oath before the grand jurors and explains the meaning of the documents and other evidence presented to them. It is the prosecutor who explains the law to the grand jury. It is the prosecutor who asks the grand jury to vote a formal criminal charge, called an indictment.

Since the grand jurors know little or nothing about the law, and since grand juries operate in secret without any input from a potential defendant's lawyers, it is the prosecutor who runs the show. The not-so-funny joke is that a competent prosecutor can persuade a modern grand jury to indict a ham sandwich. In fifty-five years of practice, I have seen only one grand jury reject a prosecutor's request for an indictment—a courageous refusal by a Nebraska federal grand jury to indict a carload of college students from Colorado arrested while bringing jars of peanut butter to a defiant encampment of Native Americans at Wounded Knee, South Dakota. The prosecutor wanted to indict the students for conspiring to cross state lines to foment an insurrection. We called it the "peanut butter" conspiracy.

Since Congress failed to conduct a serious investigation and since the federal courts could at best play only a supporting role by supervising the grand jury and protecting its prosecutor, the responsibility for getting to the bottom of Russian interference in the 2016 election rested squarely on Justice Department prosecutors and FBI agents, all of whom serve in the Department of Justice, an executive agency under the direct supervision of the president.

That was the separation of powers dilemma faced by Robert Mueller, the "special counsel" appointed to get to the bottom of whether the president or his associates had engaged in criminal activity in knowingly assisting the Russian intelligence assault on the 2016 presidential election. Unlike Ken Starr, an "independent counsel" acting outside the reach of the executive branch who made President Bill Clinton's life miserable, Robert Mueller was an employee of the executive branch, subject to the president's formal control. For good or ill, Congress had allowed the independent counsel statute to lapse, leaving the job of investigating the president up to officials of the Justice Department under the ultimate control of the president. Could Trump have unilaterally ended the Mueller investigation, just as he unilaterally fired James Comey as FBI director or unilaterally issued the travel ban? He repeatedly threatened to do so. What power did Mueller have to force the president to testify under oath before a grand jury? Why didn't he use it? What power did Mueller have to require the president to submit to an interrogation under penalty of perjury? Why didn't he use it? What power did Mueller have to recommend that a grand jury indict the president, either for conspiring with the Russians to subvert the 2016 presidential election, or criminally obstructing the investigation? Why did Mueller punt on whether the president was guilty of criminal obstruction of justice, leaving the final decision to the president's hand-picked attorney general? In retrospect, we now know that the president never followed through on his threats to force Mueller out. Why not? We now know that Mueller settled for allowing the president to answer a series of pre-negotiated questions in writing, with no possibility of follow-up questioning. Why? We now know that after forcing the disgorgement of reams of evidence resulting in the indictment of twelve Russian intelligence operatives, Mueller concluded that neither the president, nor his close aides had conspired with Russian intelligence to subvert the election. But we do not know the evidence on which Mueller's conclusion rests. We also know that Mueller, after reviewing the evidence, was unable to decide whether the president or his aides had criminally obstructed the investigation. Instead of making the decision himself on whether the president should be accused of criminal activity, Mueller delegated the final call to the president's hand-picked political appointee, Attorney General William Barr, who had campaigned for the office by arguing that the Mueller investigation was unwarranted. Why did Mueller stop short of making the call himself? We will never know the answers to those questions until Mueller's report is made public. And that will be up to Congress and the Supreme Court. It will be a cold day in July when William Barr voluntarily releases anything that harms his boss.

In assessing the importance of knowing why Mueller pulled up short, it's necessary to ask what his powers really were. In seeking to answer that question, we start with four uncontestable propositions. First, the Russian effort to manipulate the outcome of the 2016 presidential election was unquestionably criminal—not necessarily because of what the Russians said and did (ugly as it was), but because of what they failed to say. By operating in secret and through phony names, the Russians disinformation agents lied about who the real sources of the fake social media posts were, failed to register as foreign political agents, and failed to report their massive pro-Trump expenditures aimed at influencing the outcome of a presidential election. That's three federal felonies by the Russians, added to Trump's felony in directing Michael Cohen to violate the campaign finance disclosure laws by secretly using Trump's corporate funds to pay women to stop them from talking about Trump's sexual escapades on the eve of the election.

Even if every ugly, divisive thing the Russians said during the disinformation campaign was true (a highly doubtful supposition), and even if Americans have a First Amendment right to hear ugly electoral speech from foreign governments (as I think they do), Americans also have a right to know when a foreign nation (or a presidential candidate) is seeking to manipulate our electoral process. So, while Americans who admire Vladimir Putin enjoy a First Amendment right to hear from him, folks who don't like or trust Putin have an equally important First Amendment right to know when Russian intelligence agents are behind political propaganda aimed at swinging a presidential election.

Second, Mueller uncovered substantial evidence warranting grand jury indictments against twelve Russian military intelligence agents and several Russian satellites of Putin in connection with the disinformation campaign. Any reasonable American prosecutor in possession of evidence of clearly unlawful election meddling by Russian agents would be shirking her sworn law enforcement duty if she did not seek to learn whether Americans, including Donald Trump and his campaign staff, were complicit in the Russian disinformation operation. As a matter of standard prosecutorial practice, repeated communications between top Trump campaign aides and agents of the Russian disinformation campaign not only justified but compelled prosecutors to follow the trail of possible criminal bread crumbs wherever the trail might lead, even right up to the president's desk. We now know that Mueller eventually decided that the evidence of communication between persons in the Trump campaign and Russian intelligence agents was not strong enough to establish criminal activity. We are owed an explanation of what the communication consisted of and why it was not sufficient to establish criminal activity.

Third, although no separation-of-powers issues complicated Mueller's executive-branch duty to enforce the law by investigating possible violations of the criminal law by Russian agents and American politicians, efforts to investigate the president were chock-full of separation-of-powers problems.

Robert Mueller, serving as a special counsel pursuant to Justice Department regulations, was unquestionably a member of the executive branch, headed by the president, even though his job title was "special counsel." Under classical separation of powers, Congress makes the laws requiring mandatory disclosure of a Russian speaker's identity and campaign spending, but presidents get to call the shots about how the disclosure laws are enforced. Remember President Obama's arguments in the Dreamers controversy.

In an ordinary criminal investigation, that would be the end of the matter. Trump, as president, would have unquestioned power over the Mueller investigation, just the way Trump, as president, would have had unquestioned power over implementing the 1952 and 1965 immigration laws in the travel ban case. Trump could have ended the investigation, limited it, or fired Mueller, just as he fired Comey. Period.

But when it is the president—or people close to the president—who may have violated the criminal law, such a rigid application of classical negative separation-of-powers theory suffers from obvious creaks in the joints. Until Trump, the unwritten rule had been that when the president or a close associate is the target of a criminal investigation, the president should cooperate with a full investigation by the FBI and a federal prosecutor and let the criminal chips fall where they may. Maybe an Abraham Lincoln (or a Barack Obama) would possess the self-discipline and deep sense of ethical obligation needed to set the FBI on himself or his close associates, but most of us would fail that ethical test. Donald Trump never even got a copy of the ethics test paper. Our forty-fifth president has never heard of an ethical norm that can't be twisted to his own advantage.

Thus, adhering to strict separation of powers in the Time of Trump would almost certainly have resulted in a presidentially controlled, phony investigation of Russian meddling designed to whitewash the president. The Republican members of the House Intelligence Committee, headed by Devin Nunes, have already shown us what such a phony whitewash would look like.

Fourth, the fact that the Russians secretly, even unlawfully pumped ugly and divisive speech into the 2016 presidential election campaign with the aim of enhancing Trump's chances of winning does not call into question the legal validity of Trump's election victory. The content of the Russians' electoral garbage wasn't materially different from the electoral garbage poured into the campaign by Americans. Too much of the 2016 presidential election took place in Donald Trump's political sewer. In the end, the Russians merely added to and exacerbated the sludge that Americans were all too happy to pump into their own electoral process.

It's fair to speculate about whether and how much the Russian effort assisted Trump. It's even fair to assert that the Russian campaign may have put him over the top. It's also fair to prosecute anyone who cooperated with the Russians in refusing to identify themselves. But there is no justification for questioning the electoral result. Sixty-three million Americans elected Donald Trump as the forty-fifth president of the United States. He is legally entitled to exercise the full powers of his office, whatever the dents in his democratic imprimatur.

The $64,000 question that Mueller sought to answer is whether Trump or his close associates knew about and/or played a role in the Russian deception campaign. If Trump was, in fact, personally complicit in secretly using Russian criminal disinformation to gain the presidency, he is guilty of multiple felonies that fall into the category of "high crimes and misdemeanors." If that's what he did, he should be impeached, removed from office, and then indicted. Only a searching investigation could hope to get to the bottom of that factual swamp. But how would Mueller, a member of the executive branch, conduct such a searching investigation of the president if separation of powers grants Trump, as president, the power to squelch it?

We start with the fact that Mueller possessed unquestioned authority to demand that the president—or anyone else, including Michael Cohen, the president's personal lawyer—turn over potentially incriminating evidence for use by a federal grand jury, even if that put Mueller in the strange position of issuing orders to his nominal boss.

In the Nixon tapes case, the special prosecutor (the title then used in the Justice Department regulations) directed Richard Nixon to turn over the Watergate tapes for use before the federal criminal jury trying seven of the president's close advisors for planning, executing, and covering up the Watergate break-in at Democratic Party headquarters. President Nixon argued that, as president, he could not be directed by a court to follow orders issued by an inferior official of the executive branch. Such a dispute, Nixon claimed, was an intrabranch squabble beyond the power of the courts.

In *United States v. Nixon*, four Republican justices joined with four Democratic colleagues to reject that argument unanimously (Justice Rehnquist did not participate). The justices noted, first, that the evidence was demanded on behalf of a judicial body, a petit (criminal) jury; and second, that unless and until the Justice Department regulations were changed, the special prosecutor was authorized to demand the tapes on behalf of the criminal jury. If the special prosecutor had power to force the president to turn over the Watergate tapes to a criminal jury, Robert Mueller, as special counsel, almost certainly had power to force the president—just as he forced the president's lawyer—to turn over evidence to a grand jury. What we don't know is whether Mueller used all of his power.

It's also likely that, based on Supreme Court precedent established during the extended investigation into President Bill Clinton's sex life, Mueller had the power to force the president to testify under oath before a grand jury, or, in the alternative, to submit to a personal interview with Mueller's staff, under oath. In 1994, after his election as president, Bill Clinton was sued by Paula Jones for allegedly sexually harassing her while he was governor of Arkansas. Clinton argued that, as a sitting president, he could not be sued for damages in a federal court until he left office. He demanded dismissal of the Jones lawsuit, or at worst a stay of all judicial proceedings, including pretrial discovery under oath, until his term of office expired. In 1997, after Clinton's reelection, five Republican justices joined four Democratic colleagues in unanimously rejecting the president's claim to be above the law, even temporarily.

No separation-of-powers bar exists, ruled the Supreme Court, to a private lawsuit for damages against a sitting president in federal court for alleged actions having nothing to do with his official duties, especially when the allegedly unlawful conduct occurred before he became president. Jones's lawyers, seeking to bolster her story, then sought to question Clinton under oath about other alleged sexual escapades, especially his relationship with a White House intern, Monica Lewinsky. When Clinton falsely denied any sexual impropriety, he was charged with contempt of court for lying under oath and was eventually forced to resign from the Supreme Court bar.

After Jones's lawsuit was settled for $850,000, an independent counsel outside the ambit of the Justice Department launched a criminal investigation into Clinton's alleged perjury and obstruction of justice, requiring the president to testify under oath before a grand jury. Based on conflicts between the president's grand jury testimony and his testimony in the Jones case, the independent counsel recommended impeachment proceedings. The Republican-controlled House voted a presidential bill of impeachment for only the second time in the nation's history. President Andrew Johnson was impeached in 1868 and acquitted in the Senate by a single vote. In 1973 President Nixon resigned to avoid an impeachment vote.

The Republican-controlled Senate failed to convict President Clinton by the required two-thirds vote, with fifty Republican senators voting to remove the president from office for obstruction of justice and forty-five Democrats, joined by five Republicans, voting to acquit.

So, based on *Clinton v. Jones* and its aftermath, Mueller could almost certainly have forced President Trump to testify before a grand jury or be questioned under oath by the special counsel about his behavior before he became president and his private behavior after he took office.

The Clinton precedent is complicated, though, by the Supreme Court's earlier decision in *Nixon v. Fitzgerald*, where five Republican justices voted to grant Richard Nixon complete immunity from suits in federal court seeking damages for official actions taken in the discharge of his duties as president. Three Democratic justices and one Republican justice dissented. Recall that Nixon was immunized from criminal liability by President Ford's pardon.

Connecting the Supreme Court dots, illegal conduct prior to Trump's inauguration, such as alleged collusion with Russian agents or otherwise knowingly participating in the Russian scam, was undoubtedly fair game for criminal investigation by the Special Counsel. But what about illegal post-election activity allegedly engaged in by the president as part of the discharge of his official duties, such as firing James Comey in an effort to shut down the investigation or unlawfully paying hush money to conceal criminal activity? Since, under *Nixon v. Fitzgerald*, post-election official conduct would be immune from civil damages, it may well be immune from criminal sanctions also.

The outcome in the Supreme Court would turn on whether the Court's reasoning in *Fitzgerald* that a president should not be required to worry about potential damage liability when he performs his official acts carries over to a president not having to worry about being punished for violating the criminal law. It would, I believe, be an appalling mistake to place the president above the criminal law—but then, I'm a Democrat.

Mueller followed the lead of the Clinton independent counsel by issuing a comprehensive report more than four hundred pages long to the attorney general setting forth the facts. Mueller declined to recommend criminal charges against the president or his cronies based on collusion with Russian intelligence agents. He was, however, unable to decide whether to recommend the indictment of the president for criminally obstructing the investigation. The attorney general, William Barr, a hand-picked political appointee of the president who had campaigned for the office by writing a memorandum attacking the Mueller investigation, promptly issued a four-page "summary" of the four-hundred page report purporting to exonerate his boss. Much now turns on the courage and political wisdom of members of Congress who are duty-bound to see that the entire Mueller report sees the light of day. That's just what happened to the independent counsel's report on Bill Clinton. The same ground rules should govern Donald Trump. Once the Mueller report is public, the voters can decide whether President Trump deserves condemnation and punishment. The question is not whether Trump is a felon. It is whether he is a liar, a cheat, and a willing beneficiary of a massive campaign contribution from the KGB.

It turns out that Robert Mueller's failure to recommend criminal prosecution of President Trump rested on two flimsy criminal law loopholes, neither of which should exist. Loophole 1—I call it the "cooperation/conspiracy" loophole—purports to exempt unscrupulous people from criminal liability for encouraging and knowingly benefiting from someone else's crimes, unless a prosecutor can prove that a deal existed between the crook and the knowing beneficiary. Loophole 2 purports to allow a sitting president to literally get away with murder and escape criminal prosecution because, according to the Justice Department, a sitting president cannot be indicted.

I think that the special counsel was wrong about both loopholes. Based on the facts laid out in the Mueller report, the Trump campaign could—and should—have been indicted for encouraging Russian intelligence agents to break the law in order to benefit from their clearly illegal acts; and Trump himself could—and should—have been indicted for (or at least formally accused of) criminally obstructing the Russian investigation.

Let's look first at Loophole 1. The Mueller report does a brilliant job of describing the existence of massive Russian intelligence operations designed to hijack the 2016 presidential election for Donald Trump and Vladimir Putin. Mueller demonstrates that Russian operatives mounted multiple massive social media disinformation campaigns reaching more than one hundred million voters designed to help the Trump candidacy; and arranged for the theft and release of hundreds of thousands of damaging, unlawfully obtained emails from Democratic Party officials. Mueller also painstakingly chronicles 140 links between the officials of the Trump campaign and Russian agents, noting the coordination of Russian activity with the needs of the Trump campaign and the enthusiastic response of campaign officials to Russian efforts to support Trump. In the end, though, Mueller argues that merely welcoming criminal activity and knowingly benefiting from it doesn't add up to a federal crime, unless a deal exists between the crook and the unscrupulous beneficiary of the crime.

I don't think Mueller was right. If I find out that someone is in the process of burning down a building; meet with the arsonist more than one hundred times to discuss the building; cheer while the arson is going on; and then collect the fire insurance proceeds, the law does not allow me to walk away scot-free just because no deal can be proven. Now, change the crime from arson to criminal interference in a U.S. presidential election. Suppose a hugely wealthy supporter of a candidate for president decides to make a series of secret multi-million-dollar campaign contributions in blatant violation of federal law. Suppose the candidate's campaign is on notice that the secret contributions are unlawful but welcomes the cash and uses it to secure the candidate's election. The campaign would—and should—be criminally liable, even if no deal between the crooked supporter and the campaign can be proven.

The Mueller report convincingly demonstrates that the Trump presidential campaign was the knowing recipient and enthusiastic beneficiary of the largest illegal campaign contribution in history—Russia's investment of many millions of dollars aimed at hijacking the 2016 presidential election for Donald Trump and Vladimir Putin. Why should the Trump campaign be better off legally because the clearly unlawful campaign contribution came from the Russian government instead of from a crooked American supporter? Since, as Mueller demonstrates, the Trump campaign was on notice about the Russian interference in the election; failed to blow the whistle, indeed welcomed the unlawful support; and chose to accept the benefits of the ongoing unlawful action, I think the campaign broke the criminal law. Mueller should have said so.

Loophole 2 protecting the president from indictment for obstruction of justice is even flimsier. Mueller's stated reluctance to call the president's obstructive acts "criminal" rested solely on the belief that since a sitting president cannot be indicted, it would be unfair to openly call him a crook because Trump would lack a criminal trial forum in which to defend himself. With respect, that explanation barely passes the laugh test. Not only does the president command a mighty bully pulpit with which to defend himself, the absence of a public criminal trial forum was—and is—Trump's own fault. He could waive his claimed constitutional immunity from indictment tomorrow. But he won't. Trump's like the guy who murders his parents and then seeks mercy as an orphan. Even more fundamentally, the legal authority for the proposition that a sitting president is above the criminal law is awfully thin. Nixon tried the argument and failed. Clinton also tried it and failed. If Trump had been forced to try it in court, I believe that he would probably have failed, too. Remember, though, that Trump's immunity from indictment lasts only as long as he is a sitting president. The 2020 electorate will act as a nationwide grand jury with the power to remove Trump's sitting president immunity once and for all. He'll probably be forced to end his disgraceful tenure by becoming the first American president to pardon himself. In the end, I predict that the report will be made public before the 2020 elections— but not necessarily through the processes of law. This one will be a repeat of the Pentagon Papers—with one or more courageous whistle-blowers and a free press providing the voters with information crucial to an informed choice.

That will place the issue where it ultimately belongs—in the hands of the voters. If American voters, after being informed of the material in Mueller's report, do not choose to protect the electoral process from foreign subversion by punishing a president who obtained office with the assistance of a massive Russian disinformation campaign and then sought to torpedo the investigation into his conduct, no special counsel or impeachment process can preserve the integrity of our democracy.

THE DREAMERS

Throughout the eighteenth, nineteenth, and early twentieth centuries, the vast frontier, with its seemingly unlimited land and resources, and an American economy chronically short of manual labor, combined to generate a national immigration policy designed to encourage white newcomers to emigrate to the United States. Blacks were welcomed until 1808, but only if whites owned them. Chinese laborers were welcomed to build our railroads, and then kicked out. Korean immigrants were banned entirely.

On the other hand, throughout the eighteenth, nineteenth, and early twentieth centuries, white Christians from northern and western Europe were encouraged to immigrate in the millions. The pattern held into the early twentieth century, which opened with massive waves of immigration—lawful and undocumented—from southern and eastern Europe. Then things changed.

In the years following World War I, the nation's immigration policy flipped from the Statue of Liberty's wide-open "golden door" (at least for whites) to a walled racial fortress replete with moat and drawbridge. In 1924, Congress subjected long-term immigration to a national quota system, with the national quota numbers openly rigged to retain the nation's racial and religious balance as it had existed in the 1890s. Northern European nations were allocated more long-term visas than they could use. Southern and eastern European quotas were often oversubscribed. Asia, Africa, and most of South America received almost none.

When the shadow of Nazism fell across Europe in the 1930s, many Eastern European Jews desperate to escape the coming Holocaust were routinely denied entry because the Polish, Czech, or other national quotas had been filled, and Congress had not yet provided for the temporary entry of persecuted persons seeking asylum.

At the same time, Congress encouraged the temporary entry of tourists, temporary workers, and students from around the world, who brought money, broad backs, and know-how into the country without placing any significant demands on its political or social structure.

In 1965, as we've seen, Congress tried to reset what had become a racist immigration clock. It ended the national quota system. Long-term visas were to be allocated on a first-come, first-served basis. Efforts were made to reunite families by favoring the issuance of immigration visas to close relatives of people already admitted to the United States—a process since derided by President Trump (whose wife recently used her status to obtain visas for her parents) as "chain migration." And, finally, a generation late, Congress permitted the emergency entry of refugees seeking asylum from persecution.

In the years following the elimination of the national quota system, demand for low-wage workers, especially for particularly difficult jobs such as harvesting crops and working in meatpacking plants, encouraged millions of aliens seeking a better life—both documented and undocumented—to cross our national borders. Recurring worldwide plagues of civil, religious, and social strife, made worse by economic desperation and physical devastation, increased the flow of immigrants from around the world, often overwhelming the immigration system and creating a vast underclass of more than ten million undocumented aliens, vulnerable to racism and economic exploitation, and subject to deportation if discovered. An overburdened asylum system fell further and further behind in seeking to identify qualified asylum seekers.

Congress, as usual, dithered. President Obama sought unsuccessfully to encourage a bipartisan congressional compromise over immigration, seeking a middle ground that would harden the border against future undocumented aliens while providing security—even a path to citizenship—to some or all of the otherwise law-abiding undocumented immigrants already in the country. When the president was blocked by Republican senators opposed to granting any form of "amnesty" to undocumented aliens, he focused on the politically most attractive segment of the undocumented population—the approximately 1.2 million young persons who had been brought—or sent—through the cracks in the wall by their parents in search of safety and a better life. President Obama labeled them "the Dreamers."

He initially sought to persuade opponents of amnesty to accept the Dreamers by pointing out that, as children, they bore no moral responsibility for breaking the immigration laws. When he failed to persuade the Republican Congress to act, President Obama turned to unilateral presidential action, issuing regulations declining to deport Dreamers and granting them a secure, regular immigration status. He even tacked on similar unilateral protections against deportation for their parents to prevent the destruction of families.

Did President Obama violate separation of powers by acting unilaterally to help the Dreamers? If you say no, be prepared to explain why President Trump's unilateral travel ban is different.

President Obama argued that, given the scarcity of resources available for the enforcement of the immigration laws, it made no sense for immigration authorities to expend the enormous amount of resources that would be needed to deport more than one million young people who were brought into this country as children, had lived exemplary lives here, and were well on the way to becoming productive members of the community. Accordingly, the president defended his unilateral order protecting the Dreamers as a classic exercise of prosecutorial discretion designed to allocate scarce law enforcement resources.

Obama's critics argued that the regulations were far more than a mere presidential decision to allocate limited resources. They noted, first, that the usual exercise of prosecutorial discretion is an informal "retail" decision by a prosecutor who declines to enforce the criminal law against a particular person in a single case. The Dreamer regulations institutionalized a decision to forgo enforcement on a wholesale basis, directing immigration enforcement agents and prosecutors to refrain from enforcing the law against an entire category of individuals.

Critics noted as well that, unlike ordinary exercises in prosecutorial discretion, the Dreamer regulations established an institutional framework for its implementation, providing criteria for coverage, a mechanism for registration, and, most important, a regularization of immigration status that permitted a Dreamer to work, pay taxes, and enjoy a secure life in the United States. They claimed that such comprehensive regulations were more like the enactment of a statutory exemption from the immigration laws than a resource-driven inability to enforce them.

Given the intense political polarization of the immigration debate, it was only a matter of time until the Dreamer regulations were subjected to a separation-of-powers attack in court. That's just what happened. The state of Texas, governed by officials intensely hostile to undocumented immigration from Mexico, challenged the legality of the regulations before a handpicked Republican federal judge. When asked why Texas had a stake in the issue sufficient to grant it authority to mount a federal court challenge, Texas's lawyers answered that, under the Dreamer regulations, a significant number of undocumented immigrants would qualify for driver's licenses, forcing Texas to expend funds in connection with the processing and issuance of the licenses. Honest—that's what Texas claimed was the constitutionally necessary "injury in fact" it would suffer under the regulations. I guess someone forgot to tell Texas that the Dreamer kids who received the driver's licenses would also become eligible to work, and to pay sales, payroll, property, and income taxes, more than offsetting the trivial expense of issuing the licenses.

But then, Texas's real objection to the regulations was political, not financial. Lawyer-talk about the financial cost was just the usual obfuscation by American lawyers that has given them such a good name. The Republican federal judge selected to hear the case couldn't wait to get his hands on the Dreamer regulations. He grasped at Texas's tale of financial woe and, without reaching the difficult separation-of-powers issue, seized on a hypertechnical requirement that new executive regulations should have been subjected to a public notice and comment period before adoption as the justification for a nationwide injunction. The Obama administration appealed to the federal appeals court for Texas, where conservative Republican judges maintained a comfortable majority.

The appeals court focused on the hard question of whether the president was making new law or merely deciding how to implement existing law. A unilateral presidential regulation with such far-reaching categorical impact, encased in an institutional framework, was, the appeals court held, an exercise in lawmaking, something allocated solely to Congress. I'd be willing to bet, though, that the same Republican judges would have upheld President Trump's unilateral travel ban.

An immediate appeal was taken to the Supreme Court, operating with eight justices after the death of Justice Scalia. The Court split 4–4 along party lines, with the four Republican justices invalidating the Dreamer regulations as new laws promulgated by the executive in violation of separation of powers and the four Democratic justices treating them as valid exercises in executive implementation of existing law. Under traditional Supreme Court practice, while a 4–4 tie is not a final decision on the issues, it does affirm the decision below, leaving the nationwide injunction of the lower court in place.

So Texas was rewarded for winning the race to the closest Republican courthouse by securing a lower court judgment that froze the implementation of the Dreamer regulation, even though Texas couldn't persuade a majority of the Supreme Court that the president had violated the separation of powers. That's where things stood when Donald Trump unexpectedly won the 2016 presidential election.

Supporters of the Dreamers had confidently expected that a newly elected President Hillary Clinton would fill the vacant ninth Supreme Court seat with a Democratic justice who would provide a fifth vote upholding the Dreamer regulations. Instead, President Trump didn't even bother to wait for the Supreme Court. He unilaterally rescinded the Dreamer regulations as beyond the power of the executive branch, while simultaneously expressing sympathy for the Dreamers' plight and urging Congress to enact legislation rescuing them. Trump then cynically turned the issue into a bargaining chip for his border wall, refusing to support a congressional fix for the Dreamers unless Congress complied with his demands for $25 billion to fund a Mexican border wall, a massive increase in the pace of apprehension and deportation of undocumented aliens, and an end to the program of reuniting families, in favor of a "merit-based" immigration system that would avoid immigrants from "shithole" nations and favor those from prosperous countries such as Norway.

At that point, the Democrats launched a separation-of-powers counterattack, arguing that President Trump lacked power to rescind the Dreamer regulations. At first glance, it seems difficult to invoke separation of powers to challenge a president's decision to

revoke regulations that are, in his opinion, beyond his power to issue. Why shouldn't the president be allowed to eliminate an executive regulation that he believes may go beyond presidential power?
The answer, so far, lies in President Trump's characteristically
dishonest explanation for rescinding the Dreamer regulations in
the first place. In order to shield himself from political criticism for
failing to recognize the strong moral and social reasons for sparing
Dreamers from deportation, Trump professed support for allowing
them to remain in the United States with a regularized status but
claimed that he was unable to do anything about it without congressional authorization. He then blocked congressional authorization by linking it to funding his border wall.

In effect, Trump argued that he was reluctantly rescinding the
Dreamer regulations because they exceeded presidential power,
while simultaneously urging Congress to authorize him to reissue
them. Democratic federal district judges in San Francisco, Brook-
lyn, and Washington, DC, decided to take Trump at his word, overturning a presidential decision to rescind the Dreamer regulations
premised on an inaccurate understanding of his presidential powers. They ruled that the Republican Texas appeals court had been
wrong in holding that President Obama was making a new law
when his administration issued the Dreamer regulations. In fact,
ruled the three federal judges, President Obama had merely been
making legitimate, unilateral decisions about how the existing law
should be implemented.

While all three Democratic federal judges agreed that President Trump is free at any time to rescind the regulations because
he disagrees with them, they ruled that he cannot base rescission
solely on an inaccurate belief about the scope of his—and President Obama's—powers as president. Trump's lawyers then took the
unusual step of asking the by now Republican-controlled Supreme
Court to review two of the lower court decisions immediately. The
Supreme Court, led by the chief justice, rejected the application,
routing the appeals through the circuits in the ordinary course,
where they currently languish.

My bet is that the pattern will hold. Republican-dominated

appeals courts will rule for President Trump. Democratic-controlled appeals courts will rule in favor of the Dreamers. In the end, of course, the fate of the Dreamers will be decided by a Republican Supreme Court. Four Republican justices (including the chief justice) have already shown their cards in voting to affirm the Texas appeals court's finding that President Obama was improperly making new law, not deciding how to implement existing law. The four Democratic justices showed theirs in voting to uphold President Obama's power. Want to bet on the votes of Neil Gorsuch and Brett Kavanaugh?

For what it's worth, I believe that the Texas appeals court was wrong in finding that the Dreamers regulation is a new law, violating separation of powers. It's a close case, though. An exercise in prosecutorial discretion not to enforce certain laws because of scarce resources is clearly not a violation of separation of powers. But the Dreamer regulations are much more sweeping and elaborate than the usual exercise of prosecutorial discretion. So the issue could plausibly be decided either way. I would break the legal tie by asking whether President Obama's decision not to deport the Dreamers results in a dangerous concentration of powers capable of causing harm to individuals. That's what separation of powers is intended to prevent. That's how the Supreme Court upheld the independent counsel law.

To my mind, a president's decision, pending final congressional action, to refrain from deporting a vulnerable, morally innocent group of young people does not cause a dangerous concentration of powers. So in a tie case like this I would uphold the Obama regulations. But don't get too excited. The Supreme Court, with Neil Gorsuch and Brett Kavanaugh, will probably jump at the opportunity to invalidate the Obama regulations as soon as it gets the chance.

It's worth trying to stave off the inevitable, however, at least until the 2020 elections, in the hope that Congress will finally act or that a new president will find a way out of the impasse. In order to buy time, it will be crucial to throw sand in the gears of any effort to deport Dreamers before new rules can be put in place. It may come down to running out the clock. Here's one way to do it.

As part of the original Obama regulations, Dreamers were encouraged to come forward and to register for the favorable treatment promised by the president. More than 700,000 young people did so. So the government is sitting on all the information it needs to crank up the deportation machine—information obtained under a false promise of leniency. It's like enticing someone into pleading guilty by promising a lenient sentence and then backing out of the deal. Government should not be able to ensnare young people—or anyone else—by tricking them into giving officials the information the government needs to deport them by falsely promising that it would be used only to benefit them. There's a law against that. It's called equitable estoppel, and it prevents the government from benefiting from its own wrongdoing.

Thus, any effort to deport Dreamers should be met by a nationwide injunction barring deportation unless the government demonstrates that it is not relying on information wrongfully gathered under what turned out to be a phony promise of leniency. That should stall the deportation machine long enough for you—and millions and millions like you—to pass judgment at the polls. In the end, as with the fate of the Muslim travel ban and the impact of the Mueller investigation, the fate of the Dreamers will not be finally resolved as a matter of separation of powers. Their fate is up to you. The Senate managed to assemble fifty-four votes for a deal that would protect the Dreamers and build Trump's wall on the Mexican border. But, under the current filibuster rules, it takes sixty votes to enact Dreamer legislation. That's why Obama couldn't do it. Trump shot the border-wall/Dreamer deal down because he thinks he can hold the Dreamers hostage to more draconian cuts in nonwhite, non-Christian immigration.

In December 2018, President Trump doubled down on his restrictive immigration strategy by shutting down the government in an effort to force Congress to authorize billions of dollars to build a wall on our southern border with Mexico. When Congress refused and the voters turned restive, Trump resorted to authoritarian decree, proclaiming a phony "national emergency" and asserting unilateral presidential power to transfer funds from authorized military projects to build the wall. When Congress reacted by enacting joint resolutions rejecting the existence of a national emergency, Trump resorted to the veto, leaving Congress unable to muster the needed two-thirds vote to override. Unless the Supreme Court intervenes, therefore, nothing can stop Trump from unilaterally imposing draconian immigration policies except the voters. Even worse, unless the courts stop him, Trump will have built a road map for authoritarian presidential governance based on self-proclaimed national emergencies.

He'll get away with it unless the 2020 elections change the political calculus in Congress and deliver a new Congress and a new president, who will rescind the travel ban, reinstate the Dreamer regulations, and develop an enforceable but humanitarian immigration policy.

THE GREAT DEREGULATION MASSACRE

Democrats don't like to admit it, but Donald Trump, in his first eighteen months as president, may have presided over one of the most dramatic power shifts in American history. The tax bill he championed funneled vast sums to the wealthy, exacerbating a massive national divide between the very rich and the rest of us. The Trump administration and a Republican Congress also combined to repeal hundreds of executive regulations protecting consumers, the environment, employees, the elderly, the ill, children, small investors, and ordinary internet users. In industry after industry, restraints on harmful, exploitive, or dangerous behavior were gutted or repealed. The net effect shifts massive power to corporate and business leaders, who are today the real rulers of the Trump nation. Acting alone, the newly elected Democratic House of Representatives can't do much about it.

The power shift took two paths. Congress, acting under a statute from the 1990s, combined with President Trump to wipe out almost every regulation issued in the closing days of the Obama administration. As we've seen, ordinarily, under separation of powers, Congress can't unilaterally undo executive regulations because doing so would hand Congress the dangerously concentrated power of making new laws and controlling how the laws are enforced. But the 1990s legislation provides a framework for cooperative action by Congress and the president to wipe out executive regulations within sixty days of issuance. Since both the president and Congress must agree to erase a recent executive regulation, the 1990s legislation does not necessarily concentrate two powers in a single branch, although it's still not clear to me why a Congress respectful of separation of powers should be mucking around with regulations at all. Short of winning the presidency in 2020 and reissuing the regulations, there's not much the Democratic House can do to put that Humpty-Dumpty together again.

More often, though, President Trump and his appointees acted unilaterally, often through political appointees who had worked for the regulated industry prior to Trump's election, to roll back important regulations protecting the environment, climate, consumers, and health care. Technical objections to the procedures used to alter pre-existing regulations have succeeded in slowing the process of change down in twenty-eight of the thirty legal challenges to Trump's effort to alter environmental regulations, but eventually Trump's appointees will get the mechanics straight and obliterate or badly weaken a broad swath of valuable regulations. Neither the use of congressional regulation-stripping legislation nor executive repeal raises a genuine separation-of-powers issue. That's what presidents do. What one president can do by issuing regulations, another can undo. But—and here's where the hope for the future comes in—a third can redo.

In the end, the Trump deregulatory revolution is built on separation-of-powers sand. It lasts only as long as Trump is president. Its future is almost entirely in your hands.

OFF THE WALL: THE NATIONAL EMERGENCY LOOPHOLE

The Founders' idea of separation of powers may have its share of dents in the twenty-first century, but it continues to serve as a significant constitutional brake against a runaway president. The requirement that Congress authorize executive action in advance and appropriate the funds to carry out presidential initiatives gives the legislative branch a potent two-step check on presidential adventures. No congressional authorization; no presidential power. No congressional appropriation; no money to support a presidential initiative.

But President Trump has identified a potential massive "national emergency" loophole in the Founders' plan that threatens to leave it in ruins. According to our forty-fifth president, all a president need do to concentrate all three powers of government—the power to make the law; the power to enforce the law; and the power to resolve disputes about the law's meaning—in his own authoritarian hands is to issue a proclamation of national emergency vesting him with power to rule by presidential fiat. President Trump's decision to throw a "national emergency" tantrum in response to Congress's refusal to appropriate more than $5 billion to build additional walls on our southern border with Mexico threatens the very survival of our constitutional system.

The president initially refused to sign any appropriations legislation that does not provide funds for his wall, forcing a shutdown of about 25 percent of the federal government, ending paychecks for 800,000 federal workers and thousands of federal contractors, and depriving hundreds of thousands of Americans of needed governmental services. More than three weeks into the government shutdown, President Trump, facing plummeting poll ratings, caved in and re-opened the government without obtaining funding for his wall. But he then declared a national emergency on the southern border, insisted on spending disaster relief funds on the wall in the teeth of Congress's refusal to grant him funds. Both houses of Congress then voted to reject the phony national emergency, but the president overrode them with a veto. If Trump succeeds in using a national emergency declaration as a substitute for congressional authorization, separation of powers won't just have a few dents. It will cease to exist. Any president, at any time and for any purpose, can simply throw a national emergency switch turning off constitutional limits on presidential power. Vladimir Putin would smile and welcome Donald Trump to the dictators' club.

Will Trump get away with trashing the separation of powers? As usual, the problem began small and grew because of congressional willingness to cede power to the president, and Supreme Court failure to defend the separation of powers. The first presidential declaration of national emergency did not occur until February 1917, two months before war was declared on Germany. Acting pursuant to the Shipping Act of 1916, President Woodrow Wilson declared a national emergency permitting him to bar the transfer of American-owned oceangoing ships to noncitizens. Wilson was not attempting an end run around Congress. He was merely seeking to activate a non-controversial restriction that Congress had pre-approved, leaving it to the president to decide when to place it into effect.

Over the years, Congress embraced the Wilson precedent, drifting into the habit of tacking provisions onto statutes authorizing the president to take a congressionally pre-approved action only if the president deemed it necessary to meet a national emergency. By my unofficial count, a national emergency trigger was built into about five hundred statutes. In almost all of them, Congress authorized the president to activate defined regulatory sanctions, usually against foreigners, whenever a "national emergency" required the action. That's how economic sanctions are usually imposed on nations or foreign nationals. That's how President Trump has sought to justify his unilateral power to impose tariffs on Chinese products without congressional authorization.

Until now, the idea of presidentially declared "national emergencies" has functioned cooperatively as an "on-off" switch authorizing presidents to decide when, where, and against whom to deploy pre-approved congressional sanctions. In the one hundred years since Congress and President Wilson initiated the process, I know of no setting in which a president has used a unilateral proclamation of national emergency to authorize programs that Congress had refused to support. Giving presidents the power to turn congressionally approved laws on and off is bad enough. Even the best of presidents will be tempted to abuse such a broad power. But giving a president like Donald Trump power to circumvent Congress entirely by acting unilaterally in the teeth of congressional opposition is political lunacy. It is how democracies based on separation of powers die.

Congress tried in 1976 to take the national emergency power back. The National Emergencies Act, signed by President Gerald Ford in the wake of the Watergate crisis, terminated almost all presidentially declared national emergencies and imposed stringent limits on a president's ability to declare new ones. According to the act as originally written, the president was obliged to report any declaration of national emergency to Congress, which could reject it within fifteen days by a concurrent resolution adopted by a majority vote of both chambers. In 1983, however, the Supreme Court threw a monkey wrench into the National Emergencies Act's enforcement provision by ruling that a concurrent resolution that is not signed by the president, or enacted over his veto, has no legal effect. Congress then amended the Act in 1985 to require congressional rejection of a presidentially declared national emergency to take the form of a joint resolution of Congress. The problem is that a joint resolution must be submitted to the president for signature or be passed by a two-thirds vote over the president's veto before it has legal force. Since President Trump predictably vetoed Congress's effort to use the joint resolution route to block him from declaring a border wall emergency, the National Emergencies Act as currently drafted is just a paper tiger. Congress could rein in the president by amending the act to require affirmative congressional assent to the declaration of national emergency, but that would take a full-fledged new law that would also be subject to a Trump veto. So it's not going to happen because it will be impossible to marshal a two-thirds vote in both houses of Congress.

But that's not the end of the story. There will be five crucial legal issues for Supreme Court resolution. The first is whether the Constitution grants the president, as commander in chief and the nation's chief executive, an "inherent power" to act unilaterally whenever he declares a national emergency. Up until now, the Supreme Court has rejected such a dangerous assertion of unilateral presidential power. That's what *Youngstown Steel* was all about. But, ominously, the five Republican members of the current Supreme

Court did not reject the president's "inherent power" argument in the Muslim travel ban case. They simply declined to pass on it.

If the current Supreme Court majority were to recognize an "inherent emergency power" exception to separation of powers, the United States Constitution as we have known it since the founding will cease to exist. I don't think they'll do it.

The second legal issue for the Supreme Court is whether any statutory authority for a national emergency declaration exists that would permit the president to shift Defense Department funds to build his wall. The president's advisors have identified two statutes that may authorize the president to shift Defense Department funds to deal with a national emergency. But both statutes raise serious questions about whether they authorize the president to use a proclamation of national emergency to shift military funds to build a wall. One allows the president to shift money to fund otherwise "authorized" projects. The other allows the president to shift money to build facilities needed to support military activity. The president's wall is, however, neither authorized nor designed to support military activity. While the president might seek to rely on a 2006 statute authorizing the building of a wall on portions of the southern border, Congress has refused to appropriate funds to further extend the wall. A principled judge should construe the statutes literally to bar the president's effort to rely on them.

Third, Congress rejected Trump's phony emergency declaration by reenacting a bipartisan joint resolution rejecting Trump's declaration. Trump predictably successfully vetoed it.

It's something of a long shot, but it's plausible to argue that a joint resolution designed to prevent the suspension of separation of powers cannot be gutted by a presidential veto. The analogy would be to a joint resolution that commences the process of constitutional amendment, a Senate vote on ratifying a treaty or confirming a nominee, or a House vote impeaching the president, none of which are subject to presidential veto.

Fourth, assuming that the president persuades the Court that statutory authority exists and that the joint resolution of Congress rejecting it is subject to veto, the question becomes whether a proclamation of a national emergency in the teeth of explicit congressional refusal to authorize the project can vest the president with unilateral power to act. It has never been used to frustrate the will of Congress. That's why it would be such a blow to separation of powers if a tame Supreme Court deferred to the president once again in a replay of their supine approach to the president's unilateral Muslim travel ban.

Donald Trump isn't the first authoritarian leader to claim the power to dissolve legislative limits on his power by uttering the magic words "national emergency." Adolf Hitler did it in 1933 in the wake of the Reichstag fire. It was the first step in the demise of German democracy. Make no mistake about it. If Donald Trump gets away with proclaiming a manufactured national emergency to seize unilateral presidential power in the teeth of Congress's refusal to authorize his behavior, he will deliver a body blow to the United States Constitution. A unilateral presidential border wall, today, against the will of Congress; unilateral presidential responses to global warming tomorrow; presidential emergency decrees on gun violence the day after; preventing the mass murder of fetuses the day after that.

How long before we have presidentially established military internment camps for dangerous political opponents? Lock her up, indeed. That's how a constitutional democracy based on separation of powers dies.

Finally, the Supreme Court will be asked to review whether a national emergency actually exists. The justices will almost certainly duck that issue by disclaiming the expertise needed to second guess a presidential proclamation of national emergency. But the justices' skepticism about whether a true national emergency exists—and the fear of setting a precedent allowing the president to eviscerate separation of powers—will, I predict, color their decisions about inherent power, statutory authority, the legal effect of a contrary joint resolution of Congress, and the ability of a president to use national emergency power in the teeth of congressional opposition. In the end, Trump would lose on one or all of those questions.

A GLIMPSE OF THE FUTURE

A steady diet of unilateral presidential decrees flashing on and off depending on who is in office is a terrible way to govern. Think of Donald Trump unbound by limits on his personal power. It's also inherently unstable; ask the Dreamers. As long as Obama was president, they could rely on a thoughtful regulation designed to open the way to a productive life. Once Trump became president, all he had to do was flip the switch and the Dreamers were back in the cold.

That kind of instability can't be good for the economy. It's hard enough to run a business efficiently and humanely in our complex, ever-changing world. It's damn near impossible when the basic regulations governing your industry are subject to dramatic change every time one president succeeds another. Many business leaders, especially coal and oil producers, are celebrating Trump's deregulation binge. But that celebration can turn to bitter disappointment under a new president.

Maybe, when progressives get back into power, it will be time to stop governing through short-term presidential orders and executive regulations, even when we control the presidency. It's long past time to put Congress back to work as the principal architect of new law. Not only does a congressional statute more accurately reflect the will of the people, but statutes can't be turned on and off every time there's a new president. It's time to elect people to the House and Senate who are willing to shoulder Congress's separation-of-powers burden to make the law, rather than giving away that power to the president—of either party.

Maybe it's time for the Supreme Court to stop functioning as an enabler in the erosion of separation of powers, standing by as Congress repeatedly delegates the power to make new law to the executive. Once upon a time, the Supreme Court refused to permit Congress to use vague statutes to delegate lawmaking power to the president and his assistants. I agree with Antonin Scalia that the old anti-delegation precedents should be dusted off and given new life.

Maybe it's time for the Supreme Court to stop giving away its power to say what the law is. Once upon a time, the Supreme Court accepted the duty to interpret vague congressional statutes granting regulatory power to administrative agencies. Somewhere along the way, the Court gave away that power to the bureaucrats by deferring (there's that dangerous word again) to executive interpretations of the vague statutes. Once again, I agree with the critics who urge the Supreme Court to take back its classical separation-of-powers role.

Maybe it's time to rediscover the jury as ultimate fact-finder, even in administrative proceedings. Most Americans exercise direct governing power only three times in our lives—when we vote, when we serve in the nation's armed forces, and when we serve on a jury. The Constitution protects all three—the First, Fifth, and Fourteenth Amendments protect the right to vote; the Second, Fifth, and Fourteenth Amendments protect the right to serve in the military; and the Sixth, Seventh, and Fourteenth Amendments guarantee the right to a trial before a jury drawn from all the people.

Sadly, as we've seen, while the Supreme Court has provided protection for the right to vote and to serve in the armed forces, it has presided over the demise of the American jury. Most criminal cases end in a plea bargain, in large part because under our current sentencing laws prosecutors exercise so much power they can bluff defendants away from risking a guilty verdict. Civil jury trials are virtually extinct because too many cases get thrown out of court before a jury can hear them. Those that survive almost all settle. The Supreme Court has even approved the elimination of the jury from most disputes involving regulatory statutes. So in a dispute before the Securities and Exchange Commission or the National Labor Relations Board, disputed facts will be resolved by an executive official, not a jury of the people. Maybe it's time for the people to take back the fact-finding power across the board.

My seventh-grade civics notes are available if anyone needs them.

9

Which Shell Is the Power Under?

Federalism as a Protection of the Weak

For most of my career as a civil liberties lawyer, I have viewed the idea of federalism, sometimes called "states' rights," as a technique to shield pockets of racism and intolerance from efforts by the national government to protect the weak. There is, however, nothing like having an authoritarian president in the White House, a craven Republican-controlled Senate, and an ideological Republican Supreme Court to make me rethink my lifelong opposition to states' rights. When, as now, many of the instrumentalities of the national government have become at best indifferent to the idea of equality and at worst hostile to it, the idea of shoring up the powers of state governments, elected by majorities prepared to take equality seriously, suddenly looks much more appealing.

Federalism is the second pillar of what I have called the structural Constitution—the crucial but frequently overlooked provisions of our Constitution that lay out the powers and duties of the various actors in American democracy. As we've seen, the first pillar, separation of powers, defines (and limits) the relative authority of the three major components of the national government. Federalism allocates governing authority between the national government and the states (vertical federalism) and among the fifty states (horizontal federalism).

The Founders saw vertical federalism as just another way to prevent the federal government from acquiring too much power. They limited the national government to a laundry list of "enumerated" subjects, most important among them foreign policy, national defense, taxation, and the regulation of commerce between the states (interstate commerce), and gave everything else to the states, especially the powers needed to defend their status as genuine sovereigns and not merely subdivisions of the national government. When the Founders were finished, a narrowly defined slice of governing power was vested in a national government, operating pursuant to separation of powers; an important array of powers was vested exclusively in the states, operating under "republican forms of government"; and a broad spectrum of powers was jointly exercisable by both the states and the federal government, with the federal government getting the last word under the supremacy clause whenever state policy gets in the way of national policy.

One source of potential state power—called "the police power"—pre-dated the 1787 Constitution and didn't depend on the Founders. British political theory recognized the inherent right of a sovereign entity to protect the life, health, safety, and morals of its inhabitants. The original thirteen states retained their "police powers" when they entered the union, but, like all state power, even the police power must be exercised in compliance with constitutional ground rules—especially the supremacy clause.

The problem is deciding in which pot to put a given exercise of government power. What, for example, counts as regulation of interstate commerce? Thomas Jefferson and Andrew Hamilton couldn't agree in George Washington's first cabinet. The Supreme Court was no closer to an answer more than two hundred years later in 2014 when it narrowly upheld and narrowly invalidated portions of President Obama's Affordable Care Act by 5–4 votes. Five Republican justices (including Chief Justice Roberts) ruled that the power to regulate interstate commerce did not vest Congress with the affirmative power to require persons to buy health insurance. The four Democrats dissented, rejecting the difference between a negative prohibition and an affirmative command. But five justices (the four Democrats, plus Chief Justice Roberts) also ruled that Congress was empowered to impose a tax (not a penalty) on persons who fail to buy health insurance. So the chief justice won that case by a vote of 1–8.

A Republican Congress promptly repealed the tax, leaving the mandate to buy health insurance in place, but removing any legal consequences for failing to obey. Where does that leave the Affordable Care Act today? A Republican federal judge in Texas invalidated the entire act in December 2018, arguing that repeal of the tax left only an unconstitutional mandate. President Trump quickly jumped on board, directing his Justice Department to attack the constitutionality of Obamacare once again in the Supreme Court. Defenders of the act argue, first, that a "mandate" with no teeth does not go beyond Congress's commerce clause power; and, second, that, in any event, the rest of the Affordable Care Act should survive excision of the mandate. My money is on the chief justice to save Obamacare for the second time.

Conversely, what kinds of powers do the states need to maintain their sovereignty? In *Shelby County*, five Republican members of the Court thought that Section 5 of the Voting Rights Act, requiring states with a long history of disenfranchising blacks to get federal permission before they changed any voting rule, violated the equal dignity of sovereign southern states because differential treatment of the southern states was no longer necessary to protect black voters. The four Democratic justices dissented vigorously, correctly predicting that as soon as the federal restraints were removed, racists would once again make it as hard as possible for blacks to vote. We're living with the consequences of that toxic exercise in federalism today as a wave of voter restrictions sweeps the South.

Finally, how do you measure when a perfectly legitimate state policy gets in the way of a federal policy and must give way under the supremacy clause? Lawyers call it the process of preemption. For example, when states decide that imposed consumer contracts requiring compulsory arbitration are unenforceable because they unfairly burden access to the courts, does the state policy in favor of court access get in the way of a 1925 federal statute requiring courts to enforce agreements to arbitrate in settings involving interstate commerce?

In 1984, in a setting where a contract providing for compulsory arbitration had been fairly bargained, the Supreme Court ruled that the federal arbitration statute "preempted" contrary state policy. Five Republican justices then extended the 1984 precedent to all contracts, even if one side has all the bargaining power; the four Democratic justices have consistently dissented. How can an ordinary citizen decide who is right?

The truth is that there is no clear legal answer to many hard federalism issues. From the beginning, we've simply made the federalism rules up as we go along. There is no "federalism clause" to construe. Unlike separation of powers, there isn't even an underlying theory to apply. The Constitution's text is deeply ambiguous. There was no consensus among the Founders. The Civil War and the post–Civil War amendments radically diminished the power of the states but did not eliminate them. From a strictly legal standpoint, it's often just a shell game.

If the law of American federalism is just a shell game, why shouldn't progressives get in the game by taking "states' rights" seriously to: (1) preserve aspects of state autonomy needed to enable effective resistance to Trumpist policies—think sanctuary cities, protecting undocumented aliens from mass deportation by federal agents; (2) play keep-away, shifting regulatory power to the states from the federal government in order to minimize Trump's ability to harm the weak and the environment—think control over net neutrality, pollution, consumer protection, and environmental protection; and (3) funnel as much governing power as possible to state majorities willing to protect the weak—think state and local laws providing Uber drivers and other participants in the gig economy with collective bargaining rights over compensation and safety.

Using federalism to protect the weak would be a welcome relief because until now federalism has usually put the power to protect the weak under the other shell. In the beginning, southern slave owners fervently embraced states' rights because it insulated the dirty business of owning human beings from a growing national antislavery consensus. When, however, free states such as Pennsylvania and Wisconsin acted to protect fugitive slaves, southern slave owners were quick to abandon states' rights, successfully invoking national power rooted in the notorious fugitive slave clause to override efforts to protect the weak.

In the wake of the Civil War, the former slaveholders rediscovered states' rights, fighting successfully under its banner for more than a century to frustrate attempts by a national majority to protect formerly enslaved persons and their descendants, who were trapped in hostile white-majority southern states. In the late nineteenth and early twentieth centuries, corporate America copied a page from southern racists, arguing that Congress lacked power to break up monopolies, prevent stock fraud, protect consumers, end price fixing, and limit wage gouging. When, however, progressive states tried to protect vulnerable workers and consumers, the lawyers for powerful corporations pivoted on a dime and rediscovered the dominance of national power.

Things got better beginning in the late 1930s under a Democratic Supreme Court. In 1937, the Court recognized significant power over the economy vested in both state and national majorities. As one federalism shell game ended, though, another began. The "states' rights" banner was brandished successfully for more than a generation by southern racists seeking to block the enforcement of an emerging national consensus rejecting racial apartheid in the states of the old Confederacy. When at last the southern governors' ugly campaign of massive resistance to racial equality was rebuffed by a Democratic Supreme Court and a Democratic Congress, "states' rights" became the right-wing rallying cry for resistance to the Warren Court's expansive equality-driven reading of the federal Constitution.

Progressives should recognize that federalism needn't be just a shell game designed to protect the strong. A far better intellectual case can be made that American federalism, like separation of powers and the protection of individual rights, is simply another technique for protecting the weak against the tyranny or neglect of the majority. After all, that's why we established a judicially enforceable Constitution in the first place.

In every era, a shifting set of extra-legal circumstances has argued for national or local supremacy. Like an accordion, the relative power of national and state majorities has expanded and contracted in accordance with "the felt necessity of the times," to use the words of Justice Oliver Wendell Holmes. During my lifetime, three powerful social forces have combined to trigger a sustained flow of power from state to national majorities. First, the Great Depression of the 1930s generated enormous pressure to expand both state and national power to regulate the economy. The argument for national regulation was often put in terms of efficiency and superior expertise, but the real need for national norms was to avoid a race to the bottom, an inevitable series of efforts by desperate state majorities to bid for a shrinking pool of jobs by lowering minimum wages, eliminating taxes, gutting safety rules, sacrificing the environment, and ending quality controls. FDR argued that only nationwide floors could slow such a precipitous race to the bottom, which would be destructive to everyone but especially harmful to the nation's most vulnerable inhabitants.

In 1937, responding to massive electoral victories by FDR and the threat of court-packing, the Supreme Court finally realized that a race to the bottom lowers all boats. Within five years, from 1937 to 1942, a newly Democratic Supreme Court rotated 180 degrees to a new definition of constitutional federalism, moving from a Republican refusal to permit Congress to set uniform national rules governing the economy to a Democratic recognition of national power to regulate even something as local as the amount of wheat a single farmer can grow in his backyard to feed to his own pigs.

At the same time, the newly Democratic-dominated Court rotated 180 degrees in the opposite direction by removing Republican-imposed national "substantive due process" constraints on the power of states to protect vulnerable market participants, including workers and consumers. Such a double-barreled radical shift didn't take place because the justices got smarter, because they finally discovered a dictionary that correctly defined "interstate commerce," or because Alexander Hamilton and/or Thomas Jefferson spoke to them in the night.

Rather, the change was driven by sustained electoral support for Democratic candidates that eventually translated into Democratic control of the Supreme Court, with a corresponding increase in the role of equality in breaking legal ties about the allocation of power between state and national majorities.

The Depression was followed in 1939 by World War II and then the Cold War, a fight first for national survival and then for world-wide hegemony. The hot war against Nazi Germany, fascist Italy, and imperial Japan morphed into a series of Cold War military confrontations with the nuclear-armed Soviet empire, including full-scale land wars in Korea and Vietnam and a series of smaller skirmishes that continued until the collapse of the Berlin Wall in 1989 and the implosion of Soviet communism.

The almost permanent nature of such armed confrontation inevitably concentrated government power in the center. A nation that perceives itself as fighting for its life will have little patience with dissenting regional majorities out of step with the exercise of centralized power defended as necessary to preserve the nation.

Finally, beginning in the 1930s, but intensifying in the years after World War II, the Supreme Court was confronted by an ongoing refusal by recalcitrant state and local majorities in the states of the old Confederacy to defer to an emerging national consensus calling for an end to government-imposed racial apartheid and greater attention to racial fairness. Given the foreign and domestic consequences of such a racially charged confrontation, it was only a matter of time until the Democratic Supreme Court, with its tilt toward equality, empowered all three branches of the national government to act in the name of racial fairness.

Viewed as a federalism tug-of-war between conflicting state and national majorities, the Supreme Court's rejection of racial segregation in the public schools in *Brown v. Board of Education*— arguably the most important constitutional decision of the twentieth century—was really the imposition by a unanimous Supreme Court of an emerging national consensus rejecting racial apartheid on recalcitrant state and local majorities. The existence of a national consensus in three-quarters of the states for ending racial apartheid was why the *Brown* opinion was ultimately unanimous, and why its conclusion that state-imposed racial apartheid is unconstitutional continues to receive virtually unanimous support today.

The absence of a national consensus on how to deal with racial issues beyond eliminating state-imposed apartheid and intentional discrimination explains why the post-*Brown* Supreme Court was unable—and unwilling—to move beyond banning state-imposed apartheid and intentional racial discrimination.

By 1990, a year after Soviet communism had imploded at the Berlin Wall, each of the three mutually reinforcing reasons to prefer national over state majorities had diminished in intensity. The Great Depression with its race to the bottom was only a memory. While interstate competition for jobs continued to invite dilution of protections for the weak—witness the success of certain states in luring jobs from the Northeast by diluting the power of unions and dispensing with social programs impacting the tax burdens of prospective employers—the existence of national minimums enacted by Congress provided significant floors below which state majorities cannot sink in bidding for jobs.

Perhaps more important, despite a few rocky periods, the nation's economy had relentlessly improved since the end of World War II. When times are relatively good, the temptation to attract scarce jobs by gutting the social safety net is considerably less intense. So, while the risk of a race to the bottom is still with us, it became more of a slow shuffle, not a frantic sprint.

Similarly, when the collapse of the Berlin Wall signaled the end of the Soviet empire as a threat to the United States, the centralizing pressure of the Cold War evaporated overnight. Without the need to maintain a strong central shield against Soviet aggression, power began to flow back to the states, tempered only by the emergence in the years following 9/11 of a new foreign threat in the form of terrorism.

Finally, the South's regional tantrum against accepting formal racial equality ended in grudging surrender. A new generation of southern leaders accepted the legal duty to refrain from intentional racial discrimination. Race relations in the South came to resemble race relations throughout the United States, with formal racial equality coexisting with massive indirect reinforcement of inequality.

Once the perceived need for strong central rules was relaxed, power began to drift back to the states. In 1995 Congress was told by the Supreme Court for the first time in more than fifty years that it lacked power under the commerce clause to enact desired legislation. In *United States v. Lopez*, the Republican Supreme Court struck down a commerce clause–based congressional ban on gun possession in or near schools, leaving pro-gun state and local majorities firmly in control of that issue.

The newly reenergized federalism shell game continued when, in *United States v. Morrison*, the Supreme Court told Congress that it could not invoke either the commerce clause or the post–Civil War equality amendments to enact national laws protecting women from gender-based violence, locating the regulatory power solely in state or local majorities.

In *Printz v. United States*, the National Rifle Association then persuaded the Republican Supreme Court that Congress lacked power to force dissenting state law enforcement authorities to carry out federal background checks in connection with federally regulated gun purchases.

Then, in a series of cases under the Eleventh Amendment, culminating in *Alden v. Maine* and *Seminole Tribes v. Florida*, states' rights was invoked to block federal judges from imposing money judgments on the states for violating the law—even the Constitution.

The accordion shift of power back to the states continued with the stunning decision by the Republican Supreme Court in *Shelby County* to invalidate a key portion of the Voting Rights Act of 1965 that had successfully blocked state majorities from disenfranchising black voters for almost half a century.

Finally, as we've just seen, the justices drew a razor-thin distinction between Congress's power to prohibit and its power to compel, ruling 5–4 that Congress lacked power under the commerce clause to compel individuals to buy health insurance.

The seventy-five-year run of pressure for increased national power that began with the Great Depression appears to have ended—just in time for progressives to deploy the concept of states' rights as a check on a presidential bully. How can progressives get into the federalism shell game in defense of the weak? There is no all-purpose federalism dial attached to the Constitution. The pressures that drive the relative waxing and waning of state and national power play themselves out in a series of formally unconnected, maddeningly complicated legal doctrines. Progressives will have to fight the federalism battles doctrine by doctrine. Do not wade into that doctrinal swamp expecting illumination. Each of the federalism-related legal doctrines has evolved in majestic isolation from each other, and from the real-world factors that drive them.

The Trump administration's claim to a genuine electoral mandate to speak for a majority of the nation in the give-and-take of federalism is at its lowest ebb since the Civil War. As we've seen, Donald Trump is a minority president. He lost the presidential election by more than three million votes and is in the White House only because the Electoral College is unfairly tilted toward rural constituencies. Republicans control the Senate only because the constitutional mandate of two senators per state regardless of population has turned the Senate into an appallingly undemocratic body. Republicans control the Supreme Court only because confirmation of the last two justices took place in the malapportioned Senate controlled by Republican senators representing less than 40 percent of the population. Republicans are overrepresented in the House of Representatives in large part because of ruthless partisan gerrymanders protected by five Republican Supreme Court justices who have deployed the First Amendment to protect the ability of the superrich to play an excessive role in American elections but who have to this point refused to recognize a First Amendment right to vote in a genuinely competitive election.

While the undemocratic nature of the Republican hold on the national government does not erode the right of Republican officials to hold office—Trump is our lawful president, the Senate is lawfully Republican, and the Supreme Court's nine justices are lawfully entitled to exercise their powers—it should, in close cases, affect the delicate balance between state and federal power. If American federalism is really about which legitimate democratic majority, state or federal, should be empowered to rule on a particular issue, and if today's version of the national government lacks a strong democratic imprimatur, federalism issues that do not tip clearly one way or the other should, I believe, be nudged toward the state majorities as the better democratic game in town.

In deciding close federalism cases, I would ask a single question—which group of elected officials, state or national, is more likely to treat the vulnerable fairly? In short, in the Time of Trump, the power to act should be found under the shell most likely to treat the weak fairly.

Let's take a look at some likely federalism battlegrounds.

SANCTUARY CITIES

The first important federalism battleground of the Trump years will be over efforts by state and local majorities to distance themselves from President Trump's effort to deport millions of undocumented aliens. No one knows how large the pool of undocumented aliens may be, but it almost certainly exceeds ten million people, most of whom live quietly in shadowy corners of their adopted country, seeking to educate their children and trying to eke out an existence on the margins of the economy. They pick our crops and tend to the sick and aging. We let them into our gated communities only to clean our houses, cut our lawns, and collect our trash.

Donald Trump got himself elected president by demonizing them. Playing on the fears of many white Americans that non-white immigration is threatening their political, economic, and social dominance, Trump repeatedly inveighed against "Mexican rapists," "Muslim terrorists," Haitian "slackers," and Central American drug dealers. Russian oligarchs and unsavory immigrants from majority-white nations got a pass.

Not surprisingly, as president, Trump has intensified efforts by federal immigration agents (working under the acronym ICE, standing for Immigration and Customs Enforcement) to identify, apprehend, and deport undocumented aliens. There is, of course, no reason for state or local majorities to resist federal efforts to deport undocumented aliens who have committed serious crimes (although even there, thorny questions arise about what to do with innocent family members). But Trump doesn't stop with deporting serious criminals. Intensifying deportation programs begun under the Obama administration, Trump has launched a massive program of surveillance and a series of dragnet raids by a cadre of federal enforcement officials aimed at churches, libraries, courtrooms, workplaces, and residences, in the hope of sweeping as many unfortunate undocumented immigrants as possible into the deportation net, whether or not they are guilty of anything other than seeking a better life in the United States.

Many, perhaps most Americans are deeply opposed to the national government's deportation dragnets. In state after state, overwhelming majorities have directed their state officials to do all they can to distance themselves from federal dragnet arrests and mass deportations while Congress struggles to shape a humane but effective immigration policy.

In one troubling sense, the United States has been here before. This is not the first time that state majorities have sought to protect the most vulnerable among us from the unjust enforcement of oppressive national norms. During the years leading up to the Civil War, the anti-slavery Underground Railway, based in northern states, fought a battle for the bodies and souls of thousands of black human beings who had fled from slavery. Since capturing and returning escaped slaves under the Fugitive Slave Act of 1850 was an immensely lucrative business, slave catchers made little or no effort to confine themselves to pursuing proven runaways; they preyed on free blacks as well. And once a free black was captured by a bounty hunter and transported south as an alleged runaway, little chance existed that he or she would ever taste freedom again.

Responding to the kidnapping of free blacks from the streets of Philadelphia, the Pennsylvania legislature enacted an anti-kidnapping law forbidding private slave catchers from removing anyone from the state without a jury trial designed to assess whether probable cause existed to believe that the prisoner was, in fact, a fugitive slave. Southern slave owners quickly challenged the Pennsylvania statute in the Supreme Court, arguing that Pennsylvania's anti-kidnapping statute interfered with their constitutional right under the fugitive slave clause to resort to self-help to recover their "property."

Appallingly, in *Prigg v. Pennsylvania*, the pre–Civil War Supreme Court agreed with the slave owners. Trump seeks to replicate the fugitive slave model by arguing that states are powerless to shield law-abiding undocumented aliens from ICE dragnet raids. Designating themselves as "sanctuaries," states and cities have fought back by refusing to cooperate with ICE raids. Stung by the refusal of local law enforcement officials to cooperate with ICE, President Trump has threatened to punish sanctuary cities. Four principal areas of disagreement have arisen: (1) whether state or local law enforcement officials can be forced to notify ICE of the impending release of undocumented aliens from state or local custody, no matter how minor the charge, so that federal officials can pick them up for deportation with minimal effort; (2) whether state schools, such as the University of California, can be compelled to cooperate with ICE in identifying undocumented students in the student body; (3) whether state or local agencies and officials can be required to cooperate with ICE raids by providing information about the existence or whereabouts of undocumented aliens; and (4) whether private individuals, including employers and schools, can be pressured to cooperate with dragnet raids by permitting ICE agents on the premises without a warrant and providing them with information in the absence of a court order.

California law forbids cooperation with ICE in all four settings, except where the undocumented alien is deemed a threat to public safety. In retaliation, President Trump has threatened to cut off federal funding to the police forces of cities and states that decline to provide affirmative assistance to federal officials in detaining, locating, and rounding up the undocumented. It's as though southern slave owners had demanded that Pennsylvania provide affirmative help to the slave catchers.

California argues that federalism-based protection of its sovereignty should block the national government from "commandeering" the state's resources and personnel to carry out a national policy soundly rejected by the state's electorate. Ironically, the sanctuary movement's strongest legal precedent was established in *Printz v. United States* when the national government unsuccessfully sought to compel state law enforcement officials to conduct federally required background checks prior to the purchase of certain guns. A solidly Republican Supreme Court struck down the federal mandate as an unconstitutional interference with state sovereignty.

Trump will doubtless argue that withholding aid to states that refuse to cooperate with ICE is not the same thing as commanding a state law enforcement official to act. But the Supreme Court has repeatedly ruled that the national government cannot coerce individuals (and presumably states) to waive a constitutional right by threatening to withhold a benefit to which they would otherwise be entitled. It's called the "unconstitutional conditions" doctrine. The Supreme Court invoked it recently to strike down the important portions of the Affordable Care Act that required dissenting states to accept extended Medicare coverage as the price of receiving federal assistance for the rest of the program.

Thus, if respect for precedent has real meaning under a Trump Supreme Court, a sanctuary city can't be financially punished for exercising a constitutional right to decline to use state resources to carry out a federal policy with which it disagrees. Round one should go to the states on points under a combination of respect for precedent, the *Printz* anti-commandeering principle, and the unconstitutional conditions doctrine.

Round two will be tougher—probably a split decision. What happens when states such as California pass laws explicitly releasing private individuals, including employers and private colleges, from any legal duty to assist federal immigration officials in tracking down or apprehending undocumented aliens in the absence of a court order? While, under *Printz*, states, schools, government agencies, and local cops need not help in the federal immigration roundups, California may not interfere with lawful efforts by the national government to carry out a valid national program with its own resources. A state-imposed *prohibition* on private cooperation with ICE in the absence of a court order might be held unlawful as a form of sabotage. But respect for the authority of a state to preserve the peace should permit states to require that ICE provide clear legal guidance to private individuals about their rights and duties when facing a federal official with a gun. Laws merely releasing private individuals from a legal duty to cooperate with ICE in the absence of a court order merely re-state existing law and should be affirmed. Empowering a private actor to refuse to cooperate with a federal official who is attempting to carry out morally reprehensible mass deportations and who has not bothered to get a court order directing cooperation, simply forbids the federal government from engaging in self-help in the teeth of private opposition. Maybe this time we'll get the self-help issue right. One *Prigg v. Pennsylvania* is more than enough.

So, round two to the states on points—but there's a catch. Just as states can claim to speak for a legitimate state majority when declining to help President Trump to carry out his efforts at mass deportation, local majorities within many states may, as a matter of state law, opt to cooperate with the president. Some states refuse to grant local governments such operational autonomy. But most allow a form of "home rule" that would allow dissenting majorities in certain localities to make their own deals with the president. Orange County, a traditionally conservative enclave in Southern California, has done just that—opting out of California's "sanctuary state" legislation by publishing the names of all people scheduled to be released from Orange County jails so federal officials can pick them up with minimal effort. That's a matter for California law, or Orange County voters, to fix.

The third federalism skirmish over ICE will involve state laws seeking to ensure humane conditions in federal immigration detention camps located within the state. State building and public health officials routinely play constructive roles in ensuring safe and humane conditions in federal buildings, including prisons, and on federal military installations. They even played constructive roles in ensuring the health and safety of Japanese Americans confined to federal detention camps during World War II. No reason exists to exempt federal detention facilities for undocumented aliens from the reach of such traditional state concerns over health and safety, especially since the danger of contagion is apparent. Compulsory state health and building inspections of federal immigration detention facilities should be a state knockout.

NET NEUTRALITY

A classic test of the power of a minority president to issue regulations that override the will of legitimate state majorities will pit the decision to rescind Obama-era regulations ensuring net neutrality against a number of state majorities insisting on equal access to the internet.

Under the Trump administration's new rules, first-class internet access would be provided to those willing and able to pay, ensuring speedy and convenient internet service for a price, while everyone else would be required to make do with variations of second-class internet access. In effect, Trump wants to turn the internet into a commercial jetliner, with classes of service available on the basis of the consumer's ability and willingness to pay. By contrast, states such as New York and California want to treat the internet like the landline telephone, with everyone enjoying the same level of service.

The issue cries out for resolution by Congress under its power to regulate the interstate economy. Congress has the unquestioned power under the existing reading of its commerce clause authority to regulate access to the internet. As usual, though, Congress is nowhere to be found. Instead, back in 1934, Congress created the Federal Communications Commission, staffed by presidential appointees, and gave it power to develop a national communications policy "in the public interest." In 1940, the Supreme Court upheld such a ridiculously broad delegation of lawmaking power to an agency in the executive branch—it was the beginning of the end of classical separation of powers.

Over the years, the FCC has moved from left to right in deciding what is "in the public interest," initially requiring "fairness" in broadcast news coverage and then withdrawing from the field— leaving us with unregulated TV and cable propaganda networks passing themselves off as news broadcasters. Initially, in the name of encouraging a multiplicity of voices, the FCC sought to limit the power of a single broadcaster to control the airwaves and newspapers in the same local market. Now, in the name of efficiency, it encourages massive concentrations of broadcast power in the hands of a few large corporations. Through it all, Congress, by delegating uncontrolled power to the FCC, had taken itself out of the game.

As I've argued more than once, such a standardless delegation of authority to the executive should be held to violate separation of powers because, in effect, it delegates the discretionary power to make new law to the executive branch. But, so far at least, the Court has not sought to force Congress to confront its responsibilities instead of kicking the can down the road to faceless bureaucrats. In the absence of congressional guidance, the FCC has treated the question of net neutrality as just another presidential political football. After the Obama administration issued regulations requiring equal access to the internet, Trump's FCC promptly pulled the Obama regulations, substituting new executive regulations authorizing major communications players to sell unequal access to the internet.

It was simply a matter of time until state majorities seeking equal access to the internet collided with President Trump's assertion that he speaks for a national majority in authorizing unequal access to the internet. It is at this point that Trump's tenuous status as a minority president should tilt the federalism issue to the states.

Dissenting state majorities, seeking to preserve the principle of net neutrality, have fought back in two ways. Montana has insisted that any internet company with which it does business must promise to allow equal access to the internet to all Montana residents. California and New York have gone further, passing legislation requiring net neutrality in their states. How should the federalism dispute be resolved?

As president, Trump is fully entitled to provide for the issuance of FCC regulations ending net neutrality that bind the national government and, in the absence of countervailing state majorities, bind the states. But where legitimate state majorities reject Trump's effort to permit unequal access to the internet, Trump's regulations lack the democratic imprimatur of a legitimate national majority needed to override the will of a legitimate state majority. There is no expression of a congressional national majority on the issue. Nor is there a presidential national majority on the issue. That leaves the state majorities in California, New York, and Montana as the only legitimate democratic games in town.

On a more conventional resistance level, the states' residual "police power" to ensure the equal treatment of their residents should be seen as sufficiently powerful to survive an effort to override it by a federal regulation inviting internet discrimination against the weak. As we'll see in a moment, it's the same federalism issue raised by Trump's assault on the environment.

PROTECTING THE ENVIRONMENT

Much of Trump's domestic executive policy consists of unwinding Obama-era regulations designed to protect the environment. It's the regulatory neon sign in action. The underlying congressional statutes do nothing but delegate virtually standardless regulatory power to the executive. Each president, claiming to be enforcing the meaningless statute, flips a switch changing the policy mix. Executive regulations come and go like spring snowstorms.

Trump is taking full advantage of the massive delegation of lawmaking power permitted under the existing system. State majorities committed to protecting their environment can fight back by invoking state police power to protect the health and safety of state inhabitants against federal regulations inviting environmental degradation.

Newly minted federal regulations authorizing offshore drilling for oil and gas are a classic example of the coming collision over preserving the environment. No one disputes the fact that the national government exercises control over submerged lands beyond the state three-mile offshore ownership limit. As usual, though, Congress is nowhere to be found on the question of whether and when offshore drilling should take place on federal land, leaving the issue for decision by the Department of the Interior.

The secretary of the interior can't make new law. That's for Congress. But, as usual, Congress has delegated virtually unconstrained discretion to the executive branch over how to manage the submerged lands, including whether to drill for oil and gas on them. All agree that offshore drilling risks environmental degradation of the oceans and shoreline. The massive 2010 *Deepwater Horizon* oil spill in the Gulf of Mexico was only one dreadful example. On the other hand, offshore drilling may unlock substantial energy reserves, diminishing reliance on foreign sources, lowering the price of energy, and bolstering the economy.

Congress should set the balance. But, as usual, Congress is missing in action, requiring presidential appointees to step into the power vacuum left by Congress's inaction. The energy companies insist that precautions can minimize environmental risks. Environmentalists aren't so sure. The Obama administration opted to ban offshore drilling. Trump promptly lifted the ban (except for Florida, whose Republican governor successfully pleaded for an exemption because of Florida's "unique" dependence on tourism). I guess tourists only visit Republican states. No exemption for California.

Since the state's police powers stop at the three-mile limit, states cannot resist offshore drilling by simply banning it (as they can with the net neutrality issue). Instead, California has invoked its police power to ban the transportation across the state of oil and gas pumped from offshore wells. Will that work?

There is no doubt that transporting offshore oil and gas across the state would pose enhanced environmental risk, bringing California's police power into play. Pipeline leaks are not a hypothetical risk—there have been pipeline leaks all across the country. The decision of a minority president acting unilaterally to override a legitimate state democratic majority seeking to protect its environment against such a risk constitutes a weak argument for national power.

On the other hand, flatly barring the transportation of the oil and gas pumped offshore operates as a de facto veto of the president's decision to authorize the drilling. If California lacks power to prohibit the drilling directly, I question whether it may use the police power to impose a de facto prohibition. California's strongest case would be to enact stringent general regulations on energy transmission to be applied to all oil and gas pumped in or transmitted across the state—including offshore oil. Its weakest position would be to enact rules that apply only to offshore wells, leaving the state open to charges that it is exceeding its police power.

Of course, the first-best response would be to enact thoughtful congressional legislation regulating the area. Don't hold your breath. The second-best response is to vote Trump out of office before the next environmental disaster.

THE GIG ECONOMY

Once upon a time in the United States, most folks worked for someone called an "employer," who paid them something called "wages." In order to compensate for the power imbalance between an employer and an employee, Congress passed the National Labor Relations Act, ensuring employees the right to band together and bargain collectively about wages and other conditions of employment as the key to setting fair, socially stable wages and working conditions.

And then it all fell apart.

Globalization placed enormous pressure to decrease the costs of production in the United States, as countries around the world bid for jobs and investment by lowering the costs of labor, eliminating safety regulations, and polluting the environment. An identical state race to the bottom had begun in the United States during the Great Depression, leading to the enactment of nationwide floors. There is at present no mechanism for setting worldwide floors, although one could be created by treaty.

A worldwide race to the bottom caused huge numbers of union manufacturing jobs to disappear overseas, a casualty of rock-bottom labor costs and lax regulation in foreign countries, leaving Americans working in an economy increasingly devoted to the delivery of services. The union movement collapsed, except for government employees. Hours of work in service industries such as retail and fast food shrank and became increasingly erratic as employers juggled work schedules to meet fluctuating demand and sought to avoid regulatory thresholds.

The idea of long-term employees tethered to a single employer was displaced by the "gig economy," consisting of large numbers of workers performing defined tasks for one or more employers without ever attaining the protected status of an employee. Think of drivers for Uber or Lyft. Once, they would have been employees working for a taxicab company, entitled to significant, hard-won legal protections such as a minimum wage and the right to bargain collectively on wages and working conditions. Under the gig economy, though, they have devolved into something called "independent contractors" performing a compensated service for Uber and Lyft, but without most of the protections carved out for employees in the old economy.

Much of the business plan of Uber and Lyft is based on the decreased labor costs incurred by shifting its workforce from employees to independent contractors. Unlike true employees, who (at least theoretically) can bargain collectively, gig employers deal individually with each independent contractor on a take-it-or-leave-it basis, free from any risk of collective action.

Not surprisingly, faced with wage competition from abroad, denied the ability to engage in collective action to raise wages or improve working conditions, and severed from the hard-won legal protections available to employees but not to independent contractors, the substantial slice of the American labor force working in the gig economy has taken it on the chin for decades, with wages stagnating and working conditions deteriorating while employers earn large profits.

As usual, Congress has slept through the change. The statutory framework and network of labor regulations dating from the 1930s has remained relatively untouched as the economy evolved from an industrial base with employer-employee collective bargaining at its core to a service economy with millions of low-paid workers forced to operate in increasing isolation and vulnerability as independent contractors. As with so many federalism issues, the best solution would be a careful congressional updating of the 1930s-era labor laws to provide basic protections to workers trapped in the gig economy. Once again, though, don't hold your breath, especially in the Time of Trump.

If progress is to occur in ameliorating the rigors of the gig economy in the foreseeable future, it will be at the state and local levels. That makes Seattle's effort to step into the congressional void by providing drivers for Uber and Lyft with state- and local-law-based collective bargaining rights an important test of federalism. Unlike efforts to undermine federal rules in settings like offshore drilling or net neutrality—raising issues of "conflict preemption"—Seattle is seeking to reinforce a federal statute by extending its reach. Can progressive states fill voids in current federal regulatory schemes?

For years, large corporations have argued successfully that one consequence of federalism is that when Congress acts, it freezes the ability of states to regulate in the entire field, even when the state regulation seeks to reinforce or strengthen Congress's action. It's called "field preemption." Under field preemption, a federal statute or regulation imposes ceilings on the states as well as floors. Advocates of field preemption argue that Congress intended to "occupy the field" with its statute. Ironically, progressives shot themselves in the foot by inventing field preemption to protect federal labor law from erosion at the hands of state officials hostile to collective bargaining.

The question is whether Congress's decision in the 1930s to grant collective bargaining rights to employees "occupies the field," leaving no room for Seattle, acting as a proxy for the state of Washington, to supplement the 1930s legislation by providing collective bargaining rights to Uber and Lyft drivers, even though technically they may be independent contractors, not employees. The problem, of course, is that the line between employee and independent contractor is invisible to the naked eye. It is supposed to turn on the degree of supervision exercised by the employer over the worker, but that's a concept subject to infinite manipulation. It's even possible that Uber and Lyft drivers are, in fact, employees under federal law—but don't expect a Republican-dominated National Labor Relations Board to expand the envelope of protection for workers. It's just another example of how executive agencies use vague statutes to make the law, not merely apply it.

It would, I believe, be inconsistent with the Founders' view of genuinely sovereign states to insist that an eighty-year-old congressional statute designed for an industrial economy prevents states from stepping in to provide interim relief to workers in the gig economy until Congress gets its act together and promulgates rules for the modern era. If states can't step into the regulatory void, millions of workers will be trapped in limbo, falling outside the congressional safety net designed for another time, but denied access to modern safety nets designed by state majorities.

Just don't bet on a Republican Supreme Court enabling states and localities to act aggressively to protect worker equality. The Court is far more likely to use field preemption to reinforce employer autonomy. If progressives want to unleash states to protect workers, they will have to win back the right at the polls by turning Congress and the presidency blue.

The Seattle controversy also demonstrates "conflict preemption" in action. When Congress acts within its legitimate powers, its word, under the supremacy clause, is the supreme law of the land, overriding any conflicting state rules. The effort by Seattle to grant collective bargaining rights to Uber and Lyft drivers doesn't run afoul of conflict preemption with the National Labor Relations Act because it seeks to reinforce and expand, not frustrate, Congress's statute. However, it may run into conflict preemption with an even older congressional statute, the Sherman Antitrust Act, dating from 1890, barring "conspiracies in restraint of trade."

Allowing workers to bargain collectively, so the argument goes, permits them to form a cartel on wages, just like a corporate cartel on prices, and both are in restraint of free trade. If that sounds crazy to you—as it does to me—consider that when Legal Aid lawyers in the District of Columbia walked off the job, demanding better pay, smaller caseloads, and more resources to defend their poor clients, the DC Circuit found them guilty of engaging in a conspiracy in restraint of trade. There are, however, two answers to an effort to label Seattle's grant of power to engage in collective bargaining over wages as an antitrust violation. First, the Supreme Court has held, correctly, that states may empower collective action—even cartels—by weak players in the economy without violating the antitrust laws as long as the state authorizes the cartel and keeps a careful eye on its operation. It's called the "state action" exemption from the antitrust laws. The issue in the Seattle controversy is whether Washington's power to create closely regulated pockets of collective action can be delegated to local government units like Seattle.

Second, as a pure matter of economics, authorizing workers to bargain collectively with their employers on issues such as wages and hours has nothing whatever to do with the evils of corporate monopoly that led to the enactment of the Sherman Act. If anything, rules guarantying collective bargaining on wages and conditions of employment are designed to allow—not frustrate—genuine bargaining between equals. That's why Congress, in enacting the National Labor Relations Act, didn't blink in guaranteeing employees the right to engage in collective bargaining with their employers. The same thought process should allow Seattle to expand collective bargaining rights to independent contractors as well.

Most Democratic judges would do it in a minute. Most Republican judges will find a way to protect the employer. It's just another example of how important it is to participate in the process of deferred democracy by which our "apolitical" federal judges are selected.

REDISCOVERING STATE CONSTITUTIONS

After appearing to be ready—finally—to move against massive partisan gerrymandering, five Republican Supreme Court justices ducked the issue once again in June 2018, finding technical ways to get rid of the cases without ruling on the merits. While I remain cautiously optimistic that the justices will eventually recognize that excessive partisan gerrymandering is strangling American democracy, it's possible that the Supreme Court may not get around to doing anything about it as long as the Court remains in Republican hands.

That means we cannot ignore the potential of federalism as a source of electoral reform. If the Supreme Court cannot find an autonomy-based right to vote in a contested election, or an equality-based right to be free from excessive partisan gerrymandering in the federal Constitution, we must be prepared to turn to state courts—and state constitutions—to press for reform of democracy. The Pennsylvania Supreme Court has recently invalidated the state's massive partisan gerrymander under the Pennsylvania constitution. Its decision flipped four congressional seats. Since the decision was based solely on state law, the United States Supreme Court can't get its hands on it—even if Trump manages to pack the Supreme Court.

Progressives should be readying a barrage of state court challenges designed to remove unnecessary costs and increase the perceived value of voting. That's just what Common Cause has done in North Carolina, taking a challenge to a hyper-partisan gerrymander of the state's congressional districts that was languishing in the federal courts because, thus far, the Supreme Court refuses to decide it and shifting it into a North Carolina state court system headed by a state supreme court with a 5–2 Democratic majority.

Once upon a time, federal courts were the preferred forum if you wanted egalitarian reform. But that was when they were blue. Now state judges may be the constitutional forum of choice for protecting the weak. Every state is a potential battleground, especially the numerous states that elect their judges.

During my years of active practice, I tried to avoid elected state judiciaries in constitutional cases. After all, many constitutional cases are often efforts to get a second judicial opinion on something that was lost in the legislature. I found that elected judges tended to mirror the political beliefs of the very elected legislators I was asking them to overrule. So over the years I put my constitutional eggs in the federal basket. But not necessarily when it comes to partisan gerrymandering, where the people are way ahead of the judges in realizing that partisan gerrymandering is killing American democracy. It may well be that elected state judges are the best way of linking litigation seeking reform of American democracy to the widely held belief by the mass of the people that our existing law of democracy is in shambles.

RETHINKING THE INCORPORATION DOCTRINE

Finally, it may be time to rethink one of the sacred cows of progressive legal thought—an intense commitment to applying the provisions of the Bill of Rights to limit the power of the states as well as the federal government so that both operate under identical federal constitutional rules. Remember, we have two Bills of Rights. The first Bill of Rights, constituting the first ten amendments, was adopted in 1791. What is frequently called the second Bill of Rights, comprising the Thirteenth, Fourteenth, and Fifteenth Amendments, was adopted in the five years following the end of the Civil War.

The autonomy-protective aspects of the first Bill of Rights, including the rights to free speech, religious freedom, the right to bear arms, the right to be free from unreasonable searches and seizures, the privilege against self-incrimination, the right to due process of law, and freedom from cruel and unusual punishments, were initially aimed solely at the federal government. The post–Civil War equality-driven second Bill of Rights, comprising the Thirteenth Amendment's abolition of slavery and peonage, the Fourteenth Amendment's due process and equal protection clauses, and the Fifteenth Amendment's ban on racial discrimination in voting, was aimed at the states.

Until 1925, to the extent that states were bound by federal constitutional protections at all, the Republican Supreme Court usually
couched the protections as "substantive due process" guarantees
provided by the due process clause of the Fourteenth Amendment.
History taught that "substantive due process" was hopelessly vague
and subjective. Republican judges used it as a club to invalidate
minimum-wage, maximum-hours, and child-labor laws. Justices
Oliver Wendell Holmes Jr. and Louis Brandeis deeply mistrusted
the concept of substantive due process because it licensed Republican judges to turn their absolute commitment to the free market
into constitutional doctrine. During the 1920s, the two justices
sought a formula that would permit vigorous protection of social
and political rights but also would encourage substantial regulation
of the economy in order to protect the weak. They found it in 1925
by arguing that the due process clause of the Fourteenth Amendment was not an open-ended invitation to strike down anything
the justices felt was deeply unfair. Rather, it was a verbal bridge
over which fundamental textual provisions of the first Bill of Rights
could travel to bind both the state and federal governments with
the same text.

Holmes and Brandeis began in *Gitlow v. New York* (1925) by
incorporating First Amendment free speech protection into the
Fourteenth Amendment's due process clause so that it would bind
New York State as well as the United States—a brilliant exercise
in word magic. The Supreme Court followed up over the years
by marching religious freedom, protection against unreasonable
searches and seizures, the right against self-incrimination, the
rights to counsel and to a fair jury in a criminal case, and the ban
on cruel and unusual punishments over the Fourteenth Amendment's due process bridge to bind the states.

Most recently, five Republican justices marched the Second
Amendment right to bear arms across the bridge over the objection
of four Democratic justices who argued that it wasn't fundamental enough to be part of due process of law. Progressive lawyers
like me, seeking to limit the power of state majorities hostile to
racial minorities and unfriendly to political dissenters and religious

iconoclasts, have long applauded the parade of rights across the bridge—that is, until the right being incorporated into the due process clause was the Second Amendment right to bear arms. As the four Democratic justices noted in their dissent, reflex incorporation of the entire Bill of Rights into the due process clause of the Fourteenth Amendment has real federalism costs. It operates as a legal straitjacket that requires the entire nation—with all its diversity—to march to a single set of constitutional rules.

When fundamental issues such as free speech, equality, and religious freedom are at stake, I believe that the centrality of those rights to a functioning democratic society calls for uniform, robust rules throughout the United States. But many constitutional guarantees in the first Bill of Rights, including jury trials in civil cases, grand jury indictment, Fourth Amendment search and seizure rules as they govern automobile stops, and the right to bear arms, can take many forms without necessarily jeopardizing a functioning democracy. Perhaps they should not be the subject of incorporation word magic.

Respect for regional diversity may call for one set of gun ownership rules in Wyoming and Montana and another in inner-city Chicago, and one set of drunk-driving roadblock rules in New York City but another in rural Georgia. Back in the 1950s, Justice John Marshall Harlan II applauded the incorporation doctrine but argued that room for regional diversity should be built into it for certain incorporated rights. Justice Frankfurter agreed. Maybe it's time to give Harlan's views more thought.

Trump is dangerous, especially to the vulnerable. His irresponsible behavior has already launched so many dangerous spells appealing to the worst in us that we may never get the genies of racism, xenophobia, and religious bigotry back into the bottle. There is real hope, though, that the Supreme Court can contain the worst of Trump's excesses by remaining true to both red and blue precedents embedded in the purple Constitution. But even there, the capacity for slippage and deference to authoritarian governance is ever-present, especially if Trump succeeds in repopulating the Court as the current elderly justices leave the bench.

Even if the Court's membership remains stable, for the foreseeable future we will be living under the red Constitution, where close cases will be decided in favor of autonomy at the expense of equality. If you care about what happens to folks at the bottom — as well as maintaining the current level of constitutional protection for the rest of us — your only sure path of resistance is the ballot.

Let go of the belief that courts and lawyers can provide the vulnerable with bulletproof, nonpolitical legal protection. Don't give up on courts and lawyers, but, if the weak are to be protected, we'll probably have to do it ourselves through the ballot box — there is no other way.

EPILOGUE

Night Sweats—What If It All Comes Apart?

What if I'm wrong? What if the three constitutional pillars—separation of powers, federalism, and a decent balance between autonomy and equality—don't hold? What if a steady stream of lies, half-truths, and appeals to racism, xenophobia, and fear-mongering persuade enough Americans to follow Trump over an authoritarian cliff? What if a craven Republican Senate and a Supreme Court besotted with deference cease to provide a check on Trump's worst instincts? Pick your nightmare scenario.

Here are two of mine:

Trump wins the 2020 presidential and congressional elections. Justices Ruth Bader Ginsburg and Stephen Breyer leave the Supreme Court in 2021. Trump nominates fixer-lawyer replacements in the mold of Rudy Giuliani. The Republican Senate rolls over and confirms them. Justices Thomas and Alito concur with three of Trump's nominees in deferring to the president in what they characterize as a time of national crisis. *Stare decisis* is trashed—or manipulated—in favor of a populist, strongman's Constitution that provides President Trump with implied emergency powers to make America great again. The forty-fifth president, invoking Abraham Lincoln, invokes martial law, suspends the writ of *habeas corpus*, rules by executive order, silences "fake news" outlets, preventively detains dangerous subversives, and declares an end to the era of "political correctness" by rescinding all executive regulations enforcing the Civil Rights Acts and instructing the attorney general to cease enforcing the statutes.

Worse—

Trump loses the November 2020 presidential election but cries foul, claiming that the balloting was rigged by the participation of millions of fraudulent voters, many of whom are allegedly undocumented aliens or simply fictitious. Two days after the election results are announced, the president directs Attorney General Giuliani to investigate charges of widespread voter fraud. Pending the results of the investigation, Trump declares martial law; detains the apparent electoral winner, a bewildered Joe Biden; refuses to permit the Electoral College to meet; and postpones the inauguration of a new president until the will of the true electorate can be accurately determined. Pending a deferred inauguration at the close of the investigation, the president suspends the writ of *habeas corpus* and rules by executive order. He rounds up the usual suspects.

(I've left a space here for your own personal anxiety attack. Feel free to write it in by hand.)

What extralegal options would be open for resistance to such Trumpist putsches clothed in legalisms and backed by a Supreme

Court cowed into deference? What if Trump, citing Andrew Jackson, just ignores the Supreme Court?

At this point, of course, I am far beyond my expertise, such as it is. When legal institutions run out, I have little to offer but faith.

First, there's my faith in the Second Amendment right to bear arms. Not the Second Amendment you're thinking of, populated by delusional figures who think they can defeat tyranny by playing at being Rambo. That path leads to tragedy and heartbreak. I mean the real Second Amendment; the Founders' Second Amendment, the one that empowers a well-organized citizens' militia—the entire people in arms—to resist any effort by a would-be tyrant to seize power. My first act of faith is to believe that it is within the citizens' army and the professional police forces—the modern heirs to the eighteenth-century citizens' militia—that the first line of extralegal resistance must be found. No successful tyrant oppresses alone. He needs layers of armed subordinates to impose his will by force. The seeds of an effective resistance are present in every layer. Every person in the military chain of command, including the ranking officers, has sworn an oath to support and defend the Constitution of the United States against all enemies, foreign and domestic. Somewhere in that chain of command are patriots who will place that oath above executing an unlawful presidential order.

Military law frees subordinates from any duty to carry out an unlawful order. Indeed, according to the Nuremberg principles under which the Nazis were tried, "I was just following orders" is no defense to liability for carrying out orders that are formally correct but violative of fundamental norms of human decency.

In my fifty years as a civil liberties lawyer, I never met colleagues more dedicated to the preservation of the Constitution than many of the members of the armed forces with whom I have worked, especially military lawyers. I realize that my positive experience conflicts with the beliefs of many on the left who view the military and the police as hotbeds of racism and repression. There, of course, are plenty of bullies and racists who bear arms in our name. But there are also many idealists and genuine patriots. The German officer class rolled over for Hitler. A nightmare Trump won't find it so easy to subvert the American military.

My second act of faith is in the American people. Successful tyrants need more than brute force. They need a complaisant, supportive population. Hitler, Stalin, and Mao unleashed vast terror. But not one of those pathological monsters had enough bullets to rule successfully through brute force alone. Each needed the approbation, support, and cooperation of the mass of the citizenry.

When tyrants like Hitler are ultimately overthrown, their mass support vanishes retroactively—everyone always turns out to have been in the resistance—but the mass support was undeniably there. Someone enthusiastically sold Hitler the barbed wire and poison gas he used in the death camps. Someone enthusiastically informed about a skeptical neighbor. Someone marched the intellectuals to the countryside.

There will, of course, be American quislings who will enthusiastically support an American tyrant. There always are—everywhere. But I have faith that millions and millions of Americans will defend their freedom by withholding public and private support from a tyrannical regime, by declining to do business with it voluntarily, by refusing to inform on their neighbors or co-workers, and by engaging in acts of passive resistance such as mass strikes and protest. In the 1930s, the mass of German citizens became comfortable in their chains; many even reveled in them. That won't happen here.

Finally, my third act of faith is the most counterintuitive of all—faith that politicians will step forward to lead an effective extralegal resistance. While blue states may not be able to win a presidential election in a rigged Electoral College that overrepresents rural America, or to elect a majority in the appallingly malapportioned Senate, it is in the blue cities and states where the nation's resources and talent are concentrated: money, innovation, art, information, technology, communications, research, education.

How long could red America function without the massive tax subsidy provided by their blue fellow countrymen? Blue states pay huge sums into the federal tax pot and get only a fraction back in federal programs. Where do you think the difference goes? To folks in the red states, many of whom are fond of telling other people how to live their lives but are delighted to accept federal subsidies.

That's where courageous state and local political leaders could play a crucial role by turning off the blue-state tax spigots that fund a tyranny. Ordinarily, Americans pay their federal income taxes directly to the IRS. What if courageous state and local officials, driven to resistance by one of my Trump nightmare scenarios, were to take custody of all federal tax payments, agreeing to pass the funds on to the IRS after checking each return to be certain that all appropriate federal deductions have been taken? What if they were very aggressive about taking federal deductions? (Maybe they could use Trump's tax returns as a guide.) What if courageous state and local officials were to go further and deposit federal tax payments in a secure location pending the restoration of constitutional government?

Even a Trumpist Supreme Court would be obliged to dismiss any effort to prosecute ordinary taxpayers for following state law and routing their federal tax payments through their state political leaders for recalculation and transmission to the federal government. What jury would convict them? Let the president try to jail the governors of California, New York, Illinois, Pennsylvania, Michigan, Virginia, and Massachusetts for processing federal tax payments through a state strainer.

That's only the beginning of the acts of resistance available to state and local political leaders who pledge to prevent my nightmare scenarios from unfolding. They could invoke state police power to close roads and bridges for maintenance. Shut down the airports for safety checks. Withhold police or any other assistance to the federal government.

(Write in your extralegal, nonviolent resistance technique here.)

Don't worry, though. It won't come to that. In the short term, our institutions will hold. In the long term, we'll vote the narcissistic bully out.

A NOTE ON NOTES

There aren't any. This book is not an expression of objective truth backed up by footnotes designed to prove my case. It is a collection of subjective opinions about the inner workings of legal institutions—principally, the United States Supreme Court—that define and enforce our constitutional rights.

My opinions are based on six decades of active practice as a civil liberties lawyer. I formed them during my service as a staff lawyer for the New York Civil Liberties Union in the late 1960s and early 1970s, assistant national legal director during the presidency of Richard Nixon, national legal director of the ACLU during the presidency of Ronald Reagan, an active advocate before the Warren, Burger, Rehnquist, and Roberts Supreme Courts, lead counsel in the Swiss Bank and German Industry Holocaust Asset Cases, founding legal director of the Brennan Center for Justice at NYU, an active presence in hundreds of lower courts across the country seeking to enforce the Constitution, and a law teacher at NYU School of Law for almost fifty years, with teaching stints at Berkeley, Stanford, Cal Irvine, Tel Aviv, and Texas.

For those wishing to explore (or challenge) my opinions, I list the legal citations of each principal case mentioned in the book. Virtually all can be accessed free of charge online. Supreme Court opinions can readily be retrieved from the invaluable SCOTUSblog.com. Since most of the opinions expressed in this book were initially developed in my academic writings, which are chock-full of footnotes, I list, as well, a number of my books, chapters, and law review articles developing the ideas that form the core of this book. The academic articles can be accessed on my faculty page on the NYU Law website. Please read them. Sometimes, I wonder whether anyone else does.

Finally, the numbers discussed in connection with the workings of American democracy are drawn from the most recent census data and the reports of the Federal Elections Commission, both easily available online. It's probably a good idea to check my calculations. I became a lawyer only because they promised me there would be no math.

Principal Cases Discussed

Somerset's Case, 98 ER 499 (King's Bench 1772) (English law governs the status of enslaved people voluntarily brought into Great Britain)

Marbury v. Madison, 5 U.S. (1 Cranch) 137 (1803) (Supreme Court has power to invalidate acts of Congress that violate the United States Constitution)

United States v. Hudson & Goodwin, 11 U.S. (7 Cranch) 32 (1812) (federal courts lack power to create common law crimes)

Prigg v. Pennsylvania, 41 U.S. 539 (1842) (Pennsylvania anti-kidnapping law violates Fugitive Slave Clause)

Dred Scott v. Sandford, 60 U.S. 393 (1857) (invalidating Congress's effort to ban slavery from the territories as deprivation of property without due process of law; blacks cannot be United States citizens) (It doesn't get worse than this)

Minor v. Happersett, 88 U.S. 162 (1875) (denying women right to vote)

Lochner v. New York, 198 U.S. 45 (1905) (invalidating New York maximum hour law as violation of right to contract)

Hammer v. Dagenhart, 247 U.S. 251 (1918) (invalidating congressional child labor laws as beyond power to regulate interstate commerce)

Adkins v. Children's Hospital, 261 U.S. 525 (1923) (invalidating minimum wage legislation for women as violation of liberty of contract)

Gitlow v. New York, 268 U.S. 652 (1925) (upholding conviction of anarchists under New York's criminal syndicalism law)

Erie R.R. Co. v. Thompson, 304 U.S. 64 (1938) (federal courts lack power to make federal common law in civil cases)

United States v. Darby, 312 U.S. 100 (1941) (reversing course and upholding Fair Labor Standards Act setting national minimum wage)

Korematsu v. United States, 323 U.S. 214 (1944) (upholding Japanese internment during World War II)

Dennis v. United States, 341 U.S. 494 (1951) (upholding conviction of leaders of American Communist Party)

Youngstown Sheet & Steel Co. v. Sawyer, 343 U.S. 579 (1952) (invalidating unilateral presidential seizure of steel mills to avert strike during Korean War)

Brown v. Board of Education, 347 U.S. 483 (1954) (striking down government-mandated racial segregation in the public schools)

Baker v. Carr, 369 U.S. 186 (1962) (requiring equi-populous legislative districts under principle of "one-person one-vote")

Reynolds v. Sims, 377 U.S. 533 (1964) (articulating the one-person one-vote rule)

Lamont v. Postmaster General, 381 U.S. 301 (1965) (invalidating restrictions on receipt of communist political propaganda from abroad)

Harper v. Virginia Bd. of Elections, 383 U.S. 663 (1966) (outlawing property qualifications for voting)

United States v. O'Brien, 391 U.S. 367 (1968) (upholding conviction for burning draft card to protest Vietnam War)

Williams v. Rhodes, 393 U.S. 23 (1968) (recognizing right to run for office as third-party candidate)

Kramer v. Union Free School District, 395 U.S. 621 (1969) (recognizing equality-based right to vote)

Roe v. Wade, 410 U.S. 113 (1973) (upholding women's right to choose, in consultation with her doctor, whether to bear a child)

Dunn v. Blumstein, 405 U.S. 330 (1972) (invalidating durational residence requirements for voting)

San Antonio v. Rodriguez, 411 U.S. 1 (1973) (upholding unequal funding of public schools)

Richardson v. Ramirez, 418 U.S. 24 (1974) (upholding felon disenfranchisement)

Washington v. Davis, 426 U.S. 229 (1976) (requiring proof of discriminatory purpose)

INS v. Chadha, 462 U.S. 919 (1983) (invalidating legislative veto of administrative regulation)

Morrison v. Olson, 487 U.S. 654 (1988) (upholding Independent Counsel law to allow investigation of high ranking members of executive branch)

Texas v. Johnson, 491 U.S. 397 (1989) (flag burning protected by First Amendment)

Burdick v. Takushi, 504 U.S. 428, 442 (1992) (Kennedy, J. dissenting)

(dissenting on First Amendment grounds from ruling that denying write-in ballot is constitutional)

Planned Parenthood v. Casey, 505 U.S. 833 (1992) (declining to overrule *Roe v. Wade*, but diminishing its protection)

United States v. Lopez, 514 U.S. 549 (1995) (invalidating congressional effort to ban guns from vicinity of schools as beyond power to regulate interstate commerce)

Timmons v. Twin Cities Area New Party, 520 U.S. 351 (1997) (upholding ban of third-party endorsement of major-party candidate)

Printz v. United States, 521 U.S. 898 (1997) invalidating congressional effort to compel local law enforcement agents to carry out federally required background checks in connection with buying a gun)

Vieth v. Jubelirer, 541 U.S. 267 (2004) (declining to rule on constitutionality of partisan gerrymanders)

United States v. Morrison, 529 U.S. 298 (2000) (invalidating congressional effort to create a federal remedy for gender-motivated violence as beyond power to regulate commerce and protect equality)

Bush v. Gore, 531 U.S. 98 (2000) (barring Florida from completing recount of presidential ballots; awarding presidency to George W. Bush)

Crawford v. Marion County Bd. of Elections, 553 U.S. 1818 (upholding voter ID requirement that disproportionately bar poor voters despite no showing of need)

National Federation of Independent Businesses v. Sibelius, 567 U.S. 519 (2012) (holding that Congress lacks power under commerce clause to compel purchase of health insurance)

Shelby County v. Holder, 570 U.S. 2 (2013) (invalidating pre-clearance provisions of Voting Rights Act as no longer justified)

Obergefell v. Hodges, 576 U.S. (2015) (recognizing constitutional right to gay marriage)

Whole Women's Health v. Hellerstedt, 579 U.S. (2016) (invalidating Texas regulation placing undue burden on exercising right to choose)

Trump v. Hawaii U.S. (2018) (upholding Muslim travel ban)

Books and Selected Law Review Articles

Madison's Music: On Reading the First Amendment (The New Press, 2015)

Ending Lochner Lite, 50 Harv. Civ. Lib.-Civ. Rts. L. Rev. 183 (2015)

Felix Frankfurter's Revenge: An Accidental Democracy Built by Judges, 35 N.Y.U Rev. Law and Social Change 602 (2011)

The Gravitational Pull of Race on the Warren Court, 2010 Sup. Ct. Rev. 59 (2011)

Serving the Syllogism Machine, 44 Texas Tech L. Rev. 1 (2011)

Democracy and the Poor, in *Law and Class in America* 37 (Paul D. Carrington and Trina Jones, eds., NYU Press, 2006)

Reading the Bill of Rights as a Poem, 57 Vand. L. Rev. 2007 (2004)

Towards a Democracy-Centered Reading of the First Amendment, 73 Nw. L. Rev. 4 (1999)

The Origin of Rights: Constitutionalism, the Stork, and the Democratic Dilemma, in *The Role of Courts in Society* 158 (Shimon Shtreet, ed., Martinus Nijhoff Publishers, 1988)

Judicial Review and the Separation of Powers in France and the United States, 57 N.Y.U. L. Rev. 363 (1982)

The Myth of Parity, 90 Harv. L. Rev. 1105 (1977)

INDEX

About the Author

One of the nation's foremost civil liberties lawyers, **Burt Neuborne** has participated in more than two hundred cases in the U.S. Supreme Court, where he challenged the constitutionality of the Vietnam War, pioneered the flag burning cases, and worked on the Pentagon Papers, among many other issues. He is former national legal director of the ACLU, founding legal director of the Brennan Center for Justice, and currently the Norman Dorsen Professor of Civil Liberties at NYU School of Law. Neuborne is the author of *Madison's Music* (The New Press) and lives in New York.

Publishing in the Public Interest

Thank you for reading this book published by The New Press. The New Press is a nonprofit, public interest publisher. New Press books and authors play a crucial role in sparking conversations about the key political and social issues of our day.

We hope you enjoyed this book and that you will stay in touch with The New Press. Here are a few ways to stay up to date with our books, events, and the issues we cover:

- Sign up at www.thenewpress.com/subscribe to receive updates on New Press authors and issues and to be notified about local events
- Like us on Facebook: www.facebook.com/ newpressbooks
- Follow us on Twitter: www.twitter.com/thenewpress

Please consider buying New Press books for yourself; for friends and family; or to donate to schools, libraries, community centers, prison libraries, and other organizations involved with the issues our authors write about.

The New Press is a 501(c)(3) nonprofit organization. You can also support our work with a tax-deductible gift by visiting www .thenewpress.com/donate.

ALSO BY JOHN B. JUDIS

William F. Buckley, Jr.:
Patron Saint of the Conservatives

Grand Illusion:
Critics and Champions of the American Century

The Paradox of American Democracy:
Elites, Special Interests and the Betrayal of Public Trust

ALSO BY RUY TEIXEIRA

Why Americans Don't Vote:
Turnout Decline in the United States, 1960–1984

The Disappearing American Voter

America's Forgotten Majority:
Why the White Working Class Still Matters *(with Joel Rogers)*

THE
EMERGING
DEMOCRATIC
MAJORITY

John B. Judis
and Ruy Teixeira

A Lisa Drew Book

SCRIBNER
New York London Toronto Sydney Singapore

A LISA DREW BOOK/SCRIBNER
1230 Avenue of the Americas
New York, NY 10020

For information about special discounts for bulk purchases,
please contact Simon & Schuster Special Sales:
1-800-456-6798 or business@simonandschuster.com

DESIGNED BY ERICH HOBBING

Text set in Adobe Garamond

Manufactured in the United States of America

3   5   7   9   10   8   6   4

Library of Congress Cataloging-in-Publication Data
Judis, John B.
The emerging Democratic majority/John B. Judis and Ruy Teixeira.
p. cm.
"A Lisa Drew book."
Includes bibliographical references and index.
1. Democratic Party (U.S.) 2. Republican Party (U.S.: 1854–)
3. United States—Politics and government—2001-
I. Teixeira, Ruy A. II. Title.

JK2316.J83 2002
324'.0973—dc21
2002066882

ISBN 0-7432-2691-7

For James Weinstein and Eli Zaretsky
—JBJ

For Charles Falkenberg, Leslie Whittington, Zoe Falkenberg,
and Dana Falkenberg, all of whom died on Flight 77
out of Dulles Airport on September 11, 2001
—RT

THE EMERGING
DEMOCRATIC MAJORITY

CONTENTS

The Politics
of Postindustrial America

Exactly a week after the September 11 terrorist attack against the World Trade Center and the Pentagon, Virginia attorney general Mark Earley, who was the Republican candidate for governor, began airing commercials declaring that he would make "the safety and security of our families and our schools his top priority." During the last week of the campaign, Earley and New Jersey Republican gubernatorial candidate Bret D. Schundler both ran endorsement ads from New York mayor Rudolph Giuliani, who had been nationally acclaimed for his response to the terrorist attack, and Earley also touted an endorsement from President George W. Bush. The subliminal message that both Earley and Schundler meant to convey was that, by electing them, voters would be endorsing Giuliani's and Bush's responses to the terrorist attack. But the public didn't make this association. Earley was decisively defeated by Democrat Mark Warner and Schundler was routed by Democrat Jim McGreevey, ceding to the Democrats offices that Republicans had occupied since 1993.

The Democrats also scored other impressive victories in November 2001. In Dayton, Ohio; Syracuse, New York; Los Angeles; and Raleigh and Durham, North Carolina, Democrats replaced Republican incumbents. The victory in Dayton, coming on the heels of a Democratic win in Columbus in 1999, meant that all of Ohio's major cities were under Democratic control. North Carolina's Research Triangle, one of the fastest-growing areas of the state, is now entirely in Democratic hands. In the longtime Republican stronghold of Nassau County, Long Island, a Democrat won the county executive race, and Democrats also captured the county legislature. Democrats had not held the legislature and the executive in Nassau County since 1917. The one outstanding Republican victory occurred in New York City. But the Republican mayoral candidate, Michael Bloomberg, was a liberal Democrat who had rented the Republican label because he stood a better chance of winning the Republican than the Democratic primary.

When parties win elections like this, it doesn't always portend significant long-term changes. In 1946, Republicans captured the Congress from the Democrats, but the Democrats won it back in 1948. The 1946 elections reflected voters' lack of support for the new Truman administration and their weariness with fourteen years of Democratic rule. But what was remarkable about the November 2001 elections was that they took place amidst widespread support for the Bush administration's conduct of the war. After the September 11 attacks, many Republican and Democratic strategists assumed that public support for Bush would carry over to Republican candidates. That it did not is evidence that these elections were, indeed, part of a longer trend, one that is leading American politics from the conservative Republican majority of the 1980s to a new Democratic majority. Democrats aren't there yet, but barring the unforeseen, they should arrive by the decade's end.

American politics has gone in cycles where one party and its politicians have predominated for a decade or more—winning most of the important elections, and setting the agenda for public policy and debate. From 1932 to 1968, New Deal Democrats were in command of American politics, even when a Republican was president; from 1980 to 1992, conservative Republicans prevailed, even when the House of Representatives was in Democratic hands. During these periods of ascendancy, the dominant party hasn't necessarily gotten everything it has wanted, but it has set the terms on which compromises have occurred. Since the 1992 elections, we have been in the midst of a political transition, similar to the period of 1968 to 1980, in which neither party has been able to establish a clear majority. And while the transition of 1968 to 1980 led from a Democratic to a Republican majority, this one is leading in the opposite direction.

The transition is from one coalition to another. American political majorities are composed of coalitions of different interests, classes, regions, religious persuasions, and ethnic and racial groups. The conservative Republican majority of the 1980s brought together Republican managers, executives, and business and farm owners with white middle-class and working-class Democrats, many of them Protestant evangelicals, who were alienated by their party's support for civil rights and for the sixties counterculture. They also blamed the Democrats for the stagflation—combined inflation and unemployment with slow economic growth—of the late 1970s and the decline of American power overseas. This new Republican majority was based in the Sunbelt, which stretched from Virginia down to Florida, across to Texas and over to California, but also included traditionally Republican farm states. There was considerable disagreement among groups within the coalition—over abortion, free trade, and deficit spending, for instance—but the leadership was distinguished by its laissez-faire economic views (government is the problem, not the solution), its opposition to the original civil rights acts and the ongoing program of the civil rights movement, and its opposition to modern feminism. And the coalition supported the new religious right and the rollback, not merely the containment, of Soviet communism.

Much of the conservative Republicans' success—and their ability to hold together their coalition—came from widespread popular disgust with the extremes to which liberal Democrats and New Left movements had gone in the late sixties and the seventies. The civil rights movement had become identified with ghetto riots and busing; feminism with bra burners and lesbians; the antiwar movement with appeasement of third world radicals and the Soviet Union; and liberal Democrats with grandiose schemes that were supposed to stimulate the economy but that would increase taxes for the white middle class and only benefit the poor and minorities. As long as these partly justifiable stereotypes endured, Republicans were able to win elections easily. But in the early nineties, as the Cold War ended, a recession began, and the Democrats moderated their economic and social message, the conservative Republican majority finally began to erode.

The Republicans suffered significant defections in the early nineties from white working-class voters in the North and the West who became disillusioned with the party's free-market economics and from upscale suburban voters who rejected the Republicans' support for the religious right. Some of these voters supported H. Ross Perot in 1992, but enough of them backed Democrat Bill Clinton for him to defeat George Bush for the presidency. The Democrats lost these voters in the November 1994 congressional elections, but Clinton won many of them back after the Republicans, who took control of Congress, tried to revive the program of Reagan Republicanism. The new Democratic majority that began to emerge in the 1996 election included some white working-class Reagan and Bush Democrats, but it also featured three important groups of voters that were becoming a larger and more powerful part of the electorate. Professionals, who included teachers, engineers, and nurses, had earlier been one of the most Republican groups, but started moving toward the Democrats in 1972 and, by 1988, had become solidly Democratic. Women voters had once been disproportionately Republican, but, starting in 1964 and accelerating after 1980, they became disproportionately Democratic. And minority voters, including blacks, Hispanics, and Asians, who had been variously committed to the Democratic Party, became overwhelmingly Democratic in the 1990s, while expanding from about a tenth of the voting electorate in 1972 to almost a fifth in 2000.

In the three presidential elections from 1992 to 2000, the Democrats won twenty states and the District of Columbia all three times. These represented a total of 267 electoral votes, just three short of a majority. They provide the Democrats with a base on which to construct a new majority. In the 2000 election, Democratic candidate Al Gore, hobbled by Clinton-era scandals and by his own ineptitude as a campaigner, nonetheless got more votes than Republican George Bush, and together with left-wing third-party candidate Ralph Nader, won 51.1 percent of the popular vote. This emerging Democratic majority was strongest in the Northeast, the upper Midwest, and the Far West, including California, but it commanded a following in many of the new metropolitan areas. These areas join city and suburbs and include high numbers of professionals. The Virginia suburbs of Washington, D.C., helped elect Governor Mark Warner; North Carolina's Research Triangle has become solidly Democratic, as have most of Florida's high-tech and tourist centers.

The outlook of this new Democratic majority is by no means uniform, but as represented by Clinton, Gore, and other leading politicians, it is different from both conservative Republicans and from the liberal Democrats and New Left movements of the 1970s that the conservative Republicans supplanted. As columnist E. J. Dionne first noted, the new Democrats closely resemble the progressive Republicans who dominated American politics at the beginning of the twentieth century.[1] Like them, they envisage government as an instrument of public good that can be used to reduce the inequities of the private market; and they see modern science, nurtured by government, as a tool of progress rather than as a threat to biblical religion. Like the Republican Progressives, who were surrounded by socialists on one side and laissez-faire conservatives on the other, the Democrats see themselves as being neither "left-wing" nor "right-wing," but as a centrist alternative to the New Left and to conservative Republicanism. They could best be described as "progressive centrists."

The Democrats' progressive outlook is most apparent in their view of government. Unlike Republican conservatives, they do not subscribe to the gospel of deregulation and privatization. They want to supplement the market's invisible hand with the visible hand of government to ensure that the public interest is served. They favor government regulation of business to protect the environment, ensure the safety and quality of consumer goods, prevent investor and stock market fraud, and protect workers from dangers to their health and safety. They want to strengthen social insurance programs, including medicare and social security, and to widen the availability of health insurance. They uphold the freedom of companies to expand or contract as the market requires, but they also want to shield workers from the insecurities created by global trade and economic downturns. They want a larger and stronger social safety net and generous spending on education and worker training.

The new Democrats also reflect the outlook of the social movements that first arose during the sixties. They support equality for women in the workplace and their right to have an abortion. They oppose government interference in people's private lives—from censorship to antisodomy laws. They reject government imposition of sectarian religious standards on both personal behavior and on scientific research. They envision America as a multiethnic and multiracial democracy, and they support targeted programs to help minorities that trail the rest of the population in education and income.

But they also see themselves as centrists. They favor government intervention, but not, except in very special circumstances, the government's supplanting and replacing the operation of the market. They want government, in David Osborne's phrase, "to steer, not to row."[2]

They want government to equip Americans with the tools to be effective workers in a high-tech society, but they don't want government to guarantee everyone a job through public spending. They worry about budget deficits and are wary of large tax cuts. They want incremental, careful reforms that will substantially increase health-care coverage and perhaps eventually universalize it, but not a large new bureaucracy that will replace the entire private health-care market. They want aid to minorities, but they oppose the large-scale imposition of quotas or the enactment of racial reparations.

Like the old progressive Republican majority, the emerging Democratic majority reflects deep-seated social and economic trends that are changing the face of the country. At the beginning of the last century, the progressive Republicans oversaw the transition from an Anglo-Saxon Protestant society of farms and small manufacturers to an urban, ethnic, industrial capitalism. Today's Democrats are the party of the transition from urban industrialism to a new postindustrial metropolitan order in which men and women play equal roles and in which white America is supplanted by multiracial, multiethnic America. This transition is occurring in the three critical realms of work, values, and geography.

Work: In agrarian and industrial America, work was devoted primarily to production of foodstuffs and manufactured goods. Beginning in the 1920s, the United States began to shift toward a postindustrial economy in which the production of ideas and services would dominate the production of goods. The transition slowed during the Great Depression, speeded up in the decades after World War II, and then accelerated again in the 1990s with the widespread introduction of the networked computer and the Internet. New service industries arose; in addition, the production of ideas came to dominate goods production. Auto manufacturers engineered annual design changes; clothing companies no longer produced clothes, but fashions. The numbers of blue-collar factory workers shrank; the number of low-wage service workers and of high-wage college-educated professionals grew proportionately. America, once a land of farms and factories, has become a land of schools, hospitals, offices, hotels, stores, restaurants, and "schedule C" home offices.

Immigrants from Latin America and Asia filled many of the positions in the new workforce. So did women, who, freed from the imperative to produce large families and from onerous household chores, such as growing food and making clothes, joined the workforce on an increasingly equal footing with men. Over half of the new professionals were women. While the low-wage service workers thought and voted like New Deal Democrats—supporting Democrats as the party of the minimum wage, social security, and collective bargaining—the new professionals saw their work as the crafts workers of the late nineteenth century had seen theirs. They sought to create or to offer a high-quality good or service; and when they became frustrated by the imposition of market imperatives, they looked to the Democrats as the party of regulated rather than laissez-faire capitalism.

Values: In agrarian and industrial America, workers and owners were supposed to practice self-denial and self-sacrifice for the economy to grow and for their souls to ascend to heaven. The prevailing Protestantism emphasized salvation in the afterlife through sacrifice in this one. It viewed the enjoyment of leisure, including sex separate from reproduction, as idleness and sin. It envisaged the family as a patriarchal unit of production and reproduction. This view of life was reinforced by the demands of work. Aesthetic contemplation and higher education were strictly the province of the upper classes. But after the Great Depression and World War II, all this changed—due partly to the changing dynamic of American capitalism.

In the wake of the Depression, American business became concerned that workers would not be willing or able to purchase the goods and services that it produced. Advertising, buttressed by American movies and television, convinced Americans to consume rather than save; on a deeper level, it directed Americans to be more concerned about the quality than the sanctity of their lives. Graced with higher incomes and a shorter workweek, American workers also began to seek out and experience the pleasures and satisfactions that had formerly been reserved for the upper classes. American companies, in search of new outlets for investment, reinforced this new preoccupation, creating service industries aimed at popular recreation, travel, education, and physical and mental health.

During the sixties, the transformation of values came to a head. Americans' concern about their quality of life overflowed from the two-car garage to clean air and water and safe automobiles; from higher wages to government-guaranteed health care in old age; and from equal legal and political rights to equal opportunities for men and women and blacks and whites. Out of these concerns came the environmental, consumer, civil rights, and feminist movements of the sixties. As Americans abandoned the older ideal of self-denial and the taboos that accompanied it, they embraced a libertarian ethic of personal life. Women asserted their sexual independence through the use of birth control pills and through exercising the right to have an abortion. Adolescents experimented with sex and courtship. Homosexuals "came out" and openly congregated in bars and neighborhoods. Initially, these new values and pursuits inspired a sharp reaction from the religious right and conservative Republicans. Republicans used Democrats' identification with postindustrial values to pillory them among an older generation raised in a different America. But over the last decades, these values have spread throughout the society and have become an important basis for a new Democratic majority.

Geography: Industrial America was originally divided between city and country, and then after World War II among city, suburb, and country. Typically, manufacturing took place within cities, farming within the countryside, and home life in the suburbs. In the seventies, the suburbs became the focus of white flight from integrated urban public schools, and suburban areas like Long Island became prime turf for the new Republican majority. But in the last two decades, inspired in part by computer technology, a new geographical formation has emerged—the postindustrial metropolitan area. It combines city and suburb in a seamless web of work and home. As manufacturing has moved to the suburbs and even the country, cities like Boston and Chicago have become headquarters for the production of ideas. Both city and suburb have become filled with the shops, stores, and institutions of postindustrial capitalism, from café-bookstores to health clubs to computer learning centers. Many are the site of major universities, which since the sixties have been the crucible of the new postindustrial work and values. Some suburban states like New Jersey are now almost entirely composed of contiguous postindustrial metropolitan areas.

These new postindustrial metropolises—from the San Francisco Bay Area to Chicago's Cook County to Columbus, Ohio, and down to North Carolina's Research Triangle—are peopled by the new professionals who live according to the ethics of postindustrial society. Their socially liberal values and concerns with the quality of life permeate the population, including the white working class. The result is widespread and growing support for the Democrats' progressive centrism. In the past, cities like Chicago, Philadelphia, and San Francisco were Democratic, while the surrounding suburbs were Republican. Now the entire metropolitan area in many of these locations has become strongly Democratic. And as more of America becomes composed of these postindustrial metropolises, the country itself becomes more Democratic.

As we write, America is still at war and coming out of a recession. By itself, the economic downturn might have been expected to accelerate the turn toward the Democrats and was already having that effect prior to September 11. But the terrorist assault on the United States—and the Bush administration's successful prosecution of the war in Afghanistan—cast Bush and the Republicans in a far more favorable light. And even if the war did not affect the local and gubernatorial elections in November 2001, a continuing public preoccupation with national security will certainly benefit the Republicans (and generally incumbents) in November 2002 and at least mitigate whatever gains the Democrats might have expected from a recession occurring during the Bush presidency. Yet when the fear of terror recedes, and when Americans begin to focus again on job, home, and the pursuit of happiness, the country will once again become fertile ground for the Democrats' progressive centrism and postindustrial values.

CHAPTER ONE

The Rise and Fall
of the Conservative Republican Majority

In 1969, a year after Richard Nixon won the presidency, Kevin Phillips, an aide to Attorney General John Mitchell, published a book entitled *The Emerging Republican Majority*. The apparent confirmation of its thesis in 1972—not to mention Phillips's proximity to the administration—eventually landed it on the best-seller lists.

Like other books of its kind, however, it was cited more often than it was read, and its actual thesis has been clouded by its notoriety. Phillips did not argue that Republicans had already created a majority—in fact, when he wrote his book, Democrats still controlled both houses of Congress, plus the majority of statehouses. What he argued was that the era of "New Deal Democratic hegemony" was over. Phillips predicted that a new Republican majority would eventually emerge out of popular disillusionment with big government programs and the collapse of the Democratic coalition—a collapse the 1968 candidacy of Alabama governor George Wallace had foreshadowed. And a Republican majority finally did emerge in 1980, but only after the GOP had rebounded from the Watergate scandal.

Our view is that we are at a similar juncture—but one that will yield the opposite result. We believe that the Republican era Phillips presciently perceived in 1969 is now over. We are witnessing the "end of Republican hegemony." The first signs appeared in the early 1990s—not merely in Bill Clinton's victory in 1992, but in H. Ross Perot's third-party candidacy and the rise of new kinds of independent voters. The Republican takeover of Congress in November 1994 seemed to show that Clinton's win and Perot's strong showing were flukes. Indeed, many confidently predicted that 1994 heralded the beginning of still another conservative realignment. But the 1994 Republican wins turned out, in retrospect, to be the same kind of false dawn that the Democrats had experienced twenty years earlier because of Watergate.

Ever since 1994, Republicans have lost ground in Congress and in the country. Like the Democrats of the 1970s, they have also begun to suffer serious divisions within their ranks—from Pat Buchanan on the right to John McCain and Jim Jeffords on the left. Bush's aggressive prosecution of the war against the terrorists in the fall of 2001 lifted him in public esteem and may have delayed a Republican collapse in 2002. But once the clouds of war lift, and Americans cease to focus on threats to their national security, Republicans are likely to continue their slide, and the movement toward a Democratic majority is likely to resume.

The Republican majority that Phillips foresaw represented a "realignment" of American politics. A realignment entails a shift in the political coalitions that dominate American politics and in the worldview through which citizens interpret events and make political judgments. Realignments happened before in 1860–64, 1896, and 1932–36. These past realignments followed or took place during cataclysmic events—the conflict over slavery and the Civil War, the depression of the 1890s, and the Great Depression of the 1930s—that polarized the country along either regional or class lines. No similar cataclysm has shaken the political system since then, and as a result, realignments have occurred more gradually, with the fall of a prior majority and the rise of a new one separated by a decade-long transition period. It took from 1968 to 1980 for the New Deal majority to collapse and for a new conservative Republican majority to be born; and it is taking from 1992 until sometime in this decade for the conservative Republican majority to disintegrate and for a new Democratic majority to emerge.

I. HOW REALIGNMENTS WORK

Political scientist Walter Dean Burnham called realignments America's "surrogate for revolution."[1] It is a good way to think of them. Realignments respond to the sharp clashes between interests, classes, regions, religions, and ethnic groups brought about by tectonic shifts in the economy and society.* In other countries, these conflicts might have led to insurrection and revolution, but with the exception of our Civil War, in the United States they have resulted in changes in party control and the emergence of a new political zeitgeist. The tensions that industrialization stirred within a peasant economy contributed to the Russian revolutions of 1905 and 1917, but in the United States similar tensions produced the Populist Party, its absorption within the Democratic Party, and eventually the triumph of William McKinley and Theodore Roosevelt's new Republican coalition, which dominated American politics (with a brief interregnum) from 1896 to 1930. The economic collapse of the 1920s propelled the Fascists to power in Italy and the Nazis in Germany. In the United States, by contrast, the crash of 1929 simply ushered one governing coalition—Herbert Hoover's Republicans—out of power, so that another—Franklin Roosevelt's New Deal Democrats—could take over.

Realignments take place because a dominant political coalition fails to adapt to or to contain a growing social and political conflict. A political movement like the Southern civil rights movement can precipitate this sort of conflict. So can differing political responses to major changes in the country's economy or position in the world. The Jacksonian Democrats' rise in the 1820s was partly the result of conflict between the farmers of the new frontier states, who demanded easy credit, and Eastern bankers and merchants who wanted the stability of the Second Bank of the United States. The Republican Party was born in 1856 out of the conflict between the free-labor North and the plantation South over the extension of slavery. The McKinley Republicans put the United States squarely on the side of its industrial future rather than its agrarian past. And the New Deal Democrats expanded the scope and responsibilities of the federal government to overcome the inability of modern capitalism, acting on its own, to prevent poverty, unemployment, and incendiary class conflict.

*The theory of realignment, which was devised by political scientists V. O. Key and Walter Dean Burnham, is not a scientific theory like Newton's theory of motion. It can't be used to predict the exact time and circumstance of party changes, and the exact dates and degree of realignment have always been subject to debate. Did the New Deal realignment start in 1930, 1932, or 1936, for instance, and how profound was the realignment of 1896 that replaced one Republican majority with another? But it remains a valuable tool—a metaphor—for understanding a process of periodic change that has occurred in American politics.

Year	Realigning Party
1828	Jacksonian Democrats
1860–64	Lincoln Republicans
1896	McKinley Republicans
1932–36	New Deal Democrats
1968	Transition: Disintegration of New Deal Majority
1980	Conservative Republican Majority
1992	Transition: Disintegration of the Republican Majority
2004–8	New Democratic Majority

In each realignment, the emerging majority party creates a new coalition by winning over voters from its rival party and by increasing its sway over its own voters, whose ranks have typically increased through birth, immigration, and economic change. In 1896, the Republicans won over Northern workingmen who had voted Democratic in the past, but who blamed the Democrats for the depression and were turned off by presidential candidate William Jennings Bryan's agrarian appeal for free silver. The addition of these voters gave the Republicans a solid majority in the North and the Far West. And that majority held until 1932, when anger over the Great Depression drove a number of groups—industrial workers, small farmers, blacks, Catholics, and Jews—back into the Democratic Party. Together with the party's existing base in the South, this coalition gave the Democrats an enduring majority, reducing Republicans to their loyal business supporters in the Northeast and Midwest, farmers in the Western plains states, and rural Protestants in the Midwest and Northeast.

Majority coalitions are not necessarily homogeneous. They are like old cities that are periodically rebuilt. They may be recognizable by their newest buildings and streets, but they also contain older structures and streets. Similarly, a new majority coalition is distinguished by a set of leading constituencies, but also includes other groups that have traditionally supported that party and still find more reasons to support it than the opposition. At the heart of the New Deal were Franklin Roosevelt, New York senator Robert Wagner (the author of the National Labor Relations and Social Security Acts), and trade unionists like the Clothing Workers president Sidney Hillman, but it also included white Southern conservatives who had voted Democratic since before the Civil War and were typified by Roosevelt's first vice president, Texan John Nance Garner.

Realignments have been accompanied by the creation of a new dominant political worldview or zeitgeist. Like the coalition itself, a worldview is made up of heterogeneous elements, but it also has a leading set of ideas. The leading New Deal Democrats—Franklin Roosevelt rather than Garner or brain truster Rexford Tugwell rather than brain-truster-turned-critic Raymond Moley—held a far wider view of government's economic responsibility—and of what government could do—than did the Coolidge-Hoover Republicans. A Republican of the 1920s could not have conceived of, let alone condoned, the federal government paying the unemployed to go to school or to paint a mural. The New Deal Democrats also took a far more favorable view of labor unions and a far more skeptical view of business than did contemporary Republicans. But of course not all Democrats who voted for Roosevelt subscribed to these ideas about unions and government, just as, later, not all Republicans who voted for Reagan would support his ideas about banning abortion or reinstituting school prayer.

There is, finally, a kind of metaworldview that has distinguished the two parties. From Andrew Jackson through Franklin Roosevelt and Bill Clinton, Democrats have defined themselves as the party of the average American and Republicans as the party of the wealthy and powerful. The Democrats have not necessarily stigmatized the rich and powerful, but they have insisted that their priorities lie elsewhere. The Whigs and their successor, the Republicans, have been more consistently sympathetic to business and the wealthy. They have not defined themselves solely as the party of business, but they have defined America's interests as identical to those of its business class. Even when they have appeared to cast their lot rhetorically with the average American, as Reagan or former congressman Jack Kemp did, they have done so in a way that identifies the worker with the executive and the member of the middle class with the member of the upper class. They have shunned any evocation of class conflict or class resentment.*

One indication that a realignment is imminent has been the rise of third parties that defy the existing political consensus. The Liberty and Free Soil parties of the 1840s arose because both the Democrats and the Whigs were unwilling to oppose slavery. The Progressive Party of 1924, which ran Robert La Follette for president and received a respectable 16.6 percent of the vote, pointed to rising disillusionment by farmers and industrial workers with the two major parties' support for laissez-faire economics. And in 1968, Wallace's third party arose because neither the Democratic nor the Republican leadership were willing to oppose the civil rights movement. Sometimes, the revolt against the prevailing worldview occurs within the opposition party itself. In 1928, Al Smith, a "wet," a Catholic, and an advocate of liberal reform, challenged the prevailing consensus; Barry Goldwater did so in 1964; and George McGovern in 1972. The opposition gets clobbered, but it does surprisingly well among constituencies that would become the heart of a new majority. Smith was routed by Hoover nationally, but he ran unusually strongly among urban Catholic voters, who had deserted the Democrats in 1896, but would return in the 1930s.[2] Goldwater was also routed, but he created a new Republican base in the Deep South. And McGovern, as we shall soon see, tapped into the source of a future Democratic majority—one just coming into view now.

Realignments used to occur every thirty-two to forty years. By this count, a realignment should have occurred between 1968 and 1976. But the realignment cycle coincided with the business cycle. Both the realignments of 1896 and 1932 were precipitated by depressions. After World War II, Keynesian fiscal policy didn't eliminate, but did reduce, the downward trajectory of the business cycle. And by eliminating massive depressions, it made it less likely that political realignments would occur

---

*Democrats and Republicans most often put their overall rhetorical differences into practice when they formulate tax policy, with Democrats favoring progressive taxation and the Republicans some version of a flat tax that they (disingenuously) claim will benefit all classes equally. In the 1980 campaign, Reagan championed the Kemp-Roth tax plan that would cut tax rates by 30 percent for every taxpayer. In a campaign commercial Reagan declared, "If there's one thing we've seen enough of, it's the idea that for one American to gain, another American has to suffer. . . . If we put incentives back into society, everyone will gain. We have to move ahead. But we can't leave anyone behind."

exactly on time and as dramatically as before. That didn't lead to the end of realignments, but to a transitional period between the end of one majority and the beginning of another. This transition period created illusions of party dealignment and permanent equilibrium, but finally culminated in a new majority. The realignment of 1980 was prefaced by a twelve-year transition in which the old Democratic majority splintered, and the coming realignment is being preceded by a period of transition that began in 1992 in which the Republican majority has disintegrated.

II. THE COLLAPSE OF NEW DEAL LIBERALISM

In the sixties, two clear signs that a conservative Republican realignment might be imminent were Goldwater's nomination in 1964 and Wallace's independent campaign in 1968. In 1964, Goldwater directly challenged the New Deal and Cold War worldview that had united Republicans like Nixon and New York governor Nelson Rockefeller with Democrats like John Kennedy and Lyndon Johnson. The Arizonan and his conservative supporters opposed the New Deal welfare state, including social security and the minimum wage; they favored the rollback rather than containment of Soviet communism; and they rejected a commitment to racial equality, even opposing the Civil Rights Act of 1964 that guaranteed blacks equal access to public facilities. In the election, Goldwater was routed in the North and the West, but carried five Deep South states that had not backed the Republicans since Reconstruction (see chart). County by county, the pro-Republican shifts were phenomenal. For example, the average county in Mississippi moved Republican by an amazing 67 percentage points in 1964, while the average Louisiana county increased its Republican support by 34 points over 1960. These Deep South states would become bulwarks of the new conservative Republican majority.

In the 1964 Democratic presidential primaries and running as an independent candidate in 1968, Wallace challenged the consensus of both parties even more brazenly by advocating racial segregation. He waged an openly racist campaign that appealed to white Democrats who had been alienated by the civil rights movement and by the ghetto riots, which had begun in 1964. Wallace linked race to a cluster of concerns about the welfare state, taxes, spending, crime, local political power (blacks had already

Presidential Voting in Key Southern States, 1960 and 1964 Elections

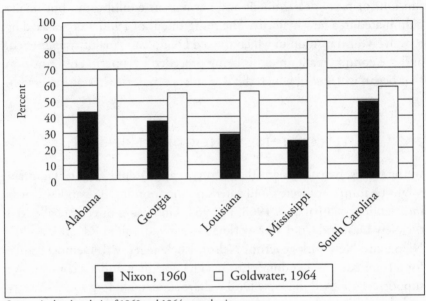

Source: Authors' analysis of 1960 and 1964 state election returns.

run for mayor in Cleveland and Gary), and the power of the federal government. This explosive cluster of issues, which had opposition to civil rights at its core, split the New Deal Democratic coalition. Phillips described this process in *The Emerging Republican Majority*:

> The principal force which broke up the Democratic (New Deal) coalition is the Negro socioeconomic revolution and liberal Democratic ideological inability to cope with it. Democratic "Great Society" programs aligned that party with many Negro demands, but the party was unable to defuse the racial tension sundering the nation. The South, the West, and the Catholic sidewalks of New York were the focus points of conservative opposition to the welfare liberalism of the federal government; however, the general opposition . . . came in large part from prospering Democrats who objected to Washington dissipating their tax dollars on programs which did them no good. The Democratic Party fell victim to

the ideological impetus of a liberalism which had carried it beyond programs taxing the few for the benefit of the many . . . to programs taxing
the many on behalf of the few.[3]

In the 1968 election, Wallace got 13.5 percent of the vote nationally,
and forty-six electoral votes from five states in the Deep South. In
twenty-four additional states, he got more votes than the difference
between Nixon and Democratic candidate Hubert Humphrey. In 1972,
Wallace's campaign for president as a Democrat was cut short by an assas-
sin's bullet. When the Democrats nominated McGovern, who endorsed
the civil rights movement agenda on welfare and crime, as well as on
school integration, Nixon inherited Wallace's vote.

In forty-five of fifty states, Nixon's vote in 1972 closely matched the
sum of his and Wallace's vote in 1968. (The exceptions were Maine,
Hawaii, Massachusetts, Rhode Island, and West Virginia.) In some
states, including seven in the South, it looked as if Wallace's votes had simply been transferred to Nixon (see chart below).[4]

Presidential Voting in Selected States, 1968 and 1972

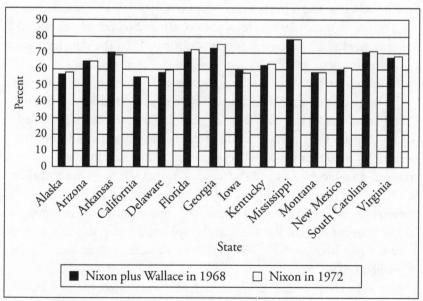

Source: Authors' analysis of 1968 and 1972 state election returns.

On the presidential level, Nixon's victory in 1972 was equivalent to Roosevelt's landslide in 1932 and seemed to augur a new conservative Republican majority. But there was one important difference: in 1932, Democrats won the White House and the Congress, while in 1972, Nixon and the Republicans were not able to win the Congress. Democrats retained a 57–43 edge in the Senate—even picking up two seats from 1970—and a 244–191 advantage in the House of Representatives.[5] Republicans failed to take the Congress partly because opposition to civil rights was not sufficiently strong in the North and Far West to overcome the voters' commitment to Democratic economics. Liberal Democrats defeated Republicans in Colorado, Delaware, Iowa, and Maine.

Republicans failed to win support in the South below the presidential level. If political position alone had mattered, the South would probably have gone solidly Republican in Congress in 1968 or 1972. Many of the Democrats it elected, such as Mississippi senator James Eastland or Arkansas Senator John McClellan, espoused exactly the same positions as the most conservative Republicans. But Southern voters, still mindful of the Republican role in the Civil War and Reconstruction, were not willing to support the creation of local Republican organizations. While the Republican Party had established a strong presence in North Carolina, South Carolina, and Tennessee, it could not recruit viable candidates in most of the South. In 1972, Democrats controlled 68 percent of both the Senate and House seats in the South, and virtually all the state legislative positions.[6]

To make matters worse for the Republicans, Nixon became embroiled in the Watergate scandal, which led to his resignation and cast a pall over Republican candidates in the 1974 and 1976 elections. The scandal was, of course, the result of Nixon's malfeasance, but it would not have become so public or led to his resignation and to Republican defeats if congressional Democrats and the national press (whom Nixon had alienated) had not been determined to do Nixon in; or, for that matter, if the Democrats had not had control of congressional investigating committees. The Watergate scandal did not simply weaken the Republicans; it happened in part because of the party's relative weakness—because a realignment had not yet occurred.

Yet while a Republican realignment had not occurred, the Democratic majority was already unraveling. Even in the shadow of Watergate,

Democrat Jimmy Carter barely eked out a victory over Gerald Ford in 1976. And while the Democrats held sixty-two seats in the Senate at the end of that year, fourteen of those senators were conservative Southern Democrats. When Carter tried to get Congress to enact the Democratic agenda of progressive tax reform, energy conservation, and consumer protection, these Southern Democrats joined their Republican counterparts to block his initiatives and to pass measures such as a reduction in capital gains taxes that would ordinarily have reflected a Republican majority.

III. THE TRIUMPH OF REAGAN REPUBLICANISM

In 1980, the Republican majority finally came to pass. Reagan won a landslide in the electoral college. He won the entire West, the South except for Carter's Georgia, and the Midwest except for Vice President Walter Mondale's Minnesota. The Republicans won a majority in the Senate and established parity in the South. The Democrats narrowly retained a majority in the House, but only because congressional results were lagging the general Republican trend in the South. Seventy of the seventy-eight Southern Democrats in the House were conservatives who would support Reagan's program and allow the Republicans to pass their legislative agenda of regressive tax cuts and reductions in social spending during Reagan's first term. In 1984, Reagan would do even better, winning 59 percent of the popular vote and every state but Minnesota and the District of Columbia against Mondale.

Two main factors propelled the Republicans into a majority. White opposition to civil rights continued to be a major factor in Democratic defections to the Republican Party. The cluster of issues that Wallace had evoked had, if anything, expanded, for now they included busing and affirmative action. As politicians were quick to understand, evoking any part of this cluster called up the whole and created a ready-made constituency among angry downscale whites who would otherwise have been expected to vote Democratic. By the time Ronald Reagan ran for president in 1980, it wasn't necessary any longer for politicians to make explicit racial appeals. He could use traditional code words such as *state's rights,* as Reagan did in his opening September campaign speech in Philadelphia, Mississippi, or could champion one of the issues at the margins of the racial cluster such as "law and order," "welfare cheating," or even capital punishment.[7]

The power of these issues was reinforced and supplemented by the stagflation of the late 1970s. Though stagflation first appeared during the 1973–75 recession, it had persisted during the Carter administration and was peaking on the eve of the 1980 election. As the economy slid once more into recession, the inflation rate in that year was 12.5 percent. Combined with an unemployment rate of 7.1 percent, it produced a "misery index" of nearly 20 percent. The stagflation fed resentments about race—about high taxes for welfare (which was assumed to go primarily to minorities) and about affirmative action. But it also sowed doubts about Democrats' ability to manage the economy and made Republican and business explanations of stagflation—blaming it on government regulation, high taxes, and spending—more plausible. In 1978, the white backlash and doubts about Democratic economic policies had helped to fuel a nationwide tax revolt. In 1980, these factors led to a massive exodus of white working-class voters from the Democratic ticket. These voters had once been the heart of the New Deal coalition, but in the 1980 and 1984 elections, Reagan averaged 61 percent support among them.[8]

In some working-class areas, race seemed like the predominant consideration. In these areas, the old Wallace vote transferred to Reagan. For instance, white working-class Lorain County, to the west of Cleveland, had once been solidly Democratic. But Nixon got 40 percent of the vote in 1968, with Wallace taking another 10. In 1980, Reagan won the county with 50 percent—exactly the sum of Nixon and Wallace's vote. White working-class Jefferson County, just south of St. Louis, had been staunchly Democratic before 1968. But in that year, Nixon had got 38 percent and Wallace 20 percent. In 1980, Reagan won the county with 52 percent.

Blue-collar Macomb County, just north of Detroit, had been the most Democratic suburban county in the country in 1960, going 63 percent for Kennedy in that year; in 1968, it had given 30 percent of its votes to Nixon and 14 percent to Wallace; in 1980, it gave 52 percent to Reagan. Then in 1984, it rewarded Reagan with a whopping 66 percent. In trying to discover why Macomb's disaffected Democrats had voted for Reagan, pollster Stanley Greenberg uncovered a cluster of issues at the center of which was racial resentment. "Blacks constitute the explanation for their vulnerability and for almost everything that has gone wrong in their lives," Greenberg wrote afterward.[9] According to Greenberg, Macomb's disaffected Democrats saw the federal government "as a black domain where whites cannot expect reasonable treatment." This view "shapes their attitudes toward government, particularly spending and taxation and the linkage between them. . . . There was a widespread sentiment, expressed consistently in the groups, that the Democratic party supported giveaway programs, that is, programs aimed primarily at minorities."

Other voters appeared to be moved primarily by doubts about Democratic economic policy. Wallace had made little headway among these voters, but they still went for Reagan in 1980 and 1984. For instance, five counties in Pennsylvania (Carbon, Erie, Lackawanna, Luzerne, and Northampton) backed Humphrey in 1968, while giving Wallace less than 5 percent of the vote. But in 1980, all except for Lackawanna went for Reagan, including predominately rural Carbon County (52–41) and blue-collar Erie (47–45). Reagan would carry these counties by similar margins in 1984. Reagan also won support from moderate Republicans who disagreed with his social conservatism and his rejection of environmental regulation and conservation, but nonetheless believed that Carter had proven incapable of managing the economy. Bergen County in northern New Jersey, just outside of New York City, and Montgomery County in Philadelphia, housed lawyers, doctors, bankers, and stockbrokers who had voted Republican for most of the twentieth century, but they were moderates who had balked at supporting Goldwater in 1964. In 1980 and 1984, however, they were back in the GOP fold, voting overwhelmingly for Reagan.

Two other factors contributed to Reagan's and the Republicans' victories in 1980—and in the next two general elections. Just as many Americans believed Carter and the Democrats had become incapable of managing the economy, many Americans also began to doubt Carter and the Democrats' leadership in foreign policy. During Carter's years, Soviet allied regimes took power in Angola, Ethiopia, Yemen, and Nicaragua and seemed on the verge of taking power in El Salvador. In 1979, the Khomeini regime in Iran, which had overthrown the shah with Carter's tacit support, took over fifty Americans hostage, creating a daily visual reminder of America's impotence. Of course, some working-class Demo-

crats had begun to harbor doubts in the early 1970s about the Democrats'
willingness to stand up to Soviet communism and third world radicalism,
but the events of the Carter years convinced voters who were worried by
Reagan's missile-rattling anticommunism that it was nonetheless time for
a change.

Reagan and the Republicans were also able to draw on some voters' dis-
comfort with the counterculture of the sixties, including feminism, gay
rights, abortion rights, decriminalization of drugs, and sexual freedom. As
early as 1966, Reagan, running for governor of California, had successfully singled out the "filthy speech movement" (a successor to the "free
speech movement") in winning blue-collar votes. In 1972, Nixon had
campaigned against "acid, amnesty, and abortion," a slogan he bor-
rowed from McGovern's Democratic critic Senator Henry Jackson. These
appeals exploited the generation gap between parents and children, but
also the gap between the blue-collar and middle-class taxpayers who
funded universities and the long-haired upper-middle-class students
who attended them.

In the 1980 election, Reagan and other conservative Republicans
were able to pick up votes from antiabortion Catholics in many former
Democratic strongholds. But the most important defection over values
came from white Protestant evangelicals in the South. These voters
made up about two-fifths of the white electorate in the South and about
one-seventh of the white electorate elsewhere.[10] In 1976, Jimmy Carter,
who identified himself as a "born-again Christian," won 52 percent of
their vote.[11]

In the late seventies, however, many of these voters began to desert the
Democratic Party. The impetus came partly from leaders like the Reverend
Jerry Falwell. Angered by the Carter administration's refusal to grant tax-
exempt status to segregated Christian academies and by Democratic
support for abortion rights, they turned to the Republicans, who, for their
part, began to court them actively. Reagan won 63 percent of their support against Carter in 1980 and then 80 percent against Mondale in
1984.[12] By the late eighties, the Protestant evangelicals had become the
most important single group within the Republican Party in the South,
while also contributing to Republican support in the Midwest and the
plains states.

Reagan's Republican coalition drew together all these voters—from the

Midwestern blue-collar Democrats that Scammon and Wattenberg had written about (who were now dubbed Reagan Democrats) to the traditional farm-state Republicans to Northeastern moderates. But Reagan's primary political base was in the Sunbelt states stretching from Virginia down to Florida, and across to Texas and to southern California. Many of these states had been the center of resistance to racial integration; they contained the bulk of the nation's Protestant evangelicals; and they were home to many of the country's military bases and defense installations and factories. While some moderate Republicans in the Northeast were put off by the conservatives' call to roll back communism and to hike military spending, these positions were extremely popular in defense-heavy states such as Virginia, North and South Carolina, Georgia, Mississippi, and Texas and in southern California. While the Republican Party still lagged in the South for historical reasons, Reagan's appeal was unmistakable. Reagan won 61 percent of white Southern voters in 1980 against a Southern candidate and 71 percent in 1984 against Mondale.[13]

Reagan Republicans incorporated the views of the Goldwater Republicans—they wanted to roll back communism, dramatically increase military spending, eliminate government intervention in the market, and end support for racial equality. Like Goldwater, Reagan adopted Andrew Jackson's antistatist populism to justify an attack on government environmental, consumer, and labor regulations. But the Reagan Republicans abandoned Goldwater's opposition to the basic New Deal programs of the minimum wage and social security and focused instead on the social welfare programs like Johnson's Great Society that had been adopted after the 1930s or that had been greatly expanded in the sixties and seventies—programs that they insinuated were aimed primarily at minorities. (Reagan would rail against the "welfare queen" in Chicago who had "eighty names, thirty addresses, twelve social security cards" and whose "tax-free income alone is over one hundred and fifty thousand dollars."[14]) In that way, Reagan, unlike Goldwater, could appeal to white working-class Democrats outside the Deep South.

Reagan also adopted the social agenda and rhetoric of the newly formed religious right. He supported a constitutional amendment banning abortion (though he had signed the nation's most permissive abortion law as governor of California); he called for restoring school prayer to the public schools; and he counseled abstinence ("just say no") to rest-less teenagers. Reagan and the Republicans put forth an older ideal of the churchgoing American family in which the husband was the sole bread-winner, in which women knew their place, and in which children went bowling and to church socials. This ideal was, of course, irrelevant to a growing number of Americans, but it also had wide appeal among what was then a growing constituency of politically active evangelicals.

Not all Republicans embraced all the tenets of this worldview, but then, majority coalitions are never homogeneous. The New Deal Democrats included Northern blacks and Southern whites, Wall Street investment bankers and Detroit autoworkers, Protestant small farmers from the Midwest and Catholic machine politicians from the Northeast. Despite their disagreements with each other and with some Roosevelt adminis-tration policies, these groups each saw reasons to remain within the coalition. Similarly, the conservative Republican coalition that Reagan forged contained disparate parts. Wealthy suburbanites from New Jersey's Bergen County might find little in common with the white parishioners at a small Baptist church in rural Southside Virginia; an unemployed Chrysler worker in Macomb County might also find little to share with Walter Wriston, the chairman of Citicorp. But in the early eighties, they all found sufficient reason to support Reagan.

This coalition was strong—strong enough, in fact, to carry a much weaker candidate, George Bush, to victory in 1988. Bush, who could not conceal his Eastern prep school pedigree, lacked credibility among the downscale Democrats who had backed Reagan. But, trailing by 17 per-cent in the polls on the eve of the Republican convention, Bush defeated Dukakis by calling forth the cluster of issues around race and the coun-terculture, as well as by criticizing him on foreign affairs (in which Dukakis had no experience). The Bush campaign repeatedly attacked Dukakis for having furloughed a black convict, Willie Horton, who subsequently attempted murder, and for vetoing a state bill requiring Massachusetts schoolteachers to lead their students in reciting the Pledge of Allegiance.[15]

Like Reagan, Bush got the support of white working-class voters, beating Dukakis 60–40 among that group. In the South, Bush won 67 percent of white voters. And he did even better among evangelical voters than Reagan, winning 81 percent of white Protestant evangelicals.[16] But this election was to be the last clear triumph for the conservative Republican coalition that Goldwater had first assembled in 1964 and that Reagan had finally consolidated in 1980.

IV. THE DISINTEGRATION
OF THE CONSERVATIVE REPUBLICAN MAJORITY

What doomed the Republican majority was the uneven growth of the Reagan economy. The Midwest—hit by the loss of manufacturing jobs— never fully recovered from the 1982 recession. The trade deficit climbed in the mideighties, creating a widespread impression that the United States was losing ground to its economic rivals. Then in 1990, the country fell into recession. In technical terms, the recession lasted barely a year, but unemployment remained stubbornly high for another five years. This economic slowdown, along with the specter of international decline, removed an important prop from under the Republican majority. Specifically, it discredited the argument that Republicans would manage the economy better than Democrats—which was, after all, the reason many moderate Republicans had voted for Reagan in spite of their distaste for his agenda on social issues and the environment. Along with the business scandals of the late eighties, it also rekindled suspicions among white working-class Democrats that Republicans favored the wealthy.

In 1986, Republicans lost control of the Senate, and in 1988, Dukakis, perhaps the dullest Democratic candidate since John W. Davis in 1924, scored surprisingly well in the industrial Midwest, winning Minnesota, Wisconsin, and Iowa while barely losing Illinois, Pennsylvania, and Missouri. Dukakis also did impressively well in some upscale moderate Republican counties. California's San Mateo County and Santa Clara County (the site of Silicon Valley) had voted for Reagan in 1980 and 1984, but Dukakis won them both easily in 1988. Then, in 1989, the Supreme Court ruled in *Webster v. Reproductive Health Services* that states could limit access to abortion, sowing fear among many women voters that a Republican would eventually overturn *Roe v. Wade*. That year, Democratic candidates for governor in New Jersey and Virginia both won strong support in upscale suburbs—and were elected— by attacking their opponent for his opposition to abortion.

But the coup de grâce to the Republican majority was delivered in 1992 by Bill Clinton and H. Ross Perot. Perot's challenge to Bush was a lot like Wallace's challenge to Humphrey. Perot claimed to be nonpartisan, but almost all of his closest aides and a large majority of his backers were former Republican voters. According to the National Election Study, over 70 percent of Perot voters had voted for Bush in 1988. And in one post-election poll, 62 percent of Perot backers said they had not only voted for Bush in 1988 but also for Reagan in either 1980 or 1984.[17] Just as Wallace had represented a dissident faction within the Democratic Party, Perot represented a dissident outlook among Republicans and among renegade Democrats who had previously voted for Reagan and Bush.

Perot's outlook was a direct repudiation of the conservative Republican worldview. He rejected the triumphalism of their outlook—"it's morning in America," Reagan had proclaimed in 1984—warning instead that America was in economic decline. He blamed the Reagan and Bush tax cuts for creating record budget deficits. He rejected Bush's continuing preoccupation with resolving the Cold War, putting forth instead a more narrowly focused economic nationalism. He rejected the religious right's intolerance and its crusade to ban abortions and restore prayer in public schools. Perot got 18.9 percent of the vote to 43 percent for Clinton and 37.4 percent for Bush. Perot didn't win any electoral votes, but he got more than the difference between Bush and Clinton in forty-seven states.

Clinton's campaign drew on several distinct political strands to weave together what would later become a new Democratic worldview of progressive centrism. With the economy faltering, Clinton tapped the Democrats' New Deal legacy to promise new jobs and greater economic security; he invoked Democratic populism, promising to "put people first" and flaying Bush and the Republicans for favoring the rich; and he sounded sixties-era commitments to protect the environment (reinforced by his choice of Al Gore as running mate) and to defend women's rights and civil rights. He was, in these respects, similar to other liberal and New Left Democrats of the seventies and eighties. But Clinton's campaign also reflected a decade-old effort to create a new post–New Deal, post-sixties Democratic politics.

In the early eighties, several Democratic politicians, including Massachusetts senator Paul Tsongas and Colorado senator Gary Hart, argued for a "neoliberal" focus on encouraging economic growth rather than redistributing existing wealth. In 1985, after Mondale's landslide defeat, two Democratic congressional staffers, Al From and Will Marshall, founded the Democratic Leadership Council (DLC), aimed at creating a new politics that could appeal to middle-class suburbanites and Southerners. The DLC preserved the Democratic commitment to civil rights, but it advocated "inoculating" Democrats against the cluster of issues with which Republicans had made covert racial appeals. The DLC proposed welfare reform; it urged Democrats to be tough on crime and to support the death penalty.

In 1992, Clinton, who had been chairman of the DLC two years before, sought to mute the older liberal and New Left message with the centrist lessons of the neoliberals and the DLC. After Clinton and Gore got the nomination in July 1992, the campaign unveiled a commercial declaring, "They are a new generation of Democrats, Bill Clinton and Al Gore. And they don't think the way the old Democratic Party did. They've called for an end to welfare as we know it, so welfare can be a second chance, not a way of life. They've sent a strong signal to criminals by supporting the death penalty. And they've rejected the old tax-and-spend politics."[18]

This eclectic worldview resonated among voters and drew together the rudiments of a new coalition. White working-class voters, who had embraced the Republicans in hopes that they could restore prosperity or put blacks in their place, gave a slight plurality of their votes to Clinton in 1992. Nationwide, over 90 percent of formerly Democratic counties like Carbon and Erie—where Wallace had never been an attraction, but which had embraced Reagan in the 1980s—went for Clinton.[19] Missouri's Jefferson County, a Wallace stronghold that Reagan and Bush had carried in the eighties, also went for Clinton. So did Monroe County in Michigan, a heavily white, working-class suburb south of Detroit, which had gone solidly Reagan. Los Angeles County, where the aerospace industry was suffering, had gone for Reagan in 1980 and 1984, but went for Clinton by 53–27 percent, contributing to Clinton's 14 percent margin over Bush in California. Moderate Republicans who had overlooked Reagan's and Bush's commitments to the religious right in the hope that they could restore prosperity now abandoned the Republicans over their social conservatism. Clinton, for instance, won Pennsylvania's Montgomery County, and California's historically Republican Santa Barbara and San Luis Obispo counties.

The 1992 election demonstrated that the old conservative era was over: without California, and without moderate Northeasterners and Reagan Democrats, the Republicans simply could not command a consistent political majority in the country. And yet 1992 didn't demonstrate a new Democratic majority, either. In fact, Clinton didn't get significantly more votes than Democrat Michael Dukakis had received in 1988. He won because many erstwhile Republicans and Reagan Democrats voted for Perot rather than for Bush. For them, Perot represented either a protest against Bush's brand of Republicanism or a way station between their apostasy and their return to the Democratic fold.

Clinton, alas, didn't grasp how tenuous his victory was. Convinced that he was the second coming of Franklin Roosevelt, and that his first year should be comparable to Roosevelt's "First Hundred Days,"[20] he proposed a comprehensive national health-insurance plan. (He even called it a campaign for "health security," consciously evoking the language of FDR's signature achievement.) Republicans and business opponents of the plan were able to discredit it by stoking popular anxiety about Democratic "tax and spend" policies. Clinton further antagonized his white working-class supporters by championing causes like the admission of gays into the military. And to make things worse, he hadn't yet delivered on his promise to bolster the economy, which did not really begin to grow strongly until the spring of 1996.

In November 1994, Democrats paid a dear price for Clinton's miscalculation, as Republicans won the House and Senate for the first time since 1952. Yet the Republicans failed to understand the basis of their victory. Even though the Republicans had campaigned on an apolitical antigovernment platform designed to appeal to Perot voters, they portrayed the 1994 election as the dawn of a new conservative era. Lobbyist Grover Norquist wrote, "Winning control of the House of Representatives is as historic a change as the emergence of the Republican Party with the election of Lincoln or the creation of the Democratic Party majority in the 1930–1934 period with the Depression and Franklin Roosevelt."[21] Former Bush administration official William Kristol said, "The nation's long, slow electoral and ideological realignment with the Republican Party is reaching a watershed."

But the Republicans' victory in 1994 turned out to be similar to the Democratic congressional victory in 1974 and presidential victory in 1976. It represented the Indian summer of an older realignment rather than the spring of a new one. For one thing, some of the GOP's gains reflected completion of the old Republican majority—not the formation of a new one. In the House, twenty-one of the fifty-eight new Republican seats were from the South, including Kentucky and Oklahoma. In the Senate, half of the net gain of eight seats were from the South.[22] These new Southern seats were simply the final step in the South's partisan realignment dating back to Goldwater's run in 1964, rather than a new Republican breakthrough.

And it soon became clear that the new Republican Congress had no greater mandate than Clinton had had two years earlier. Once in power, Newt Gingrich and the Republicans, after briefly adopting some of the good-government reforms in the Contract With America, began trying to complete the "Reagan revolution" that they had promised their business and religious-right backers. They introduced measures that would virtually have eliminated government regulation of the environment and workplace health and safety and would have threatened medicare and medicaid. They passed a huge cut in capital gains taxes. And they tried to do away with the Department of Education, a Christian-right bugaboo, and to ban abortion and reinstitute school prayer. The result was a massive backlash among voters in the North and West, who wanted no part of such aggressive conservatism, and a renewed mobilization effort by Democratic interest groups, particularly the AFL-CIO. Indeed, for the AFL-CIO, the Democratic losses in 1994 were instrumental in provoking a revolt against its president, Lane Kirkland, and his replacement by a new leadership explicitly committed to using labor's clout to defeat Republicans and elect Democrats.[23] In the 1996 elections, Bill Clinton routed Bob Dole by hitting the Republicans on medicare, education, and the environment, and Democrats in the House and the Senate began to recoup the losses they had suffered outside the South.

More important than the actual wins, though, was the way Democrats had won. In 1996, Democrats continued to win among moderate, well-to-do voters who had supported Reagan and Bush. For example, Bush had won New Jersey's Bergen County in 1988 by 58–41 percent; in 1992, he edged Clinton there by 2 percent. But in 1996, after the Republican takeover of Congress, Bergen County threw its support to Clinton by a substantial margin—53–39 percent. Four years later, it would back Gore by 55–42 percent. Reagan Democrats also continued to desert the Republicans. Bush narrowly won Michigan's Macomb County in 1992, by 42–37 percent, but Clinton would win it by 49–39 percent in 1996, and Gore would take it by 50–48 percent in 2000. (Nader would get 2 percent in Macomb, bringing the potential Democrat total to 52 percent.) Clinton won California, the linchpin of the conservative Republican majority of the 1980s, by 13 percent in 1996, and Gore would win it by 12 percent in 2000, despite never having campaigned there. The old conservative Republican majority was finally, and very clearly, dead.

V. AN EMERGING DEMOCRATIC MAJORITY?

But what will take its place? Among those for whom the present is always the future, it's become popular to predict that the current rough parity between the parties, with third parties and political independents tipping the balance one way or the other, will continue indefinitely. But the rise of third-party candidates like Perot and Ralph Nader have usually foreshadowed a partisan realignment; after one election, most of their supporters settle back into one of the two parties. (That Nader tipped the election to Bush will, after all, quite likely discourage future third-party bids from the left.[24]) As for the increased importance of independents, that's a bit murky, too. Yes, there are more of them: according to the University of Michigan's National Election Studies, voters who are willing to identify themselves as "independent" have increased from 23 percent in 1952 to 40.4 percent in 2000.[25] But while independents are making a political statement of a sort, they do so not with a single voice and not in a way that finally affects the two-party system itself.

In the South after 1960, many former "yellow dog" Democrats who couldn't reconcile themselves to registering Republican described themselves as independent. But, as far as election arithmetic is concerned, they have been reliably Republican voters. In the Northeast, upper Midwest, and Far West, many voters now identify themselves as independents as a protest against the venality and corruption they see in Washington and in party politics. But although they occasionally vote for an independent candidate—as Minnesotans did for Jesse Ventura in 1998—they usually support candidates from one of the major parties. Indeed, when the new independent vote is broken down, it reveals a trend toward the Democrats in the 1990s and a clear and substantial Democratic partisan advantage. The National Election Studies show that about 70 percent of independents will say which party they are closer to, and, once these "independents" are assigned to the party they are closer to, Democrats enjoy a 13 percent advantage over the Republicans, which is close to the advantage Democrats enjoyed among the electorate in the late 1950s and early 1960s.[26]

The Democratic leanings of the new independents are even clearer if one looks at the states that boast the highest percentage of independents. Ten of the top fifteen—Connecticut, Illinois, Iowa, Maine, Massachusetts, Minnesota, New Jersey, Rhode Island, Vermont, and Washington—are solidly Democratic, two—Arkansas and New Hampshire—are swing states, and only three—Alaska, Montana, and North Dakota—are dependably Republican in national elections.[27] Thus, a close look at today's independent voters suggests that the most likely successor to the dying Republican majority is another major-party majority—a new Democratic majority.

There is also a striking analogy between the period from 1968 to 1976, which preceded the birth of the last realignment, and the period from 1992 to the present. The Wallace defection of 1968 had a similar effect on the Democratic Party that the Perot defection of 1992 had on the Republican Party. Nixon and Clinton were both transitional presidents who maneuvered amidst shifting coalitions. Nixon had to face a Democratic Congress, and Clinton after 1994 a Republican Congress. Both were capable of sharp turns in their political outlook that bedeviled their supporters—Nixon on China and wage-price controls, Clinton on government itself ("the era of big government is over") and on the provisions of welfare reform. Both understood that they were on the verge of assembling new political majorities, but both were prevented from doing so by scandals. These scandals were partly the result of their own misdeeds or misbehavior but also of a fierce political opposition that was determined to undermine them.

Both men unwittingly inspired a political revival among their opponents—the Democratic congressional victories of 1974 and 1976 and the Republican congressional victory of 1994. By leaving a trail of scandal behind them, they also made it difficult for the men who tried to succeed them. Both Ford and Gore had to overcome problems of political trust that they were not principally responsible for creating. If not for Watergate, Ford—indeed, almost any Republican candidate—would have been elected president in 1976. And if not for the shadow of the Clinton scandals, Al Gore would almost certainly have defeated George W. Bush. According to Gore pollster Stanley Greenberg's extensive postelection poll, lack of trust in Gore was the single most important factor dogging his candidacy and seriously hurt him among voters that had begun moving Democratic in Clinton's successful 1996 campaign.

There are even remarkable similarities between Carter, who won in 1976, and George W. Bush, who won in 2000. Bush, like Carter, is a relatively inexperienced governor who was elected president on a platform that stressed character rather than program, and who took office amidst growing divisions within his own party and an opposition determined to foil him. And Bush, like Carter, will have to face a sputtering economy that could easily be the final catalyst for a new realignment.

There is also an analogy between the South's role in the conservative Republican realignment and the North's role in this new realignment. Just as the Democrats' continued hold on Congress depended on the partisan loyalty of Southern Democrats, the Republicans' narrow 221–213 margin in the House depends on the partisan loyalty of about thirty moderate Republicans—ranging from Maryland's Connie Morella to New York's Peter King—who often vote with the Democrats.[28] These House members generally represent districts that strongly backed Clinton in 1996 and Gore in 2000, but they continue to be reelected based on their personal popularity. In the absence of strong provocation—a conflict with their leadership, the recapture of the House by the Democrats—they are unlikely to switch parties, but once they retire, they are likely to be replaced by Democrats. In the Senate, one Republican, Vermont's Jim Jeffords, did leave the party in May 2001, turning the Senate itself over to the Democrats.

But the most important arguments for a new Democratic majority do not rely on analogies. A look at the voting patterns for president and Congress during the 1990s clearly indicates that while the conservative Republican majority was crumbling, a new Democratic majority was germinating. It would include white working- and middle-class Democrats, such as those from Lorain or Jefferson counties, who have returned to the Democrats in the nineties because they (or their progeny) believe the Democrats are more responsive to their economic situations. They are responding primarily to the Democratic Party's Jacksonian and New Deal past—its commitment to economic security for the average American.

But it would also include three groups of voters who clearly appeared in George McGovern's loss to Richard Nixon: minority voters, including blacks, Hispanics, and Asian-Americans; women voters, especially single, working, and highly educated women; and professionals. While the ranks of white working-class voters will not grow over the next decade, the numbers of professionals, working, single, and highly educated women, and minorities will swell. They are products of a new postindustrial capitalism, rooted in diversity and social equality, and emphasizing the production of ideas and services rather than goods. And while some of these voters are drawn to the Democratic Party by its New Deal past, many others resonate strongly to the new causes that the Democrats adopted during the sixties. These new causes help ensure that these groups of voters will continue to support Democrats rather than Republicans, paving the way for a new majority.

CHAPTER TWO

George McGovern's Revenge:
Who's in the Emerging Democratic Majority

Nothing has inspired such scorn as George McGovern's 1972 campaign. Immediately afterward, Jeane Kirkpatrick, who was then a Democrat, described McGovern's constituency as "intellectuals enamored with righteousness and possibility; college students, for whom perfectionism is an occupational hazard; portions of the upper classes freed from concern with economic self-interest; clergy contemptuous of materialism; bureaucrats with expanding plans to eliminate evil; romantics derisive of Babbitt and *Main Street*."[1] Even today, liberals still regard the campaign as having been quixotic and destructive. Margaret Weir and Marshall Ganz compare it unfavorably to Goldwater's campaign in 1964: "Although the 1964 Goldwater campaign laid a foundation for subsequent grassroots organization on the right, the equally unsuccessful 1972 McGovern campaign seemed to have just the opposite effect on the left."[2]

Perhaps it is time to reappraise the McGovern campaign—not as a model of how to win presidential elections, but as an election that foreshadowed a new Democratic majority in the twenty-first century. Although McGovern lost to Richard Nixon 60.7–37.5 percent, the third-largest margin ever, several groups that would become important components of today's Democratic Party made a clear statement during that election. According to the Gallup Poll, McGovern actually did slightly better among nonwhite voters than Hubert Humphrey did in 1968—winning 87 percent of their vote. And though McGovern lost the vote among women as well as men, he showed unforeseen strength among working women. The Democrats had opened up a gender gap among employed voters starting in 1964, but this gap ballooned in

1972. McGovern did 13 percentage points better among working women than among working men.[3]

McGovern also won college communities that had once been Republican. These included the University of California at Berkeley's Alameda County, the University of Wisconsin's Dane County, and Washtenaw County, where the University of Michigan is located. And he did astonishingly well among highly skilled professionals. This group, which had been solidly Republican and had given Humphrey only 36 percent of its vote, gave McGovern 42 percent.[4] He did better among these voters than he did among blue-collar workers.

At the time, of course, these results were scant consolation. What did it matter if McGovern won Alameda County and San Francisco but decisively lost Los Angeles and San Diego? Or that he did better among working women than working men, and among professionals than blue-collar workers, but still lost a majority of all these voters? Thirty years later, however, these anomalies loom larger. Women are still voting more Democratic than men, but they are also voting much more Democratic than Republican, particularly women who now work outside the home, single women, and women with college degrees. Minorities, once about 10 percent of the voting electorate, now constitute 19 percent; extrapolating from recent trends, they could make up nearly a quarter of voters by 2010. They, too, are continuing to vote Democratic. Democrats are winning even more decisively in college towns, and these towns and their schools have become linked to entire regions such as Silicon Valley and North Carolina's Research Triangle. And skilled professionals have become a much larger and a dependably Democratic voting group.

The outlook of these groups differs from that of the white working-class voters who were the heart of the New Deal Democratic majority. Professionals, working women, and minorities have been shaped by the political and economic events of the last half century: the tumultuous sixties—a period that really stretches from 1956 to 1974—which saw the rise of the civil rights movement, the revival of the women's movement, and the growth of consumer and environmental movements; and by the transition from an industrial to a postindustrial economy, which really begins in the 1920s, but erupted in the sixties, and then accelerated during the "information revolution" of the nineties. As a new Democratic majority began to emerge in the 1990s, these three groups joined forces with white working-class voters, many of whom had voted for Nixon, Reagan, and Bush, but returned to the Democratic fold in 1992 or 1996. The resulting coalition, evident in Clinton's 1996 victory, reflected the diverse outlooks of all these groups, but above all, that of professionals.

I. POSTINDUSTRIAL SOCIETY AND THE RISE OF THE PROFESSIONALS

No group used to be as dependably Republican as highly skilled professionals, a group that includes architects, engineers, scientists, computer analysts, lawyers, physicians, registered nurses, teachers, social workers, therapists, designers, interior decorators, graphic artists, and actors. This group dutifully backed Eisenhower in 1952 and 1956, Nixon in 1960, 1968, and 1972, Ford in 1976, and Reagan in 1980 and 1984. But their anti-Democratic proclivities began to soften as early as 1972, and by 1988, they were supporting Democrats for president and have continued to do so. In the fifties, their political choices didn't matter that much: they made up only about 7 percent of the workforce. But by 2000, they made up 15.4 percent.[5] Moreover, they have the highest turnout rate of any occupational group.[6] As a result, they compose about 21 percent of the voting electorate nationally and are likely near one-quarter in many Northeastern and Far Western states.[7]

The growth of professionals as a group is partly a function of the introduction of technology into the production process, which has increased the role of scientists and engineers in relation to blue-collar workers and has fueled the growth of public and private education. In 1900, there was one engineer for every 225 factory workers; in 1950, one for every 62; now, it is one for every 8.[8] But engineers make up only 11.4 percent of professionals.[9] The main reason for the growth of professionals is the transition from an industrial society, in which labor was primarily devoted to goods production, to a postindustrial society, in which the labor is primarily directed at producing ideas and services.

In the industrial society of the late-nineteenth and early-twentieth centuries, most workers were engaged in manufacturing and farming. In 1900, 38 percent worked on farms, and 36 percent were manual workers, primarily in factories—together making a total of three out of four

American workers. Twenty years later, the number of farm laborers had declined to 27 percent, but the proportion of manual workers had climbed to 40 percent. It looked as though America were going to become a giant factory, divided between a small white-collar managerial-professional class, which in 1920 made up about 12 percent of the workforce, and a huge blue-collar proletariat, much of which lived on the edge of poverty.[10] But in the 1920s, America began the transition to a postindustrial society.[11]

During the 1920s, the introduction of electricity and scientific management on the factory floor and of the gas-driven tractor and harvester in the fields made it possible for the goods-producing workforce to shrink while goods production expanded dramatically. Potentially, this promised release from unremitting toil and sacrifice, but in the near term, it created a threat of overproduction. If the wage-earning class shrank, while production grew, who would buy the growing array of new food-stuffs and cars? America failed to find a solution to this problem during the Great Depression, but over the next decades, government and business adapted to the challenge posed by the new productivity. Government's role in the economy was transformed. The federal government began to use fiscal and monetary policy to temper the business cycle. The federal government even did the unthinkable—encouraging consumer demand through running deficits. It would fund consumer housing purchases and college attendance and use public investment to build roads, bridges, schools, and hospitals, as well as aircraft carriers, and to reward farmers for not planting crops.

Private industry would also alter its practices. Businesses had begun offering installment plans in the 1920s, but after World War II, they established charge accounts and later credit cards to encourage consumer spending. Advertising also exploded after the introduction of television. Advertising budgets went from $1 billion in 1929 to $6.5 billion in 1951 to $12 billion in 1962.[12] Advertising encouraged Americans to spend rather than save, and to seek happiness on earth rather than in the afterlife—to worry about the "quality" of their life. Businesses expanded into new realms that had been previously reserved for upper-class luxuries or for production at home. They built restaurant chains, hotels, theme parks, casinos, auditoriums, and opened television and movie studios. They sold sexual pleasure and mental and physical health. They imbued the material objects they produced with the new ethic of consumerism. They marketed not merely edible food, but gourmet delights and prepackaged and frozen food. They sold fashion and not merely clothes. They didn't just sell a standard car like the Model T or Model A; they produced a new model or style annually.

These measures transformed the face of the economy, as the production of things became secondary to the production of services and ideas. By 1970, only 35 percent of the workforce was devoted to goods production; the rest was devoted to services and ideas.[13] Since then, computer automation has accelerated the transition from industrial to postindustrial society. During the 1990s, manufacturing output increased by over a third, while factory employment declined by 4.4 percent. By the decade's end, manufacturing employment accounted for only 14.3 percent of the nation's jobs. About eight in ten American workers were producing services or ideas[14]—a dramatic change from the beginning of the century, when the corresponding figure was only about three in ten.[15]

If you look at this new postindustrial workforce, it is far more diverse than the workforce of 1900 and 1920. At the top are executives, administrators, and managers. At the bottom are unskilled manufacturing and service workers, still a considerable, though shrinking, portion of the workforce. Among those groups in between are professionals, now the largest of the major occupational groups.* They are the workforce, above all, of the new postindustrial society.

In the 1990s, the ranks of professionals swelled 30 percent[16]; and the

---

Professionals is a term used by the Census Bureau to distinguish white-collar, highly skilled, credentialed workers from managers, administrators, and executives, on the one hand, and technicians and blue-collar mechanics and repairers, on the other hand. But in terms of the critical characteristic we cite—identification with the quality of the service or idea rather than with the market result—there is a blurring of the categories. The census lists airline pilots and navigators as technicians, but we would include them within professionals. We would also include school administrators, who have their own professional associations, as professionals rather than managers, even though they perform management functions. And we would probably cede certain kinds of public relations people and corporate lawyers—for instance, in-house counsels—to managers, administrators, and executives. All in all, the category of professionals, as we would use it, is slightly broader than, but roughly congruent with, the census category. To maintain consistency, and due to data limitations, all data cited here on professionals, in terms of occupational statistics and voting behavior, are based on the Census Bureau definition.

Labor Department projects that from 1998 to 2008, professionals will be the fastest-growing of any major occupational group. Among the professions expected to increase by more than 20 percent are a startling combination of jobs that either didn't exist or were of marginal significance in the industrial age: actors, directors, and producers, artists and commercial artists, designers and interior designers, camera operators, public relations specialists, counselors, registered nurses, therapists, coaches, special education teachers, preschool teachers, social workers, electrical and electronics engineers, architects and surveyors, agricultural and food scientists, conservation scientists and foresters, medical scientists, computer systems analysts, computer scientists and engineers, physicists and astronomers, and directors of religious activities.[17] Of course, some of these start from a small base, but their projected rapid growth tells us much about where the economy is headed.

The political views of professionals have been shaped by their experience in this transition to postindustrial society. From 1900 to 1960, when they were a tiny minority within the workforce, they saw themselves clearly linked to managers and executives. They disdained unions, opposed the New Deal and "big government," and adopted an ethic of individual success that made them the most Republican of the occupational groups. In the 1960 presidential election, professionals supported the Republican Nixon 61–38; managers backed Nixon by a more modest 52–48. But in the last four presidential elections, professionals have supported the Democrats by an average of 52–40 percent, while managers have averaged 49–41 support for the GOP.[18] Why did professionals turn so abruptly toward the Democrats?

One key to the change is the different relationship that managers and professionals have to the private market. While corporate and financial executives, accountants, and property managers are creatures of the private market who tend to gauge their own success in profit-and-loss terms, many professionals identify their success with the quality of the service they offer or the idea they produce. Software programmers worry about the "coolness" of their code; architects about the beauty and utility of their buildings; teachers about whether their pupils have learned; the doctor and nurse about the health of their patient. AnnaLee Saxenian wrote about Silicon Valley engineers of the 1990s that "status was defined less by economic success than by technological achievement. The elegantly designed chip, the breakthrough manufacturing process, or the ingenious application was admired as much as the trappings of wealth."[19]

One survey of different kinds of professionals conducted by Hart Research[20] confirmed the strong emphasis professionals put on "making a contribution," "the opportunity to be creative," and "excelling at my job" (see table below). The professional could draw a distinction, which neither the manager nor the alienated blue-collar worker could, between the quality of his or her product and the demands of the market.

As long as professionals felt that they had the opportunity to pursue excellence in their jobs, they identified themselves with the successful entrepreneur and CEO. They saw themselves as case studies of how capitalism could reward quality. But as the numbers of professionals have grown within postindustrial capitalism, they have become subject to higher authority within the private and the public sectors. And they don't

What Professionals Value

	Teachers	Nurses	Engineers	Information Technology Workers
Making a contribution	68%	54%	47%	37%
Creative opportunities	29	8	27	28
Excelling at my job	26	27	25	29
Professional autonomy	8	16	16	11
Salary and benefits	10	16	11	16
Voice on the job	4	10	7	8

Source: David Kusnet, *Finding Their Voices* (Washington, D.C.: Albert Shanker Institute, 2000).

like it. They have been forced to accede to what they see as alien market standards of performance that conflict with their own standards of excellence. They have had their autonomy undercut by corporate and institutional managers who have introduced work rules, overseen their output, controlled the prices they charge and the income they receive, and even divided up their work among more specialized but less highly trained technicians. As a result, they have increasingly made a distinction between their own priorities and those of business and the market. That has placed them much closer in outlook to the Democratic Party than to the unequivocally pro-market Republican Party.

Many midlevel professionals, including teachers, aerospace engineers, social workers, and software testers, have had a similar experience to late-nineteenth-century crafts workers—the smiths, machinists, and carpenters who evaluated their work by the quality of their product and jealously guarded their prerogatives. "In each craft," labor historian Harry Braverman recounts, "the worker was presumed to be the master of a body of traditional knowledge, and methods and procedures were left to his or her discretion."[21] When they saw their autonomy threatened by industrial capitalism, they helped to form and lead the American Federation of Labor in 1886. Similarly, many of today's professionals have responded in the last four decades by joining unions. In 2000, 19.3 percent of professionals belonged to unions—a higher percentage than all other white-collar workers and close to the level of operators and laborers.[22] And many of these unions, such as the American Federation of Teachers and the National Education Association, have become bulwarks of the Democratic Party.

Even the highest-level professionals have become subject to what Marxists called proletarianization. Doctors used to enjoy the privileges and security of a medieval guild and the income of the most highly paid executive, but in the last three decades, their work has increasingly become subject to direction from insurance companies through managed-care plans and health maintenance organizations. They are told what procedures to follow, what prices to charge, and how much they can make. About 40 percent of doctors are now salaried employees.[23] Marcia Simon, the director of government relations for the American College of Obstetricians and Gynecologists, says, "Doctors had always been quintessential small businesspeople, but now they're essentially employees of large corporations. It represents a real sea change in the role of doctors in the economy."[24]

Doctors who are not self-employed have begun joining unions. From 1997 to 1999, the number of unionized doctors went from twenty-five thousand to about forty thousand.[25] That year, the AMA also pledged support for unionization among doctors. Politically, doctors used to be one of the most dependable Republican constituencies. The American Medical Association and other doctor lobbies could be expected to give the bulk of their funds to Republicans. But as doctors have tried to fight the control of the insurance companies, they have found allies among Democrats rather than Republicans. In the first half of 2001, when Congress was considering a patients' bill of rights, the majority of AMA contributions—67 percent—went to Democrats rather than Republicans.[26] Says one doctor who used to raise money for Republicans, "The chicks have come home to roost on the GOP." The doctors' vote, he says, "is now up for grabs."[27]

The other key to the political outlook of professionals is the experience of the sixties, in which many future professionals, while attending college, became supporters and leaders of the civil rights, women's, antiwar, consumer, and environmental movements. These movements had their own rationales and impetus, but the women's, environmental, and consumer movements were shaped by the transition to postindustrial society. One feature of that transition—transmitted in the new variety of jobs and products and by the new appeal to the consumer crafted by advertisers—was a far more expansive definition of what Americans could expect from their lives and, by extension, their government. Americans of the last half of the twentieth century learned to value not only automatic transmissions on automobiles, but also clean air and water, physical and mental well-being, and safe and reliable products. And when they didn't get these from the invisible hand of the market, they demanded them from the visible hand of government.

This new understanding was nurtured in the universities, where the professionals were trained. The post–World War II members of the baby-boom generation would spend their late adolescence and early adulthood on college campuses. In 1900, 5 percent of eighteen-to-twenty-one-year-olds attended college. By 1970, 51.8 percent did. In college, they were insulated from parental authority and from labor market discipline. The college campus became ground zero for the development of a new postindustrial ethic and for the development of new political movements. One of the leading civil rights organizations was the Student Nonviolent Coordinating Committee, and the leading antiwar group was Students for a Democratic Society. The environmental movement was born on Earth Day at the University of Michigan, and the consumer movement grew out of the law schools.

Of all occupational groups, professionals would be the most clearly touched by these movements. To this day, they exhibit the most support for civil rights and feminist causes and for environmental and consumer regulation. Moreover, professionals would bring their own special outlook to them—an outlook that was markedly different from New Deal Democratic politics. New Deal Democratic politics were defined largely by industrial unions and blue-collar workers, who by the nature of their jobs were adversaries of business managers and executives. The New Deal Democrats envisaged American politics as a contest of interest groups, and they sought a "fair deal" (the name of Harry Truman's platform) for workers and ordinary Americans. But the growing army of professionals occupied a place between the alienated blue-collar worker and the manager and executive. They didn't see themselves primarily as winning a better deal from the rich and powerful. Instead, they believed they were acting on behalf of the public as a whole rather than on behalf of workers or management. They thought they represented the "public interest," and they envisaged the movements they founded as "public interest" groups. The model was Harvard Law School graduate Ralph Nader's Public Interest Research Group and Public Citizen and John Gardner's Common Cause.

These environmental, consumer, and political reform groups were initially nonpartisan, identified with neither the New Deal Democrats nor the pro-business Republicans, but by the mid-1970s they found themselves opposed by an alliance of business groups and conservative Republican politicians and think tanks. In 1977, for instance, the Business Roundtable teamed with Republicans to defeat a Nader plan, backed by the Carter administration, to establish a consumer protection agency. Four years later, Reagan appointed a host of officials to the Federal Trade Commission, Interior Department, and Environmental Protection Agency who were hostile to the environmental and consumer movements. As a result, the consumer and environmental movements—and the larger public interest movement of which they are a part—found themselves at odds with the Republican Party and increasingly identified with the Democratic Party. The many professionals who actively supported these groups or merely subscribed to their goals followed suit. It became another impetus for professionals to abandon the Republicans for the Democratic Party. (As we will see, professionals' support for feminist goals would have a similar effect on their party allegiance.)

If you look at the voting history of professionals in the light of these influences, it becomes more comprehensible.[28] Professionals began in the 1950s as a thoroughly Republican group. They identified with the market and opposed the "big government" initiatives of the New Deal and the Great Society. Like managers, and every other occupational group, they supported Johnson against Goldwater because of the latter's seeming readiness to plunge the United States into nuclear war, but they reverted to strong support for Nixon against Humphrey in 1968. In 1972, they backed Nixon, but much less so than managers because many of them supported the movements of the sixties. In 1976, they supported Gerald Ford and in 1980 and 1984, Reagan.

They continued to support Republicans largely because professionals still tended to share the economic outlook of small businessmen: they were suspicious of government spending on jobs and feared deficits were imperiling the economy. Like many Americans, they were skeptical of Carter and the Democrats' economic policies. And they distrusted government in general. Johnson's conduct of the war and Nixon's Watergate scandal had reinforced this attitude. By 1980, 81 percent of professionals believed government was "too powerful." Even so, many professionals balked at supporting Reagan. Instead, 15 percent of professionals voted for the fiscally conservative and socially liberal Anderson—a higher percentage than he got from any other occupational group.

The professionals' move toward the Democratic Party continued in the 1984 election. In that election, professionals increased their support for the Democratic presidential candidate by about 9 percent to 45 percent, while only 30 percent of managers backed Mondale. One of the reasons professionals moved to the Democrats and managers did not was their support for environmental regulation. In 1984, 52 percent of professionals favored spending more on the environment compared to 32 percent of

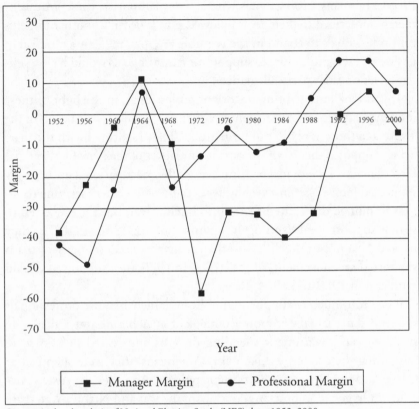

Democratic Margin among Professionals and Managers, 1952–2000

Source: Authors' analysis of National Election Study (NES) data, 1952–2000.

managers. Of all the occupational groups, professionals were also most sympathetic to civil rights and women's rights and the most supportive of campaign finance reform and other good-government issues.[29] Since 1988, professionals have strongly backed Democratic presidential candidates, while managers have remained mostly Republican (see chart).

Professionals might not have moved toward the Democratic Party, however, if the party itself had not moved toward them. If the 1972 election marked the Democrats' identification with the sixties, the 1984 election marked the end of the Democrats as the party of indiscriminate big spenders and the beginning of the party's commitment to more incremental reform. It was the first intimation of the Democrats' progressive centrism. In that election, Mondale attacked Reagan for running deficits and promised to reduce the deficit, even if that meant raising taxes. Such a stance probably hurt him among blue-collar Democrats, but it may have helped him among professionals worried by looming deficits. Dukakis, Clinton, and Gore continued in their campaigns to promise fiscal restraint. Clinton, for example, despite the more ambitious experiments of his first two years in office, would end up running on a program of moderate, fiscally prudent reform in the 1996 campaign, and Gore followed in 2000 with a similar approach that emphasized the importance of not endangering the budget surplus. This general approach has helped to reassure professionals leery of overly ambitious government programs and to make the Democratic Party the natural home of the professional voter.*

II. WOMEN AND THE FEMINIST REVOLUTION

Like professionals, women used to vote more for Republicans than Democrats. They also used to vote disproportionately more Republican than men did. In 1956, according to the National Election Study survey, women supported Eisenhower 63–37 percent while men supported him 56–43 percent. In 1960, women supported Richard Nixon 53–46 percent against Democrat John Kennedy, but men backed Kennedy 52–48 percent. In 1964, women began to vote slightly more Democratic than men, and in 1968 and 1972 the trend grew.[30] Then, after subsiding for the 1976 election (when the Republican candidate was pro-choice, pro–equal rights Gerald Ford along with his outspoken wife, Betty), in 1980 it reappeared in force. According to the CBS/*New York Times* exit poll, men in 1980 supported Reagan over Democrat Jimmy Carter 55–36 percent— while women supported him only 47–45 percent.

---

*In 2000, however, some professionals, concerned about the Clinton-Gore campaign-finance scandals, voted for Nader rather than Gore. In the NES 2000 survey, professionals and technicians were the most supportive of Nader's candidacy, and professionals registered the greatest concern with reforming campaign finance of any of the occupational groups. This, of course, didn't alter the Democratic trend among professionals.

In the 1980s, women not only began voting disproportionately more Democratic than men—the so-called gender gap—but what is more important they began to vote more Democratic than Republican. As a result, Democratic candidates began to win elections on the strength of the women's vote the way they had won elections on the strength of the union vote. In 1982, Mario Cuomo got 56 percent of the women's vote—but just 48 percent of the men's—in defeating Republican Lew Lehrman for the New York governorship. In 1984, Illinois Democratic Senate candidate Paul Simon defeated incumbent Republican Charles Percy by winning 55 percent of the women's vote and only 46 percent of the men's vote.

In the 2000 elections, women's support helped the Democrats win eight Senate races. In Florida, Democrat Bill Nelson won 56 percent of the women's vote, but only 45 percent of the men's vote. In Minnesota, Democrat Mark Dayton lost the men's vote to incumbent Rod Grams 44–47 percent, but he won the women's vote 54–40 percent. In the presidential race, men supported Bush 53–42 percent, but women supported Vice President Al Gore 54–43 percent.[31] In twelve of the nineteen states that Gore won, women made up a Democratic deficit among male voters and enabled Gore to win. This change in women's voting was due to the way that the parties responded to the transformation of women's role and status that occurred after the sixties—a transformation that was itself closely bound up with the transition to postindustrial society.

In industrial society, women of all classes were defined by their subordinate role within the family to men. If they were in working-class families, they had many other duties besides mother and homemaker—they might, for instance, do piecework to supplement the family income—but their primary identity and responsibility was as wife and mother under a husband's authority. Working-class single women like Theodore Dreiser's Sister Carrie got jobs, but their goal in life was to leave the workplace when they married. Few middle- and upper-class women worked outside the home, especially if they were married. As late as 1910, only 9.2 percent of married women worked outside the home.[32] "The economic position of women in the world," Charlotte Perkins Gilman wrote in 1898, is "that of domestic servant."[33] Women's personal lives were circumscribed by the dictates of nineteenth-century Protestantism and the demands of industrial society for new workers. Sex was for reproduction—

and for creating large families. Women's cares, interests, and wants were to be directed at their children and husband.

The transition to postindustrial society after World War II changed women's lives, but didn't really change their place in society. Business and the public sector increasingly took over many of the functions that women had performed within the home—from making clothes and educating children to preparing food. New technology reduced the time women had to spend on cooking, cleaning, and doing laundry. Work itself was changing—toward the kind of service and professional jobs that women had been deemed capable of filling. And more women began to attend college. Yet married women were still discouraged from working outside the home. Wrote Betty Friedan in 1963 in her groundbreaking book, *The Feminine Mystique,* "It is more than a strange paradox that as the professions are finally open to women in America, *career woman* has become a dirty word."[34]

Women's personal lives were also in flux. Freed from the social imperatives of the farm and factory, they were no longer enjoined to have large families. Through birth control, they could have sex without the threat of reproduction (and with the introduction of the pill, they could have some control over the process themselves). The new ethic of consumerism and personal fulfillment—put forth by advertisers and reflected in popular entertainment—depicted women as sexual beings. The fashion of the fifties—epitomized by Dior's "New Look"—emphasized women's curves.[35] Yet women were still constrained by Victorian ideals of feminine behavior. They were educated to have minds of their own, but were discouraged from displaying them by the official culture.

In the sixties, these looming contradictions gave rise to the modern women's movement. While the older movement had limited itself to demanding political equality for women, the new movement of the sixties demanded equality within the home, school, and workplace. NOW was founded in 1966 and Friedan became its first leader. Its membership climbed to 15,000 in 1972 and to 220,000 in 1982. In the late sixties, hundreds of local women's groups also grew up under the aegis of the New Left's women's liberation movement—which was modeled on the black liberation movement. While the women's movement's membership was largely drawn from college students, young educated women in their twenties, and professionals, its impact was universal. It changed the way women envisaged all aspects of their working and personal lives—from their responsibility as parents to their sexuality.

The women's movement challenged the barriers to women's equality—whether in the workplace or in university funding of athletics; the movement pressured states and finally the Supreme Court into eliminating most restrictions on abortion. The women's movement also spearheaded women's massive entry into the workplace, which began in the 1960s. Women's labor force participation went from 37.7 percent in 1960 to 43.3 percent in 1970 to 51.5 percent in 1980 and to 57.5 percent in 1990 (see chart). Among twenty-five-to-thirty-four-year-old women—those who would be expected to leave the workforce after marriage—participation rates went up by 20.5 percent during the 1970s.[36] As women entered the labor force, they also moved up within it. In 1970, fewer than 10 percent of medical students and 4 percent of law students were women; by the early 1990s, more than 40 percent of first-year law and medical students were women.[37] By the end of the twentieth century, 55 percent of professionals were women.[38]

Women's Labor Force Participation: 1950–2000

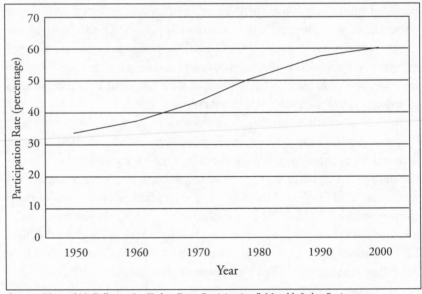

Sources: Howard N. Fullerton Jr., "Labor Force Participation," *Monthly Labor Review,* December 1999; and Bureau of Labor Statistics Web site.

The rise of the women's movement and women's accelerated entry into the labor force also changed the way women thought about politics. Women's disproportionate support for Republicans before 1964 was largely attributable to the political outlook of women who did not work outside the home. These homemakers made up almost two-thirds of female voters, and they were much more likely to support Republicans than working women or men were.[39] (Even then, working women were more Democratic than working men.) In 1952, for instance, only 38 percent of nonworking women supported the Democrat Stevenson against Eisenhower, compared to 44 percent of working men and 48 percent of working women. While demographic differences had some influence, the main reason nonworking women were disproportionately Republican was because their position in the home made them more politically conservative. They represented the vestiges of an earlier ethic, and as such, they were more likely to favor the Republicans, who still represented the small-town mores of the Protestant Midwest.

The presixties women's movement was also pro-Republican. The members of the main women's organization, the National Woman's Party, were often Republican businesswomen. In addition, Republicans were more likely before 1973 to back the Equal Rights Amendment (ERA), which the NWP championed. The first major party candidate to endorse the ERA was Republican Thomas Dewey in 1948, and Eisenhower was the first president to endorse it (in 1957). New Deal Democrats from Franklin Roosevelt through John Kennedy opposed the ERA because they feared that it would undercut state labor legislation aimed at protecting working women from overtime and heavy lifting.[40] But Friedan and many of the leaders of the new women's movement came out of the political left and were inclined to link the women's movement, if at all, with the Democratic rather than the Republican Party. In 1972, feminist political leaders, including Congresswoman Bella Abzug and *Ms* magazine founder Gloria Steinem, attended the Democratic convention. Actress Shirley MacLaine and Los Angeles official Yvonne Braithwaite Burke headed the California delegation. In 1968, 13 percent of the Democratic delegates were women; by 1972, 38 percent were. McGovern staffers talked of a "nylon revolution" in the party.[43]

But the great divide between women and the parties did not occur until after 1973. Liberal feminists and labor Democrats had come out in favor of the ERA after an amendment to the 1964 Civil Rights Act prohibited discrimination in employment on the basis of sex. That, and the fact that women were increasingly working in services and in professions that didn't need special protection, undercut the older liberal objections to the ERA. In 1972, Nixon and Republicans had backed the ERA, but in 1973, new right leader Phyllis Schlafly began a successful crusade to turn the Republicans and the country against the amendment. In January of that year, the Supreme Court ruled in *Roe v. Wade* that states could not outlaw all abortions. While Democrats endorsed abortion rights in 1976, conservative Republicans got the Republican Party to come out in favor of a constitutional ban.

In 1980, the religious right became an important constituency of the Republican Party, and the party went on record in favor of women's traditional place in the family. It even removed support for child care from the platform. Reagan spoke repeatedly for banning abortion and in opposition to affirmative action for women. In 1983, the Reagan administration attempted to gut Title IX, which required federally subsidized colleges to offer equal facilities to women.[42] The women's organizations moved closer to the Democrats, and in 1984 NOW actually endorsed Mondale for president.

Of course, women in this era were concerned about a range of issues from affirmative action to breast cancer research. Evidence is particularly strong that working women, as they experienced the vagaries of the marketplace, developed distinctly positive views of government's role in providing services and mitigating economic insecurity. These views disposed working women naturally toward the Democratic Party and account for much of the move toward the Democrats among women as a whole.[43]

But one issue that concerned female voters directly as women and clearly turned many college-educated women toward the Democratic Party was the Republican Party's opposition to abortion. It struck at the heart of women's claims to a new independence and identity outside the traditional role of mother and wife. It impinged on women's ability to work outside the home and to have sex for pleasure rather than for reproduction. Tanya Melich, a longtime Republican Party activist who finally broke with the party in the 1990s over its hostility to women's rights, wrote later of the centrality of abortion as an issue: "A woman's right to determine whether she has a child strikes at the core of her being, affecting how she lives and what she does, who she is, and what she will be."[44]

One poll taken after the 2000 election showed that abortion was still a defining issue for many women. Stanley Greenberg, who served as Gore's pollster, asked over two thousand respondents to identify three reasons (out of eighteen choices) why they voted, or considered voting, for Gore and three reasons (out of thirteen choices) why they had doubts about voting for George Bush. Among all women voters, Bush's "opposition to a woman's right to choose" was the single biggest reason for opposing him. In addition, Greenberg found that for white college-educated females and white females making over $75,000, protecting a woman's right to choose was both their most important reason for supporting Gore and for having doubts about Bush. Thirty-nine percent of white college-educated females said defending a woman's right to choose was their main reason for supporting Gore, and 33 percent said it was their main source of doubt about Bush.

Some women's support for Democrats can, of course, be attributed to factors other than their experience as women. It could be argued, for instance, that African-American women support Democrats simply because they are African-American. Yet even here there is good evidence that the feminist revolution has had its special effect. African-American women voted for Gore by 94 percent, a 9 percent gender gap over their male counterparts.

Women's support for Democrats is also not universal. It is particularly concentrated among working and single women and among college-educated women, especially those with a postgraduate education—exactly those groups that would experience most clearly the effect of feminism and of the transition to postindustrial society. Single working women, for instance, backed Dukakis in 1988 by 57 to 42 percent; Clinton in 1992 by 62 to 24 percent; and Clinton in 1996 by 72 to 21 percent. Women college graduates supported Gore by 57 percent compared to 39 percent for Bush, and 63 percent of women with advanced degrees backed Gore.[45] But these are the groups that, as a proportion of the female electorate, have been steadily growing since the end of World War II and will continue to do so.

III. MINORITIES AND THE DEMOCRATIC MAJORITY

Until recently, America's minority groups—defined in distinction to the white Indo-European majority—had widely differing political allegiances. Mexican-Americans, typical of many new immigrants, generally voted for Democrats. African-Americans were Republicans from the Civil War to 1936. Chinese and Cuban-Americans were anticommunist Republicans. But over the last few decades, these diverse minorities, with the exception of Miami's Cubans, have converged on the Democratic Party and have given it a large potential advantage in national and some state elections over Republican candidates.

Blacks

Blacks did begin voting for Democrats during the New Deal, but as late as 1960, almost a third of the black electorate voted for Republican Richard Nixon for president.[46] The big change came after 1964 when Democrats sponsored the Civil Rights Act of 1964, and when Republicans, who as a party had been supportive of civil rights legislation, nominated Goldwater for president, who had voted against it. That November, blacks voted for Johnson against Goldwater 94–6 percent.[47] As Democrats cemented their commitment to civil rights and conservatives took over the Republican Party, blacks supported Democrats overwhelmingly. Between 1968 and 2000, they never gave Democratic presidential candidates less than 83 percent of their vote and usually quite a bit more.[48] In 2000, blacks gave Gore 90 percent, Nader 1 percent, and Bush 9 percent.

At the same time as blacks were voting Democratic, the black vote increased as a proportion of the electorate. In 1960, only 29 percent of Southern blacks were registered to vote; by 1976, after passage of the Civil Rights Act of 1965 guaranteeing blacks the right to vote, 63 percent of Southern blacks were registered.[49] The black proportion of the electorate went from less than 6 percent in 1960 to 10–12 percent in the 1990s.[50]

The single most important reason why blacks supported Democrats was, of course, civil rights. They saw Democrats supporting civil rights and

Republicans doing what they could to take advantage of the white back-lash to it—from Nixon's thinly veiled pledge to restore "law and order" to Reagan's stories about the "welfare queen" in Chicago. Many blacks also supported Democrats for economic reasons. African-Americans dispro-portionately occupied the lower rungs of the occupational ladder, and many lived in cities beset by poverty and crime. They saw government not only as providing much needed aid and benefits, but also as an important source of upwardly mobile employment. They backed the New Deal and the Great Society. They wanted the minimum wage raised, and welfare payments expanded. They favored national health insurance and a mas-sive program of urban aid. While Democratic politicians like Clinton and Gore balked at the most ambitious of these programs, they still repre-sented to black voters a viable alternative to Republicans, who tended to oppose or to seek to weaken even basic New Deal programs.

Hispanics

Some Mexicans had settled in the Southwest and West before American settlers had wrested these lands from Mexico. In the late nineteenth and early twentieth century, Mexican laborers were lured into the South-west and West to help build the railroads and work on farms. They were given citizenship but were discouraged from voting and denied ade-quate schooling. In the 1930s, some were forcibly deported. But unlike blacks, they were never enslaved. Instead, they faced the kind of dis-crimination that blacks experienced in the North in the twentieth cen-tury. Like Northern blacks, many Mexican-American and Central American immigrants have also occupied the lower rungs on the occu-pational ladder. They worked as migrant farm laborers and, over the last three decades, have filled many of the service industry jobs created by the postindustrial economy.

Except for the Cubans who emigrated after the revolution, a majority of Hispanics have voted Democratic. John and Robert Kennedy both wooed Mexican-Americans, and in 1972, Mexican-American political leaders became active in the national party. In McGovern's California del-egation to the national convention, 17 percent were Mexican-Americans.[51] In the 1960s, the Hispanic civil rights movement, which included sepa-

California Latino and White Views of Economic Issues, May 1998

Taxes and Spending	Latinos	Whites
Should spend more on social programs, even if it means increasing taxes	58%	46%
Should reduce taxes, even if it means spending less on social programs	38	46
Government Regulation		
Regulation of business is necessary to protect public interest	63	49
Regulation of business does more harm than good	33	48

Source: Mark Baldassare, *California in the New Millennium: The Changing Social and Political Landscape* (Berkeley, Cal.: University of California Press, 2000).

rate Chicano and Puerto Rican organizations, followed on the heels of the black civil rights movement; and many Hispanics supported Democrats as the party of affirmative action and opposition to discrimination. But Hispanic voters probably placed more emphasis on economic issues. Hispanics, who were concentrated in the working class, were Democrats on grounds of economics as much as on grounds of civil rights. Primarily working class, they supported the New Deal and the Great Society and wanted government to do still more (see table).

When the Democrats appeared to falter in their economic leadership in the late 1970s, some Hispanics voted for Reagan. Reagan got as high as 47 percent of the Hispanic vote in one poll taken in 1984.[52] But Hispanics returned to the Democratic Party in the 1990s—not only because of Republican support in California and in the U.S. Senate for punitive measures aimed at Mexican illegal and legal immigrants, but because they saw Democrats as the party of economic opportunity and security. Growing union membership seems to have had an important impact on

Hispanic support for Democrats, particularly in California, Illinois, New York, and New Jersey.* In the 2000 election, for example, working-class Hispanics who belonged to unions supported Gore by 37 percent (66–29); those who did not supported Gore by just 17 percent (57–40).

Hispanic support is a crucial part of a new Democratic majority. Hispanics are the minority group that is growing the most in terms of both absolute numbers and percentage of population. In 1990, they made up 9 percent of the population compared to 11.7 percent for blacks. They now make up 12.5 percent compared to 12.4 percent for blacks and are also at virtual parity in terms of the voting-age population: 11 percent compared to 11.3 percent for blacks.[53] In a quarter of the country's congressional districts, there are at least one hundred thousand Hispanic residents.[54] They are 29 percent of the potential electorate in Texas, 28 percent in California, 21 percent in Arizona, 16 percent in Florida, 15 percent in Colorado, and 14 percent in New York.[55] Their voting turnout continues to be low, albeit gradually improving, but their share of active voters has been steadily increasing thanks to their rapid increase in numbers. In 1992, they made up 3.7 percent of the presidential voting electorate. In 2000, they made up 5.4 percent of voters and possibly more.[56]

Asian-Americans

Like the term *Hispanic,* the term *Asian-American* imputes a spurious unity of belief to a diverse group of nationalities. Chinese, Japanese, Vietnamese, Korean, Indian, and Filipino immigrants have followed different political trajectories and also very different histories in America. While the Vietnamese and South Asian Indians are recent immigrants, the Chinese, for instance, began coming in the nineteenth century as "coolie" labor to build the railroads. Chinese, Japanese, and Indian immigrants have also prospered in recent decades. They are the most educated nationalities in

---

*In New Jersey's Fifth District, which includes Paterson, Democrat Bill Pascrell challenged incumbent congressman Bill Martini in 1996. According to Martini's polls, he was well ahead on election eve, but he lost by 51 to 48 percent to Pascrell. The reason appeared to be a Democratic surge among Hispanic voters in Paterson, inspired by organizers from the textile union UNITE.

America and have the highest proportions of professionals and managers. Nearly a quarter of Silicon Valley firms are run by Chinese or Indian immigrants.[57] On the other side, Filipinos are primarily working class and are heavily unionized. Among Asians, as among Hispanics, union members are much more likely to vote Democratic.

In the 1990s, Asian-Americans[58] had the fastest rate of increase of any minority group. Their numbers swelled 59.4 percent compared to 57.9 percent for Hispanics.[59] They have gone from 2.8 to 3.9 percent of the population[60] and are now about 2 percent of the voting electorate.[61] The largest numbers of Asians are found in California, New York, Hawaii, Texas, New Jersey, Illinois, and Washington state.[62] Since World War II, Japanese-Americans and Filipinos have been the most consistently Democratic voters. The Japanese supported the Democrats' commitment to civil rights and the Filipinos were drawn by the Democrats' New Deal economics. The Chinese who emigrated after World War II and the Vietnamese who came after the war were the most Republican, largely because they identified the Republicans with opposition to Chinese and Vietnamese communism. In addition, many of the Chinese owned small businesses and opposed Democrats as the party of labor unions and blacks.

In the nineties, however, these different groups came together in the Democratic Party. The Chinese, who are by far the single largest group of Asian-Americans, were impressed by Clinton's "new Democratic" politics and his appointments of Chinese-Americans. Says David Lee, the executive director of the Chinese American Voter Education Committee, "Clinton was a different kind of Democrat, he was a founder of the DLC, and they had distanced themselves from the party's labor and African-American roots." At the same time, Chinese-Americans were offended by a succession of Republican actions in Washington. In 1996, Wyoming senator Alan Simpson introduced a bill restricting immigration, and Republicans adopted a welfare reform measure that denied benefits to legal residents. After the 1996 election, Republicans tried to tar Asian-American contributors to the Clinton campaign, and in December 1997 Senate Republicans refused to confirm a prominent Chinese-American, Bill Lann Lee, as assistant attorney general for civil rights. By 1998, Chinese-Americans were voting Democratic. An extensive national postelection poll found Chinese-Americans backing Al Gore over George W. Bush 64–21 percent.[63]

Vietnamese also shifted their political allegiance in the 1990s. As memories of the war faded, many working-class Vietnamese began supporting the Democrats on economic grounds. A *Los Angeles Times* survey of Vietnamese voters in Orange County's "Little Saigon" concluded that these voters were becoming Democratic because they were "becoming more concerned about issues such as medicare, social security, and programs for the poor."[64] According to the national survey just cited, Vietnamese voters supported Gore over Bush 54–35 percent.[65] All in all, the survey suggested that Asian-American voters favored Gore 55–26 percent (with 18 percent refusing to state or not sure).[66]

Writing in *The Emerging Republican Majority*, Kevin Phillips mused that it was possible for Republicans to cede the minority vote and still win elections. Reagan's victory in the 1966 California gubernatorial contest tended "to disprove," Phillips wrote, that "minority group support is a mandatory ingredient of Republican victory in a big-city state." But that was when minorities were not much more than one-tenth of the electorate. Asian, Hispanic, black, and other minority voters, swelled by the enormous wave of immigration during the 1990s, now are about 19 percent of the voting electorate, and they gave Gore at least 75 percent support in the 2000 election.[67] Over the next decade, this bloc of voters is expected to continue to increase and, extrapolating from recent trends, could make up nearly a quarter of the electorate. If these voters remain solidly Democratic, they will constitute a formidable advantage for any Democratic candidate.

Democrats could suffer from an embarrassment of political riches. As Democrats have gained majorities in cities or states, assuring a politician with united Democratic support of victory, turf battles have begun to break out among the members of the Democratic coalition. These have pitted blacks against Hispanics or both against whites. In Los Angeles's 2001 mayoral election, a Hispanic candidate lost out to a white candidate who had black support. Both were Democrats, but the tension that the election caused could weaken Democratic prospects in future city elections. In New York City that year, Mark Green, a white liberal Democrat, fought a bitter primary battle against a Puerto Rican opponent, who was backed by Al Sharpton, an African-American demagogue who has thrived on creating racial division.[68] Green won the primary, but defections from Hispanics and blacks helped elect his opponent Michael Bloomberg, a former Democrat who had become a Republican because he thought he had a better chance of winning the Republican than the Democratic primary. New York remained a Democratic city, but racial divisions had prevented the Democratic candidate from winning the mayoralty. These kind of intraparty battles could eventually disrupt a national Democratic majority the way conflicts between the religious right and moderates have undermined the conservative Republican majority, but that danger probably lies well in the future—*after* the Democratic majority has emerged.

IV. THE WHITE WORKING CLASS

From 1932 to 1964, the Democrats were the party of the white working class, and particularly of blue-collar and service workers, who in 1950 constituted about half the workforce.[69] The Democrats enjoyed the overwhelming support of these workers just as Republicans enjoyed the support of upper-income business executives and professionals. From 1932 through 1960, voting for Democrats among whites was inversely proportional to their income and the power and status of their occupation. You could put a line through a pyramid depicting the distribution of income and the status of occupational groups, and you'd have a rough estimate of Democratic and Republican support (see chart). In 1960, for instance, 57 percent of blue-collar whites identified themselves as Democrats and only 26 percent as Republicans.[70] Heavy Democratic support among these and other white working-class voters, who made up well over half of the voting electorate, was enough to win elections.[71]

The Democrats sustained this support by their populist rhetoric branding the Republicans as the party of the rich and powerful (Truman asked voters in 1948 to elect a Congress "that will work in the interests of the common people and not in the interests of the men who have all the money"[72]) and by their support for New Deal reforms, including social security, the minimum wage, unemployment insurance, and the Wagner National Labor Relations Act. They also benefited from the postbellum commitment of the Confederate South to the Democratic Party and by the support of unions, which, by the late 1940s, could claim around 60 percent or more of the Northern blue-collar workforce.[73]

Since 1964, the white working class has undergone two dramatic

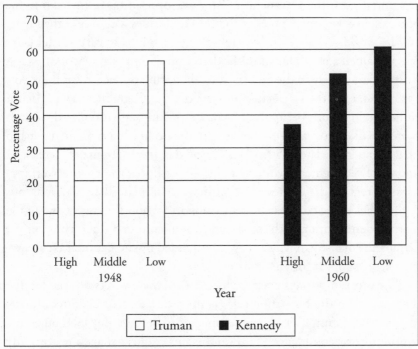

**Democratic Presidential Vote among Whites
by Socioeconomic Status: 1948 and 1960**

Source: Everett Carll Ladd Jr. with Charles D. Hadley, *Transformations of the American Party System: Political Coalitions from the New Deal to the 1970s* (New York: Norton, 1975).

political shifts. First, in the 1960s, it turned against Democratic candidates. In the 1968 election, 64 percent of white working-class voters supported either Nixon or Wallace against Democrat Hubert Humphrey. In 1972, 70 percent backed Nixon against McGovern. In 1980, 57 percent voted for Reagan against Carter; in 1984, 65 percent voted for Reagan against Mondale; and in 1988, 60 percent voted for Bush against Dukakis.[74] Then in the 1990s, some of these voters began to return to the Democratic Party. In the 1992 election, Clinton actually won the white working-class vote from Bush 39–38 percent (the remainder voted for Perot); and in 1996, he won it again from Dole by doing particularly well among white working-class women. Gore lost back some of these votes, but there were still significant gains for Democrats from 1988 to 2000 among these voters.

As we saw in chapter 1, the main reason that white working-class voters initially left the Democratic Party was opposition to the civil rights movement—and more broadly, the cluster of issues with race at their core. White working-class identification of the Democratic Party with blacks has remained a major factor in the defection of some white working-class voters, particularly in the South. The other principal factor was these voters' belief, after the Carter administration, that Republicans were better at maintaining prosperity than Democrats. Although unionized workers were less likely to reach this conclusion, the decline in union membership that began in the late 1950s and accelerated in the 1970s made these views more prevalent among white workers.[75] In addition, some white working-class voters in the Protestant South were influenced by the religious right. They objected to Democratic support for abortion rights and to the party's identification with the sixties counterculture. Other whites in the rural and small-town Midwest were offended by the national Democratic Party's support for gun control.

The most important reason why many of these voters returned to the Democrats in the early nineties was the recession that occurred during the Bush administration. The recession wiped out not only jobs, but white working-class confidence that Republicans could manage the economy better than Democrats. Clinton also successfully countered the image of the Democrats as the "black party" by his advocacy of welfare reform and the death penalty and by a publicized spat with the Reverend Jesse Jackson on the eve of the Democratic convention. Clinton's success in 1992 and 1996 was particularly notable among unionized white working-class voters—a group that would be most susceptible to the Democrats' economic argument. Reagan had won these voters in 1980 and 1984, and Bush had barely lost them 52–48 percent in 1988, but Clinton won them by an average of 23 percent in 1992 and in 1996.

Gore's problems with white working-class voters were due partly to his political ineptitude and to the shadow that the Clinton scandals had cast over his campaign. But they were also due, ironically, to the boom of the late 1990s; in such flush times, working-class voters thought less about the economy and more about the issues on which they preferred Republicans, such as gun control, abortion, or affirmative action. Gore did particularly poorly among white working-class voters in rural areas and in the South—the two groups most susceptible to Republican appeals on these issues. (White working-class voters in rural areas, for instance, preferred Bush over Gore by 35 percent.) But the economic slowdown that began soon after George W. Bush took office is likely to lead many of these voters to pay renewed attention to economic issues, especially as their focus shifts back from the war on terror to domestic concerns. This should benefit Democratic candidates for years to come.*

The white working class's move back to the Democrats has also been spurred by the change in the composition of the working class. In 1948, about two-thirds of the workforce was white men, and the bulk of these white men worked at blue-collar manufacturing and construction jobs or at blue-collar service jobs like janitor or warehouseman. By 2000, working-class whites still constituted about 70 percent of the working class, but they had become a much more diverse group. There were almost as many women workers as men, and only three out of ten working-class whites were engaged in goods production. Many now worked in hospitals, schools, offices, and stores. Many were government employees.

Different influences impinged on this new group. White working-class women began voting much more Democratic than white working-class men. In the states that Gore won in 2000, he got 52 percent of white working-class women, and just 40 percent of their male counterparts. Overall, white workers who lived in large metropolitan areas were more

---

*Some indication of how this might happen appeared in the results of the 2001 Virginia gubernatorial election. The small-town, rural districts in southern Virginia, dominated by tobacco growing and textiles, had been overwhelmingly Democratic until 1964, when, in response to the national Democrats' support for civil rights, they backed Goldwater in 1964, and Nixon and Wallace in 1968. In subsequent elections, this area, dubbed Southside, supported either Republicans or very conservative Democrats. But in 2001, as unemployment in the area rose, moderate Democratic candidate Mark Warner, promising to bring high-technology growth, won the area's voters in the November election. Warner did not fudge his commitment to civil rights, but he did promise not to strengthen the state's gun control laws and appealed to the area's voters by sponsoring a NASCAR team and recruiting country singers for campaign ads. By contrast, the Democratic candidate for attorney general, an African-American who called for tougher gun laws and a moratorium on the death penalty, lost overwhelmingly to his Republican opponent among the same voters. See John B. Judis, "Coming Attractions," *American Prospect*, December 3, 2001.

inclined to vote for the Democrats than workers who lived in small towns or rural areas. In 1988, for instance, Dukakis lost to Bush among working-class whites in large urban areas 57–44 percent. Gore won these voters in 2000, 49–46 percent. Meanwhile, Gore actually lost white working-class voters in rural areas by almost 20 points more than Dukakis did. Fortunately for the Democrats, many more white working-class voters live in metropolitan than in rural areas.

Democrats did best among those white working-class voters who had been most dramatically affected by the experience of the sixties and by the transition to postindustrial society. These included not only working women, but men and women who lived in large metropolitan areas that have been transformed over the last four decades from manufacturing centers to centers for production of services and ideas. A white working-class voter in Seattle's King County or in the Boulder-Denver area is likely to support the right to abortion and the need for environmental regulation and to place some importance on being racially tolerant. In the Denver-Boulder area, for example, working-class whites backed Gore 53–38 percent, with only a few percentage points separating men and women in the group.

The key to Democratic victories in the 1990s was combining majorities in the three McGovern constituencies—women (especially the working, single, and highly educated), professionals, and minorities—with a respectable showing among white working-class voters. This is true nationally, as well as in state-level races Democrats have won, including in those states where the national ticket has not done well. For example, if you compare Mike Easley's gubernatorial win in North Carolina to Gore's loss there, or compare Bill Nelson's five-point senatorial win in Florida to Gore's (very narrow) loss there, the key in both cases was the winning Democratic candidate's ability to attract a reasonable level of white working-class support to add to Democratic support among the McGovern constituencies.

What makes it likely that a Democratic majority will emerge over the next decade? First of all, as a result of the transition to postindustrial society, each of the McGovern constituencies will continue to grow as a percent of the electorate. And barring a sea change in Republican politics, these constituencies will continue to vote Democratic. Second of all, as postindustrial areas continue to grow, white working-class and professional voters in these areas are likely to converge on a worldview that is more compatible with Democrats than with Republicans. A continuing economic slowdown could also move white working-class voters back to the Democrats. Of course, all these constituencies overlap with one another— for instance, many working women are professionals as well as white working class—but even so, it is fair to assume that if Democrats can consistently take professionals by about 10 percent, working women by about 20 percent, keep 75 percent of the minority vote, and get close to an even split of white working-class voters, they will have achieved a new Democratic majority.

Elections in America aren't finally won, however, by collections of constituencies. Our national elections are determined by who wins states. Who controls Congress is determined by who wins state and district elections. If a new Democratic majority is to emerge, it will have to stake out a geographical as well as a numerical majority. The outlines of that geography have also become apparent during the last decade.

CHAPTER THREE

The Geography of the New Majority

After the 2000 election, political commentators began referring to the Democrats as the "blues" and the Republicans as the "reds"—terms corresponding to the blotches of states that Gore and Bush won on the electoral map. And the question of America's political future has been posed in terms of who will dominate—the blues or the reds. In American politics, that's entirely appropriate, because as the 2000 election agonizingly demonstrated, presidents don't get elected by winning national majorities, but by winning states. And longstanding majorities are not constructed out of random voters, but out of support from certain states and regions.

Until the Great Depression, the Republicans were the party of the North and Midwest and the Democrats the party of the segregated South. In the 1930s, the New Deal Democrats put the Solid South together with the growing cities of the North, Midwest, and Far West to form a new majority. The Republican "reds" were confined to New England and the farm states. In the 1980s, the Reagan Republicans turned the New Deal configuration upside down by capturing the South. They combined traditional Republican support in the prairies with a new majority in the Sunbelt—a large swath of land stretching southward along the Virginia tidewater down to Georgia and Florida, around to Mississippi and Texas and across to southern California.

The emerging Democratic majority looks as if it will mirror the conservative Republican majority it is replacing. Its strength lies in the Northeast, the upper Midwest through Minnesota, and over to the Pacific Northwest. But like the old McKinley majority, it includes the Sunbelt prize of California. Over the last three elections, Democrats were able to win states with 267 electoral votes in these areas. That's only three short of a majority. In the 2004 election, these states will account for 260 elec-

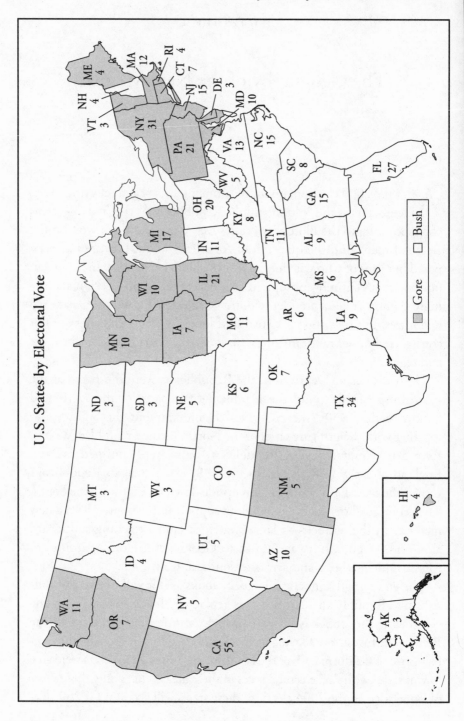

U.S. States by Electoral Vote

Gore　☐ Bush

toral votes, ten short of a majority. This suggests that the Democrats are on the verge of establishing the same kind of "lock" on the electoral college that the Republicans enjoyed in the 1980s (see map). They won't automatically win all these electoral votes—a Republican presidential candidate from Pennsylvania, for instance, might win that state just as Mondale won Minnesota in 1984, and Republican George W. Bush, buoyed by his success in fighting terrorism, could overcome underlying trends—but, all else being equal, Democrats can be assured of beginning an election campaign at a distinct advantage over the Republicans.

The major parties also represent certain kinds of industries, which are primarily located in certain states and regions. The Jacksonian Democrats united Southern and Western farmers with urban workingmen; the McKinley Republicans spoke for the new industrial corporations and banks; and the New Deal Democrats captured the new mass-production industries in the North. The conservative Republicans were the party of the military bases, shipyards, aerospace firms, and space centers that dotted the Sunbelt. Indeed, in the 1980s, the Sunbelt had 142 military bases—more than the rest of the nation put together.[1]

The emerging Democratic majority is closely linked to the spread of the postindustrial economy. Democrats are strongest in areas where the production of ideas and services has either redefined or replaced assembly-line manufacturing, particularly in the North and West, but also including some Southern states like Florida. Republicans are strongest in states like Mississippi, Wyoming, and South Carolina (as well as in former Democratic enclaves like Kentucky) where the transition to postindustrial society has lagged. There are exceptions to this pattern, of course, but they are anomalies—states like Utah where cultural conservatism runs deep or regions like California's San Diego County where the Sunbelt military ethos is still strong. Since America is moving toward a postindustrial economy, that gives the Democrats a significant advantage in the decade to come.

This new postindustrial politics is not defined by states, however, but by metropolitan regions within states. These postindustrial metropolises, which we call ideopolises, are the breeding ground for the new Democratic majority. Insofar as they are not confined to the Northeast, Far West, and upper Midwest, but are also found in the South and Southwest, the Democrats have a chance of building a large majority and of rewriting today's political map. By our count, Democrats could enjoy by 2008 a state-by-state advantage of 332 electoral votes, well more than they need for a majority, plus a competitive position in a number of additional states that might swell that majority. The key to the development of this electoral dominance will be the spread of these ideopolises.

THE ROLE OF IDEOPOLISES

The transition to postindustrial society has transformed the economic geography of the country. After World War II, industrial society was divided into three domains: cities, which housed offices and manufacturing plants; suburbs, where many of the workers lived; and rural areas of farms, mines, and forests. Postindustrial society is organized around metropolitan areas that include both suburbs and central cities.[2] Goods production has moved out of the central city into the suburbs, or even into semirural areas in the south-central Midwest. There is a clear contrast between metropolitan and rural areas, and also a sharp difference between metropolitan areas like Silicon Valley that bear the marks of postindustrial society and other metropolitan areas like Muncie, Indiana, or Fresno, California, that are still relatively backward in telecommunications, computers, and high-tech jobs.[3]

Some of the new postindustrial metropolitan areas like Silicon Valley or Colorado's Boulder area contain significant manufacturing facilities, but it is the kind of manufacturing—whether of pharmaceuticals or semiconductors—that applies complex ideas to physical objects. The amount of labor time expended in researching and developing these ideas far outweighs that in producing the final goods. That has become true even of automobile production in eastern Michigan. While much of the actual production has moved southward, much of the research and development and engineering of automobiles (which now make extensive use of computer technology) is conducted in Michigan.[4]

Some of these metro areas specialize in producing what Joel Kotkin and Ross C. DeVol call soft technology—entertainment, media, fashion, design, and advertising—and in providing databases, legal counsel, and other business services. New York City and Los Angeles are both premier postindustrial metropolises that specialize in soft technology.[5] Most of these postindustrial metropolises also include a major university or several major universities, which funnel ideas and, more important, people into the hard or soft technology industries. Boston's Route 128 feeds off Harvard and MIT. Silicon Valley is closely linked to Stanford and the University of California at Berkeley. Dane County's biomedical research is tied to the University of Wisconsin at Madison. And all of them have a flourishing service sector, including computer learning centers, ethnic and vegetarian restaurants, multimedia shopping malls, children's museums, bookstore–coffee shops, and health clubs.

Professionals and technicians are heavily concentrated in the workforces of these postindustrial metropolises. A quarter or so of the jobs in Austin (Texas), Raleigh-Durham, Boston, or San Francisco are held by professionals and technicians.[6] Plentiful, too, are low-level service and information workers, including waiters, hospital orderlies, salesclerks, janitors, and teacher's aides. Many of these jobs have been filled by Hispanics and African-Americans, just as many of the high-level professional jobs have been filled by Asian immigrants. It's one reason that the workforces in these areas we call ideopolises tend to be ethnically diverse and more complex in their stratification (various combinations of employers, employees, contract workers, temps, consultants, and the self-employed) than the workforce of the older industrial city.

The ethos and mores of many of these new metropolitan areas tend to be libertarian and bohemian, because of the people they attract. Economists Richard Florida and Gary Gates found a close correlation between the concentration of gays and of the foreign-born and the concentration of high technology and information technology within a metropolitan area. They also found a high percentage of people who identified themselves as artists, musicians, and craftspeople.[7] Concluded Florida, "Diversity is a powerful force in the value systems and choices of the new workforce, whose members want to work for companies and live in communities that reflect their openness and tolerance. The number one factor in choosing a place to live and work, they say, is diversity. Talented people will not move to a place that ostracizes certain groups."[8]

Within metropolitan areas, ideopolises come in different stages and configurations. In the San Francisco Bay Area or the Chicago Metro area, the work and culture of the ideopolis pervades the entire metropolitan area. Many of the same people, the same businesses, and the same coffee shops or bookstores can be found in the central city or in the suburbs.

These are the most advanced and integrated ideopolises. Politically, many of these areas used to be Republican, but have become extremely Democratic in their politics. In the 2000 election, Al Gore didn't campaign in Colorado, but still carried the Denver-Boulder area 56–35 percent.[9] He won Portland's Multnomah County 64–28 percent. Princeton University's Mercer County went for Gore 61–34 percent. Seattle's King County was 60–34 percent for Gore.

The Democrats' vote in these integrated ideopolises included, of course, professionals, women, and minorities, but it also included relatively strong support from the white working class—the very group that had begun to abandon the Democrats during the sixties and that formed the backbone of the Reagan majority. In the most advanced ideopolises, the white working class seems to embrace the same values as professionals, and in some of them, white working-class men vote remarkably similarly to their female counterparts. As a result, Republican appeals to race (or resentment against immigrants), guns, and abortion have largely fallen on deaf ears, and these voters have not only rejected Republican social conservatism, but also reverted to their prior preference for Democratic economics. In Seattle's King County, white working-class voters backed Gore 50–42 percent. In Portland's Multnomah County, it was 71–24 percent.[10] By comparison, working-class whites nationwide supported Bush 57–40 percent.

Sometimes, of course, high-tech development has taken place either on the outskirts of the central city or in the suburbs—with the inner city impoverished and underdeveloped. Predictably, the politics of these areas are different, too. St. Louis, Cleveland, and Detroit, though pro-Democratic as a whole, have politics marked by familiar race and class cleavages. The most Democratic groups are minorities and college-educated women, while many, and sometimes most, white working-class and college-educated males still vote Republican. In Cleveland's Cuyahoga County, for instance, white college-educated men backed Bush 55–38 percent and white working-class voters supported him 45–42 percent, while white college-educated women backed Gore 67–28 percent.[11] Voters in St. Charles County, across the river from the black section of St. Louis, used to be Democrats, but gave Wallace 19.4 percent in 1968. Since then, these suburban voters have consistently identified Democrats with St. Louis blacks and have voted heavily for Republicans.* In 2000, St. Charles voted for Bush 56–42 percent and for extreme-right-wing Republican congressman Todd Akin.

Also, in some burgeoning metropolitan areas, a county or city has become a center of high technology or information technology, but the surrounding semirural counties have been largely unaffected by these developments. Some of the counties that surround Charlotte, North Carolina, Columbus, Ohio (where Ohio State University and the state capitol are located) and Lansing, Michigan (where Michigan State University and the state capitol are located) tend to be rural or small-town and very Republican, while the central area has become increasingly Democratic. Eventually, the culture and politics of the city will spread farther into the metropolitan area, but in the meantime, the core city or county will vote much more Democratic than the surrounding suburbs.

Finally, some postindustrial metropolitan areas are well integrated between city and suburb, but have not adopted the libertarian ethos of the ideopolis. In Salt Lake City or Colorado Springs, for instance, a conservative religious culture precludes the bohemian and libertarian spirit that normally accompanies the development of the most advanced ideopolises. But nationally these areas are the exception. In most areas where an ideopolis has arisen alongside a conservative religious culture—as in the Kansas suburbs of Kansas City—the two soon find themselves at war.

To gauge the effect of these ideopolises nationally, we looked at 263 counties that are part of metro areas with the highest concentrations of high-tech economic activity or that contain a front-rank research university.† Most of these areas used to be Republican and voted for Repub-

---

*When the metropolitan St. Louis area wanted to run its commuter Metrolink line out to St. Charles in the midnineties, its white inhabitants balked out of the fear that it would attract minorities to their county. Said St. Louis University political scientist Ken Warren, who did polling on the decision, "They turned it down because blacks could cross the river from St. Louis."

†For this statistical survey, we took the fifty top metropolitan areas for high-tech concentration as determined by the Milken Institute's Ross C. DeVol in his study *America's High-Tech Economy*. DeVol's study, besides having a sound methodology, is distinctive in that it rated virtually all (315) of the nation's MSAs (Metropolitan Statistical Areas) and PMSAs (Primary Metropolitan Statistical Areas), allowing us to look at metropolitan America as a whole, rather than a small subset defined by size or job growth as in other studies. To DeVol's top-fifty list, which he termed tech-poles, we added a handful of counties not included in the Milken list, but that contain one of the fifty top national universities desig-

lican presidential candidates in 1980 and 1984. In 1984, for instance, they went 55–44 percent for Reagan. But in 2000, Gore garnered 54.6 percent of the vote in these areas compared to 41.4 percent for Bush. And since Nader got 3.3 percent in these counties, the total Democratic-leaning vote in America's ideopolises can be reckoned at close to 58 percent.

By contrast, Democrats have continued to lose in rural areas in Missouri and Pennsylvania and in many low-tech metropolitan areas like Greenville, South Carolina, that have not made the postindustrial transition. In all, Gore lost the nonideopolis counties 52.9–43.6 percent. Indeed, if you compare 1980, the beginning of the Reagan era, to today, it is clear that almost all of the pro-Democratic change in the country since then has been concentrated in America's ideopolis counties (see chart).

The Democrats' victory in these postindustrial metro areas is likely to translate into a national majority over the next decade. Together, the ideopolises account for 43.7 percent of the vote nationally. They represent the most dynamic and growing areas of the country. Between 1990 and 2000, the average ideopolis county grew by 23.2 percent compared to 11.1 percent for the average U.S. county and 10 percent for the average nonideopolis county. And ideopolis counties start from a large population base—an average of 475,000 inhabitants, compared to 90,000 for all counties and just 54,000 for the typical nonideopolis county.[12] Their vote should, if anything, increase in the next decade, and if the trend toward the Democrats in these areas continues, that would give the Democratic Party a solid base for a new majority.

To see how this would translate into a presidential majority—and also a majority in Congress—we will analyze the vote in each region and

---

nated 'by *U.S. News & World Report.* There was considerable overlap, but this allowed us to include a number of worthy areas such as Nashville's Davidson County, Madison's Dane County, and Princeton's Mercer County that would not otherwise have made the list. We would like to have included several other counties, such as Salt Lake City's Salt Lake County, Charlotte, North Carolina's Mecklenburg County, Columbus, Ohio's Franklin County, Las Vegas's Clark County, and Lansing, Michigan's Ingham County in our statistical analysis, but we did not want to seem arbitrary in our criteria. In the text itself, however, we refer to all these counties as postindustrial areas. (Including these additional counties in our analysis would not have substantially altered the statistical results we present.)

Presidential Voting, Ideopolis vs. Nonideopolis Counties, 1980 and 2000

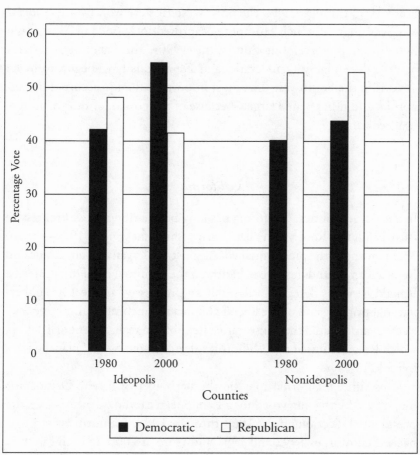

Source: Authors' analysis of county election returns, 1980 and 2000.

the key states. This survey is for readers who want to see how the new majority is actually emerging in states from California and Oregon to New Jersey and North Carolina and the major role that is being played by the development of ideopolises.

THE WEST

From 1968 through 1984, the only Western state won by a Democrat was Washington, which Humphrey captured in 1968. The West was a Republican preserve. But during the 1990s, the Pacific coast states became dependably Democratic, and Democrats have begun to make inroads in the Southwest. The most important change occurred in California, and it happened largely because of the growth of the postindustrial economy.

California

In American politics, California has long been a trendsetter. Progressive Party candidate Robert La Follette's astonishing showing in 1924—he got 33.1 percent of the presidential vote against conservative Democratic and Republican candidates—foreshadowed the coming New Deal majority. Ronald Reagan's defeat of a Republican progressive in the 1966 gubernatorial primary and of the liberal Democratic incumbent in the general election anticipated the conservative Republican realignment of 1980, in which Reagan himself and California's electoral votes would play the leading role.

This time, California may be the harbinger of a new Democratic majority. After having voted for a Republican candidate in six successive presidential elections from 1968 through 1988, Californians strongly backed Clinton in 1992 and 1996 and Gore in 2000, in each case by a margin of 12 to 13 percent. Starting in 1992, Californians elected and subsequently reelected two Democratic senators. Republicans controlled the governor's office from 1982 to 1998, but in November 1998, Democrat Gray Davis won in a landslide, and Democrats won every other state office except one. This political shift was the result of factors that also prevailed, although less dramatically, in other parts of the country: the transition to postindustrial society, which created large ideopolises in northern and southern California; the GOP's dogged and continued turn to the right; the Democrats' move to the center; and the growth of the state's minority population.

The key development was the political reconciliation of northern and southern California, which had been sundered by Reagan's candidacy in 1966. In that election, by three to one, Reagan won the support of formerly Democratic white working-class voters in the Los Angeles area. These voters, many of whom worked for the aerospace industry, took umbrage at the rise of the antiwar left on California's campuses and were disturbed by the Watts riot of 1965 and by the growing civil rights movement in the state.[13] Over the next two decades, voters in southern California, except for minority and Jewish enclaves, backed Republican conservatives, while the Bay Area in northern California remained generally Democratic, with a strong current of moderate, upscale Republicanism in San Mateo, Santa Clara, and Contra Costa counties.[14] But in the nineties, the differences between the Bay Area and Los Angeles County suddenly disappeared, and the two most populous areas in the state, making up about 45 percent of the population, both began voting strongly for Democrats.

Beginning in 1988, the Bay Area ideopolis, which includes Silicon Valley (the area with the highest concentration of high-technology and information-technology jobs in the country[15]), became even more Democratic. Voters in San Francisco and Alameda County backed Dukakis by two to one, and voters in the formerly moderate-Republican bastions in Santa Clara, San Mateo, and Contra Costa counties—wary of the Republicans' identification with the religious right—also supported Dukakis against George Bush. By 2000, the area immediately around San Francisco was supporting Gore by well over two to one, with San Francisco turning in some staggering figures—76 percent for Gore, 16 percent for Bush, and 8 percent for Nader—and even Contra Costa, the least Democratic of the Bay Area counties, going for Gore 59–37 percent. Befitting the culture of the most advanced ideopolis, there were no sharp differences between working-class and professional voters. Both college-educated and working-class white voters in the Bay Area backed Gore by roughly equal amounts—65–29 percent among the former and 70–25 percent among the latter.[16] And white female voters as a whole backed Gore 78–19 percent.[17]

As northern California went even more Democratic, the south began turning back to the Democrats. The impetus was economic. In the early 1990s, the recession and the cutbacks in military spending elimi-

nated more than three hundred thousand manufacturing jobs in the
state, many of them in the Los Angeles aerospace industry. Some of these
workers, who had been essential to the conservative Republican majority, moved out of state or to neighboring Ventura, Orange, or Riverside
counties. Others found employment in the new postindustrial economy
that grew up in the 1990s. This economy, centered around computer
services, biotechnology, and entertainment, relied on highly skilled professionals, technicians, and unskilled service workers. In 1983, there
were almost twice as many aerospace workers as workers in the motion
picture industry. By 2000, almost three times more workers were
employed in motion pictures than in aerospace (see chart). Los Angeles
County had become one of the nation's leading ideopolises.

As the economic cultures of these areas became similar, so, too, did their
political cultures. According to an extensive survey conducted in 1998 by

The Transformation of Los Angeles County

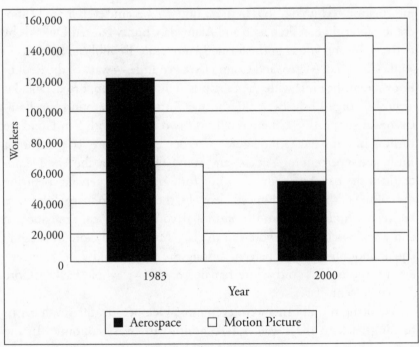

Source: California Employment Development Department Web site.

California's Public Policy Institute, Bay Area and Los Angeles residents held similar favorable views on the need for environmental regulations and the importance of government regulating business in the public interest, both thought religion should be kept out of politics, and both favored affirmative action programs.* As many as 35 percent of Los Angeles residents and 36 percent of San Francisco Bay Area residents described their views as "liberal"; all together, 69 percent of both Los Angeles and San Francisco residents described their views as either "liberal" or "middle of the road."[18]

The views in these two ideopolises are in striking contrast to those in California's primarily agricultural Central Valley, where the workforce is largely divided between manager-owners and workers, and where, except in Sacramento, there is no flourishing service sector. Even when Democratic Sacramento is included in this survey, residents of the Central Valley took a far less favorable view of government regulation of business, affirmative action, immigrants, and government assistance to the poor and were more likely to approve of politicians invoking religion. For example, residents of the Los Angeles area (61–33) and the San Francisco area (67–30) strongly endorsed the view that environmental regulation is worth the costs over the view that environmental regulation costs too many jobs. In contrast, residents of the Central Valley, again even including relatively liberal Sacramento, were split about down the middle, 48–45 percent.

As might be expected, the state's major ideopolises voted Democratic and its nonideopolis counties went Republican (see map). In 1992, Clinton defeated Bush 53–29 percent in Los Angeles and 57–25 percent in the Bay Area.[19] In 1996 and 2000, Clinton and Gore won both Los Angeles and the Bay Area by two-to-one margins.† On the other hand,

---

*The only anomaly in the survey was that while 74 percent in San Francisco supported a woman's right to choose, only 58 percent did in Los Angeles. The anomaly is the result of Los Angeles's Latino population, which is generally antiabortion, but which also doesn't typically evaluate candidates or parties on that basis.

†Significantly, in Los Angeles County in the 2000 election, working-class and professional voters both apparently favored the Democrats. In the city of Los Angeles, working-class whites voted 63–36 in favor of Gore, while in suburban L.A. County, where most of them live, the same group supported Gore 50–47 percent. By contrast, in the Central Valley, working-class whites backed Bush 56–34 percent. Even working-class white women voted 55–39 percent Republican. (Authors' analysis of VNS data.)

California's Counties

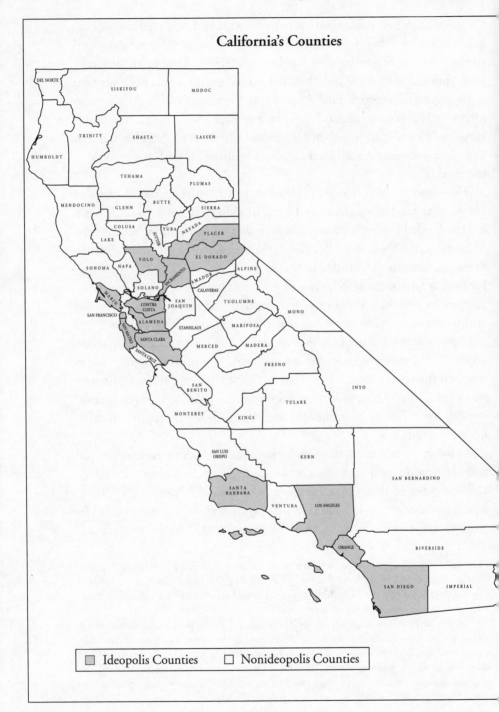

☐ Ideopolis Counties   ☐ Nonideopolis Counties

Clinton just tied 39–39 percent in the Central Valley in 1992 and lost the region by 4 percent to Dole in 1996.[20] Then, in 2000, even while winning Sacramento, Gore was handily defeated by George W. Bush 54–42 percent in the overall Central Valley.

In the state as a whole, Gore won the ideopolis counties, but lost the counties that have not yet been transformed by the postindustrial economy. California's fourteen ideopolis counties, which made up 69 percent of the overall vote, supported Gore 57–38 percent, while the forty-four nonideopolis counties supported Bush 49–46. Bush did win two areas of high-tech concentration in Orange County and San Diego County south of Los Angeles, but in these counties, the religious right has had a strong presence, and the military continues to be a leading employer. Even so, both these areas have become far less Republican over the last two decades—a result of the impact of the postindustrial economy and of the growth in the Hispanic and Asian populations. George Bush carried San Diego by 22 points in 1988, but his son carried it by only 4 points, 50–46.

The other factor that has transformed California into a Democratic bulwark is growing support from Hispanics and Asians, who by 2000 made up 44 percent of the population in California and about 20 percent of the voting electorate statewide and 57 percent of the population in Los Angeles County (see chart[21]). Latinos had been pro-Democratic throughout the twentieth century, but Reagan and other Republican candidates could hope to get as much as 40 percent of the California Latino vote. Until the 1990s, Democrats were lucky to get half of the Asian vote, which included pro-Republican Chinese-Americans and Vietnamese-Americans.

But over the next eight years, Hispanics became decidedly more Democratic than before, especially in state elections, and Asians became dependably Democratic. What moved many new Hispanics into the Democratic column was the 1994 governor's race. In that race, the Republican incumbent, Pete Wilson, faced with a stagnant economy, played a version of the race card that the party had successfully used in the sixties and seventies to win office. He tried to blame the lingering slowdown in the California economy on illegal Mexican immigrants. Wilson championed Proposition 187 to deny public services to the children of these illegal immigrants. Wilson won against an inept opponent, but he deeply alienated Hispanic voters. After Proposition 187, the Republicans' share of the Hispanic vote has consistently been low. In the 1998 guber-

California's Population by Race and Ethnic Group

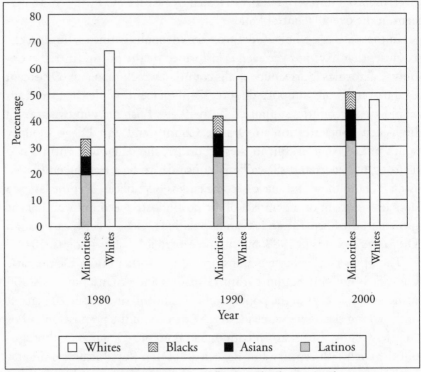

Sources: Mark Baldassare, *California in the New Millennium: The Changing Social and Political Landscape* (Berkeley, Cal.: University of California Press, 2000); and authors' analysis of 1990 and 2000 census data.

natorial race, the Republican candidate, Dan Lungren, only got about 20 percent of the Hispanic vote, which by then accounted for 14 percent of the electorate in California. In the 1996 presidential election, Clinton got about 73 percent of the Hispanic vote against Bob Dole, who championed an English-only requirement, and in 2000, Gore got 71 percent against Bush, even though Bush, speaking Spanish, vigorously campaigned among Hispanics.[22]

Asians, too, have moved Democratic. As we recounted in chapter 2, Chinese-Americans and Vietnamese-Americans, in particular, became more Democratic in the 1990s. In the 2000 election, Gore easily defeated

Bush by about 57–40 percent in California among Asian voters (one survey had the margin as high as 63–33).[23]

The growth of the Hispanic population has been particularly important in changing Orange County's politics. Hispanics make up about 31 percent of Orange County's population, but 62 percent of the forty-sixth congressional district, which includes Santa Ana, the largest city in Orange County. Until 1996, the congressional seat was held by arch-conservative Republican Robert Dornan, who won with a coalition of white and Vietnamese-American voters. But in 1996, Dornan was defeated for reelection by Mexican-American businesswoman Loretta Sanchez. And Clinton also beat Dole in the district, which had always been Republican, 49–41 percent. After the election, Dornan charged that Sanchez had stolen the election with votes from illegal immigrants. Dornan's charge further inflamed California's Hispanics and ensured that in their rematch in 1998, Sanchez would defeat Dornan easily, 56–39 percent. In 2000—a final indication of how Orange County had changed—Gore would carry this district 54–42 percent and Ralph Nader would get 2 percent of the vote.

Oregon and Washington

Both Oregon and Washington went Democratic in 1988, the same year that Democrats began to win Silicon Valley in California. Both states had residual New Deal voters, especially among unionized workers in Washington, but their dramatic shift into the Democratic column occurred because of the growth of the ideopolises around Portland's Multnomah County, which accounts for 45.7 percent of Oregon's votes, and around Seattle's King County, which accounts for 43.3 percent of Washington's vote.

Both states typify the new progressive centrist politics. The voters back regulatory capitalism, but are wary of ambitious social engineering. Perot got 24 percent in Washington in 1992, and in 1994, the state's voters, alienated by Clinton's policy failures, backed Republicans, leading to a seven-to-two Republican edge in Congress. But Clinton's increased effectiveness, especially on economics, and move to the center, combined with the Republican Party's capture by Southern conservatives, moved Washington voters back into the Democratic column. By November 2000, Democrats had six of nine congressional seats, both Senate seats (both of which were held by women), control of every major state position except commissioner of public lands, and control of both legislative houses. In both states, the Democrats' hold looks as if it will strengthen. Along with Hawaii, New Mexico (which combines a Hispanic and high-tech vote), and California, they form a solid Democratic majority in the West for years to come.

Arizona, Colorado, and Nevada

Much of Nevada votes like California's Central Valley, but the fastest-growing area in Nevada—and one of the fastest in the country—is Las Vegas's Clark County. It added about 630,000 residents in the 1990s, over a third of whom were Hispanic. Las Vegas's economy, based around entertainment, resembles that of Los Angeles, and it is voting increasingly like Los Angeles. After voting for George Bush in 1988 by 56–41 percent, it supported Clinton twice, and Gore in 2000, giving the Democratic candidate a higher percentage of the vote each time. If Clark County's population continues to grow at the rate it has been and continues trending politically as it has, Nevada could become dependably Democratic in the next decade.

In Colorado and Arizona, Democrats have begun to make inroads. Democratic hopes in Arizona, which backed Clinton in 1996, depend upon the growing Tucson-area ideopolis, which is pro-Democratic, and upon the rising Hispanic population, which went from 19 to 25 percent of the state in the 1990s. In addition, the Democrats could benefit from a continuing pro-Democratic trend in Phoenix's Maricopa County, the largest county in Arizona and the county with the largest growth in the nation. In 1988, Bush senior carried Maricopa 65–34 percent; in 2000, his son's margin was down to just 53–43, a swing of 21 points toward the Democrats.

Colorado might also go Democratic over the next decade. Granted, rural Colorado votes like Wyoming, while Colorado Springs's El Paso County is influenced by the religious right and the culture of the military. (It is home to the Air Force Academy and to conservative evangelist James

Dobson's Focus on the Family.) But the Denver and Boulder area votes like the San Francisco Bay Area. And Colorado's pro-Democratic Hispanic population grew from 13 to 17 percent of the state in the 1990s. After backing Clinton in 1992, Colorado did support Dole in 1996 and Bush in 2000, but Clinton barely lost in 1996—Nader's vote provided the difference—and Bush benefited in 2000 from an even larger Nader vote—5.25 percent—and from Gore's failure to campaign in the state. Democrats should stand a good chance of winning Colorado in the future.

The Republican West

Idaho, Wyoming, Montana, and Alaska vote like western Washington, rural Oregon, and parts of the Central Valley of California—which is to say, they view the national Democratic Party as an alien force dominated by labor, Eastern cities, and minorities. What helps Democrats in suburban California or New Jersey—support for gun control, federal land management, environmentalism, and feminism—kills them in many of these states. To win in these states—or in Nebraska, Kansas, South and North Dakota—a Democrat has to be deeply rooted in the state's culture,

Summary: Democratic Prospects in the West in the Next Decade

Solid Democratic	Leaning Democratic	Leaning GOP, but Competitive	Solid GOP
California	Nevada	Arizona	Alaska
Hawaii		Colorado	Idaho
New Mexico			Montana
Oregon			Utah
Washington			Wyoming
82 electors	5 electors	19 electors	18 electors

fight fiercely for the state's special interests, and, if necessary, distance her- or himself from the national party. A national Democratic candidate can generally only win in these states if the Republican is unpopular—as Clinton showed in Montana in 1992.

Utah contains a postindustrial area in Salt Lake City and several other smaller concentrations of high-tech research and development, but it has not adopted the bohemian culture of the ideopolis. Instead, its culture and its politics are shaped by the omnipresent Mormon religion, which opposes homosexuality, looks askance at feminism, and until 1978 prohibited blacks from being pastors. As a result, it is dependably Republican.

THE NORTHEAST

After the Civil War, the Northeast was the most Republican area in the nation for a long while. Even during Roosevelt's New Deal years, Vermont and Maine remained solidly Republican. In the 1948 presidential election, the Northeast, from Maine down to Maryland, except for Massachusetts and Rhode Island, voted for Republican Thomas Dewey. But Northeastern Republicanism bore little resemblance to the conservative Sunbelt Republicanism of Goldwater and Reagan, and after the recession of the early nineties and the capture of the Republican Party by the extreme right, the Northeast began to move strongly into the Democratic column.

The Northeast has become to the emerging Democratic majority what the South was to the conservative Republican majority of the 1980s. In the last three presidential elections, only New Hampshire and West Virginia went Republican, and only once. And while Republicans still hold some key congressional seats and governorships, it's mostly out of historical habit. Northeastern Republicans like New York congressman Jack Quinn, Maryland congresswoman Connie Morella, or Rhode Island senator Lincoln Chafee are moderates whose voting records are largely indistinguishable from moderate Democrats—and in a few cases, a little more liberal. Eventually, when these senators and House members retire, Democrats are likely to replace them. And in some cases, it may not even take that long, since there's always the possibility of defecting as did Long Island congressman Michael Forbes (who was then denied reelection when a left-wing Democrat defeated him in the primary) and as did Vermont senator James Jeffords in 2001.

New Jersey

One of the latest, and most significant, states to go Democratic has been New Jersey. Like California, it has been a bellwether state that went with the winner in the presidential election twenty-two of twenty-five times in the twentieth century. It supported the Republican nominee from 1968 through 1988, but has now backed Democrats three times in a row. Republicans controlled the governor's office and a majority of the House seats in the midnineties, but all the major state offices and a majority of House seats are now in Democratic hands.

New Jersey went Democratic for many of the same reasons that California did. In the nineties, its minority population, which votes overwhelmingly Democratic, grew from 26 to 33 percent[24]; the state's white working class, after abandoning the Democrats in the eighties, began returning to the fold with the recession of 1991; and the state's economy, once dependent upon heavy industry, has now become a leader in high-tech and information technology. New Jersey still has over four hundred thousand manufacturing jobs, about a tenth of the labor force, but many of these jobs are in the high-tech telecommunications and pharmaceutical firms that run along Highway 1 through Princeton's Mercer County and Middlesex County then eastward to Monmouth County.

New Jersey also used to be known as a collection of suburban bedroom communities, most of whose citizens actually worked in either New York or Philadelphia. But in the last two decades, firms have increasingly located in counties like Bergen and Hudson that are across the Hudson River from New York. These counties have become headquarters for securities, banking, health care, telecommunications, and publishing. The state's largest single occupational group—and the fastest growing—is professionals, who make up 23.3 percent of the workforce compared to 15.4 percent nationally.[25] And these professionals, like those in California, are now strongly Democratic.

New Jersey's shift to the Democratic Party came in an initial lurch forward, followed by a stagger backward, and then a resumption of the original movement. In the eighties, New Jersey voted for Reagan and Bush for president, and for moderate Republican Tom Kean for governor. Reagan and Bush won the biggest and third-biggest counties, Bergen in the north and Middlesex in the center, by comfortable margins. Bergen's professionals and managers were moderates who supported Republicans like Kean and Bergen County congresswoman Marge Roukema. In the eighties, Bergen's moderates backed conservative Republican presidential candidates out of opposition to Democratic economics. Blue-collar Middlesex voters, many of them pro–New Deal Irish Catholics, began voting Republican as part of the racial backlash. The same thing happened in the predominately white counties that bordered Trenton and Camden in the south. Wallace had gotten 11 percent in Middlesex in 1968 and from 12 to 15 percent in the predominately white southern counties. These votes would go to Nixon in 1972 and to Reagan and Bush in the 1980s.

But in the 1989 gubernatorial election, the Democrats reemerged as a force in state politics. Democratic representative Jim Florio, an environmentalist known as the author of Superfund legislation, ran as a moderate, pro-choice, pro-gun-control candidate against Representative Jim Courter, who was identified with the religious right's views on abortion and the National Rifle Association's position on guns. Florio won decisively, 62–38 percent, with large margins in Bergen and Middlesex counties. One key factor was women's support for Florio in the wake of the Supreme Court's *Webster* abortion decision.[26] Florio won 60–39 percent support among women under thirty.[27] Florio also gathered support in both counties for his strong environmental record and for his pledge not to raise taxes and to hold down auto insurance rates.

Although Florio's victory showed the potential for a Democrat, he squandered it by raising taxes and by championing an unpopular plan to redistribute school funds from predominately white to predominately black districts. (The school plan was mandated in some form by the state court.) Florio and his advisers believed they would mobilize the old New Deal majority on his behalf by framing the tax increase as a progressive levy. They were wrong—in a big way.[28] In 1990, the vitriolic backlash very nearly claimed the career of incumbent senator Bill Bradley simply because Bradley refused to publicly repudiate Florio. In 1992, Clinton won New Jersey, but by a smaller percentage than in neighboring states, as 19 percent of New Jerseyans backed Perot. And in 1993, Florio was defeated for reelection by moderate Republican Christine Whitman. Yet the underlying conditions for a Democratic upsurge were, if anything, stronger than before. New Jersey's recovery after the 1991 recession led to a boom in information services. Formerly blue-collar counties like Middlesex became dotted with telecommunications firms. Many of the older chemical refineries were replaced by pharmaceutical plants. The central and northeastern sections of the state became almost a continuous ideopolis.

Politically, the breakthrough came after the November 1994 election. Southern Republicans took over Congress and attempted to roll back environmental regulations—an affront to New Jerseyans, who suffer from pollution and toxic waste. The Republicans also tried to cut medicare and proposed banning abortion. At the same time, Clinton and the Democrats tailored their message so as not to scare professional and white working-class voters wary of overly ambitious social programs. As a result, New Jersey voters forgot about Florio and resumed their movement to the Democratic Party. In 1996, Clinton defeated Dole 54–36 percent, and in 2000, Gore defeated Bush by 56–40 percent, with Nader getting 3 percent. And in the 2001 gubernatorial contest, Democrat Jim McGreevey, who had been chairman of the state's DLC chapter, easily defeated a conservative Republican opponent.

In these elections, women and professionals backed the Democrats. Gore won Bergen County 55–42 percent, Mercer 61–34 percent, and Middlesex 60–36 percent. In Bergen County, Gore won 65 percent of college-educated white voters, including 77 percent of college-educated white women. In the state, he won voters with postgraduate degrees (usually a good indication of professionals) 62–34 percent. At the same time, he won 88 percent of the black vote and 58 percent of the Hispanic vote (which includes pro-Republican Cubans from Union City).[29]

The Democrats eventually picked up many of the white working-class voters who had backed Wallace in 1968 and Nixon, Reagan, and Bush from 1972 to 1988. In the face of the recession of 1991, these voters abandoned the Republicans, but many of them voted for Perot rather than Clinton. In 1996 and 2000, they went for Clinton and Gore. For instance, in white working-class Gloucester County, outside Camden and Philadelphia, where chemical plants are still located, Wallace had gotten 15 percent in 1968. The county went overwhelmingly for Reagan and

Bush in the 1980s. In 1992, Clinton got 41 percent to 36 percent for
Bush and 23 percent for Perot. By 2000, however, Gore was getting 57
percent and the Republicans were still stuck under 40 percent (see
chart). In New Jersey's southern counties overall in 2000, white working-
class voters backed Gore 55–38 percent and white female professionals
supported him 78–22 percent.[30]

In New Jersey, Democrats have created a powerful coalition of professionals, working women, minorities, and the white working class. The
Republicans' principal strength is in sparsely populated rural counties
such as Somerset (where billionaire Malcolm "Steve" Forbes lives), Hun-
terdon, and Warren. The danger that Republicans face in New Jersey is
that as moderate voters abandon their party for the Democrats, they will
increasingly be dominated by the most conservative voters, who will

Presidential Vote in Four Southern New Jersey Counties, 1988–2000

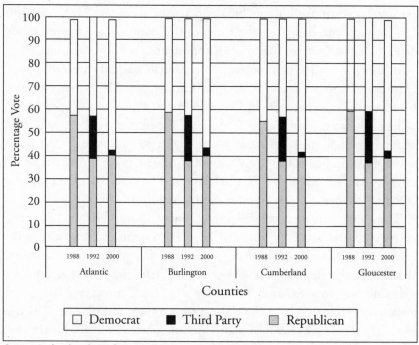

Source: Authors' analysis of county election returns, 1960–200..

nominate candidates who can't win a general election. That clearly happened in the 2001 Republican primary for governor when New Jersey Republicans chose Bret Schundler, an antiabortion, anti-gun-control conservative, over moderate former congressman Bob Franks, dooming the party to ignominious defeat in November.

New York and Pennsylvania

New York has followed a pattern similar to New Jersey's. New York City, once a manufacturing center, has become an ideopolis, with its own "Silicon Alley." Its professionals, minorities, and white working class vote Democratic. Gore defeated Bush 80–15 percent in the city, which would have made it virtually impossible for Bush to win the state even if he had carried Long Island and upstate counties. But what has turned New York into a dependable Democratic state is the movement of the populous Long Island counties of Suffolk and Nassau into the Democratic column in presidential elections.

These Long Island counties were settled by the Italian middle and working class who called themselves Republicans primarily for the sake of ethnicity, not philosophy. (The Irish controlled the city's Democratic machines, so the Italians became Republicans.) During the tumultuous sixties, however, when New York was rocked by ghetto violence, racial tension, and rising crime, Long Island politics became consumed by the white backlash against New York liberal politics. As Jonathan Cohn has written, "Fear of, and hostility toward, New York City became the defining characteristics of Long Island politics."[31] But as New York quieted under Republican mayor Rudolph Giuliani (who, like New York's mayor during the 1930s, fellow Italian Republican Fiorello La Guardia, was closer to the national Democratic than the Republican Party), the white backlash receded. And as national Republican politics became the preserve of conservative Southerners, Long Island voters increasingly turned toward the Democrats in national elections. Like New Jersey's white working-class voters, large numbers of these voters journeyed out of the Republican Party by way of Perot, but finally ended up with the Democrats (see chart).

Pennsylvania was a dependable New Deal state. After World War II,

Presidential Vote in Two Long Island Counties, 1988–2000

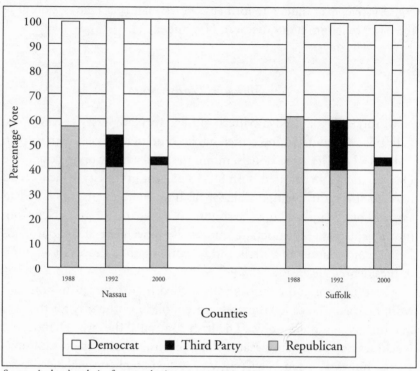

Source: Authors' analysis of county election returns, 1988–2000.

Democrats carried the state in presidential elections by overcoming the Republican vote in the primarily agricultural parts of the state and in the growing upscale Philadelphia suburbs. Democrats racked up big margins in Philadelphia and Pittsburgh and in the steel towns around Pittsburgh. In the eighties, enough blue-collar Democrats joined traditional and suburban Republicans for Reagan and Bush to carry the state, but Democrats have won it three times since then.

What changed in the nineties, though, was the way they carried it. Democrats still won the steel counties west and south of Pittsburgh, but by lower margins. Much of the disaffection is cultural, although these voters may also have blamed free-trade Democrats for the decline in the steel industry in the late nineties. (In 2000, a pro-gun, antiabortion Republican won a congressional seat in western Pennsylvania that had long been in Democratic hands.) But Democrats have made up for these losses by winning over the Philadelphia suburbs. The Philadelphia area now shows the voting traits of an ideopolis, including 58–39 percent Democratic support in 2000 among white, college-educated, suburban women and similar levels of support among white working-class voters, particularly women.[32] Overall, Gore carried Philadelphia and its Pennsylvania suburbs 61–36 percent. And the suburban counties in this area remain the fastest growing in the state—giving reason to believe that Democrats will be able to hold Pennsylvania over the next decade.

New Hampshire and West Virginia

The Democrats won every Northeastern state from 1992 to 2000 except for New Hampshire and West Virginia, which Bush narrowly won in 2000. But Republican support in both states could prove to be fleeting. What has distinguished New Hampshire in the eighties and nineties from its neighbors was that, because it did not have an income or sales tax, it became a haven for professionals and managers who worked in Massachusetts, but wanted to avoid paying its taxes. These antitax voters joined New Hampshire's rural Republicans to keep the state on the political right. But in the nineties, New Hampshire began to move left, partially out of disillusionment with Republican economics, but also because New Hampshire was developing a high-tech corridor whose voters, like professionals elsewhere, were beginning to prefer moderate Democrats. New Hampshire voted for Clinton twice and elected and reelected a Democratic governor. Gore lost New Hampshire in 2000 by 48–47 percent because he failed to anticipate Nader's 4 percent vote. Gore didn't campaign or run ads in the state and allowed Nader and Bush to brand him as a foe of the environment.[33] New Hampshire will continue to be more Republican than its neighbors, but a progressive centrist Democrat should be able to win the state in the future.

West Virginia has historically been one of the most Democratic states—it even went for Carter in 1980 and Dukakis in 1988. But the state, dependent on its declining coal industry, has been largely untouched by the high-tech boom of the 1990s. This, in turn, has fueled antipathy toward a Democratic Party identified not only with gun control but environmental regulation. In 2000, coal operators were able to rally many West Virginians against Gore and the Clinton administration, which they blamed for pushing environmental regulations that would potentially close mines throughout the state.[34] The Bush administration's political strategy is to turn West Virginia into another Republican Idaho or Wyoming. The administration has already given priority to coal in its energy plan, and the EPA chief for the West Virginia region has announced his support for letting states police their own industries—a recipe for lax enforcement of clean air standards.[35]

Summary: Democratic Prospects in the East in the Next Decade

Solid Democratic	Leaning Democratic
Connecticut	New Hampshire
Delaware	West Virginia
District of Columbia	
Maine	
Maryland	
Massachusetts	
New Jersey	
New York	
Pennsylvania	
Rhode Island	
Vermont	
110 electors	9 electors

And yet, ultimately, the state's struggling economy could push its politics back the other way. By November 2000, unemployment was also nearing 10 percent in coal counties that Democrats had carried easily in the past. Democrats can still claim the allegiance of the United Mine Workers and the support of West Virginians who look to them as the party of social security, medicare, mine-safety legislation, and the minimum wage. Plus Democrats control every major state office, both statehouses, both Senate seats, and two of three House seats. If the downturn in West Virginia's economy continues, the state is almost sure to go back to the Democrats.

THE MIDWEST

The Midwest has always been a battleground in American politics and will continue to be during the next decade. Republicans will undoubtedly retain their hold over the prairie states of Kansas, Nebraska, and North and South Dakota and over traditionally Republican Indiana. But the Democrats have established their own grip over the western Great Lakes states. The key to Democratic strength in Illinois, Minnesota, Michigan, and Wisconsin has been the revival of blue-collar support and the growth of ideopolises where older manufacturing cities used to exist. That has nowhere been more apparent than in Chicago and Illinois. It has set the pace for the emerging Democratic majority in the Midwest.

Illinois

Illinois voted for the winning presidential ticket twenty-one out of twenty-four times in the last century. It also voted for the Republican candidate from 1968 through 1988. But since then, it has gone Democratic. In 2000, Gore won the state easily, 55–43 percent, with Nader garnering 2 percent. Democrats have gained ground in the ideopolis around Champaign and in Chicago's outlying "collar" counties, but where Illinois has become irretrievably Democratic is in Chicago and its immediate Cook County suburbs.

The enormity of Chicago's shift can be gauged by looking back at the

1960 election. "In Cook County, Illinois," historian Stephen Ambrose writes, "Mayor Richard Daley . . . turned in an overwhelming Kennedy vote."[36] Nixon supporters charged that Daley had achieved this "overwhelming" vote through fraud. That may or may not have been true, but what is interesting is that Democrat John F. Kennedy's actual margin in Cook County was only 56–43 percent. It was probably closer to 65–35 percent in the city. By contrast, Al Gore defeated George Bush in Cook County in 2000 by 69–29 percent, and Gore won Chicago by an incredible 80–17 percent. With Cook County tallying about 40 percent of the votes in the state, Bush would have had to win 65 percent outside of Cook County to carry Illinois. That's an insuperable obstacle in a state that, even outside of Chicago and Cook County, is beginning to trend Democratic.

Chicago's movement to an 80 percent majority in 2000 has not been inexorable. In 1972, Nixon actually won Chicago and Cook County, and Mondale won the county by only 2.6 percent in 1984. The big shift came in the 1990s, and it coincided with important changes in Chicago's economy and politics (see chart). Like Boston, San Francisco, and Los Angeles, Chicago was once known for its manufacturing. It packed meat and made such things as household appliances, plastics, railroad equipment, televisions and radios, diesel engines, telephone equipment, candy, soap, and of course, steel.[37]

But between 1970 and 1997, Chicago lost 60 percent of its manufacturing jobs.[38] While Chicago still manufactured goods, what it made was often high-technology computer equipment such as modems or semiconductor chips. In the nineties Chicago became one of the leading areas for high technology and information technology. According to a Humphrey Institute study, the Chicago metropolitan area has the greatest number of high-technology and information-technology jobs of any metropolitan area.[39] All in all, the metro area had twice as many professionals and technicians as production workers. These included 103,910 computer and mathematical professionals; 71,000 architects, surveyors, and engineers; 49,690 community and social service professionals; 22,450 lawyers; 204,460 teachers; and 46,900 artists, designers, media professionals, athletes, and entertainers.[40]

The city itself was transformed. Once a larger version of Kansas City, it became a much larger version of San Francisco, with its theater and music, its restaurants, its funky lofts, its artists, and its visible gay popu-

Democratic Vote in Cook County

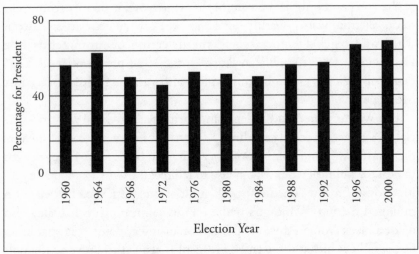

Source: Authors' analysis of county election returns, 1960–2000.

lation on the North Side. Once a city divided between white and black, Chicago became multiethnic in the nineties as its Asian and, particularly, its Hispanic populations continued to increase. The percentage of blacks in Cook County went from 25 to 26, Hispanics increased from 14 to 20, and Asians from 4 to 5. Neighborhoods, particularly on the North Side, that used to be demarcated by ethnic loyalty now became integrated.

This shift toward a postindustrial metropolis was accompanied by a dramatic change in the city's politics. Richard J. Daley governed the city from 1955 to 1976 through a New Deal coalition that combined the city's unions, ethnic groups, and blacks with its leading business interests. By the time he died, the Democratic machine was already coming apart—a victim of racial division and also of Chicago's declining industrial base. By the early eighties, Chicago looked as if it were going to become a racial Beirut. In 1983, black Democrat Harold Washington won the Democratic nomination over a divided white field. Any Democrat should have had an easy time against an unknown Republican, but Chicago's white working-class voters flocked to Bernard Epton. The low point of the campaign came on Palm Sunday when Washington and former vice president Walter Mondale were heckled by an angry crowd during a visit to a Polish-American church on the city's northwest side. "Die nigger die" was inscribed on the church door. Washington won with only 51 percent of the vote, and only 19 percent of the white vote, primarily from well-to-do lakefront wards. Washington's first term saw pitched battles between white and black Democrats and the defection of prominent white Democrats to the Republican Party. In the 1984 presidential election, many of Chicago's white ethnic voters also supported Reagan against Mondale.

But Washington died suddenly after being reelected in 1987. In a special 1989 election to succeed him, Richard M. Daley, the son of the former mayor, won the nomination over a divided black field. Daley sought to heal the political wounds, but also to redirect the city's Democratic politics toward a new postindustrial, multiethnic Chicago. His election mollified many of Chicago's white ethnic community, but Daley also made a black woman the city spokeswoman and appointed Hispanics to be the police chief and fire chief. He instituted an affirmative action policy. And he did what would have been inconceivable to his father—in June 1989, he led the Gay and Lesbian Pride Parade through Chicago's North Side. More than anything, that gesture—and Daley's subsequent overtures to gay Chicago—indicated that he knew he was dealing with an entirely different Chicago from that which his father had governed.[41] Aided by the city's boom during the nineties, Daley would not only bring Chicago together, but he would also erase the political division between Chicago and its suburbs. Chicago suburbanites, like New York City suburbanites, would no longer define themselves against Chicago, but see themselves as part of the city. That was crucial to the change in the voting pattern of the Chicago suburbs.

Chicago and its suburbs began to move Democratic in 1988, but the most dramatic change came in the 1990s. In the 1992, 1996, and 2000 elections, the Republicans would never get more than 30 percent of the vote in Cook County, and the Democratic total would rise from 58 percent in 1992 to 69 percent in 2000. In the 1992 election, Chicago's minorities and professionals voted heavily for Clinton, but some white ethnic voters hedged their bets by backing Perot, who got 13 percent in Cook County. Like voters in Long Island and southern New Jersey, these white Democrats were still leery of the national party, but in the face of a recession, they were no longer willing to vote Republican. In 1996 and 2000, these voters would return to the Democratic fold. Chicago's Polish voters, for instance, had backed Reagan both because they identified the Republicans with support for Poland in the Cold War and because they identified the Democrats with Chicago's insurgent blacks. By 1996, the Cold War was over, and Daley had largely healed the racial divisions in the city. As a result, many of these voters began to vote Democratic again. Says Chicago political consultant Don Rose, "With the Cold War's end and more of a cessation of racial hostilities, they began to vote their pocketbook and their issues."[42]

Chicago voting patterns were similar to those in other advanced ideopolises. There was not a dramatic difference between professional and working-class whites within the city. Working-class whites backed Gore 78–11 percent; and college-educated white voters (which includes many managers and business owners) backed him 69–20 percent. Overall, white men in the city supported Gore 67–32 percent and white women 78–10 percent.[43] In the past, the Cook County suburbs had been Republican in contradistinction to the city, but during the nineties, the suburbs became Democratic and backed Gore 56–41 percent in the 2000 election.*

Chicago's political shift has spilled over to the "collar counties" around Cook County that have also taken part in the transformation of Chicago's economy (see map). In the past, these counties voted like California's Orange County. Indeed, they still send Republican Phil Crane, one of the most right-wing members of the House, to Congress. But they have begun moving toward the Democrats over the last decade. Lake County backed Bush against Dukakis in 1988 by 64–36 percent; in 2000, it supported his son by just 50–48 percent, with 2 percent going to Nader. Will County backed Bush senior in 1988 by 59–40 percent. In 2000, it backed his son 50–47 percent with 2 percent to Nader. Both counties have become toss-ups and will probably become Democratic by the decade's end. The ideopolis in the Champaign-Urbana area has gone Democratic.

*In that shift, however, working-class white, minority, and women voters played the crucial role. Working-class white voters, for example, backed Gore 56–38 percent, and white college-educated women backed Gore 57–41 percent. In contrast, college-educated white men backed Bush 65–34 percent, suggesting the continued presence of managers and business owners in the suburbs who identify with Republican free-market policies. (Authors' analysis of 2000 VNS Illinois exit poll.)

Illinois's Counties

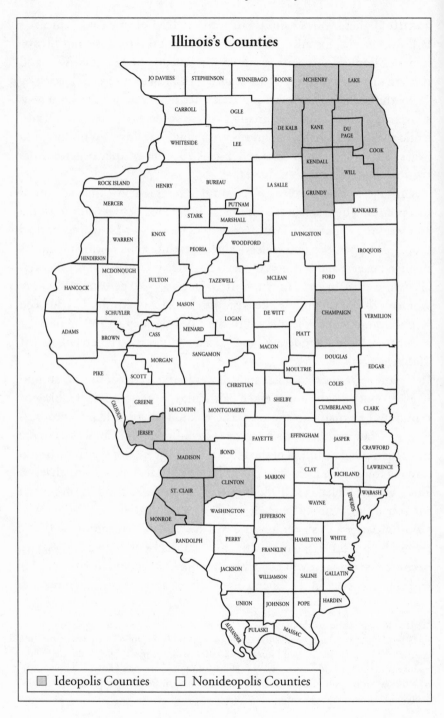

☐ Ideopolis Counties   ☐ Nonideopolis Counties

In 1988, Bush won Champaign County 52–47 percent; in 2000, Gore won it 48–47 percent, with 5 percent going to Nader.

Across the entire state, the Democrats' gains in Illinois are almost exclusively in the state's ideopolises. In 1988, these counties gave Bush and Dukakis each just under 50 percent, but in 2000, Gore won them collectively 59–39 percent. By contrast, Democrats lost the nonideopolis counties by 6.7 percent in 1988 and by 6.3 percent in 2000. Fortunately for the Democrats, the state's growth has been concentrated in the ideopolis counties. The greatest increases in population during the 1990s came (in this order) in the four ideopolis counties of Cook, Du Page, Lake, and Will. If this continues, the Democrats' hold over bellwether Illinois looks secure for the early twenty-first century.

The Upper Midwest

Minnesota and Wisconsin have voted in a similar manner to Washington and Oregon, the other states that form "greater New England." After a brief Republican interregnum in the early eighties (Minnesota supported Democrats for president, but at one point had two Republican senators and a Republican governor), both states have become dependably Democratic. The Democratic coalition has changed, however, from the New Deal days. Once dominated by blue-collar workers and small farmers, it now includes a large contingent of professionals. In Wisconsin, Democrats are strongest in Milwaukee and in Dane County, which houses the capitol and the University of Wisconsin and has become strongly Democrat in the last four decades, going 61–33 percent for Gore in 2000, with 6 percent for Nader. Dane is also the fastest-growing county in the state and together with Milwaukee accounts for about 26 percent of the voting electorate.

Minnesota is dominated by the Minneapolis–St. Paul metro area, which makes up 59 percent of the state vote. It is the home of the University of Minnesota and was the birthplace of Control Data, Honeywell, 3M, and other innovative high-tech companies. The city itself has almost always been Democratic, but in the last decades, the formerly Republican western suburbs in Hennepin County, the largest county in Minnesota, with the largest growth, have trended Democratic. In 2000, Gore won the county 54–39 percent with Nader getting over 6 percent. Along with strongly Democratic Ramsey County (57–36 for Gore, with 6 percent for Nader) this gives the Democrats overwhelming dominance of over one-third of Minnesota's vote.

Like Washington and Oregon, Minnesota and Wisconsin also have a history of supporting political reform and third-party efforts—from the farmer-labor parties of the 1920s to John Anderson, Perot, Minnesota governor Jesse Ventura, and Nader. Gore should have won easily in 2000, but barely won both states because the campaign ignored them and allowed Nader to flourish. Nader got 5 percent in Minnesota and 4 percent in Wisconsin. Many of the states' independent-minded voters supported Nader out of a commitment to political reform and good government and in opposition to the Clinton administration's scandals. In Minnesota, Gore did worse compared to Clinton in 1996 in exactly those counties that had voted for Ventura in 1998. Democratic Senate candidates—Herb Kohl in Wisconsin and Mark Dayton in Minnesota—ran far ahead of Gore. A Democrat untainted by scandal should be able to capture these states easily in the next decade.

Democrats continue to have a following among Iowa's farmers, who suffered under Republican policies in the 1980s. But more important, Democrats are strongest in the three counties that registered the largest increases in population—Des Moines's Polk County, Cedar Rapids's Linn County, and Iowa City's Johnson County. These counties, which are the sites of the state's major universities, have also moved the farthest toward a postindustrial economy. Gore failed to win decisively in Iowa, as in Minnesota and Wisconsin, because of Nader's vote and because of the shadow of Clinton's scandals. If Nader's vote is factored in, the total Democratic-leaning vote was 51 percent, more than Clinton got in 1996.

Republicans carried Michigan from 1972 to 1988 through a coalition of traditional Republicans in western and central Michigan and white working-class voters disgruntled about black Democrats and stagflation. But the Democrats revived in the late eighties and have now won the state three times in a row. One key to the Democratic revival was the return to the fold of white working-class counties like Macomb and Monroe around Detroit, Flint, and Toledo. Monroe, just north of Toledo, whose biggest single employer is a Ford auto parts factory, voted for George Bush in 1988 by 54–45 percent, grudgingly favored Clinton in 1992 by

42–34 percent (with Perot getting 23 percent), but then gave Clinton 50 percent in 1996 and Gore 51 percent in 2000. The Democrats' success in these counties signaled the diminution of race as a divisive factor and the reidentification of the Democrats as the party of prosperity.

But the other key to the Democratic revival was the growth of Michigan's postindustrial areas around Detroit–Ann Arbor, Lansing, and Kalamazoo in the 1990s. These areas have all become increasingly Democratic, going from 51–48 Republican support overall in 1988 to a 57–41 Democratic advantage in 2000, a swing of 19 percent.[44] For instance, upscale and predominately white Oakland County outside of Detroit is the home of the high-tech side of the auto industry, including Chrysler's research and development facility, Electronic Data Systems, and Fanuc Robotics. It was overwhelmingly Republican in the 1980s (Bush won it 61–38 percent in 1988), but it turned Democratic in 1996. In 2000, Gore won it 49–48 percent, with 2 percent to Nader. Oakland County also recorded the largest population growth of any Michigan county in the 1990s.

Missouri, Ohio, and Kentucky

Gore lost three Midwestern states in 2000 that Clinton had won in 1992 and 1996: Missouri, Ohio, and Kentucky. In Kentucky, Democrats still control the governor's office and one of two statehouses, but Republicans occupy both Senate seats and five of six House seats, and Gore lost decisively to Bush 57–41 percent. And while Democrats historically have had a strong working-class following in Louisville and in rural areas, many of the state's working-class voters in or around the coal and tobacco industries have abandoned the national Democrats over their environmental and public health policies. The state also lacks a postindustrial metropolis—it's thirty-ninth among states in the percentage of high-tech workers.[45]

Missouri and Ohio, by contrast, are developing politically and economically in ways that will make it very possible for a capable Democrat to win those states. Missouri, which was under Republican rule during the 1980s, began to go Democratic in the 1990s. Democrats now control one of two Senate seats and every state office except secretary of state. The shift toward the Democrats was the result of the same factors that worked in

Michigan. Many white working-class voters in the Kansas City and St. Louis areas who had backed Republicans because of race and stagflation returned to the Democrats after the recession. Jefferson County, south of St. Louis, backed Clinton in 1992 and 1996 and Gore by 50–48 percent (with Nader getting 2 percent) in 2000. And upscale voters in St. Louis's St. Louis County (which encompasses the suburbs and not the city) and in Kansas City's Clay County—both of which have become part of high-tech ideopolises—also turned Democratic in the 1990s. The Democrats had lost St. Louis County, the home of aerospace and biotechnology firms, 55–45 percent in 1988; in 2000, they won it 51–46 percent.

Gore's defeat in Missouri—at the same time Democratic candidates for Senate and governor were winning—may have been due to several special circumstances of his candidacy. He did much worse than Clinton or other Missouri Democrats among white working-class voters in rural areas and small towns. In the north and southeast parts of the state outside of the St. Louis metro area, Clinton had won white working-class voters 50–38 percent in 1996, but Gore lost them 60–38 percent, a 34-point swing. The late Mel Carnahan, running for Senate against Republican John Ashcroft, ran 11 percent better than Gore in the north and southeast parts of the state.[46]

Gore may have been hurt, ironically, by the prosperity of the Clinton years. According to St. Louis University political scientist and pollster Ken Warren, working-class voters, who had focused on jobs and the economy in the two earlier elections, focused in 2000 on "luxury" issues such as personal morality, abortion, and guns, on which they favored the Republicans. Exit polls also suggested that Missouri voters, mindful of Clinton administration scandals, were worried about whether they could trust Gore.

According to Warren, Gore suffered as well from being unable to communicate with rural voters in Missouri. While they had seen Clinton as a neighbor from Arkansas who, like them, had been born to humble circumstances, they saw Gore as a "Northeastern stuffed shirt." Says Warren, "Rural people tend to have an inferiority complex. They are intimidated by city people. Gore came across as a snob and a Northeast, Washington bureaucrat. Clinton never came across that way. And Bush came across as folksy. You have no idea how rural people hate that Northeast, Washington image."[47] The same problems seem to have affected

Gore in other Midwestern states and in Southern states such as Arkansas, Louisiana, and Tennessee, where white working-class voters are reluctant to support Democrats with whom they feel little cultural affinity.

In Ohio, Republicans control the governorship and both Senate seats. Its southern tier, including Cincinnati, is traditionally Republican, and Democrats have proven unable to field candidates with broad appeal. But Ohio's unionized industrial working class—after flirting with Republicans in the eighties—returned to the fold in 1988; and Democrats have fared increasingly well in the state's two postindustrial areas, Cleveland and Columbus's Franklin County, the site of Ohio State University and the state capitol. Democrats lost Franklin County in 1988 by 60–39 percent, but Gore won it 49–48 percent in 2000, and Nader got 3 percent. Even though the Gore campaign withdrew from Ohio almost a month before the campaign was over, Gore only lost the state 50–46 percent. With Nader's 3 percent, that amounts to a 49 percent vote for Democratic politics.

Gore suffered in Ohio from the same disabilities that sank him in Missouri: rural and small-town voters' concerns about guns, abortion, and the Clinton scandals, and Gore's difficulty in communicating with them. According to exit polls, 61 percent of Ohioans had an unfavorable view

Summary: Democratic Prospects in the Midwest in the Next Decade

Solid Democratic	Leaning Democratic	Leaning GOP, but Competitive	Solid GOP
Illinois	Missouri	Kentucky	North Dakota
Iowa	Ohio		South Dakota
Michigan			Indiana
Minnesota			Nebraska
Wisconsin			Kansas
65 electors	31 electors	8 electors	28 electors

of Clinton as a person; of those, 70 percent voted for Bush and only 26 percent for Gore. As in Missouri, a Democrat who evoked a reasonable level of trust could have won Ohio in 2000 and could win it in future elections.

THE SOUTH

The Republicans have been winning most of the South in recent elections, but the region is by no means as solid for Republicans as it was for the Democrats from 1876 to 1960. A few states, such as Mississippi, Alabama, and South Carolina, would be very unlikely to vote for a national Democrat. But one very important state, Florida, has been turning Democratic, and several other states, including North Carolina and Virginia, could go Democratic before the decade is over. These states could veer Democratic because of the growth of a postindustrial economy in their key metropolitan areas.

Florida

Of all the Southern states, the one most clearly moving toward the Democrats is Florida. Clinton won Florida in 1996, and Gore lost it only because of ballot irregularities in Palm Beach and Duval counties. In the same election, Democratic Senate candidate Bill Nelson easily defeated Republican congressman Bill McCollum. And Florida should get easier not harder for the Democrats in the future. Since 1988, Democratic strength has dramatically increased in all five counties of the state that added the most people during the last decade: Fort Lauderdale's Broward County, Miami-Dade, Palm Beach, Orlando's Orange County, and Tampa's Hillsborough County (see table).

In Palm Beach County, for instance, Bush defeated Dukakis in 1988 by 55–44 percent, but Gore won it in a landslide 62–35 percent, with 1 percent to Nader, a swing of 38 percent toward the Democrats. Similarly, Bush overwhelmingly defeated Dukakis in Orange County, 68–31 percent, but Gore won it 50–48 percent with 1 percent to Nader, a pro-Democratic swing of 39 percent. Even in Hillsborough County, where the

Democrats slid slightly backward in 2000 (although Senate Democratic candidate Nelson easily won the county against Republican McCollum), there was still a swing of 17 percent toward the Democrats over that period.

Behind this dramatic shift were the same factors that made states in the West or Northeast more Democratic. Florida has one of the most advanced economies in the South, and its largest metropolitan areas have moved toward becoming postindustrial and high-tech. In Palm Beach County, Pratt and Whitney makes jet engines; Motorola, pagers; and Siemens, communications equipment. Miami-Dade, the home of the University of Miami, is a major center for health care, fashion, and entertainment. Fort Lauderdale's Broward County has more workers employed in education than in direct goods production. Orange County is, of course, a major entertainment center with Walt Disney World and Universal Studios, but it also a home for computer services. In these areas, college-educated women and white working-class voters both tend to vote Democratic as they do in the more advanced ideopolises. For example, white working-class voters in the Miami area supported Gore 51–47 percent, while college-educated white women backed him 68–30 percent.[48]

During the 1990s, Democrats have also benefited from the growth of Florida's minority population, which accounted for about 2 million of the 3 million additional residents of the state. The Hispanic population went from 12 to 17 percent, African-Americans from 13 to 15 percent,

Democratic Margin in Five Largest-Growth Florida Counties, 1988–2000 (in percentages)

County (increase in population)	1988	1992	1996	2000
Broward (368,000)	0	+21	+35	+36
Miami-Dade (316,000)	-11	+4	+19	+6
Palm Beach (268,000)	-11	+12	+25	+27
Orange (219,000)	-37	-11	0	+2
Hillsborough (165,000)	-20	-6	+2	-3

Source: Authors' analysis of 1988–2000 county election returns and 1990 and 2000 census data.

and Asians from 1 to 2 percent of the state.[49] Most of the new Hispanics were from Central America and Puerto Rico and, unlike Cubans, have tended to vote Democratic. The influx of Puerto Rican voters into Orange County—Hispanics went from 10 to 19 percent of the county's population during the decade—was clearly a factor in that county's shift toward the Democrats.

The Republicans remain strong in rural Florida—exactly where the Democrats used to get their votes.[50] Escambia County, in the panhandle near the Alabama border, and Nassau County, near the Georgia border, formerly went heavily for Democrats. In 1960 these counties went for Kennedy by almost two to one even though Nixon won Florida. But these voters, angered by national Democratic support for civil rights, would support Goldwater in 1964 and Wallace in 1968. Since then, both counties have become increasingly Republican. In 2000, Bush carried Escambia 63–35 percent and Nassau 69–29 percent. Needless to say, however, the votes in these small, rural counties are eclipsed by those in Orange or Palm Beach. In Florida, growth is very definitely on the side of the Democrats.

North Carolina and Virginia

North Carolina and Virginia have voted Republican in presidential elections since 1980 but, because of the influx of minorities and the growth of postindustrial metropolises, could turn Democratic in the next decade. Three decades ago, North Carolina led the nation in low-wage manufacturing. Since then, its tobacco and textile industries have shrunk, but it has become a national leader in banking, biotechnology, pharmaceuticals, environmental services, and in computer research and development. These new industries are centered in Charlotte's Mecklenburg County and in the Raleigh-Durham–Chapel Hill Research Triangle, the centers of population growth in North Carolina during the 1990s. Once primarily a small-town rural state, North Carolina is increasingly organized around these new postindustrial areas.[51]

Like other Southern states, North Carolina was traditionally Democratic, although there were always Republicans in the Appalachian regions to the west. But in the sixties, many of the state's white working-class voters abandoned the Democrats over the national party's support for

civil rights and began to vote Republican, helping to elect conservative
Republican Jesse Helms to the Senate in 1972. But in contrast to neighboring South Carolina, where the Democrats became identified with
blacks and with political corruption, North Carolina whites continued to
back moderate Democrats like Jim Hunt, who was elected governor in
1976, and after serving for two terms, was elected for another two terms
in 1992. Since Hunt's election, Democrats in North Carolina have
increasingly relied not only on votes from minorities but also from the
professionals, women, and other relatively liberal whites in the state's growing postindustrial areas (see map). Since 1988, all these areas have
become more Democratic. Dukakis lost Mecklenburg County 59–40 percent in 1988, but Gore lost it only 51–48 in 2000, even though he did not
campaign in the state. The Democrats' edge in Durham County increased
from 54–45 percent to 63–35 percent over the same period. In the
Raleigh metro area, Gore won with 50 percent, including 55–42 percent
among college-educated white women voters.[52]

State Democratic candidates have done even better in these high-tech
areas. North Carolina democratic senator John Edwards, who defeated
incumbent Lauch Faircloth in 1998, won Raleigh's Wake County 51–48
percent. In 2000, Democratic gubernatorial candidate Mike Easley won
it 55–43 percent. Edwards and Easley also won Charlotte's Mecklenburg
County. Significantly, Edwards did not repudiate the national party,
but ran in 1998 on national Democratic issues such as the patients' bill
of rights. It's not hard to envision a Democrat who could establish a rap-
port with the state's voters winning North Carolina's electors.

Like North Carolina, Virginia has gone Republican in presidential elections, but has alternated between Democrats and Republicans in Senate
and gubernatorial elections. Who wins these latter elections has depended
on who carried the increasingly vote-rich northern Virginia suburbs of
Washington, D.C. In the late seventies, alienated by liberal Democratic
spending and criticisms of the military, these suburban voters swung the
state Republican. In the eighties, alienated by the rise of the religious right,
which was headquartered in Falwell's Lynchburg and Robertson's Chesa-
peake, they backed Chuck Robb for governor and the Senate and Doug
Wilder and Gerald Baliles for governor. In the nineties, wooed by "com-
passionate conservatism" and tax cuts, they elected George Allen to the
governorship and Senate and James Gilmore as governor.

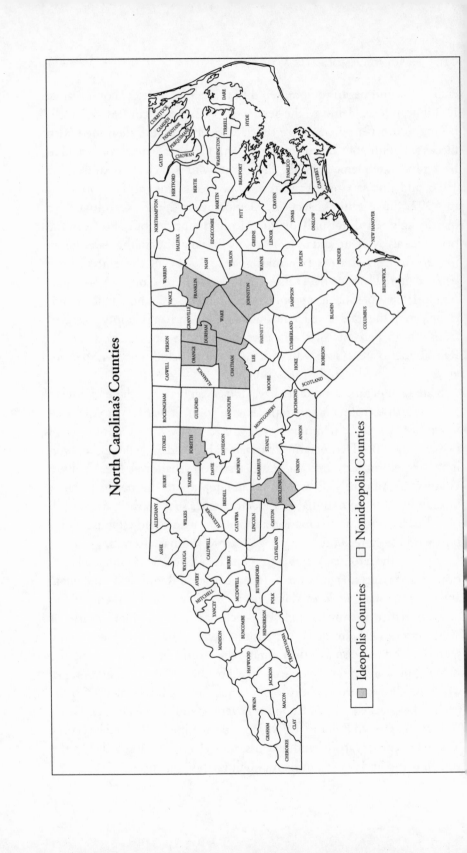

North Carolina's Counties

■ Ideopolis Counties   □ Nonideopolis Counties

But Virginia may be swinging back to the Democrats. In the 2001 state elections, Democrats won two out of three of the major offices. Democratic gubernatorial candidate Mark Warner carried northern Virginia's Fairfax County, also the state's largest, 54–45 percent. And in spite of Democratic indifference to Virginia in presidential elections, a clear trend toward the Democrats exists in these same high-tech suburbs, which contain the second-greatest concentration of computer firms in the country. Fairfax has gone from a 61–38 percent Republican margin in 1988 to a 49–47 percent Bush margin in 2000, with 3 percent to Nader. Loudon County went from a 66–33 Republican margin to a 56–41 percent Republican advantage. Arlington went from a 53–45 Democratic edge to a 60–34 percent Democratic advantage, with 5 percent to Nader, over the same period. If these suburban voters keep increasing their proportion of the Virginia vote, and if they continue to trend Democratic, they could very well tilt Virginia back to the Democrats, even in presidential elections. Certainly, Democrat Mark Warner's victory suggests this is a real possibility.

The Republican South

Republicans are strongest in some of those states, such as Mississippi, Alabama, and South Carolina, with the largest percentage of black voters. In these states, race is not just one political issue, but the most important issue, by far. Mississippi and South Carolina have recently had raging controversies over whether to fly a Confederate flag, a symbol of Southern racism, over their state capitols. In South Carolina, a Republican governor lost his bid for reelection in 1998 partly because he favored taking down the flag. "The intensity of the debate over the flag reveals that the economic issues that have dominated South Carolina's political discourse in recent years have yet to displace racial concerns at the core of South Carolina's political culture," wrote Glen T. Broach and Lee Bandy in a perceptive study of the state's politics.[53] In April 2001, Mississippi voted by two to one to retain the flag.[54]

In these states, there remains a close correlation, dating back to the Wallace era, between the Republican vote and white racial concerns. Mississippi's DeSoto County, which voted six to one for the flag, went for

Wallace by three to one in 1968 and for George W. Bush by a similar margin in 2000, giving him 71 percent of the vote. All the other Mississippi counties where Bush's vote exceeded 70 percent were also lopsided for Wallace in 1968.

The strongest Republican states are also those that have lagged behind Northern and Western states in developing a postindustrial economy. Mississippi's principal innovation over the last two decades has been riverboat gambling. Oklahoma is still dependent on a declining oil industry. The standard of living in these states is well below the national average. Taking 100 as the national norm in per capita income, Oklahoma's fell from 89 in 1978 to 80.3 in 1997. Mississippi's per capita income is at 71.6 and Alabama's at 81.7. Democrats can still win elections in these states, but generally only if they repudiate the national party and tailor their message to the state's voters. Democratic gubernatorial candidates in Alabama, Mississippi, and South Carolina have won elections this way, but national Democrats face an uphill battle.

In two of the states with lagging development, Louisiana and Arkansas, Democrats still have a good chance of winning the state's presidential electors. Democrats won both states in 1992 and 1996. Clinton's favorite-son status was certainly a factor in Arkansas, but by the same token Clinton's popularity in that state over two decades showed that its white voters, who make up 87 percent of the voting electorate, will support a progressive centrist Democrat. White workers in Arkansas and Louisiana—and particularly in Cajun country—still respond to New Deal Democratic appeals. But in 2000, Gore failed to win these voters. Clinton had won Jefferson Davis parish in Cajun country 53–33 percent in 1996. Even Dukakis won it in 1988. But Gore lost it to Bush 55–41 percent. Just as in southeast Missouri, these voters were probably heavily motivated by cultural considerations in their 2000 vote choice; they felt more comfortable with Bush, a Texas oilman, than with Gore. With a different set of candidates, the result could have been quite different.

Over the next decade, a Democratic presidential candidate could also win the electoral votes of Georgia, Tennessee, and yes, even Texas. In all three of these states, the same conditions obtain, though to a lesser degree, that might make it possible for the Democrats to win North Carolina and Virginia. All three have large minority populations that, in the case of Georgia and Texas, are getting larger at a rapid clip and that vote primarily Democratic. In Georgia, the Hispanic population increased from 2 to 5 percent and blacks from 27 to 29 percent during the 1990s. (The increase in black population was primarily a product of a reverse migration back from the North to the South.) In Texas, the Hispanic population increased from 26 to 32 percent in the 1990s, while the black population remained at 12 percent.

Each of these states also has postindustrial areas where the Democrats are doing well. Dukakis lost Nashville's Davidson County by 5 points in 1988, but Gore won it by 17 percent in 2000. In Texas, Clinton won Austin's Travis County in 1996 by 52–40 percent, and the county elects a Democratic congressman. But the other postindustrial areas in these states are not culturally and politically integrated. They and their white voters begin from an overwhelmingly Republican base, so even though the Democrats have been doing better in most of them, Republicans generally remain far ahead.

Texas's ideopolises in the Dallas and Houston metro areas and Georgia's Atlanta metro area are constructed around the model of St. Louis. Most high-tech economic development has taken place outside the core urbanized area, and the residents of many primarily white suburbs that surround the minority-dominated central area define themselves politically and economically against it. The professionals in these suburbs are likely to identify with managers and to vote Republican rather than Democratic. Even white college-educated women in these suburbs, a strong Democratic group in most ideopolises, tend to vote Republican. In the primarily white suburbs that form the outer ring of the Atlanta metro area, college-educated white women were only marginally less Republican than their male counterparts, preferring the Republican Bush 70–26 percent, while in the racially integrated suburbs immediately adjoining Atlanta, college-educated white women voted Democratic 59–39 percent.

In all three of these states, white working-class voters began moving away from the Democrats in the sixties, and while they have fitfully come back when Republicans appear to be responsible for a recession, many of them abandoned the Democrats in 2000—probably for the same reasons that rural Democrats in Missouri or Cajun Louisiana did. In Georgia, Gore got only 23 percent of the white working-class statewide vote. In Tennessee he did better with 34 percent, but a Democrat would probably need close to 40 percent to carry the state.

Still, the Democrats have a chance in all three of these states if the minority vote continues to grow, if white voters eventually experience the same kind of cultural change that residents of other ideopolises have, and if white working-class voters become convinced (as they do periodically) that their jobs, social benefits, and general quality of life depend on having Democrats in office.

A warning: This survey is not intended to show that a Democratic majority is inevitable. What it shows is that over the next decade, the Democrats will enter elections at an advantage over the Republicans in securing a majority. Whether Democrats actually succeed will depend, in any given race, on the quality of the candidates they nominate and on the ability of candidates and their strategists to weld what is merely a potential majority into a real one. Whether they can do that will depend upon the politics of the new majority.

Summary: Democratic Prospects in the South in the Next Decade

Leaning Democratic	Leaning GOP, Very Competitive	Leaning GOP, Competitive	Solid GOP
Florida	Virginia	Georgia	Alabama
	North Carolina	Tennessee	Mississippi
		Texas	South Carolina
		Louisiana	Oklahoma
		Arkansas	
27 electors	28 electors	75 electors	30 electors

CHAPTER FOUR

The Politics
of the Emerging Democratic Majority

It should be constantly borne in mind that a coalition is just that—it is not a consensus. Both the opportunities of John-son and Nixon—after massive victories—were lost when the responsible people came to believe that they could achieve consensus and basically ignore politics. A coalition is com-posed of many different factions of people who basically don't like each other much and are competing for various rewards and favors that a government can offer. The trick is finding a mixture of rewards and factors that will hold 51 percent of the voters together in a reasonable stable block.

—Pat Caddell, 1976[1]

Political majorities are always coalitions. They combine different, and sometimes feuding, constituencies, interest groups, religions, races, and classes often united by nothing other than greater dislike for the opposing party, candidate, and coalition. What, after all, united the white Southern Bourbon and the Northern black who voted for Roo-sevelt in 1940, or the upscale suburbanite from Bergen County and the white working-class evangelical from Greenville who voted for Reagan in 1984? Like these past majorities, the new Democratic majority will be made up of disparate groups and voters—from the autoworker from Jef-ferson County, Missouri, concerned, above all, about his job and wages, to the Boston corporate lawyer concerned about her daughters' right to choose. To unite these disparate groups and voters is the role of politics and politicians—and of the political strategists that they rely on.

117

The strategy, or worldview, that unites these disparate groups has not consisted of a simple formula or commitment. Only small third parties such as the Libertarian or Natural Law Party boast a unified, homogeneous appeal. Instead, the political strategies of major parties resemble the heterogeneous groups that they are attempting to unite. From 1912 to 1920, Woodrow Wilson's Democrats stood for progressive economics, a foreign policy based on national self-determination, and white Southern racism. In the 1980s, Reagan conservatives advocated a libertarian economic policy and an authoritarian social ethic. What seemed like inconsistencies to the political philosopher reflected attempts to unite politically divergent constituents behind a common set of candidates.

The search for a new Democratic majority began after the debacle of 1968. Over the next decade, Democrats would search for a strategy and a set of constituencies that would make up a majority. Three alternatives would emerge that would frame the debate over Democratic strategy: first, a *New Left liberalism* that fused a Johnsonian–New Deal optimism about government intervention with a commitment to the social movements of the sixties; second, a *restorationist* strategy that tried to re-create the status quo ante of New Deal and Cold War liberalism; and third, a *revisionism* that tried to rebuild a new majority primarily on college-educated suburbanites. The proponents of each of these political alternatives insisted that only their own held the path to success for the Democrats. But as it turned out, success did not lie in traveling only one of these paths, but all three simultaneously. The Democrats needed a strategy, and a worldview, that could accommodate the white working class, the political remnants of the sixties, and the suburban baby boomers and yuppies.

I. MCGOVERN, CARTER, CADDELL, AND KENNEDY

In 1972, George McGovern drew upon the social movements of the sixties and the broader parts of society that they would eventually represent. His candidacy was based not only on ending the war, but on the assumption that the social ills facing the country, including those unearthed by the environmental, consumer, and civil rights movements, could be cured through large-scale government intervention, financed by taxes on the wealthy and by the diversion of funds from the military. He advocated, among other things, a national health insurance system and a guaranteed annual income (a "Demogrant") to replace welfare. With Johnson, he became the model of the "tax and spend liberal" that Republicans would later attack.

The counterreaction to McGovern's candidacy set in even before the election was over. A group of Democrats led by Washington senator Henry "Scoop" Jackson and former Johnson administration speechwriter Ben Wattenberg formed the Coalition for a Democratic Majority (CDM). The CDM's purpose was to reclaim the Democratic Party for Jackson, Hubert Humphrey, and other Cold War liberals who believed that it had been hijacked by McGovern and sixties New Leftists. Their lodestar was Wattenberg and Richard Scammon's *The Real Majority*, which recounted how the white working class had abandoned the Democrats over what Wattenberg and Scammon called "the social question."[2] Their book was the Democratic equivalent of Phillips's *Emerging Republican Majority* and proved no less prophetic. What they described as the prototypical Democratic defector of the 1970s—a "forty-seven-year-old housewife from the outskirts of Dayton, Ohio, whose husband is a machinist"—became the Reagan Democrat of the 1980s. But as strategists, they were as blind to reality as the McGovernites they opposed. The constituency they championed was a dwindling part of the electorate, and at least some of the voters they coveted—white Southerners who had left the Democratic Party over race issues—simply weren't ready to come back unless the party was willing to repudiate its commitment to civil rights.

In 1976, CDM members backed Jackson for president, while many of the former McGovernites supported Congressman Morris Udall. But neither proved any match for former Georgia governor Jimmy Carter. There was plenty about Carter that McGovern supporters could like. He had been a "new South" governor who prided himself on his support for civil rights; he was a conservationist and environmentalist; he had reservations about the Vietnam War; and he favored extensive campaign finance and lobbying reform. But Carter rejected the McGovernites' "big government" utopianism. Among other things, he refused to endorse the New Left and liberal Democrats' cause célèbre, the original Humphrey-Hawkins Full Employment bill, which would have required government to guarantee every American a job.

Carter, of course, would go on to win—but only by a slim margin, particularly given the long shadow Watergate had cast over the country. Which is one reason that just a month after Carter's election, his pollster, Pat Caddell, drafted a memo spelling out how Carter could create a new realignment out of his majority. Caddell, who had also served as McGovern's pollster in 1972, produced an astute piece of analysis—the first tract of post–New Deal revisionism. While the CDM had urged Democrats to focus on blue-collar Midwesterners, Caddell argued that if Democrats wanted to create a new "political realignment," they had to reach "the younger white-collar, college-educated, middle-income suburban group that is rapidly becoming the majority of America."[3] Wrote Caddell, "If there is a future in politics, it is in this massive demographic change. We now have almost half the voting population with some college education, a growing percentage of white-collar workers, and an essentially middle-class electorate." These "white-collar and professional" voters, Caddell warned, were "cautious on questions of increased taxes, spending, and particularly inflation."

Caddell also urged Carter to pay attention to twenty-five-to-thirty-five-year-old baby-boom voters. Like white-collar, suburban voters, Caddell said, these voters, too, couldn't be expected to fall in line behind traditional Democratic appeals. "Younger voters," Caddell wrote, "are more likely to be social liberals and economic conservatives. More importantly, they perceive a new cluster of issues—the 'counterculture' and issues such as growth versus the environment—where the old definitions don't apply. . . . We must devise a context that is neither traditionally liberal nor traditionally conservative, one that cuts across traditional ideology." But Caddell couldn't tell Carter what that new ideology was. "What we require is not a stew, composed of bits and pieces of old policies, but a fundamentally new ideology. Unfortunately, the clear formulation of such an ideology is beyond the intellectual grasp of your pollster."

Caddell had grasped, if imperfectly, what the electorate of the future would look like, particularly the impending dominance of the suburbs, the rise in educational levels, the shift away from blue-collar work, and the importance of professionals. But during Carter's term, he failed to devise a political appeal and set of policies for winning over this future electorate. Carter and his political consultant were ahead of their time. They were presiding over what by then was the inexorable wreck of the New Deal coalition, from which a new progressive centrist coalition was not yet ready to emerge. Carter was faced with continuing racial tensions that divided whites from blacks in the Democratic Party and rising unemployment, along with inflation, that the traditional Democratic tool of deficit spending would only exacerbate. To stem inflation, Carter had the impossible choice of wage-price controls, which had not worked for Nixon, and a Federal Reserve–induced recession, which his own party rejected. Politically, he was pinioned on one side by a rising Republican conservatism, augmented by Washington's business lobbies, that frustrated his attempt to enact even modest reforms, and on the other side by a New Left and labor bloc within the Democratic Party that blamed him for his failure to enact even more ambitious reforms, such as the original Humphrey-Hawkins bill.

As the 1980 election approached, liberals, including some leaders of industrial unions, rallied behind the presidential candidacy of Massachusetts senator Edward Kennedy. Kennedy advocated exactly what Carter refused to champion—a massive government jobs program, comprehensive national health insurance (even though Congress had blocked Carter's modest plan for hospital cost containment), and mandatory price controls. In the primaries, Carter defeated Kennedy—not only because of voters' initial support of Carter during the hostage crisis and their disapproval of Kennedy's abandonment of a drowning woman off Chappaquiddick Island a decade earlier, but also because of public skepticism about Kennedy's programs. Public support for Great Society–style social engineering had disappeared, but Kennedy acted as though it were still there.

Carter's popularity, which was initially buoyed by Kennedy's challenge, began to sag, however, once the fall campaign began. The Iranian hostage crisis raised doubts about the Democrats' willingness to confront third world militants and a Soviet Union that had just invaded Afghanistan. The growing misery index (inflation plus unemployment), combined with higher taxes and deficits, raised doubts, particularly among the white working and middle class, about the Democrats' ability to manage the economy and fed fears that Carter was giving precedence in his policies to minority interests. Reagan's campaign took ample advantage of these fears and doubts. Carter's defeat that fall by Reagan ended the first attempt to build a new kind of Democratic majority.

II. HART, MONDALE, AND JACKSON

After Reagan's victory and the Republican capture of the Senate in 1980, Democratic strategists once again confronted the question of how to regain a majority. In Congress, a group of Democrats—dubbed Atari Democrats for their interest in the "information revolution"—advanced a strategy that would define Democrats as the party of economic growth rather than of economic redistribution and that would remove the label of "tax and spend liberal" that Johnson's presidency, McGovern's candidacy, and Kennedy's primary challenge had hung around the party's neck. A leading member of this dissident group was Colorado senator Gary Hart.

Hart was a product of the politics of the sixties who had learned the hard political lessons of the seventies. After graduating from Yale Law School, he had helped draft environmental legislation for the Johnson administration.[4] In 1972, he managed McGovern's campaign and hired Caddell as McGovern's pollster. McGovern's crushing defeat chastened him. In 1974, when he ran for Senate, his stump speech was entitled "The End of the New Deal." The title was more interesting for what it suggested politically than for its historical accuracy. In his speech, Hart argued against a standard sixties bugaboo, big government, and the alliance between business and government, which characterized at best the first New Deal of 1933–34. In the Senate, Hart became a champion of military reform and of an industrial policy that would encourage new high-tech industries rather than rescue older factories.[5]

In October 1983, Caddell produced another grand analysis, "The State of American Politics." He described a division within the Democratic Party between "its younger baby boom cohort, who came to politics through the antiwar movement and are now coming of age as elected and party leaders, and its older traditional leadership."[6] He noted that "unlike their parents, these people tend to be far more liberal on social issues, more concerned about the environment, skeptical about institutions, but also more conservative on economic issues, e.g., government. . . . The party, ideology, or individual who could mobilize the bulk of this cohort as a base support group could dominate politics for well into the twenty-first century." Caddell called for the creation of "new ideas" that would "eschew the current instinct toward incrementalist problem-solving." These ideas would not be Johnsonesque expansions of government, but "the most vigorous departure from statist government since Franklin Roosevelt's first and second New Deals." What they would actually look like Caddell didn't say.

Caddell's emphasis on generation rather than social group was off-target, as would become obvious in the 1990s. What was important was not just when people were born and what they had experienced growing up, but also the kind of jobs they were filling in the new postindustrial economy. His rejection of the New Deal, like Hart's, was also aimed at the Humphrey-Hawkins advocates of the seventies, but was silent on key programs such as social security or medicare, which were also part of the New Deal tradition. This made his rejection of the New Deal somewhat incoherent and susceptible to misinterpretation. But these failings aside, Caddell, like Hart, was trying to adapt Democratic politics to a new postindustrial society. Caddell's paper provided a framework for Hart's political campaign. Hart, who enlisted Caddell as his adviser, became the candidate of new ideas and of the baby-boom generation.

Hart's main opponent was former vice president Walter Mondale. Initially, Mondale had feared that he would have to face Kennedy in the primaries, so he had cultivated some of the same unorthodox thinkers that Hart had. But when Kennedy declared he would not run, Mondale hastily locked up the endorsement of party regulars and of the AFL-CIO. Emboldened by Democratic victories during the 1982 congressional election, Mondale eschewed new proposals and adopted a standard liberal attack against the unfairness of Reagan conservatism. He promised a jobs program and government aid to Midwestern smokestack industries. And he would later attack Hart for criticizing the government bailout of Chrysler and for rejecting the United Auto Workers' plan to require foreign automakers to produce their cars in the United States. Hart, in turn, attacked Mondale as the candidate of special interests rather than the public interest—which was a key postsixties theme and one that Reagan would later use effectively against Mondale.

Mondale deployed his support from labor-union and party regulars to win the nomination by defeating Hart in the crucial Southern and Midwestern primary states where organization mattered, but the final primary results bore out Caddell's thesis. While the overall electorate was certainly changing, so, too, was the Democratic primary electorate. In the 1984 primaries, over half of the Democrats interviewed in exit polls had at least some college—a figure that is probably too high, but even if substantially discounted, is indicative of serious change in the electorate—and these voters supported Hart over Mondale 39–32 percent.[7] Almost half the voters made $25,000 and over, and this relatively affluent group, too, had preferred Hart to Mondale.[8] And Hart had obliterated Mondale among voters under thirty by 39–26 percent. Mondale's most loyal voters had been those over sixty, union members, and those who did not possess a high school diploma—the voters least likely to be part of the new postindustrial economy. To make matters worse, while Mondale had defeated Hart in the Deep South, Hart had easily defeated Mondale in California, winning two-thirds of its convention delegates. (In northern California, the vanguard of postindustrial society, Hart had won ninety-one delegates to four for Mondale.)

Once Mondale had secured the nomination, he tacked back to the center to lure Hart's voters and the independents who had been attracted to Anderson in 1980. In his convention speech, Mondale focused on the threat of growing deficits and called for a tax increase. Mondale's newfound moderation may have helped him with upscale professionals, among whom he actually did better than Carter in 1980. But pressured by NOW president Eleanor Smeal, who had boasted that "Reagan can be defeated on the woman's vote alone," he gambled by picking an untested woman running mate, Congresswoman Geraldine Ferraro, rather than Hart.[9] Mondale and Smeal were certainly correct in perceiving a shift in women's voting, but their strategy for exploiting it underestimated women's intelligence. Ferraro was not particularly qualified to succeed Mondale as president—she was a second-tier congresswoman with no experience in foreign policy. Ferraro also quickly became embroiled in a scandal concerning her husband's business associations.

The third candidate in 1984 was the Reverend Jesse Jackson, a former Martin Luther King lieutenant who had backed McGovern in 1972 and had co-led the Illinois delegation that had ousted Chicago mayor Richard Daley and the party regulars. Jackson, whose following was largely confined to the black community and the campuses, attempted to craft a New Left message. He wanted to build a "rainbow coalition," but it would not be based on what Kennedy in his 1980 convention speech had called "the cause of the common man and woman." Instead, it would represent what Jackson called "the damned, the desperate, [and] the dispossessed."[10] Jackson's candidacy in 1984—initially fueled by Harold Washington's victory in Chicago—would founder on racial divisions (which he exacerbated in 1984 through his alliance with Nation of Islam head Louis Farrakhan) and on white voters' unwillingness to endorse a radical expansion of Johnson's Great Society that they perceived to be aimed primarily at blacks and inner cities.

In 1988, Jackson ran again, but this time sought to broaden his coalition to include small farmers threatened with foreclosure, gay rights activists, and Midwestern industrial workers whose plants were moving overseas. His platform was again reminiscent of McGovern's—one of his main appeals was to convert military spending into social spending—but he also advocated trade protection against Asian imports. Jackson would ask audiences how many of them owned MX missiles and how many owned Japanese VCRs.[11] Jackson won five primaries in the Deep South, then scored a surprising victory in the Michigan Caucus in March, garnering some support from white UAW members. But once Jackson began to be seen as a genuine presidential candidate and not merely as a protest candidate, his white support deserted him. After Michigan, he would lose every succeeding primary except for predominately black Washington, D.C., to eventual nominee Michael Dukakis.

Jackson's candidacy failed because he was seen as a black activist whose primary allegiance was to African-Americans rather than as a Democratic politician (such as Los Angeles mayor Tom Bradley) who happened to be African-American. Jackson was, as Amiri Baraka wrote in July 1988, "the chief spokesman of the African-American people."[12] White Americans might have reconciled themselves to a politician who was black, but they would not accept a candidate who they believed gave priority to blacks over whites. Jackson was a victim not only of the legacy of racism, but of the identity politics that the American left had encouraged over the prior two decades. And his defeat in 1988 marked his own last attempt at the presidency—and the end of any similar effort to be both a black protest candidate *and* a credible candidate for the nomination. It cleared the way for a candidate who could try to unite black and white working-class Democrats around common objectives.

III. THE FOUNDING
OF THE DEMOCRATIC LEADERSHIP COUNCIL

In the 1980s, the task of developing a new strategy eventually fell to an organization of moderate Democrats, the Democratic Leadership Council (DLC), that had been founded in 1985 to counter the embattled Democratic National Committee. The DLC would try to craft a politics and a platform that could overcome the obstacles that Democrats had faced in the 1980s. And the DLC leaders would look for a candidate who could carry out this politics.

The initial impetus for the DLC came from Louisiana congressman Gillis Long, the head of the Democratic Caucus and of its Committee on Political Effectiveness (CPE).[13] The CPE brought together Atari Democrats like Gore, Colorado's Tim Wirth, and Missouri's Richard Gephardt (who would not move sharply left until late 1987) with Southern Democrats like Long who were worried that the party was abandoning the South. Long stressed the importance of gearing Democratic politics to the "national interest" rather than "special interests." He wanted to downplay Democratic support for abortion rights and gun control and emphasize Democratic vigilance on crime and support for basic New Deal reforms and for a strong national defense. The positions of CPE were an interesting hodgepodge of CDM-style restorationism on defense and economics with the Atari Democrats' attention to high technology, free trade, and white-collar workers.

At the 1984 Democratic convention in San Francisco, Long held meetings with Georgia senator Sam Nunn, Arizona governor Bruce Babbitt, Virginia governor Chuck Robb, Gephardt, and others to work out a long-term strategy that could allow the party to survive the coming disaster. After the November election, the talks began to focus on the idea of a new organization that would parallel and rival the Democratic National Committee. When Long died of a heart attack in January 1985, leadership over the project passed to his chief aide, Alvin From. From had backed liberal Democrat Ed Muskie in 1972, but in 1984, disenchanted with the party's direction, he had supported Hart against Mondale. Working with another former House aide, Will Marshall, From pulled together a new organization, the Democratic Leadership

Council, that the two of them staffed, but that was composed of elected officials and financed primarily by Washington business lobbyists who were sympathetic to congressional Democrats. The DLC got going in March of 1985 with forty-three members and with Gephardt as its chair, but almost from the beginning its direction was in the hands of From, Marshall, and Robb, who succeeded Gephardt as chairman in 1986, and of Nunn, who would succeed Robb in 1988.

In a memo to the future DLC members, From had expressed his concern about the Democrats' decline, which he blamed on the "consistent pursuit of wrongheaded, losing strategies."[14] From was particularly critical of Mondale's strategy of "making blatant appeals to liberal and minority interest groups in the hopes of building a winning coalition where a majority, under normal circumstances, simply does not exist." He worried that with union membership declining the Democrats "are more and more viewed as the party of 'big labor,'" and that with liberalism in disrepute, Democrats are "increasingly viewed as the 'liberal' party." From was most at home with Southern Democrats like Nunn, Robb, and Long. He supported social security and other basic New Deal reforms, was concerned about poverty, was committed to civil rights, and wanted a strong defense, but he was also sympathetic to business's view of its problems, hostile or indifferent to labor unions, and opposed to any ambitious new government social programs.

Yet in the DLC's first years, the organization did not seek to sell this politics publicly. Instead, From and the DLC adopted an insiders' factional strategy. They attempted to alter the way presidential nominees were chosen so that someone like Robb would be nominated for president in 1988. Robb could then transform the party in his image. And the DLC did take the first step in its strategy. It got the Democratic Party to schedule an early "Super Tuesday" of Southern primaries that would, presumably, allow a Southern moderate to compete for the party's presidential nomination. But the DLC's strategy completely backfired. Robb didn't run, and Gore, the other Southerner who did, wasn't ready for prime time. Indeed, the big winner on Super Tuesday was the DLC's ultimate political nemesis, Jesse Jackson, who captured five Deep South states, one more than Gore.

The DLC, as well as New Left Democrats, had seen the 1988 election as a prime opportunity to recapture the White House. The Reagan administration was mired in the Iran-contra scandal and financial scandals. Republican nominee George Bush was a weak candidate presiding over what was already becoming a divided party. But the Democrat field, dubbed "the seven dwarfs," was even weaker. Massachusetts governor Michael Dukakis finally won the nomination only because he was the most credible alternative to Jackson. A fiscal moderate, he had no experience in foreign policy at a difficult time when the Cold War looked as if it could be ended through skillful diplomacy. And because of his opposition to capital punishment, his strong civil rights record, and his reliance on Jackson in the fall campaign, Dukakis was vulnerable to the Bush campaign's subtle use of the race card.

After the 1988 fiasco, From, Marshall, and the DLC decided to develop a philosophy and a platform for the Democratic Party. With money raised primarily by Wall Street Democrats, the DLC set up the Progressive Policy Institute (PPI), with Marshall at the helm, and hired policy experts to draft papers and proposals.[15] The most important of these was an 1989 paper entitled "The Politics of Evasion," written by William Galston, Mondale's former issues director, and PPI fellow Elaine Kamarck, who would later become Gore's policy adviser in the first Clinton administration. Galston and Kamarck argued that in the late sixties, the liberalism of the New Deal had degenerated into a "liberal fundamentalism," which "the public has come to associate with tax and spending policies that contradict the interests of average families; with welfare policies that foster dependence rather than self-reliance; with softness toward the perpetrators of crime and indifference toward its victims; with ambivalence toward the assertion of American values and interests abroad; and with an adversarial stance toward mainstream moral and cultural values."[16]

Galston, Kamarck, and the DLC advocated fiscal conservatism, welfare reform, increased spending on crime prevention through the development of a police corps, tougher mandatory sentences, support for capital punishment, and policies that encouraged traditional families. Another PPI fellow, David Osborne, developed a strategy for "reinventing government" by contracting out services while retaining control over how they were performed. Government should "steer, not row" in Osborne's formulation.[17]

The DLC wanted to counter the reputation of the Democrats as the party of "big government" and "tax and spend liberalism" and also as the party that took its cues from black militants. Opposition to capital punishment and to increased spending on police and public safety, for instance, was part of the cluster of issues around race that had driven white voters out of the Democratic Party. Bush had cleverly exploited this cluster during the 1988 campaign against Dukakis. By abandoning these positions, Democrats would be preventing Republicans from using these issues to distract working-class voters from those areas of economic policy where they might agree more with Democrats than with Republicans. Galston and Kamarck spelled this objective out clearly: "All too often the American people do not respond to a progressive economic message, even when the Democrats try to offer it, because the party's presidential candidates fail to win their confidence in other key areas such as defense, foreign policy, and social values. Credibility on these issues is the ticket that will get Democratic candidates in the door to make their affirmative economic case. But if they don't hold that ticket, they won't even get a hearing." From referred to this strategy as "inoculating" Democrats from criticism on other fronts so that they could make their economic case.

But what was that economic case, and to whom would it be made? The DLC's advice about inoculation applied to just about any Democratic economic proposal—from the defense of social security to a proposal for a single-payer national health care system.* Instead, the DLC and PPI argued, the Democratic Party should develop programs that achieved traditional goals, while avoiding charges of "big government." They advocated, for example, using market incentives and penalties to enforce environmental regulation; they wanted to use "managed competition" to hold down health-care costs while broadening access to insurance; they favored charter schools and public school choice (as opposed to private school vouchers) to improve education; they didn't call for large jobs programs, but they wanted more money for worker training; they wanted increases in government spending targeted at creating growth and limited to increases in per capita income.[18]

If the DLC had one overarching ideological creed, it was something like

---

*Massachusetts congressman Barney Frank would make arguments similar to Galston and Kamarck's in his book *Speaking Frankly* (New York: Thunder's Mouth Press, 1992), but Frank did so in the interests of gaining an audience for the Democrats' more liberal economic proposals.

the communitarian, "national interest" approach first favored by Long. The DLC expressed its proposals in terms of a "new social compact that demands individual responsibility from everyone and ties public benefits to public service." Welfare recipients should seek education and work; students who receive government aid should enroll in a new national service program; and corporations that receive government subsidies should invest in competitiveness and "treat their workers as assets who are partners in productive enterprises."

The DLC and PPI strategists didn't detail the constituencies they were trying to reach. But they were implicitly targeting Caddell's middle-class, white-collar suburbanites, as well as the blue-collar Reagan Democrats that Wattenberg and Scammon had described. They also didn't talk about how a majority would appear on a map, but their focus seemed to be primarily on winning the Midwest and the South for Democrats. The DLC was skeptical about California being the anchor of a new majority—Galston and Kamarck derided this idea as "the California dream." The DLC also didn't put stock in the power of the women's vote to deliver a new majority. Galston and Kamarck wrote that "the gender gap that has opened up in the past twelve years is not the product of a surge of Democratic support among women, but rather the erosion of Democratic support among men."[19] The DLC's 1990 platform didn't even explicitly support abortion rights.

In other words, the DLC didn't yet understand the special role that professionals, women, and minorities would play in the new Democratic majority, nor the central role that California and the Northwest would play. But the DLC and PPI's post-1988 strategy nevertheless represented an enormous step forward for the Democrats. While other Democrats were putting their faith in increased voter turnout or a steep recession to alter their national prospects, From, Marshall, and the organization's members boldly confronted the image of the Democrats as the party of big government and racial favoritism that had led to a string of embarrassing defeats for the party's presidential candidates. And they tried to advance proposals that altered that image but that did not compromise the party's commitment to economic justice and civil rights.

IV. THE THREE FACES OF BILL CLINTON

In March 1990, From succeeded in convincing Bill Clinton to succeed Nunn as chairman of the DLC. From saw Clinton as the DLC's chance to have its own candidate and platform in the 1992 presidential race. A year and a half later, Clinton fulfilled From's wishes—he resigned as DLC chair to run for president, taking several DLC advisers with him and incorporating parts of the DLC's strategy and its themes into his campaign. He championed welfare reform, increased spending on police and public safety, and capital punishment to inoculate himself against Republican attacks. He spoke of a "new covenant" between the people and the government—"a solemn agreement between the people and their government, based not simply on what each of us can take, but what all of us must give to our nation."[20]

But as From had recognized, Clinton's commitment to the DLC was only one part of his complex political makeup. Like many successful politicians, he was a combination of disparate and seemingly contradictory influences that allowed him to appeal to a wide range of constituencies. Clinton was a Southern politician, but of an entirely different lineage from Robb and Nunn.* Raised in humble circumstances and brought up politically in the Democratic Party of a poor state, Clinton was the heir of a Southern-Southwestern populism that had also claimed Lyndon Johnson, Albert Gore Sr., Dale Bumpers, and Oklahoman Fred Harris. He envisaged Democrats as the representatives of the people against the powerful, even if, at times, he acted on behalf of the powerful. When he was first elected to office in 1976 as Arkansas's attorney general, he made his reputation fighting utility-company rate increases.

At the same time, Clinton, who graduated from Georgetown and Yale Law School and attended Oxford as a Rhodes scholar, was a product of the sixties' student movements. In 1972, he volunteered for the McGovern campaign and was sent by Hart to Texas. He remained close to a group

---

*Robb and Nunn were heirs of the Southern Whig tradition, which had flourished briefly before the battle over slavery and the creation of the Republican Party forced Southerners to embrace the Democratic Party. Even then, the Whigs were the party of business and of class harmony rather than conflict. Nunn was an admirer of Georgia Whig Alexander Stephens. See John B. Judis, "Nunn of the Above," *The New Republic*, October 30, 1995.

of liberal intellectuals who included Robert Reich, Ira Magaziner, Taylor Branch, Eli Segal, and Derek Shearer. And, of course, Hillary Clinton had been part of the same circles. Veterans of the sixties, they brought to the Clinton campaign not only an emphasis on consumer rights, civil rights, the environment, and women's rights, but also a New Left penchant for big government proposals that would cure major social ills. They wanted large-scale public investments in infrastructure and a national health insurance program. They disdained the DLC's concern about deficits and big government.[21] They thought they could use the power of government to transform and revive.

Clinton expressed these different sides of himself during the campaign, but circumstances led to his giving more prominence to the populist, New Deal side than From and the DLC would have wished. Clinton had expected that his main foe in the Democratic primaries would be New York governor Mario Cuomo, a proponent of New Left liberalism. Clinton had expected to parry Cuomo's politics with the DLC's "new Democrat" politics, but Cuomo decided not to run, and the other unreconstructed liberal, Iowa senator Tom Harkin, quickly fell by the wayside. Clinton's main opponent turned out to be former Massachusetts senator Paul Tsongas.

Tsongas's views resembled those of the nonpopulist Clinton. He embraced the DLC's experimental approach to economics and the New Left's commitment on social issues and foreign policy. A Peace Corps veteran, Tsongas had been elected to the House in 1974 from a suburban Massachusetts district that included Route 128's electronics and computer firms. He moved up to the Senate in 1978, but retired in 1984 after he was diagnosed with cancer. Tsongas was, perhaps, the original neoliberal and Atari Democrat. In 1980, he had shocked the audience at an Americans for Democratic Action gathering by urging them to focus on economic growth rather than the redistribution of wealth and by advocating the deregulation of natural gas prices. Tsongas was a strong, almost ideological, fiscal conservative who believed in using market incentives rather than government control to solve economic problems, but he was also an ardent environmentalist and outspoken defender of abortion rights, gay rights, and affirmative action and was a human rights internationalist. Claiming that he had been cured of cancer, Tsongas ran for president in 1992.

Tsongas was running second to Clinton in New Hampshire until the uproar over Clinton's affair with Gennifer Flowers and his exemption from the draft caused the Arkansas governor's popularity to fall. Tsongas won New Hampshire and battled Clinton for the nomination over the next six weeks. To defeat Tsongas, Clinton emphasized his populist streak. Like Mondale in 1984 against Hart, Clinton also ran as a champion of the New Deal. He charged Tsongas with a lack of faith in social security; Clinton promised a large middle-class tax cut, massive public investments, and national health insurance. He avidly courted unions, blacks, and senior citizens. As a result, Clinton won the primaries against Tsongas.

Naturally, this move to the left had made him vulnerable in the general election, as more conservative voters began to see him as another liberal Democrat who would squander their tax money. By mid-June, potential third-party candidate Ross Perot was running ahead of Bush and well ahead of Clinton in national polls. So, during the summer, Clinton set about righting his campaign—first by distancing himself symbolically from Jesse Jackson, then by choosing the more explicitly centrist Gore as his running mate. Clinton still trumpeted his support for women's rights and for the environment, and with the country mired in recession, he continued to promise ambitious new programs in a first "hundred days" that would rival FDR's. But Clinton also emphasized his support for reducing government bureaucracy and for "ending welfare as we know it." In the end, Clinton's campaign was a blend of Caddell revisionism, the DLC, seventies-style Humphrey-Hawkins liberalism, and old-style populism, epitomized by his platform statement, "Putting People First." With a strong assist from Perot's candidacy, which in 1992 took more votes from Bush than from Clinton, the former Arkansas governor reclaimed the White House for the Democrats.

Of course, Clinton had actually gotten a smaller percentage of the popular vote than Dukakis. But Clinton did not heed it as a warning—a mistake for which he, and the party, would pay dearly. The first stumble came over gay rights, as Clinton got drawn into supporting a controversial proposal to allow gays to serve openly in the military. Gay rights did not enjoy the popular support of women's rights, particularly in conjunction with military service. Clinton also backed an economic stimulus package weighted toward poor city neighborhoods, which allowed Republicans to paint Democrats as busting the budget to pay off New York City's

African-American mayor, David Dinkins, for his campaign support. And Clinton postponed welfare reform in favor of a complex, almost unintelligible, plan for national health insurance, which, while relying on the existing health-care system, evoked fears of an overweening government bureaucracy. These proposals did much to alienate voters who had backed either Clinton or Perot in 1992, an alienation that was deepened by the continued sluggishness of the economy. In November 1994, many of them abandoned the Democrats and voted for Republicans, giving the GOP control of the Congress for the first time since the 1953–54 session. (In 1992, almost half of Perot voters had backed Democratic congressional candidates. In 1994, only 32 percent did.[22])

After November 1994, Clinton changed course. Prompted by political consultant Dick Morris, he reverted to the DLC's inoculation strategy. He invoked the "new covenant" in his 1995 State of the Union, and in his 1996 address declared that "the era of big government is over." He committed himself to backing welfare reform and a balanced budget and tried to co-opt the Republican "family values" agenda through supporting school uniforms and a proposal that an antiviolence V-chip be installed in television sets. At the same time, he and the Democrats advanced proposals for raising the minimum wage, extending health insurance coverage, and protecting the environment. These proposals were of a piecemeal, incremental nature that could not easily be labeled "big government."

Clinton's change of course might have proved too little too late, but he was aided by the conservative Republicans who took over Congress after November 1994. They introduced legislation to gut the EPA and the Occupational Safety and Health Administration; to abolish cabinet departments, including the Department of Education (which enjoyed public support except among the religious right); to crack down on immigration; and to cut medicare expenditures while reducing taxes for the wealthy. In the fall of 1995, the Republicans shut down the government to force Clinton to accept these proposals. This action did for Clinton and the Democrats what they might not have been able to do on their own: it united liberal and moderate Democrats, independents, and moderate Republicans behind Clinton and his administration.

In Clinton's 1996 campaign, he was able to bring together all the different sides of his complex political character—and by extension the different strategies for a Democratic majority that had swirled around

Washington for a decade or more. The campaign, buoyed by the strong economic growth that began in early 1996, was a success on multiple fronts, which foreshadowed a Democratic majority. Its strategy and worldview was that of progressive centrism. Clinton the populist— reinforced by an AFL-CIO reinvigorated politically under its new president, John Sweeney—flayed the Republicans for cutting medicare to pay for a tax cut to the wealthy; Clinton the former DLC chairman boasted of reforming welfare and advanced incremental, not "big government" reforms to make higher education affordable, put computers in classrooms, and provide child care and increased access to health care. Clinton the child of the sixties campaigned earnestly for civil rights, women's rights, and the protection of the environment. And Clinton, the tribune of postindustrial America, promised to "build a bridge to the twenty-first century."

The results bore out the strategic insight of Clinton's campaign. He increased his proportion of the vote from 1992 among all the key groups of the emerging Democratic majority: by 9 percent among women, by 4 percent among professionals, by 5 percent among the white working class, by 13 percent among Asians, by 11 percent among Hispanics, and by 10 percent among eighteen-to-twenty-nine-year-olds.[23] In Ohio, Clinton bettered his vote among college-educated whites by 12 percent. In New Jersey, he improved among white working-class voters by 10 percent.[24]

At the beginning of his second term, Clinton set about solidifying Democratic support among these constituencies through a series of reforms in education, health care, child care, and housing. These reforms were incremental, but like Clinton's proposal for extending medicare to younger retirees, they could represent steps toward major reforms. "Quantity would lead to quality," explained Clinton aide Sidney Blumenthal, harking back to Hegel's theory of the dialectic.[25] The new majority seemed there for the taking.

But it was not to be. In January 1998, as Clinton was about to unveil a raft of proposals in his State of the Union address, federal prosecutor Kenneth Starr revealed that Clinton had been having an affair with a White House intern. Clinton, facing calls for resignation from Republican conservatives, was kept off-balance for the next thirteen months and lost what chance he had to put the political synthesis of 1996 into permanent programmatic form. Clinton survived impeachment, thus avoiding Nixon's fate, but on the eve of the 2000 elections Democrats found themselves in precisely the same situation as the Republicans of a generation before. Instead of handing down to his successor a solid majority, Clinton had bequeathed to him a shadow of scandal that dogged his campaign and contributed to his defeat.

V. GORE, GREENBERG, AND PENN

Al Gore was a product of many of the same influences as Bill Clinton. He had been a founding member of the DLC and was the choice of some of its leaders for president in 1988. As a student at Harvard, he had become familiar with, and participated in, the social movements of the sixties, and particularly the environmental movement, for which he later wrote a book, *Earth in the Balance*. And he had inherited his father's populist convictions. But there was an important difference between Clinton and Gore as politicians. Gore had populist convictions, but having been raised as a child of wealth and power in Washington, D.C., he did not come naturally to the style of Jacksonian Democratic populism. He was an intelligent, diligent, but uninspiring congressman, and a wooden campaigner who sounded scripted even when he was extemporizing. Like Clinton, he had different sides and faces, but in public he could only exhibit them over time, and in a manner that made his audience question whether they were seeing the real Al Gore or a campaign contrivance.

In his presidential campaign, which began in early 1999, he shifted every few months from one face and strategy to another. During the first phase of his campaign, Gore relied heavily on New York pollster Mark Penn. Penn had been brought into Clinton's 1996 campaign by Dick Morris. Afterward, Penn had gone back to working for corporations, but the DLC had hired him to do polls and provide strategic analysis. As Gore began running, Penn advised him not to worry about the effect of the Clinton scandals on his campaign. Penn helped to craft a message aimed at white-collar suburbanites, or what he and the DLC now called "wired workers." This message stressed the threat of "suburban sprawl" to a better "quality of life." And it eschewed any hint of populism or class conflict, which Penn argued was antithetical to the spirit of wired workers.

The DLC and Penn had gotten the idea of wired workers from Morley Winograd, an AT&T executive in California who was close to the DLC and would later go to work for Gore. They defined them as workers who "frequently use computers that are part of a network and work together in teams."[26] The DLC claimed these workers had become "the dominant force in the new economy." According to From and Marshall, they "are optimistic about their economic prospects; they are for choice and competition in education and against race and gender preferences; they are impatient with the ideological ax-grinding of the left-right debate; and they favor a smaller, nonbureaucratic form of government activism that equips people to help themselves." From and Marshall also insisted that these workers took umbrage at a politics of "class warfare." "Outdated appeals to class grievance and attacks on corporate perfidy only alienate new constituencies and ring increasingly hollow to the modern workforce."[27]

Like Caddell and Hart, the DLC understood that as the workforce and population were changing, so, too, was the Democratic electorate. And the concept of wired workers was an advance upon Caddell's theory of the baby-boom generation. It described the new constituency not in terms of its age or date of birth, but in terms of its relation to the postindustrial economy. And it also suggested that the Democrats should align themselves with the country's future rather than its past. But the category itself had little explanatory value because there was no evidence that "wired workers"—who ranged from a telemarketer in West Virginia to an airline clerk in Springfield, Missouri, to an insurance executive in Hartford to a computer programmer in Redmond—were making political judgments based on their using computers, being part of a computer network, or working together as part of a team. If anything, the term blurred the important distinction between professionals and managers—and between workers who were inclined to question the imperatives of the market and those who were not.

By October 1999, Gore believed that Penn's strategy was not working. He trailed Bush by 19 percent in one opinion poll and had lost his lead to his Democratic challenger, former senator Bill Bradley, in Iowa and New Hampshire. And to make matters worse, Bradley and Bush seemed to have hurt Gore by linking him repeatedly to the Clinton scandals. Gore fired Penn and hired Harrison Hickman, a more conventionally liberal pollster. Gore also enlisted former Kennedy speechwriter Bob Shrum, who had written Kennedy's paean to New Left liberalism at the 1980 Democratic convention.

Gore now adopted the same strategy against Bradley that Mondale had used against Hart and that Clinton had used against Tsongas. He defended Democratic orthodoxy and the party's most loyal constituencies. His campaign manager, Donna Brazille, described these groups as "the four pillars of the Democratic Party . . . African-Americans, labor, women, and what I call other ethnic minorities."[28] Gore adopted a highly mannered populism, repeating the verb *fight* and looking stern and determined. Gore declared that he would "fight for the people against the powerful." He described "the presidency" as "a long, resolute, day-by-day fight for people." He accused Bradley of undermining medicaid and tried to outbid him in his support for gay rights and gun control. The strategy worked for Gore, as it had for Mondale in 1984. He secured the AFL-CIO's endorsement in October and, with solid support from union members and blacks, defeated Bradley for the nomination.

But having vanquished Bradley, Gore found himself once more trailing Bush. And so, like Mondale and Clinton before him, his initial reaction was to grasp for the center. He attacked Bush's tax program as a "risky" threat to the fiscal health of the country and promised to maintain the budget surplus even in the face of a recession. In June 2000, he launched a "prosperity and progress" tour to remind voters of what two terms with Clinton and Gore had brought. But this time the trick didn't work. A month had passed and Gore was still consistently trailing Bush, with a double-digit deficit in many opinion polls.

That's when Gore brought Stan Greenberg on board.[29] Greenberg, a former Yale political scientist, had been the pollster for Clinton's 1992 campaign. He remained with Clinton and the DNC until after the 1994 November election, when Clinton fired him—reportedly because he blamed Greenberg for not warning him about the looming public opposition to his health-care bill. Afterward, Greenberg went to work for foreign candidates, including Britain's Tony Blair and Israel's Ehud Barak, but he continued to write about American politics and what the Democrats should do. Greenberg's priority for the Democrats was winning back the white working class. He recognized that Democrats would win votes among minorities, professionals, and women, but he thought that without substantial support from the white working class, Democrats could not win elections. Greenberg had written, "Democrats cannot aspire to dominate this period and lead the country unless they can reinvent their links with and regain the confidence of downscale voters—working- and middle-class voters—who want nothing more complicated than a better life."[30]

Greenberg, who had done polling for the DLC, agreed with Galston and Kamarck that to reach white working-class voters, Democrats had to counter the perception of the party that Republicans had fostered and some Democrats had reinforced. Greenberg believed that Clinton's victory in 1992 was due in large part to his support for "values" issues such as welfare reform, but he worried that Clinton's affair with Monica Lewinsky had "once again identified" the party with "1960s-style irresponsibility."[31] Greenberg also believed that to reach these voters, Democrats had to embrace a populist message that identified Democrats as the party that stands up for workers "who are vulnerable to the whims of more powerful forces in society."[32] Greenberg certainly had history on his side. Democrats from Andrew Jackson to Franklin Roosevelt to Bill Clinton had effectively used such populist appeals to win the support of working-class voters.

Greenberg advised Gore to use his biography, particularly his service in Vietnam, to counteract voters' identification of him with the Clinton scandals, to steer clear of Clinton himself, and to underplay his support for issues like gun control and abortion that could alienate working-class voters.[33] Gore followed this strategy. Given the opportunity in the debates to attack Bush's support in Texas for carrying concealed weapons or his cavalier administration of the death penalty, Gore held back and equivocated. Gore also made a point of distancing himself from Clinton and even from the administration's accomplishments. Gore's reluctance to use Clinton as a campaigner may have won him votes in some parts of the country, but probably lost him at least Arkansas.[34]

Greenberg also recommended that Gore resume the populist rhetoric of the primary campaign, but without committing himself to any large government programs. Gore's convention speech did exactly this. He said of the Republicans, "They're for the powerful, and we're for the people." Gore promised to "stand up and say no" to "big tobacco, big oil, the big polluters, the pharmaceutical companies, the HMOs." After the convention speech, Gore suddenly sped past Bush in the opinion polls and remained ahead for more than a month—until the fateful debates, when his personal limitations as a candidate shone through.

Gore's defeat was the narrowest ever—and made even more so by the third-party candidacy of the Green Party's Ralph Nader. Nader, who played a key role in founding the modern consumer and environmental movements, decided to run in 2000 as the candidate of the tiny Green Party. Unlike Jackson in 1988 or Perot in 1992, Nader was not running to win, but to register his disapproval of Clinton and Gore, whom he believed had betrayed the left liberal cause. He also hoped to gain the Green Party ballot status in the 2004 election by securing 5 percent of the vote nationally. Nader succeeded at least partially in his first objective. He not only won attention from the media, but he actually cost Gore the election by providing Bush's margin of victory in Florida and New Hampshire and by forcing Gore to divert precious resources in the last weeks of his campaign to states like Minnesota and Oregon that, in the absence of Nader, Gore would have been assured of winning easily.

In the end, though, Nader failed to attain the 5 percent that he and the Green Party sought, getting only 2.7 percent of the vote. Which is one reason why Nader's campaign in 2000 probably spelled the end of his political career and of similar efforts by his supporters. Many of Nader's youthful followers did not understand how American politics worked. They believed that they could build an American Green Party similar to the European parties. But the American presidential system has always encouraged two major parties and discouraged third parties, except as spoilers. The major parties do not represent a single unified philosophy. They are coalitions of constituencies and views. Those who attempt to build a party of uniform conviction invariably suffer disillusionment, as Nader's followers did in 2000, and either withdraw from politics or adopt a more realistic view of how change is made.

VI. THE NEW SYNTHESIS

In his December 1976 memo, Caddell described the need for a "synthesis" of views and strategies: "I think it can be argued clearly that we are at one of those points in time, when—as Marx or Hegel would have argued—neither the thesis nor the antithesis really works. We need a synthesis of ideas."[35] In the wake of Gore's defeat, Democratic strategists brought forward thesis and antithesis, but not a new synthesis. They insisted that the Democrats were faced with stark and opposing choices in what direction to take. But behind these polarities lay a rough kind of synthesis.

The DLC and Penn blamed Gore's loss on his adoption of a populist appeal in the last months of the campaign. "Gore chose a populist rather than a New Democrat message," From wrote. "As a result, voters viewed him as too liberal and identified him as an advocate of big government. Those perceptions . . . hurt him with male voters in general and with key New Economy swing voters in particular. By emphasizing class warfare, he seemed to be talking to Industrial Age America, not Information Age America."[36]

Penn wrote that Gore "missed the new target of the twenty-first century: the wired workers." He failed to reach "middle-class, white suburban males, many of whom had voted for Clinton in the past." Gore's "old-style message sent him tumbling in key border states . . . they were turned off by populism."[37] According to Penn, "Clinton fatigue" was not a "key factor that cost Al Gore the presidency . . . postelection polls showed little evidence of such a phenomenon." In other words, the legacy of the Clinton scandals did not hurt Gore's candidacy. What hurt him was his populist rhetoric, which cost him votes among wired workers, and in particular middle-class, white suburban males.

Greenberg took the antithesis. He blamed Gore's defeat primarily on the decline of the Democratic vote among white working-class voters, particularly white working-class men. According to Greenberg, they backed Bush rather than Gore because they didn't trust Gore—a sentiment traceable to the Clinton scandals—and because they rejected Gore's stands in favor of gun control and abortion. They were not put off by Gore's populism. On the contrary, it was a major reason that many of them backed him.[38]

Who was right? In explaining Gore's defeat, Greenberg's analysis was much closer to the truth. In the border states like Missouri and West Virginia, and in the states like Ohio, Arkansas, and Louisiana that Clinton had won in 1996, but Gore lost in 2000, Gore lost votes compared to 1996 primarily among the white working-class rather than among "middle-class, white suburban males." For instance, in Missouri, Clinton won working-class white men by 3 percent in 1996, while Gore lost the same voters by 25 percent, a swing of 28 percent against the Democrats. In contrast, Clinton lost college-educated white men by 8 percent in 1996, while Gore lost the same voters by 15 percent, a much smaller anti-Democratic swing of just 7 percent. Gore lost Missouri in the working-class north and southeast, not in the affluent St. Louis or Kansas City suburbs.

Gore didn't lose support among these voters because of his populist rhetoric. In some states, such as West Virginia and Kentucky, Gore lost votes because of his specific stands on the environment, tobacco, and coal. Many rural and small-town voters objected to Gore's support for gun control. And in most of the states, the single most important reason for voting against Gore was distrust of him stemming in large part from the Clinton administration scandals.

Greenberg backed up this analysis with an extensive postelection poll conducted among 2,036 respondents. When he asked respondents their three main reasons for not voting for Al Gore, 29 percent cited his "exaggerations and untruthfulness," 20 percent his "support for legalizing the union of gay couples," 19 percent his "pro-abortion position," and 17 percent his "being too close to Bill Clinton." Among white, non-college-educated male voters, 31 percent cited Gore's untruthfulness, 29 percent cited his "antigun positions," and 21 percent cited his being too close to Clinton. In other words, their doubts stemmed from the Clinton scandals and Gore's position on gun control. When Greenberg asked these voters what three factors most contributed to their voting, or considering voting, for Gore, the one that far outnumbered all the others—mentioned by 49 percent of these respondents—was his New Deal–style "promise to protect social security and add a prescription-drug benefit for seniors."[39]

Moreover, there is little evidence that white, suburban, college-educated voters were put off by Gore's populist rhetoric. According to Greenberg's poll, only 10 percent of white, college-educated male voters said that Gore's populist attacks had contributed to their doubts about him—an even lower percentage than the 13 percent of working-class white men who said they were put off by Gore's populist attacks. These figures seem paradoxical until you remember that many of these college-educated voters are white-collar professionals whose positions have put them in conflict with market imperatives—a fact that is entirely obscured by categories like "wired workers." What primarily drove these voters away from Gore was distrust of him stemming from the scandals. Gore's "untruthfulness" was cited by 38 percent of white, college-educated male voters as a reason for not voting for him; no other reason came close.

Greenberg was mostly right about why Gore lost, and the DLC and Penn were mostly wrong, and Greenberg was also right earlier in his insistence that populism—understood broadly to be the party's identification with the "common man and woman" and its defense of their interests against the powerful—was essential to the Democratic majority. Indeed, it has been a defining difference between Democrats and Whigs, and then Democrats and Republicans, since the 1830s.

But while the DLC and Penn were wrong about 2000, they were ultimately right about where the party's future lies. It may not lie in "wired workers," which is much too vague an appellation, but it does lie in the new workforce of postindustrial America and in the fast-growing metropolitan areas where they live and work. The key for Democrats will be in synthesizing Greenberg and Penn—in discovering a strategy that retains support among the white working class, but also builds support among college-educated professionals and others in America's burgeoning ideopolises. To do that, they don't have to choose between a populist politics and a politics that emphasizes the "quality of life." They can do both, as Clinton began to demonstrate in 1996, but as Gore failed to in 2000, largely because of factors that had nothing to do with the appeal of his politics. The Democrats' future, and the promise of its new majority, lies in the rough synthesis represented by this progressive centrism.

CHAPTER FIVE

The Tenuous Case
for a Republican Majority

Some political strategists argue that what is most likely over the next decade is a new Republican majority. Karl Rove, Bush's political director, has compared the Bush presidency to that of William McKinley and the election of 2000 to the election of 1896:

> Under Rove's theory, America is experiencing a "transformational" era comparable to the Industrial Revolution more than a century ago. He sees parallels to the election of 1896, when Republican governor William McKinley of Ohio—"a natural harmonizer," according to one admirer—rode to victory on a belief that the GOP could no longer base its appeal on old divisions from the Civil War because the nation had utterly changed. Today, Rove argues, the "new economy," based on technology, information, and entrepreneurship, is again transforming America, along with a new wave of immigrants from Latin America, Asia, and elsewhere. And the country is eager for a new leader who will, in Bush's inelegant phrase, be a "uniter, not a divider"—just like McKinley was.[1]

Rove sees Bush as the candidate of the "new economy," and his victory in 2000 as a harbinger of the kind of thirty-four-year Republican majority that McKinley initiated.

What are the grounds for believing that this kind of a new Republican majority is imminent? And are any of them valid? The most widely cited proponent of Rove's view is journalist Michael Barone, the lead author of the biannual *Almanac of American Politics*. Barone makes a case that while Republicans and Democrats currently divide up the electorate evenly, the country is moving toward what he calls the "Bush nation."

Barone sees religious observance as a primary difference between Republicans and Democrats. The Bush and Gore voters, he writes, represent "two nations of different faiths. One is observant, tradition-minded, moralistic; the other is unobservant, liberation-minded, relativist."[2] He sees a parallel difference in the two parties' view of markets, choice, and government. The 2000 election, he writes, was "a contest between more choice and more government." Barone argues that in both respects, Bush's views will eventually prevail. "Demography is moving, slowly, toward the Bush nation," he writes.

Barone's argument and those of like-minded Republican strategists can be broken down into three assertions: first, that the growth of the population, based on the 2000 election and census, will favor the Republicans rather than the Democrats; second, that the trends in religious observance and belief favor the Republicans rather than the Democrats; and third, that the trends in economic philosophy and practice favor the Republicans rather than the Democrats. We will consider each of these arguments in turn.

The September 11 terrorist attack has produced a fourth argument for a Republican majority. Most Democrats, as well as Republicans, have acknowledged that the administration's success in prosecuting the war against terror has benefited Bush, and by extension, Republicans in Congress. But some Republican conservatives argue that the war against terror has permanently altered the policy agenda in Washington and has created the opportunity for Bush to redraw the boundaries between the parties. David Brooks wrote in *The Weekly Standard* that Bush had gained an opportunity to turn the Republicans into the "party of patriotism" and to occupy the political center by relegating the party's "cultural warriors" and business lobbyists to the sidelines.[3] By doing this, Bush could regain the moderates and independents who deserted the party in the 1990s. If he could also retain the religious conservatives, he could have a version of the Reagan majority, but with a somewhat different center of gravity.

I. THE PARTIES AND THE POPULATION

Barone argues that demography favors the "Bush nation" because Republicans enjoy an advantage in "the fastest-growing parts of the United States." Barone is absolutely right: in the fifty counties that grew the fastest during the 1990s, Bush averaged 62 percent of the vote compared to 33 percent for Gore. But the Republican advantage in these counties doesn't suggest that there will be a growing Republican advantage in the electorate as a whole. Most of these pro-Bush counties are relatively small, and their rate of growth is less significant than their actual numbers, which pale before the growth of larger metropolitan counties. And as they become more densely populated over the decades, these "edge" or "collar" counties, initially populated by rural émigrés, will tend to become more Democratic and less Republican.

Barone's argument takes advantage of a simple mathematical fact: it is easier for a county to grow fast when it starts from a smaller base. Elbert County, Colorado, which was the third-fastest-growing county, doubled in size in the nineties from under 10,000 to just under 20,000. It went for Bush 69–26 percent. The fifth-fastest-growing county was Park County, Colorado, which doubled from 7,000 to 14,000, and supported Bush 55–36 percent. Boise County, Idaho, the ninth-fastest-growing, went from 3,500 to 6,700, and Bush won it 66–24 percent. But the picture changes completely if you consider the fifty counties with the largest population growth. In these counties, Gore won 54–42 percent overall, with 3 percent going to Nader. These large-growth counties average 1.46 million in size compared to an average of 109,000 for the fifty fastest-growth counties. This difference in size means that Gore came out of the fifty largest-growth counties with a 2.7-million-vote lead, compared to Bush's margin of half a million from the fifty fastest-growing counties.

Moreover, the Democrats are also gaining ground in a number of still-Republican large-growth counties that are losing their rural character and becoming more tightly integrated into metropolitan areas. The elder George Bush carried California's San Bernadino County, the eleventh-largest-growth county, by 21 percent in 1988; his son carried it by only two points, 49–47. In 1988, George Bush carried Maricopa County, Arizona, the largest-growth county in the United States, by 65–34 percent;

in 2000, his son's margin was down to just 53–43, a swing of 21 percentage points toward the Democrats. Bush senior carried Clark County, Nevada, the thirteenth-fastest-growing county, and the third largest in actual population increase, 56–41 percent in 1988. Gore defeated George W. Bush 51–45 percent in Clark County in 2000. The trends in these large-growth counties are the likely future of many fast-growth counties as they become larger and go through the same metropolitan integration process.

What Barone's numbers really show is that Bush and the Republicans enjoy an advantage in rural areas and in counties that are being formed primarily by white émigrés from rural areas. And because nonmetro or rural counties make up about three-fourths of all counties, and occupy about four-fifths of the land area in the United States, this creates an impression of Republican geographical dominance. But these counties don't include enough people, and when they do, they start to become less Republican. If American history were running in reverse, and if the country were becoming a primarily rural nation again, then the Republicans would enjoy a distinct demographic advantage. But history continues to run in the exact opposite direction. Rural America is shrinking—its share of the country's population down a hefty 17 percent over the last four decades—and densely populated metropolitan America is growing.[4] And so are Democratic chances.

As we already noted in chapter 2, Democrats benefit from other prominent population trends. Two of the fastest-growing parts of the population are Hispanic and Asian minorities, both of whom have tended to vote Democratic. The major occupations projected to grow the fastest in this decade are professionals and low-level service workers, both of whom have tilted Democratic. Among women, the proportions of working women, single women, and highly educated women, all of whom tend to vote heavily Democratic, are growing, while the least Democratic group, married homemakers, is shrinking. All in all, demography is moving toward a Democratic majority.

II. OBSERVANT REPUBLICANS

Barone also argues that religious observance separates Republicans from Democrats and implies that this division favors Republicans over the next decade. According to exit polls, Bush won the support of voters who say they attend church more than weekly by 63–36 and voters who say they attend church weekly by 57–40. And these voters make up 43 percent of the electorate. According to a study by John C. Green and other political scientists, Bush defeated Gore among "more observant" evangelical Protestants 84–16 percent and among "more observant" Roman Catholics 57–43 percent.[5] If one assumes that these groups are growing as a percentage of the electorate, then Bush and the Republicans should be in good shape for years to come.

But this assumption is not warranted. Surveys of religious attitudes and church attendance are notoriously inaccurate. As sociologists Penny Long Marler and C. Kirk Hadaway have demonstrated, Americans exaggerate their church attendance when asked by pollsters.* But even leaving aside the question of exaggeration, there is reason to believe that Americans as a whole are not as strongly devout as conservative evangelicals

---

*In a 1993 article for the *American Sociological Review*, "What the Polls Don't Show: A Closer Look at U.S. Church Attendance," Marler and Hadaway, along with Mark Chaves, found that Protestants in an Ohio county and Catholics in eighteen dioceses around the country were exaggerating by almost 100 percent their church attendance. In Ohio's Ashtabula County, they found, for instance, that "among Protestants, 19.8 percent attended a church workshop . . . during a typical week in 1992, compared to 35.8 percent who said they attended." Challenged and heavily criticized, Marler and Hadaway repeated the experiment at a large Protestant evangelical congregation in the Deep South. This time, they literally counted who attended and found the same results ("Testing the Attendance Gap in a Conservative Church," *Sociology of Religion*, 1999). While 70 percent of the church's parishioners said they attended a service, only 40 percent actually did. In a communication with the authors, Hadaway suggested on the basis of several studies they have done that the gap in reporting wasn't as wide forty or fifty years ago as it is now. This suggests that the decline in church attendance from that period to the present is probably even steeper than it appears. It also sheds light on a problem in current polling. In exit polling, the VNS survey, which asks cursory and limited questions in a public space where normative influences can be particularly strong, seems much more likely to have elicited exaggerated responses about attendance than the more careful and detailed questions asked by the National Election Study and the National Opinion Research Center. For this reason, we attach more credence to the latter than the former in assessing the level of religious observance in the United States.

claim and that over the last decades they have become less rather than more devout. While Bush did better than Gore among those who said they attended church weekly or more, even according to the unusually high VNS figures, they made up only a bit over two-fifths of the electorate in 2000.[6] Each of the groups in the less observant three-fifths of voters—those who said they attended church a few times a month, a few times a year, or never—preferred Gore over Bush, with support particularly strong among never-attenders, who gave Gore a 61–32 percent margin.

Moreover, in surveys taken over the last thirty years, it is the ranks of those who never or rarely attend church that have grown the most. According to a National Opinion Research Center (NORC) study, those who said they never attended church or attended less than once a year went from 18 percent in 1972 to 30 percent in 1998. Confirming this latter figure, the National Election Study found that those who say they never attended was at 33 percent of the citizenry and 27 percent of voters in 2000.[7] This group is about twice the size of those who identify themselves as members of the religious right and has tended to vigorously support Democrats rather than Republicans.

Some of the growth in the nonattenders came out of the mainline Protestant churches. In the seventies and eighties, white evangelical Protestants, the group out of which the religious right came, grew considerably in both numbers and proportion. But in the nineties, this group did not grow as a percentage of the electorate. According to an extensive survey by John C. Green and other political scientists, white evangelicals accounted for 25 percent of the electorate in 1992 and 26 percent in 2000, a statistically meaningless difference.[8] Those who identify themselves as members of the religious right (another highly subjective, but suggestive, designation) fell from 17 percent of the electorate in 1996 to 14 percent in 2000. And according to sociologist David Leege, the proportion of observant Catholics—one of the Bush campaign's targeted groups—also dropped during the 1990s.[9] In other words, trends among the religious do not favor Republicans over Democrats. If anything, they favor Democrats.

Republican strategists don't like to say so aloud, but Republicans have paid a heavy price for their avid support from the religious right. As members of the Christian Coalition and other groups have gained strength and controlled nominations or taken over state parties, they have tended to drive out old-guard and moderate Republicans. Divisions among Republicans in some congressional and state races have allowed Democrats to win seats that had long been held by Republicans. Perhaps the most vivid example is in Kansas's third congressional district, which until 1998 had always been held by Republicans. The district is dominated by the suburbs outside Kansas City, which includes upscale moderates from Overland Park, many of whom work for high-tech firms like Sprint, and ex-rural religious conservatives from the edge city of Olathe.[10] In 1996, a conservative Republican backed by the Christian Coalition won the seat. He quickly alienated the moderate Republicans in Overland Park, who were up in arms over an attempt by the religious right to impose the teaching of creationism on Kansas's public schools. In 1998, these voters, along with the voters from Lawrence, where the University of Kansas is located, swung the election to a moderate Democrat, Dennis Moore. In 2000, Moore was reelected when Republicans nominated another religious-right candidate over a moderate in the primary.

Even in the Deep South, where the religious right has bolstered the Republican Party, moderate Democrats have sometimes been able to defeat Republicans who were closely identified with the religious right. In 1996, Democrat Jim Hunt easily won the North Carolina gubernatorial election after the Republicans, in a bitter primary battle, chose Christian Coalition candidate Robin Hayes over a moderate. In Georgia, Democrat Zell Miller won the governor's office in 1994—a heavy Republican year—after a Christian right candidate won the Republican nomination in a primary against a moderate. In Alabama, Democrat Don Siegelman won the governor's office in 1998 against Christian right Republican Fob James. In all these cases, Democrats were able to create a coalition that included upscale white moderates who had been voting Republican, but who were unwilling to back a candidate of the religious right.

III. THE FREE MARKET PARTY

Conservative Republicans from Goldwater to Mississippi senator Trent Lott have always championed a laissez-faire theory of the government and the economy. They have blamed government intervention for whatever economic ills the country suffers. As Reagan put it in his 1981 inaugural address, "Government is not the solution to our problems; government is the problem." Conservative Republicans have called for the deregulation of industry, the privatization of government functions, including social security, and the dispersal of government funds to the private sector through tax cuts. Republican strategists believe that this laissez-faire philosophy could still be the basis of a new majority. Barone thinks such an approach is "in line with the increasingly decentralized character of American society."[11] Republican speechwriter Daniel Casse, writing in *Commentary* after the 2000 election, concurs, arguing that Republican proposals to privatize social security and to eliminate federal control of medicare will eventually be the basis for a new majority. Asks Casse, "For how long will voters abide Democratic leaders who remain steadfastly against any use of private accounts for social security?"[12]

Barone, Casse, and the Republican strategists really raise different kinds of questions. First, are these free market policies of deregulation and privatization as popular as the authors make out? Are Americans increasingly supportive of proposals for privatizing social security or reining in the Environmental Protection Agency? Second, will these proposals, if enacted, accomplish what their proponents claim? Will privatization rescue the social security system from the threat of insolvency and put more money in retired Americans' pockets? A policy need not work to get politicians elected; but it has to show results to get them reelected and to secure more than a fleeting majority for their party. Yet on both of these counts, the Republican argument for a laissez-faire majority fails to be convincing.

American support for laissez-faire rather than interventionist government policies has gone in cycles like the economy. By the late 1970s, continued stagflation and rising tax bills had undermined support for the interventionist policies advocated by the Carter administration and the even more ambitious programs advanced by liberal Democrats like Ted Kennedy. A growing number of Americans had come to believe that government intervention had caused the stagflation of the late 1970s. The change in opinion was captured in the Harris Poll. In September 1973, only 32 percent of Americans agreed that "the best government is the government that governs the least"; by February 1981, 59 percent agreed (see chart). They were willing to give Reagan's program of privatization and deregulation a chance to work.

**"The Best Government Is the Government
That Governs the Least"**

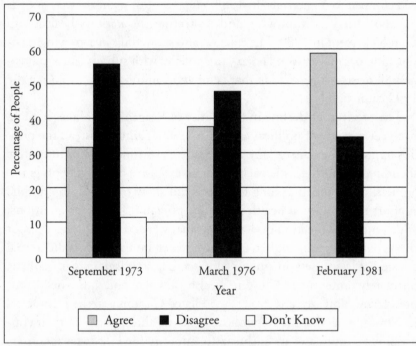

Source: William G. Mayer, *The Changing American Mind: How American Public Opinion Changed Between 1960 and 1988* (Ann Arbor, Mich.: University of Michigan Press, 1992).

The Reagan-era policies—if those of the Federal Reserve are included—did finally end the stagflation and helped restore business's incentive to invest, but by the end of Reagan's second term, these policies had also led to massive budget and trade deficits and to a series of squalid business scandals, topped off by the savings-and-loan collapse. By the late eighties, the public had become disillusioned with the conservative Republican approach. The reaction showed up most clearly in a dramatic increase in how many people thought the government was doing "too little" to protect the environment, improve the nation's health, and the country's educational system. In 1980, for instance, 48 percent thought the government was doing too little to protect the environment; by 1988, after two terms of conservative Republican rule, 65 percent believed the government was doing too little.[13] In 1980, 53 percent thought we were spending too little on education; by 1988, it had climbed to 64 percent. In 1988, 66 percent thought we were spending too little on "improving and protecting the nation's health," up from 55 percent in 1980. The reaction also showed up in a growing identification of conservative laissez-faire policies with subservience to business lobbyists—a perception that Perot and Clinton would exploit in the 1992 campaign.*

The precipitous decline in popularity of Reagan-era policies began a five-year comedy of political errors. In 1993, Clinton misread the public's opposition to laissez-faire conservatism as strong support for public spending and enthusiastic backing for an extensive health-care program. Some simpleminded polling questions did show overwhelming public support for a national health insurance program. But other questions, which included the kind of drawbacks that were eventually raised about the program—from higher taxes to greater bureaucracy—did reveal considerable softness in public support. These misgivings, of course, ultimately undermined Clinton's health-care plan and, quite nearly, his presidency. Similarly, after voters repudiated Clinton and the Democrats in November 1994, the Republicans misread the victories of their congressional candidates as enthusiastic support for laissez-faire conservatism. They soon discovered they, too, were sorely mistaken.

By the 1996 election, it had become abundantly clear that the public opposed both a revival of Great Society–style social engineering and laissez-faire conservatism. Instead, as the Clinton administration recognized, the public backed a more incremental approach to improving health-care delivery and insurance and to strengthening existing environmental and consumer regulations. They wanted more money spent on social needs, but they wanted it spent carefully. Indeed, in an extensive

---

*Lee Atwater, George Bush's campaign manager and later chairman of the Republican National Committee, recognized the problem as early as 1985. In a symposium on "baby-boom politics," Atwater warned that the Republicans were in danger of losing this generation of voters. "What we as Republicans have always got to be aware of is that they're also anti-big-business, and if we once again become viewed as the party that caters solely to big business, we would be in trouble with this group," Atwater said. See David Boaz, ed., *Left Right and Baby Boom: America's New Politics* (Washington, D.C.: Cato Institute, 1986).

1998 poll, 73 percent of the public thought the government was not spending enough on education, 70 percent thought it was spending too little on health care, and 65 percent thought it was unduly ignoring the environment.[14]

Perhaps the clearest public endorsement of regulatory capitalism came in the 2000 campaign when Republican candidates discovered that they, too, would have to profess support for new government regulations even if they had no intention of enacting them. When Gore accused George W. Bush at the last presidential debate of not supporting "a strong national patients' bill of rights," Bush responded, "Actually, Mr. Vice President, it's not true. I do support a national patients' bill of rights. As a matter of fact, I brought Republicans and Democrats together to do just that in the state of Texas, to get a patients' bill of rights through." In point of fact, the Texas bill had passed over Bush's opposition, and once in office as president Bush would oppose a similar bill.

Even the most conservative Republicans embraced regulatory capitalism. Missouri Republican senator John Ashcroft had fought attempts to regulate HMOs and to include prescription-drug coverage in medicare. He was a darling of the health and drug industry lobbyists. Yet in his campaign for reelection in 2000, facing a moderate and popular Democratic governor, Ashcroft ran as a *proponent* of a patients' bill of rights and a foe of the drug companies. "John Ashcroft stood up to the drug companies for unfair drug prices," one campaign commercial intoned. Ashcroft recognized that the public itself no longer supported the conservatives' laissez-faire agenda.

Casse and other Republicans insist that the public does support privatization of social security, but they couldn't be more mistaken. They are relying on the same kind of misinterpretation of polling data that convinced Clinton and the Democrats in 1993 that they could press ahead with a bold national health-insurance plan. For example, the Cato Institute, which is funded by the same securities firms that would enjoy a windfall from privatization, has conducted surveys that purportedly show Americans back privatization by more than two to one. But these surveys simply ask questions like "How likely would you be to support social security privatization if it allowed you to take your social security money and invest it in a retirement account of your choosing?"[15] Such surveys fail to ask respondents the questions other surveys do: whether they would support privatization if it resulted in reduced guaranteed benefits, lower over-all benefits, or higher taxes—all of which could happen because of reduced payroll tax revenues, the transition costs of a new system, and the vagaries of the stock market. In just one recent example, when the American Association for Retired Persons asked respondents whether they would favor the chance to invest part of their payroll taxes, 54 percent said that they would; when asked if they would still favor privatization if that meant lower guaranteed benefits from the government, only 42 percent backed privatization.[16]

The Republicans also contend that there is widespread public support for a voucher-based system for medicare. Under such a system, seniors would get a set amount from medicare and then have to shop around among a number of basic plans for their health insurance. If they wanted a better plan than the ones available at the base amount, they would have to pay extra to get it. But advocates, who say that consumers will embrace the system because it gives them more choice, use the same kind of ten-dentious polling evidence to make their case. They cite questions such as this one, which Republican pollsters John McLaughlin and Associates asked: "Should senior Americans have the right to choose between different health-care plans with different benefits just like members of Congress and federal employees?" Unsurprisingly, the public is over-whelmingly supportive of such an idea.

But any attempt to put this proposal in a realistic context that mentions something besides choice—that turning medicare into a voucher system would strictly limit the amount medicare would contribute to recipients, that recipients might be financially penalized if they wanted to continue standard medicare fee-for-service coverage and not move into an HMO, and that they might have to pay more money out of pocket for their health expenses—results in a precipitous drop in support.[17] Indeed, it is difficult to find realistic descriptions of the medicare choice idea that elicit more than about one-third support from the public. The laissez-faire agenda is no more popular in the area of health—probably less—than it is in the area of retirement.

If support for laissez-faire and regulatory capitalism goes in cycles, we are, if anything, at the end of a period in which laissez-faire has reigned, and at the beginning of a new period in which greater government intervention will occur. Barone argues that the onset of postindustrial capitalism inspires laissez-faire approaches, but in the late nineties, the contrary was true. In Bush's first eighteen months, the onset of a recession and of a war against terrorism has strengthened support for government spending, while the electricity crisis in California and the Enron scandal have put Republican proponents of continued deregulation and privatization on the defensive.

That has become evident even for tax cuts—always a key part of the Republican argument for shrinking government. Bush's tax cut that passed in August 2001 contributed to his falling popularity prior to the war. In the November 2001 gubernatorial elections in New Jersey and Virginia, the Republican candidates promised to cut taxes while accusing their Democratic opponents of being tax-and-spenders. In Virginia, Mark Earley promised to continue eliminating the state's car tax and to veto a referendum in the northern-Virginia suburbs to determine whether local taxes should be raised to improve the area's transportation system. In New Jersey, Bret Schundler promised to eliminate the tolls on the Garden State Parkway. But in the light of falling revenues and growing social needs, voters repudiated both candidates. A *Washington Post* poll showed four-to-one support in northern Virginia for a tax referendum.[18]

In the late 1970s, many citizens believed that they were paying high taxes for programs they didn't want. In the early part of this new century, many citizens believe that their states are suffering from insufficient revenues to pay for programs in health care, transportation, and education that they do want. In the 2001 elections, eleven of twelve states passed referenda approving infrastructure spending proposals.[19]

IV. THE PARTY OF PATRIOTISM

George W. Bush and the Republicans can't build a new majority by trying to revive the conservatism of Newt Gingrich, the U.S. Chamber of Commerce, and the Heritage Foundation. In 2000, Bush would not have won the presidency, even against a tarnished opponent, if he had not disguised his own conservative convictions on environmental and health-care issues. During his first nine months, governing within a conservative framework, except on education, Bush found himself and the Republicans sinking in popularity. On the eve of September 11, a Zogby poll found his job approval rating at 50 percent—a historical low for a first-year president.[20] It looked likely that, with the recession deepening, Bush and the Republicans would be routed in November 2002, giving birth prematurely to a Democratic majority. But the terrorist attack on September 11, and Bush's effective response to it, boosted his popularity and that of his party.

Even before September 11, Bush and Republicans had enjoyed greater public support than the Democrats on handling foreign policy and national security. The war against terror made national security the most important issue in the country, completely overshadowing and even redefining the recession in the immediate post-9/11 period. Prior to September 11, much of the public had blamed Bush for the flagging economy; after September 11, many shifted blame to the terrorists and saw whatever privation they suffered as a necessary sacrifice to defeat terror. As long as the war continues, and as long as the administration is seen to prosecute it effectively, Bush's popularity should remain unusually high, and the Republicans should benefit (although it is not clear by how much) in the polls. But the question for the future of American politics is, what will happen once the obvious imperative for war abates. Will Bush and the Republicans be able to sustain their popularity? Or will the trends that have led toward a Democratic majority reassert themselves?

David Brooks and some other Republican conservatives argue that Bush has been using the post–September 11 mood of national emergency to reposition the Republicans as a more centrist party of patriotism—to distance it from business and religious conservatism and to move closer to his former rival John McCain. While such a move might not create what Brooks calls a "reemerging Republican majority," it could create a continued stalemate in American politics—what W. D. Burnham has called an "unstable equilibrium"—over the remainder of the decade.[21] But there is not a great deal of evidence that Bush has moved closer to the center and distanced Republicans from their older base.

In national party affairs, the Bush administration has been willing to countenance a more politically diverse Republican Party. Bush befriended New York mayor Michael Bloomberg, even though Bloomberg remains at heart a liberal Democrat, and Bush and his political director, Karl Rove, encouraged liberal, pro-choice former Los Angeles mayor Richard Riordan to seek the Republican nomination in California's 2002 gubernatorial race. But Bush has continued to govern domestically from the right rather than the center, and the Republican leaders in the House and Senate have, if anything, hardened their own conservative convictions. Rather than using his newfound popularity to reposition the party, he and other Republicans have used it to deflect opposition to their continued conservative direction on taxes, the environment, social security, and worker protection.

Bush has had numerous opportunities since September 11 to reposition himself and his party politically, but has not done so. His first chance came in the debate over how to improve the nation's private and notoriously incompetent airport security system, which had failed to detect a terrorist threat on September 11. Instead of backing a coalition of Democrats and moderate Republicans who favored federalizing the airport security force, Bush backed the House Republican leadership, which had been heavily lobbied by the security firms. Republican Marshall Wittmann, who had backed McCain in 2000, commented about the president's decision to back the House Republicans: "While the president enjoys stratospheric poll ratings, these numbers will eventually return to earth. That is why it is surprising that the administration has displayed little political imagination in building a broader governing coalition that is sustainable for the long haul. They were presented with a golden opportunity to rebuke DeLay and assume a law-and-order position on airport security. But, no, the White House continues to slavishly adhere to pre-9/11 'base' politics."[22]

Since then, Bush has continued to tack right. He used the threat to national security to justify rolling back environmental regulations and pressing for his plan to turn the Arctic National Wildlife Refuge over to oil companies.[23] Facing criticism for withdrawing from the global-warming treaty, he introduced a plan, backed by business, to limit voluntarily the carbon dioxide emissions that are causing global warming. Even the most moderate environmental groups denounced it. He also opposed a continuation of corporate taxation for Superfund cleanup efforts, shifting these costs onto the taxpayer.

Bush has tried to appeal to white working-class Democrats in Pennsylvania and West Virginia by making concessions on steel and coal production, but these are dwindling constituencies. On the broader economic and social issues, he has failed to advance the kind of themes or proposals that would attract the constituencies that would potentially compose a new Democratic majority. Bush's stimulus program was filled with additional tax breaks for the wealthy and for corporations, including a plan to eliminate the alternative minimum tax on businesses that might otherwise pay no taxes at all to the government. He presented a ten-year budget at the beginning of 2002 that was heavy with tax cuts for business supporters and that cut money for job training and environmental enforcement. He abandoned any attempt to protect the social security fund surplus, guaranteeing the emergence of budget deficits, and at the same time reintroduced a plan to privatize part of social security.

Bush responded to the Enron debacle with a cosmetic reform in securities regulation that stressed self-regulation. Brooks and the McCain Republicans wanted him to champion reforms in corporate governance, but faced with alienating his corporate support, Bush balked at doing so. He also continued to cultivate social conservatives by appointing conservative judges and taking every opportunity to inject evangelical Christian discourse into politics. And he abandoned his effort to win over Hispanic voters by liberalizing immigration rules. Of course, congressional conservatives proved to be even more intractable. During the recession, for instance, House Republicans even opposed extending unemployment benefits for the jobless unless they could be tied to tax cuts for business and the affluent. And the Republican primary electorate, which chose conservative over moderate gubernatorial candidates in New Jersey in 2001 and California in 2002 (over Bush's own choice of Riordan), has proven equally inflexible.

In the wake of 9/11, Bush and the Republicans did fashion a party of patriotism, but one as conservative on social and economic issues as the pre-9/11 party. As long as the war was at its height, Bush and the Republicans did not have to pay a political price for continuing to back bigger tax cuts for the wealthy or reductions in environmental enforcement. But these kind of positions, and the Republican association with firms like Enron, are likely to resurface—like early childhood traumas—once the public ceases to be preoccupied with the war against terror. When that happens, American politics is likely to turn toward a new Democratic majority rather than a reemerging Republican one.

*   *   *

There is one last possibility, which hinges on the outcome of the war against terror. By December 2001, the United States had defeated the Taliban government in Afghanistan and destroyed most of al Qaeda's bases there. The war itself appeared to be devolving into an international police action, punctuated by the use of American Special Forces and military advisers and by less frequent terror alerts from the attorney general. But in George W. Bush's January 2002 State of the Union speech, he suggested that the United States would expand the war from Afghanistan to an "axis of evil" in Iraq, Iran, and North Korea. That would mean using American forces and troops against those of other foreign governments whose militaries are far more powerful than those of the Taliban. Some Bush advisers advanced a strategic argument that the United States needed to pursue such a wider war to protect its citizens from future threats, but it remains unclear as of this writing whether Bush will act on their arguments.

If the United States were to score relatively easy victories, such as occurred before in Kosovo or Afghanistan, then this success would redound to the popularity of the Bush administration. But if the expansion of the war were to lead to protracted fighting and military occupation, and to terrorist reprisals, then it could spark the kind of sharp debate within the country and the parties that occurred during the Korean War, the Vietnam War, and the later stages of the Cold War. Here the Republicans would probably benefit immediately, but over a lengthier period, support for Republican foreign policy could erode, leading to a Democratic advantage. Thus, in the event of a wider war, either party could gain a temporary majority for reasons having little to do with the long-term trends toward a progressive centrist politics. These trends would be likely to reassert themselves, however, and give birth to a new Democratic majority, once peace was secured and Americans could look toward the pursuit of happiness rather than the prevention of terrorist assaults.

The Progressive Center

These are turbulent and unusual times. In the 1990s, America saw its longest peacetime economic expansion, including a half decade of spectacular economic performance, led by computer automation and the Internet. Although superficially identified with twenty-something millionaires making a killing on dotcom stocks, the period presaged a postindustrial society in which advanced electronic technology would progressively liberate human beings from repetitive drudgery and toil; in which knowledge and intelligence would displace brute physical power as the engine of economic growth; and in which citizens could increasingly devote their lives to the pursuit of knowledge and happiness. The boom of the nineties was followed, of course, by a recession and by the onset of a war against radical Islamic terrorists who, if successful in their jihad, would have undermined the promise of postindustrial society and plunged the world back into the dark uncertainty and otherworldly fanaticism of the Middle Ages.

In the midst of these tumultuous times, the United States has been undergoing a significant political transition from a conservative Republican majority, which dominated American politics during the 1980s and maintains a weak grip on national power, to a new Democratic majority, which began to emerge during the Clinton presidencies of the 1990s. This new majority is intimately bound up with the changes that America began to go through in the last part of the twentieth century: from an industrial to a postindustrial society, from a white Protestant to a multiethnic, religiously diverse society in which men and women play roughly equal roles at home and at work, and from a society of geographically distinct city, suburb, and country to one of a large, sweeping postindustrial metropolises.

The conservative Republican realignment of the 1980s was in large part a reaction to the turmoil of the sixties and seventies. It sought to contain or roll back the demands of civil rights protesters, feminists, environmentalists, welfare rights organizers, and consumer activists. It was also a reaction to the changes wrought in family structure, work, neighborhood, and ethnic composition by the transition to postindustrial capitalism. And it was a protest against government programs that cost too much and accomplished too little in the midst of a stagnating economy.

Much of that political reaction was inevitable and understandable. Some government programs did waste resources and did little to promote better citizens and a better society. Welfare, as originally devised, did encourage family breakup; much public housing fostered ghetto crime. And the intersection of war and social protest gave the movements of the sixties an apocalyptic edge. The civil rights movement degenerated into ghetto riots and gun-toting militants; feminists ended up challenging the utility of the family and of marriage; consumer activists looked down upon the tastes and habits of average Americans; the counterculture championed drugs and mocked traditional religion in favor of fads and cults; and community organizers encouraged the poor to depend on government handouts.

But the conservative reaction has ranged to extremes of its own. It exploited white Southern resistance to racial desegregation; it denigrated single mothers and working women while stigmatizing homosexuals; it rejected any government intervention into the market and called for abolishing whole sections of the federal government; and it sought to impose the strictures of sectarian religion on education and scientific research. The emerging Democratic majority is a corrective to this Republican counterrevolution—an attempt to come to terms with what was positive and enduring in the movements of the sixties and in the transition to postindustrial capitalism. It does not represent a radical or aggressively left-wing response to conservatism, but a moderate accommodation with what were once radical movements. Like the Republican realignment of 1896, it seeks to ratify and consolidate progressive views that increasingly dominate the center of American politics.

I. SECURITY, STABILITY, AND FREE MARKETS

In the early twentieth century, Republican progressives pioneered the idea of a regulatory capitalism that stood between laissez-faire capitalism and socialism. This kind of public intervention through government attempted to reduce the inequities and instability created by private growth without eliminating the dynamism of markets. It preserved private ownership of farms, factories, and offices, but subjected them to regulation on behalf of the public interest. Franklin Roosevelt's New Deal expanded the scope of government regulation and intervention, creating a system that worked well for many decades. By the 1970s, however, the system was breaking down and became mired in a crippling stagflation that government seemed helpless to correct. Many liberal Democrats came to believe that measures like nationalization of the energy industry, the control of wages, prices, and even investments, and publicly guaranteed full employment were necessary to get the system back on track.

At that point, Republican conservatism provided a useful corrective, a reassertion of the importance of markets and entrepreneurial risk to economic growth. But the Republican support for markets became hardened into a laissez-faire dogma. By the midnineties, the economy was booming, aided by technology-driven productivity growth, but it was also generating new kinds of inequity, instability, corruption, and insecurity— problems that would become even more apparent during the downturn that began in late 2000. Yet Republican conservatives continued to argue for reducing regulations and for cutting taxes for corporations and the wealthy even further. They were motivated partly by laissez-faire ideology, but also by alliances with business lobbies in Washington that heavily funded their campaigns.

By the nineties, the Republican approach put them at odds not only with public opinion, but with the demands that the new postindustrial economy was putting on Americans. For one thing, Republicans seemed oblivious to Americans' concern about their quality of life. Air pollution continued to pose a risk to public health and, through global warming, to the planet's future. But after winning the Congress in 1994, Republicans tried to virtually close down the EPA. When Democrats tried to toughen air standards in 1997, Republicans and their business allies blocked the new rules through a court suit.[1] A decade before, Democrats had used the same legal tactics to block Republican attempts to weaken regulations. What was a sign of political weakness in the Democrats of the eighties was equally a sign of political weakness and desperation in the Republicans of the nineties.

When George W. Bush became president, he undid Clinton administration environmental regulations and pulled the United States out of negotiations for a global-warming treaty. Bush equally ignored popular concern about product quality and safety, appointing regulatory foes to head the Federal Trade Commission and the Consumer Product Safety Commission. Bush's moves were so controversial that he eventually had to back off on some of them, including the reduction of clean water standards. Mindful of potential public opposition, the administration resorted to eliminating regulations by quietly negotiating them away in response to industry suits that were brought against them.[2]

Republicans also ignored public concerns with the corruption of the campaign finance system. In the aftermath of 1996 campaign finance scandals, Democrats and a few moderate Republicans, including John McCain, backed a modest measure—well short of public financing of elections—that would have eliminated unlimited "soft money" contributions by corporations, unions, and wealthy individuals to candidates. But conservative Republicans, led by Kentucky senator Mitch McConnell, blocked the legislation. After George W. Bush took office, a campaign finance bill passed the Senate over Bush's objection, but conservative Republicans were able to stop it in the House. Finally, in the wake of the Enron scandal, moderate Republicans in the House banded together with Democrats to pass the campaign bill and Bush, facing a public revolt, finally signed it, though with a conspicuous lack of enthusiasm.

Republicans seemed equally oblivious to the insecurities created by the postindustrial economy. In the older industrial economy, a blue-collar worker at an automobile or steel factory could expect to hold his job until he retired and to enjoy health insurance and a pension. So could a white-collar worker at a bank or insurance company. In the postindustrial economy of global competition and automation, these kinds of jobs declined in number and could also suddenly disappear as companies moved overseas or reorganized or automated at home. Many of the newer jobs in low-wage services and professions were without the kind of fringe benefits that American workers of the 1950s had enjoyed. From 1979 to 1998, the percentage of private sector workers with employer-provided health insurance went down 7.3 percent. The drop was the sharpest among the lowest-paid workers. Of those in the bottom fifth of wage earners, coverage went down by 11.1 percent.[3] Americans also lacked the kind of job protections they had enjoyed earlier. Their sense of insecurity rose, even during a period of recovery. In 1978, 29 percent of workers believed they were in some danger of losing their job; by 1996, the percentage had risen 10.7 percent to 39.7 percent.[4] During the recession, these figures rose still further. In 2001 alone, 1.2 million Americans lost their health insurance.[5]

Democrats sought to respond to this new insecurity through a national health insurance program, but when the public balked at that level of government intervention, they began considering a series of incremental measures. These included extending medicare downward to Americans fifty-five years and older and to children under eighteen; providing prescription drug coverage as part of medicare; eliminating abuses by health maintenance organizations; making health insurance and pensions portable; and providing universally available retirement accounts that workers can use to increase their old-age pensions. By contrast, Republicans have insisted that Americans would be best off in the hands of private markets and with government removed entirely from the economy. "We do have an economic game plan," the House Republicans declared in *Restoring the Dream*, "and its central theme is to get bureaucratic government off of America's back and out of the way."[6] They advocated turning medicare into a voucher system and partially replacing social security with private investment accounts. Only in the face of widespread public support for the Democratic programs did they sponsor their own version of a patients' bill of rights or medicare prescription drug coverage—and in both cases, their proposed alternatives were intentionally so full of loopholes as to be virtually ineffective.

The rise of postindustrial capitalism and the increase of global competition has also put a premium on educated workers. Over the last three decades, only workers with a four-year college degree or more have seen their real wages increase, while workers with less than a college degree have seen their real earnings actually decline. Workers with a high school degree, for instance, made $13.34 an hour in 1973 and $11.83 an hour in 1999 (in 1999 dollars). In the same period, workers with advanced degrees saw their income rise from $23.53 an hour to $26.44 an hour.[7] The clear message to workers was to acquire more education. That message was reinforced by changes in the global economy in which manufacturing work—the most remunerative of noncollege occupations —increasingly shifted from the United States to less developed capitalist countries.

Democrats have advocated more money for job retraining and early childhood education and to allow every high school graduate to attend a two-year college. They have also called for more money for school buildings, science and computer equipment, and teacher salaries. By contrast, Republicans, after taking control of Congress in 1994, tried unsuccessfully to shut down the Department of Education. In many states, Republicans, led by the religious right, have promoted home schooling or exotic theories of education. Nationally, Republicans have made a special priority of vouchers—a program with particular appeal to some white Catholic and evangelical Protestant voters, but remarkably unpopular with much of the electorate. Republicans have deservedly criticized some Democratic efforts as merely "throwing money at problems" and correctly emphasized the need for high standards, but they have used these deficiencies in the Democrats' approach as an excuse to neglect needed spending. Even in a recession, the Bush administration cut funds for worker training— a key component of any education program—in the fiscal year 2002 budget.

Democrats, reflecting their New Deal heritage, have also tried to use government policy to reduce the income inequality created by the new postindustrial economy. In 1993, the Clinton administration dramatically raised the earned income tax credit (EITC) for low-wage workers, while raising the top rate for upper-income Americans. According to the Harvard political scientist Jeffrey B. Liebman, the increase in the EITC worked wonders for low-income workers: "As recently as 1993, a single-parent family with two children and a full-time minimum-wage worker made $12,131 (in today's dollars) with the EITC. . . . Because of the expansions of the EITC during the 1990s, that family now makes $14,188—a 17 percent boost above the poverty line. The Census Bureau estimates that the EITC lifts 4.3 million people out of poverty, including 2.3 million children."[8]

By contrast, the Republican efforts of Reagan, the Republican Congresses of the 1990s, and the George W. Bush administration have widened income inequality by bestowing tax breaks disproportionately on the most wealthy and on corporations. In the Bush plan that Congress passed in August 2001, the tax cuts, phased in over ten years, will primarily benefit the top 10 percent of income earners. After 2001, they will receive 70.7 percent of the tax benefits, while the bottom 60 percent will get 6.5 percent of the benefits.[9]

These broad differences between the parties became even more apparent after the September 11 terrorist attacks. With the economy slumping, Democrats wanted to give the bulk of money in a stimulus package to unemployed workers who would spend it immediately, with some extra money thrown in to help the newly jobless buy health insurance. By contrast, Republicans in the House, with the Bush administration's support, passed a bill that would primarily have provided tax benefits to corporations and wealthy individuals. Under the bill, almost three-quarters of the tax benefits would have gone to the top 10 percent of income earners, and incredibly, no benefits whatsoever would have gone to a typical family of four with an income of $50,000.[10] In addition, *Fortune* 500 companies would have gotten a $25-billion windfall through the retroactive elimination of the corporate "alternative minimum tax." Almost all of the tax measures in the Republican bill would have taken effect too late to help the economy.[11]

Democrats blocked the Republican stimulus package in the Senate, but in its 2002 budget, the Bush administration was back at redistributing the country's wealth to the wealthy. With deficits rising, the administration actually proposed accelerating when the ten-year tax cuts that Congress had passed would take effect. The administration also proposed making them permanent after ten years rather than subject to congressional review.

II. RACE AND REALIGNMENT

Republicans were the original party of racial equality. In the 1950s and early 1960s, leaders from both parties attempted to come to terms with the new Southern civil rights movement. But after 1964, the Democrats embraced, and the Republicans rejected, the cause of civil rights. The new conservative movement took root in opposition to the federal civil rights acts of 1964 and 1965. It gained a wider following and credibility in the 1970s and 1980s—attracting many whites without any animus toward black civil rights—because of the extremes to which some black militants, such as New York's Reverend Al Sharpton, the author of the infamous Tawana Brawley hoax, went and because of the corruption and venality of some black Democratic officials, such as Washington, D.C.'s Marion Barry. The backlash was also sustained by white voters' frustrations with 1970s stagflation and by the utter inadequacy of many of the civil rights remedies proposed by liberal Democrats. School busing, for instance, often had the effect of encouraging white flight rather than integrating schools. Some public housing programs put the entire onus of integration on working-class white neighborhoods. But Republicans used the corruption of the black officials and the inadequacy of these programs to stigmatize the Democrats and to avoid offering any constructive remedies of their own.

Republicans, particularly in the South, sought to build a new majority by wooing the whites who had backed segregationist George Wallace in 1964 and 1968. South Carolina Republican Hastings Wyman, a former aide to Strom Thurmond, recalled the tactics by which Republicans built this new majority in the South: "I was there, and I remember denouncing the 'block vote'; opposing busing so long and so loud that rural voters thought we were going to do away with school buses; the lurid leaflets exposing 'the integrationist ties' of our Democratic opponents—leaflets we mailed in plain white envelopes to all the white voters in the precincts that George Wallace had carried. . . . Racism, often purposely inflamed by many Southern Republicans, either because we believed it, or because we thought it would win votes, was a major tool in the building of the new Republican Party in the South."[12]

In 1980, when the realignment finally occurred, it was based to some extent on disenchantment with Democratic economics and foreign policy. But opposition to the civil rights movement and to a cluster of race-based or race-identified policies was particularly important in the South and in the ethnic suburbs of the Midwest and Northeast. In many of those areas, the two parties became identified with their different racial compositions—the Republicans as the "white party" and the Democrats as the

"black party." Such an identification was inimical to the cause of racial reconciliation. It created a dynamic by which the Republicans, to maintain
their majority, sought to divide whites from blacks. It also created an
incentive for Republicans to ignore black economic inequality in their policy proposals and legislation.

Some Republican politicians, such as former congressman Jack Kemp,
tried to develop a multiracial Republican Party and strategy, but they
were ignored. (Kemp was popular among Republicans because of his outspoken advocacy of tax cuts, not because of his support for racial equality.) Most Republican politicians were swept away by the racial logic
underlying the Republican majority. Faced with the prospect of defeat at
the hands of a Democratic opponent, Republicans from Jesse Helms to
the elder George Bush used racial wedge issues to win over erstwhile white
Democrats. And while Bush's son avoided these sorts of tactics in his own
run for president, as recently as fall 2001 two other Republicans—both
of whom, interestingly, had reputations for racial reconciliation—pulled
out the race card once they found themselves trailing in the polls.

Early on in his run for the governorship of Virginia, Republican
attorney general Mark Earley had boasted of his membership in the
NAACP and vowed that he would not ignore the black vote. But by the
summer's end, Earley was trailing Democrat Mark Warner by 11 percent
in the polls. Warner was even ahead in Southside Virginia, where small-
town white voters had deserted the Democrats for Wallace in 1968 and
had subsequently backed Republican presidential candidates. To win
back Southside whites, who were drawn to Warner's message of encouraging high-tech growth, Earley and the Virginia Republican Party ran
radio ads and passed out leaflets in the area accusing Warner and the
Democratic candidates for lieutenant governor and attorney general of
supporting gun control, same-sex marriage, and the abolition of capital
punishment. The charges were false, and without foundation. And they
grouped together the candidates in spite of the fact that they had been
nominated separately, disagreed on a range of issues, and were running
entirely separate campaigns. What was most striking about the leaflets,
however, was not what they said about the candidates' positions, but
what they showed: a photograph of Warner with that of attorney general
candidate Donald McEachin. Warner is white and McEachin is African-
American. Such a technique, pioneered by Helms's political machine in

North Carolina, was designed to demonstrate to these white Southside voters, who had a history of racial voting, that Warner was the candidate of the "black party."

In New Jersey, Republican Bret Schundler had captured the mayor's office in Jersey City twice, winning substantial black votes each time. But, as he fell far behind Democrat Jim McGreevey in the race for governor, Schundler increasingly resorted to issues with a strong racial component. In New Jersey, these issues pivot around the differences between the primarily black cities and primarily white suburbs. In his first debate with McGreevey, Schundler, without any prompting, raised his opposition to the New Jersey Supreme Court's Mount Laurel decision. This 1975 decision forced developers in affluent suburbs to devote a "fair share" of their new properties to affordable housing. Schundler said he wanted to "get rid of" the decision because it increased "suburban sprawl."[13] Although people tend to worry about suburban sprawl because they're concerned about pollution or want to ease congestion on the roads, the link to the Mount Laurel decision made it obvious that Schundler had something other than the environment or traffic in mind: Schundler was proposing to curb the movement by the poor—overwhelmingly black and Hispanic—into more affluent, mostly white suburbs.

In the closing month of his campaign, Schundler also highlighted his plan to provide vouchers. Some conservatives have advocated vouchers so that ghetto children could afford to go to private schools as an alternative to failing public schools. But in his campaign, Schundler brazenly appealed to Catholic and religious right parents who already send their children to private schools. He attacked spending on public education as a subsidy to urban—that is, minority—schools and presented vouchers as a way of rewarding suburban parents who send their children to private schools. Schundler charged that McGreevey, who opposes vouchers, "wants to just throw more money into urban school districts and cut money for suburban and rural school districts." McGreevey, in Schundler's coded words, was guilty of favoring primarily black cities over primarily white suburban and rural school districts.

Earley and Schundler, like the elder Bush, showed no sign of personally being racist. But as Republicans, they inherited a coalition and a strategy that divided the parties along racial lines and that encouraged Republicans, when in trouble, to stress their opposition to race-based or race-identified programs. In the seventies and early eighties, these tactics frequently worked. But as Democrats abandoned programs like busing, and as a new generation of black leaders, including Washington, D.C., mayor Anthony Williams and Detroit mayor Dennis Archer, replaced the old, race-baiting began to backfire on Republicans, particularly among professionals and women voters who were raised in the sixties ethos of racial tolerance. In Virginia's 1989 gubernatorial race, African-American candidate Douglas Wilder's standing in the Washington, D.C., affluent suburbs shot up after a Virginia Republican attempted to paint Wilder as a black militant. And in the 2001 Virginia and New Jersey races, Republicans had no success whatsoever using these kinds of tactics.

III. STEM CELLS, GAY RIGHTS, AND THE RELIGIOUS RIGHT

In 1980, when Ronald Reagan called on Americans to affirm the values of "family, work, and neighborhood," he was drawing a distinction between these values and those that the extremes of the sixties counterculture had embraced. Republicans became the party opposed to the drug culture, bra burning, sexual promiscuity, teenage pregnancy, and the New Age denigration of religion. And they won elections on this basis. But in the 1980s, as Republicans embraced the religious right of Falwell and Robertson, they went well beyond repudiating the most extreme movements of the sixties. They rejected the new values and social structure that postindustrial capitalism is creating and nourishing.

Most important among these are women's equality at home and at work. The transition to postindustrial capitalism has profoundly altered family structure and the role of women, as the public sector and private industry have increasingly absorbed tasks at home that women traditionally performed. The imperative to have large families has disappeared. Women, no longer consigned to the home, have entered the workforce and many have taken up professional careers. The numbers of divorced women and single mothers have risen; so has the number of college-educated women professionals. *Father Knows Best* has given way to *An Unmarried Woman*. Modern feminism arose in response to these changes. Like other political movements, it included apocalyptic and utopian extremes, but at its core, it represented an attempt to remove the contradiction between an older patriarchal ideology and the growing potential for equality between men and women.

The Republicans, prodded by the religious right and by conservatives who sought its support, rejected the Equal Rights Amendment and the right of women to have an abortion. They balked at federal money for child care and held up the older ideal of the family. (Pat Robertson stated the case in 1992: "I know this is painful for the ladies to hear, but if you get married, you have accepted the headship of a man, your husband. Christ is the head of the household and the husband is the head of the wife, and that's the way it is, period."[14]) Republicans highlighted the most extreme aspects of the women's movement in order to reject the whole. By contrast, Democrats absorbed the mainstream of the new feminist movement, exemplified by the abortion rights organizations and the National Organization for Women. Democrats also advanced proposals for child care and paid family leave to accommodate the reality that so many mothers were now working outside the home.

Democrats and Republicans have similarly parted ways on encouraging sexual education among teenagers and on preventing discrimination against homosexuals in housing or employment. Like the controversies about prohibition in the 1920s, these seem peripheral to the heart of politics, but in fact arise directly from the transition from one way of life to another. Prohibition was the cause of the small town against city, the ordered life of the farmer and craftsman against the chaos and squalor of the factory city, and of Anglo-Saxon Protestants against ethnic immigrants. Similarly, the Republicans, goaded by the religious right, have become the defenders of the mores of Middletown against those of the postindustrial metropolis.

Republicans, as the party of the religious right, have upheld the older ideal of sexual abstinence and of family life as not merely the norm, but as a moral imperative. They have opposed sexual education, if not sex itself, for teenagers. In December 1994, congressional Republicans forced the Clinton administration's surgeon general, Jocelyn Elders, to resign because she responded favorably to an off-the-cuff question at a press conference about the advisability of discussing masturbation as part of sexual education. Republicans have also adopted the religious right's attitude toward homosexuals as purposeful sinners who represent a threat to public morals. They opposed not only Clinton's unpopular proposal to allow gays to serve openly in the military, but also began to mount initiative campaigns to deny gays protection from discrimination in housing and employment. In Congress, Senate Republicans even refused to confirm a Clinton administration choice for ambassador to Luxembourg because he was a homosexual. They have also indicted homosexuals for causing the AIDs epidemic. In Virginia's 2001 contest for lieutenant governor, the Republican candidate, Jay Katzen, declared that AIDs "is the product, sadly, in most cases of a choice that people have made. . . . We recognize that homosexuality is a choice. It's a lifestyle with public health consequences."[15]

These Republican attitudes were common, of course, fifty and a hundred years ago, but they have lost ground in postindustrial America. Americans today see sex not simply as a means to procreation, but as a source of pleasure and enjoyment. Many still cringe at the sight or prospect of homosexuality, but recognize it as a possibly inherited form of sexual expression that, if denied and closeted, could prevent a person's pursuit of happiness. They may not want gays to be honest about their sexual preference in the military, but they see conservative attempts to punish and stigmatize gays as bigotry and intolerance.

Conservative Republicans and Democrats also part ways on the relationship of religion to science. Here, there was little provocation by the Democratic left or even from the counterculture, unless the arch-Victorian Charles Darwin is seen as representative of the left-wing counterculture. In search of votes, the conservative Republicans of the 1980s made a devil's pact with religious fundamentalists that entailed their indulgence of crackpot religious notions. While Democrats have opposed the imposition of sectarian religious standards on science and public education, the Republicans have tried to make science and science education conform to Protestant fundamentalism. Throughout the South and the Midwest, Republicans have promoted teaching creationism instead of or in competition with the theory of evolution. Creationists hold that the Bible is the literal truth and that the world began several thousand rather than billions of years ago. One leading creationist, for instance, holds that dinosaurs roamed the earth in the twentieth century.[16]

Prominent Republican politicians and intellectuals, including Irving Kristol, William Bennett, and Robert Bork, have refused to repudiate these notions.[17] Instead, they have sanctioned the idea that creationism and Darwinian evolution are merely two competing theories. In the 2000 presidential campaign, George W. Bush endorsed this view: "I believe children ought to be exposed to different theories about how the world started." Later Bush's official spokeswoman said, "He believes both creationism and evolution ought to be taught. He believes it is a question for states and local school boards to decide but he believes both ought to be taught."

The Republican rejection of modern science reached an apogee during Bush's first year in office when he became embroiled in a controversy over whether the government should fund stem-cell research. Stem cells were finally isolated and reproduced for research purposes in 1998 by a University of Wisconsin scientist. These cells could provide the basis for a new "regenerative medicine" that would aid, and even cure, victims of Parkinson's, Alzheimer's, heart disease, stroke, diabetes, and some forms of cancer by replacing or regenerating cells. Stem cells have been garnered from embryos at fertility clinics. Some one hundred thousand embryos are currently frozen and, if not used, will eventually be discarded. Scientists want to use them for scientific research, and the Clinton administration agreed to fund research on new stem cells.[18]

But Republicans sided with the religious right who argued that these embryos are living beings that cannot be "murdered" for the sake of scientific research.* This notion of life prompted journalist Michael Kinsley to ask in *Time* magazine, "Are we really going to start basing social policy on the assumption that a few embryonic cells equal a human being?"[19] But Bush, after claiming to spend months pondering the issue of life in a petri dish, finally announced in a nationwide address that researchers could only use stem cells that had already been created from embryos. They could not use new embryos. Such a decision bore out the degree to which conservative Republicans had become hostage to the religious right's campaign against modernity and postindustrial America.

On many of these economic and social issues, conservative Republicans initially won support by standing resolutely against the excesses of

---

*Bush also solicited the views of the pope and other Catholic leaders on whether to fund stem-cell research. Bush was not similarly concerned about Catholic views on capital punishment or on government aid to the poor. His interest in Catholic views seemed to flow from the interest of his political adviser Karl Rove in winning votes for 2004.

the sixties and of post–New Deal liberal Democrats. But clearly they have gone to extremes of their own. They are putting forth remedies for problems that no longer exist and ignoring problems that do. They are fighting the future on behalf of the past. In the meantime, Democrats, chastened by defeat during the eighties, have repudiated their own extremes and moved to the political center, which itself has gravitated in a broadly progressive direction. Ironically, the party that the Democrats most clearly resemble is the one that Bush and Rove claim for themselves—the progressive Republicans of the early twentieth century. Like the progressive Republicans, today's Democrats stand between the extremes of right and left and at the gateway at the end of one era of capitalism and the beginning of another. They are the new party of progressive centrism.

Today's Americans, whose attitudes have been nurtured by the transition to postindustrial capitalism, increasingly endorse the politics of this progressive centrism. They want government to play an active and responsible role in American life, guaranteeing a reasonable level of economic security to Americans rather than leaving them at the mercy of the market and the business cycle. They want to preserve and strengthen social security and medicare, rather than privatize them. They want to modernize and upgrade public education, not abandon it. They want to exploit new biotechnologies and computer technologies to improve the quality of life. They do not want science held hostage to a religious or ideological agenda. And they want the social gains of the sixties consolidated, not rolled back; the wounds of race healed, not inflamed. That's why the Democrats are likely to become the majority party of the early twenty-first century.

APPENDIX: DATA SOURCES

NATIONAL ELECTION STUDIES (NES)

The National Election Study is a biennial academic survey about politics conducted in every election year by the University of Michigan's Center for Political Studies. The survey has been conducted since 1948 and collects a wide range of data about attitudes, opinions, and voting behavior. The continuity of the survey and the richness of the data make it the premier data source used by academics in the study of American politics.

These factors also made the survey useful for some of the research conducted for this book. In fact, to the extent we were interested in political attitudes and the demographics of voting behavior going back to the 1960s, there was really no choice. The NES is the only survey that allows you to go back that far and investigate these issues.

The NES has interviewed from 1,200 to 2,700 respondents over the years. In recent years, the totals have been 2,485 (1992), 1,795 (1994), 1,714 (1996), 1,281 (1998), and 1,807 (2000). Since the NES surveys the adult citizen population, the actual number of (self-reported) voters is less than these numbers would indicate, since some adults choose not to vote. However, even with this diminution of the sample, the survey is still quite adequate for looking at broad political and attitudinal trends among voters. For more elaborate analysis of smaller subgroups of the voting electorate (e.g., Hispanics, married working-class whites with children), the NES sample does start to have limitations due to the small number of respondents in such subgroups. Fortunately, an alternative with a much larger sample size, exit polls (discussed below), allows us to perform more elaborate analyses for recent elections.

BUREAU OF THE CENSUS DATA

We use three different Bureau of the Census data sources. First, of course, we use the decennial censuses of 1990 and 2000 to track demographic changes in the 1990s. This was particularly useful in looking at changes in population and race/ethnic distribution nationally, by state, and by counties within states.

In doing so, we faced the difficulty common to all who have used these data to compare 1990 and 2000 race/ethnic distributions: the change in race coding in the 2000 census made it possible for respondents to check more than one race. This creates the problem of comparing a distribution from 1990, where it was only possible to check one race, with a distribution from 2000, when two or more races could be selected.

The solution we used, as outlined in a paper by geographers James P. Allen and Eugene Turner, was to assign race fractionally based on other data that showed how likely a biracial individual was to have designated a given race as his or her primary race. Individuals who selected three, four, or five races were simply divided up equally among the races in question.

We also linked the 1990 and 2000 census data to a database of county-level presidential voting results going back to 1960. This allowed us, for example, to look at how counties that had added the most people in the 1990s voted in recent presidential elections.

Second, we used the Current Population Survey (CPS) Voter Supplement data to look at the demographics of voters. The CPS is the Bureau of the Census's large-scale monthly survey to track changes in the labor market, particularly unemployment rates. In addition, the CPS periodically collects supplementary information about selected social and economic topics. One such effort is the Voter Supplement, administered as part of the November CPS in every election year (presidential and off-year). The Voter Supplement collects basic information about whether respondents voted, whether they were registered, and a small number of other items (for example, what time of day the respondent voted). No information is collected about whom the respondent voted for or what the respondent's political attitudes and partisan preferences are.

The lack of political information means the Voter Supplement is useless for examining what any given election is about. But its huge size—90,000 to 100,000 respondents eighteen and over—combined with the rich demographic information always collected by the CPS, makes it a superb source for analyzing how the demographics of the voting pool have changed over time.

The Voter Supplement data are particularly useful as a corrective to the exit polls' apparent tendency to overstate the educational credentials of voters. For example, in the 2000 election, the exit polls said that 42 percent of voters had a four-year college degree; in contrast, the census data said that only 31 percent had a four-year college degree. Similarly, in 1996, the exit polls said 43 percent of voters were college-educated; the census data said only 29 percent. This is quite a substantial difference and suggests the exit polls should be used mostly for what they were intended for: to project the results of elections and, secondarily, to compare the political attitudes and preferences of different voter groups.

The question has been raised, most forcefully by political scientists Samuel Popkin and Michael McDonald,[1] whether this is a fair judgment, since the census data are based on self-reports of voting, whereas the exit polls, with all their flaws, are at least based directly on voters. Therefore, perhaps it is the exit poll data that are accurate and the census data that are biased.

A number of things are wrong with this argument.[2] Most importantly, if one believes the exit poll data, implied turnout levels by education are literally unbelievable. For example, according to the 1996 VNS exit poll, 43 percent of voters were college graduates. Based on the total number of votes cast and the education composition of the population, this implies a turnout rate for college-graduate citizens of 102 percent. This is impossible and clearly indicates a serious problem with the exit polls.

Popkin and McDonald's main reply has been that the exit poll question on education is flawed, and that this, not education bias in the exit poll sample, mostly accounts for the difference between the two surveys. They pointed out that the education question on the exit poll, until recently, typically listed the some-college category as "some college but no degree." Given this wording, it seemed a reasonable assumption that some unknown proportion of those with a two-year AA degree didn't check this category but selected the "college graduate" category instead. But this didn't make the exit polls right; it merely meant they overstated the proportion of four-year college graduates for a different reason (question wording instead of sample bias).

More seriously—and fatally for the substance of their question-wording thesis—VNS *did* change their question wording in 2000 so that voters with associate degrees were included in the some-college category. But the 41.7 percent in the 2000 VNS college category still translates into an implied turnout rate for college-educated citizens of 99 percent—a preposterously high figure, though a slight improvement on 1996's absurd implied rate of 102 percent. Thus, there does appear to be a serious exit-poll-sample education-bias problem, and it seems prudent to rely on the CPS voter supplement data for estimates on the education distribution of voters.

The third census data source we used was the CPS Outgoing Rotation Group (ORG) files. These files are particularly useful for looking at labor force characteristics such as occupation and union membership. When collected for an entire year, the large number of labor force cases (about 150,000) allows for good estimates of these characteristics in the nation, individual states, and selected metropolitan areas.

NATIONAL EXIT POLLS

A consortium of television networks and newspapers sponsors large national exit polls during every presidential and off-year election, currently conducted by Voter News Service (VNS). The number of questions asked is small compared to the NES, but the sample size is much larger (11,000 to 16,000 voters in recent years, compared to just 800 to 2,000 for the NES). This makes it an ideal data source for looking at recent trends in voting support among various demographic subgroups (though not for looking at the demographic composition of voters, particularly education, as discussed in the previous section).

Since VNS conducts exit polls in every state, it is possible to use their surveys to look at voting patterns in various states, rather than just nationally, as is the case with the NES. In addition, since the VNS state data sets typically include a variable that indicates roughly where in the state a respondent was interviewed, it is possible to use these "geocodes" to look at voting patterns among various demographic groups in different regions of states.

We should point out that only some of the VNS geocodes are clear enough in terms of their geographic coverage to be useful. We should also stress that the VNS data are not really designed for this kind of substate analysis, and in fact, the VNS cautions against it. However, we elected to use the data anyway in selected instances because no alternatives exist if one is interested in asking certain questions about substate voting behavior.

COUNTY PRESIDENTIAL ELECTION RESULTS

We made extensive use of presidential voting results by county going back to 1960. We copied most of these data from Dave Leip's excellent Web site of presidential election results. Data we took from Leip's Web site was carefully cross-checked against hard-copy data in the *America Votes* series of election data compilations. We also used the *America Votes* volumes to fill in gaps in the data on Leip's Web site.

Finally, we took these data and linked them by county FIPS (Federal Information Processing Standards) code to an extensive set of 1990 and 2000 county-level data from the decennial censuses of those years. We also created a special county-level variable for whether a county could be considered part of an ideopolis. A footnote in chapter 3 explains our procedure for doing this.

NOTES

INTRODUCTION

1. See E. J. Dionne, *They Only Look Dead* (New York: Simon & Schuster, 1996).
2. See David Osborne and Ted Gaebler, *Reinventing Government* (New York: Plume, 1993).

CHAPTER 1

1. See Walter Dean Burnham, "Party Systems and the Political Process," in *The American Party Systems,* ed. William Nisbet Chambers and Walter Dean Burnham (New York: Oxford University Press, 1975). V. O. Key first described a theory of realignment in "A Theory of Critical Elections," *Journal of Politics,* 1955.
2. See Key, "Theory of Critical Elections."
3. Kevin Phillips, *The Emerging Republican Majority* (New York: Arlington House, 1969).
4. The University of Michigan's authoritative National Election Study confirmed what these patterns imply: an overwhelming proportion of Wallace voters who voted in 1972 cast their votes for Nixon.
5. These and other figures on changes in the House and Senate by party for different elections are taken from *National Journal,* November 11, 2000, pp. 3557, 3562.
6. Norman J. Ornstein, Thomas E. Mann, and Michael J. Malbin, *Vital Statistics on Congress, 1995–96* (Washington, D.C.: CQ Press, 1996).
7. See Thomas Edsall with Mary Edsall, *Chain Reaction* (New York: Norton, 1991).
8. Authors' analysis of National Election Study data.
9. Stanley Greenberg, "Report on Democratic Defection," The Analysis Group.
10. Authors' analysis of 1980 National Election Study data; figures based on white voters only.
11. *New York Times/*CBS News exit polls.

185

12. Ibid.

13. Ibid.

14. Edsall, *Chain Reaction*. Senator Phil Gramm, who would switch parties in 1982 to become a Republican, talked about some Americans who "rode in the wagon" and others who "pulled the wagon" and put himself and other conservative Republicans clearly on the side of the latter.

15. See Sidney Blumenthal, *Pledging Allegiance* (New York: HarperCollins, 1990).

16. *New York Times*/CBS News exit polls.

17. See Stanley Greenberg, *Middle Class Dreams* (New York: Random House, 1995).

18. Quoted in Alexander P. Lamis, ed., *Southern Politics in the 1990s* (Baton Rouge: LSU Press, 1999).

19. Authors' analysis of county-level election returns, 1960–2000.

20. See "Clinton's Revolution," *Newsweek,* March 1, 1993.

21. Grover Norquist, *Rock the House* (Fort Lauderdale: Vytis, 1995), 2.

22. Ornstein, Mann, and Malbin, *Vital Statistics,* tables 1-5 and 2-3.

23. See Taylor E. Dark, *The Unions and the Democrats* (Ithaca, N.Y.: Cornell University Press, 1999).

24. On third parties, see Micah L. Sifry, *Spoiling for a Fight* (New York: Rutledge, 2001).

25. See Herbert Weisberg and Timothy Hill, "The Succession Presidential Election of 2000: The Battle of the Legacies" (paper delivered at 2001 American Political Science Association annual meeting). Note however that many of these independents are "leaners," who admit to favoring one party when pressed.

26. Ibid.

27. Authors' analysis of 2000 Voter News Service (VNS) state exit-poll data.

28. See John B. Judis, "The Hunted," *The New Republic,* April 17, 2000.

CHAPTER 2

1. Jeane Kirkpatrick, "The Revolution of the Masses," *Commentary,* November 27, 1972.

2. Margaret Weir and Marshall Ganz, "Reconnecting People and Politics," in *The New Majority,* ed. Stanley Greenberg and Theda Skocpol (New Haven, Conn.: Yale University Press, 1997).

3. Authors' analysis of National Election Study (NES) data.

4. Ibid.

5. Figure for 2000 from authors' analysis of Current Population Survey occupation data provided on Population Reference Bureau Web site; 1950s estimate is derived from deflating the combined figure for professional, technical, and kindred workers in *Historical Statistics of the United States.*

6. See Ruy Teixeira, *The Disappearing American Voter* (Washington, D.C.:

Brookings, 1992), chapter 3. The pattern is also observed in 1996 Current Population Survey Voter Supplement data.

7. National figure based on analysis of 2000 NES survey; it includes both those professionals who are currently working and those who are retired, as well as students, homemakers, and disabled who do professional work. Estimates for the comparison among states are based on analysis of the 1996 Current Population Survey Voter Supplement, using the 2000 NES figure as a baseline.

8. Figures for the past are from Daniel Bell's introduction to Thorstein Veblen, *Engineers and the Price System* (New York: Harcourt Brace & World, 1963), and for the present from Stephen Rose's unpublished tables on factory work and SESTAT (NSF) tables on U.S. scientists and engineers.

9. *Current Statistics on Scientists, Engineers, and Technical Workers* (DPE, 2000).

10. *Historical Statistics of the United States.*

11. This account of American economic history draws heavily upon Martin J. Sklar, *The United States as a Developing Country* (New York: Cambridge University Press, 1992), chapter 5; and Daniel Bell, *The Coming of Post-Industrial Society* (New York: Basic, 1973). See also John B. Judis, *The Paradox of American Democracy* (New York: Pantheon, 2000), chapter 4.

12. See Paul A. Baran and Paul M. Sweezy, *Monopoly Capital* (New York: Monthly Review Press, 1966), chapter 5; and David M. Potter, *People of Plenty* (Chicago: University of Chicago Press, 1954), chapter 8.

13. See Bell, *Coming of Post-Industrial Society.*

14. Figures here and before in this paragraph based on Lawrence Mishel, Jared Bernstein, and John Schmitt, *The State of Working America, 2000–01* (Ithaca, N.Y.: Cornell University Press, 2001), table 2.27, slightly adjusted to take agricultural employment into account.

15. *Historical Statistics of the United States.*

16. Authors' analysis of Current Population Survey occupation data provided on Population Reference Bureau Web site.

17. *Monthly Labor Review,* November 1999.

18. Authors' analysis of National Election Study data.

19. AnnaLee Saxenian, *Regional Advantage: Culture and Competition in Silicon Valley and Route 128* (Cambridge, Mass.: Harvard University Press, 1994).

20. David Kusnet, *Finding Their Voices* (Washington, D.C.: AFL-CIO, 2000), poll by Peter Hart Associates.

21. Harry Braverman, *Labor and Monopoly Capital* (New York: Monthly Review Press, 1998).

22. Authors' analysis of 2000 Current Population Survey Outgoing Rotation Group files.

23. See *Modern Physician,* February 26, 2001.

24. *Praxis Post,* October 4, 2000.

25. AP, June 25, 1999.

26. *Wall Street Journal,* August 8, 2001.

27. *Praxis Post,* October 4, 2000.

28. On voting by professionals, see Steven Brint, *In an Age of Experts* (Princeton: Princeton University Press, 1994); and Clem Brooks and Jeff Manza, *Social Cleavages and Political Change* (New York: Oxford University Press, 1999).

29. Based on authors' analysis of NES data for various years.

30. All data for elections prior to 1976 from authors' analysis of NES data.

31. All data in paragraph from authors' analysis of VNS national and state exit polls.

32. Kevin White, *Sexual Liberation or Sexual License* (Chicago: Ivan R. Dee, 2000).

33. Charlotte Perkins Gilman, "Economic Basis of the Woman Question," *Women's Journal,* October 1, 1898. On this subject, see Eli Zaretsky, *Capitalism, the Family and Personal Life* (New York: Perennial Library, 1975).

34. Betty Friedan, *The Feminine Mystique* (New York: Norton, 1963).

35. See Ruth Rosen, *The World Split Open* (New York: Viking, 2000).

36. Howard N. Fullerton Jr., "Labor Force Participation," *Monthly Labor Review,* December 1999.

37. Claudia Golden and Lawrence F. Katz, "On the Pill," *Milken Institute Review,* second quarter, 2001.

38. Authors' analysis of Current Population Survey occupation data provided on Population Reference Bureau Web site.

39. Authors' analysis of 1956 NES data.

40. See Jo Freeman, "Who You Know versus Who You Represent," in *Women's Movement in the United States and Europe,* ed. Mary Katzenstein and Carol Mueller (Philadelphia: Temple University Press, 1987); and Jo Freeman, *A Room at a Time* (Lanham, Md.: Roman and Littlefield, 2000).

41. White, *Sexual Liberation or Sexual License.*

42. See Tanya Melich, *The Republican War Against Women* (New York: Bantam, 1996).

43. For data and a useful discussion, see Brooks and Manza, *Social Cleavages,* chapter 5.

44. Melich, *The Republican War Against Women,* 70.

45. All data in paragraph based on authors' analysis of national exit polls for years indicated.

46. Gallup and NES data.

47. Gallup data; note that Gallup labels the category *nonwhite,* but it can safely be assumed to be almost exclusively black at that point in time. Also, the NES data, which does disaggregate blacks, shows every black respondent in the survey saying he or she voted for Johnson, so the Gallup 94 percent figure seems reasonable.

48. Data for 1968 and 1972 from the NES; 1976 to 2000 data from national exit polls.

49. Paul R. Abramson, John H. Aldrich, and David Waruhde, *Change and Continuity in the 1980 Elections* (Washington, D.C.: CQ Press, 1982), 60.

50. Teixeira, *The Disappearing American Voter;* authors' analysis of exit-poll and Current Population Survey data.

51. See Theodore White, *The Making of the President, 1972* (New York: Atheneum, 1973), 236.

52. ABC News/*Washington Post* poll.

53. Authors' analysis of 1990 and 2000 census data. We allocate bi- and multiracial individuals in the 2000 census according to the procedure suggested by James P. Allen and Eugene Turner in their paper "Estimating Primary Single-Race Identities for Reported Biracial Populations in the 2000 Census" (Department of Geography, California State University–Northridge).

54. Census data for 2000, cited on Hispanictrends.com Web site.

55. Authors' analysis of 1990 and 2000 census data.

56. This 5.4 percent figure is from the Current Population Survey (CPS) Voter Supplement. The exit poll estimate was higher, at 6.5 percent. However, we generally consider the CPS estimates to be more reliable.

57. *Los Angeles Times,* July 6, 2001.

58. Here and throughout we include Pacific Islanders with Asians as is customary in most analyses, including those done by the Census Bureau.

59. Authors' analysis of 1990 and 2000 census data.

60. Ibid.

61. VNS 2000 exit poll and 2000 Current Population Survey Voter Supplement.

62. Authors' analysis of 2000 census data.

63. See "Pilot Study" of the National Asian American Political Survey by Pei-te Lien, Margaret Conway, Taeku Lee, and Janelle Wong.

64. *Los Angeles Times,* May 23, 2001.

65. "Pilot Study."

66. The VNS exit poll had Gore with 55 percent and Bush with 41 percent, only a fourteen-point margin. Officials with the "Pilot Study" believe that the margin was wider, as indicated in their poll, and explain the difference by VNS's failure to include poll-takers who knew Chinese and other Asian languages. Note also that the *Los Angeles Times* national exit poll had Gore by twenty-five points (62–37) among Asians, close to the "Pilot Study" margin.

67. The 19 percent figure is drawn from both the 2000 VNS exit poll and from the 2000 CPS Voter Supplement; the 75 percent figure is based on the 2000 VNS exit poll but could be higher if the correct figure for the Asian-American pro-Democratic margin is close to that indicated by the "Pilot Study."

68. See Harold Meyerson, "Race Conquers All," *American Prospect,* December 3, 2001.

69. *Historical Statistics of the United States.* This 50 percent was composed of 40 percent who were blue-collar workers and 10 percent who were service workers.

70. Everett Carll Ladd Jr. with Charles D. Hadley, *Transformations of the American Party System: Party Coalitions from the New Deal to the 1970s* (New York: Norton, 1975), 231.

71. Authors' analysis of NES data; actual size of white working-class vote would be largest using an education-based (noncollege) definition, but virtually any reasonable occupation-based definition appears to still yield a figure well over 50 percent.

72. Robert J. Donovan, *Conflict and Crisis* (New York: Norton, 1977), 396.

73. Authors' analysis of the 2000 Current Population Outgoing Rotation Group files shows that Northern (that is, Northeastern and Midwestern) blue-collar workers still have a 29 percent unionization rate. Data from Derek C. Box and John T. Dunlop, *Labor and the American Community* (New York: Simon & Schuster, 1970), show that unionization rates in the early 1960s—when the overall unionization rate for nonagricultural workers was close to its level in the late 1940s—for various blue-collar occupations were generally two to three times higher than they are today. It is therefore a reasonable estimate that Northern blue-collar workers in the late 1940s had a unionization rate approaching, and probably exceeding, 60 percent.

74. Authors' analysis of NES data for years indicated; note that when we use the term *working class* without further specification we are referring to the non-college-educated—that is, those without a four-year college degree. See Ruy Teixeira and Joel Rogers, *America's Forgotten Majority: Why the White Working Class Still Matters* (New York: Basic, 2000), chapter 1, for more discussion and justification of this specification.

75. See Michael Goldfield, *The Decline of Organized Labor in the United States* (Chicago: University of Chicago Press, 1987).

CHAPTER 3

1. See Kirkpatrick Sale, *Power Shift* (New York: Random House, 1975).

2. See Robert Atkinson, "Technology and the Future of Metropolitan Economies" (Federal Reserve of Chicago, November 1995).

3. See Robert D. Atkinson and Paul D. Gottlieb, *The Metropolitan New Economy Index* (Washington, D.C.: PPI, April 2001).

4. On this point, see Richard Kaglic and William Testa, "Midwest Prospects and the New Economy," *Chicago Fed Letter,* October 2000; and Ann Markusen et al., *High-Tech and I-Tech: How Metros Rank and Specialize,* Humphrey Institute of Public Affairs, University of Minnesota (August 2001).

5. See Joe Kotkin and Ross C. DeVol, "Knowledge-Value Cities in the Digital Age" (Milken Institute, February 2001).

6. Authors' analysis of 2000 Current Population Survey Outgoing Rotation Group files; note that figures refer to metropolitan areas, not cities.

7. See Richard Florida and Gary Gates, "Technology and Tolerance" (Brookings Institution, June 2001).

8. Richard Florida, *Information Week,* November 13, 2000.

9. Authors' analysis of 2000 VNS exit poll for Colorado.

10. Authors' analysis of 2000 VNS exit poll data for states indicated.

11. Authors' analysis of 2000 VNS exit poll for Ohio.

12. All data in this paragraph from authors' analysis of county-level 2000 census data. Note that if one looks at total population growth across all ideopolis and nonideopolis counties, this considerably narrows, but does not eliminate, the growth gap discussed in the paragraph.

13. See Lou Cannon, *Ronnie and Jessie* (Garden City, N.Y.: Doubleday, 1969).

14. When we speak of the Bay Area, we generally mean the Bay Area ideopolis, which includes the San Francisco, Oakland, and San Jose PMSAs, areas tightly clustered around the city of San Francisco. This includes the counties of Alameda, Contra Costa, Marin, San Francisco, San Mateo, and Santa Clara. Sometimes the Bay Area is more broadly defined to include several counties farther north of the city: Napa, Sonoma, and Solano. And the San Francisco CMSA (Consolidated Metropolitan Statistical Area) includes all these and Santa Cruz County besides. But we will generally use the narrower definition where data permits.

15. See Markusen et al., *High-Tech and I-Tech.*

16. Democratic support was 72–23 percent among white voters with a postgraduate education, the closest approximation of professionals that the VNS affords.

17. Authors' analysis of 2000 VNS exit poll data for California; note that the VNS Bay Area designation may or may not correspond to the definition we prefer (the San Francisco, Oakland, and San Jose MSAs).

18. See Mark Baldassare, *California in the New Millennium: The Changing Social and Political Landscape* (Berkeley, Cal.: University of California Press, 2000).

19. Ideopolis-based definition, as specified earlier.

20. Central Valley defined as in Baldassare, *California in the New Millennium,* to include Butte, Colusa, Fresno, Glenn, Kern, Kings, Madera, Merced, Placer, Sacramento, San Joaquin, Shasta, Stanislaus, Sutter, Tehama, Tulare, Yolo, and Yuba counties.

21. Other races not shown in chart.

22. California is unique among states in having two credible and roughly equally sized exit polls to choose from, one conducted by VNS and the other by the *Los Angeles Times (LAT).* Here we report an average of the top-line findings from the two polls, which for Hispanics tend to be quite close.

23. The 57–40 figure is an average of the VNS and *LAT* exit polls; the 63–33 figure is the *LAT* figure.

24. Authors' analysis of 1990 and 2000 census data.

25. New Jersey Department of Labor statistics in "Projections 2008," July 2000.

26. See William Schneider, "The Battle for Saliency: The Abortion Issue in This Campaign," *The Atlantic,* October 1992.

27. *Washington Post,* November 12, 1989.

28. See John B. Judis, "A Taxing Governor," *The New Republic,* October 15, 1990; and "Bill Folds," *The New Republic,* January 28, 1991.

29. All data in paragraph except overall county results from authors' analysis of 2000 VNS New Jersey exit poll.

30. Operationalized as those with a postgraduate education (VNS collects no occupation data).

31. Jonathan Cohn, "Fade to Black," *The New Republic,* November 13, 2000.

32. Authors' analysis of 2000 VNS Pennsylvania exit poll.

33. Authors' interview with Ray Buckley, former political director of the Gore campaign in New Hampshire.

34. See Beth Gorczyca, "Peering into a Murky Future," *Herald Dispatch,* September 17, 2000. See also *Wall Street Journal,* June 13, 2001.

35. *Charleston Gazette,* November 7, 2001.

36. Stephen E. Ambrose, *Nixon: The Education of a Politician* (New York: Simon & Schuster, 1987), 606.

37. See Neal R. Pierce, *The Megastates of America* (New York: Norton, 1972).

38. Kotkin and DeVol, "Knowledge-Value Cities."

39. See Markusen et al., *High Tech and I-Tech.*

40. Bureau of Labor statistics for 1999.

41. See Paul Green and Melvin Holli, eds., *The Mayors: The Chicago Political Tradition* (Carbondale, Ill.: Southern Illinois University Press, 1995). John Kass, "The New Mayor Daley," *Chicago Tribune,* August 25, 1996.

42. Interview with authors.

43. Authors' analysis of 2000 VNS Illinois exit poll.

44. Note that this calculation does not include Lansing's Ingham County for reasons previously outlined; however, inclusion of Ingham County in this calculation would only make the result stronger.

45. MDC, Inc., *State of the South 2000* (Chapel Hill, N.C.: MDC, Inc., 2001).

46. All data in this paragraph from authors' analysis of 1996 and 2000 VNS exit polls for Missouri.

47. Interview with authors.

48. Authors' analysis of 2000 VNS Florida exit poll.

49. Authors' analysis of 1990 and 2000 census data.

50. Lance deHaven-Smith, "George W. and Jeb, a Rogue Legislature, an Activist County, Cuban Republicans, and Puerto Rican Democrats, Blue Dogs and Yellow Dogs, Dixiecrats and New Dealers, the Old South and the New South" (unpublished paper, December 2000).

51. See Michael I. Luger, "Spontaneous Technopolises and Regional Restructuring: The Case of Research Triangle, N.C.," Department of City and Regional Planning, University of North Carolina, Chapel Hill, unpublished, June 8, 1998.

52. Raleigh metro figure from analysis of North Carolina county election returns;

figure on college-educated white women from authors' analysis of 2000 VNS North Carolina exit poll.
53. "South Carolina," in *Southern Politics in the 1990s*, ed. Lamis.
54. *Decatur Daily*, April 19, 2001.

CHAPTER 4

1. Memo, Pat Caddell to President Carter, December 10, 1976, Press Files: Jody Powell, Jimmy Carter Library.
2. Richard Scammon and Ben Wattenberg, *The Real Majority* (New York: Coward-McCann, 1970).
3. This and following quotations from Memo, Caddell to Carter.
4. See Sidney Blumenthal, "Hart's Big Chill," *Our Long National Daydream* (New York: Harper & Row, 1988).
5. See Gary Hart, *The New Democracy* (New York: William Morrow, 1984).
6. Patrick Caddell, "The State of American Politics," October 25, 1983.
7. Exit polls have a long-term and consistent problem with overestimating the educational credentials of voters, particularly the numbers of college graduates. See appendix to this volume and appendix to Teixeira and Rogers, *America's Forgotten Majority*, for discussion of this problem.
8. Income data only available for two breaks, under and over $25,000. This translates into under and over $41,500 in 2000 dollars.
9. See Karen Paget, "The Gender Gap Mystique," *American Prospect*, Fall 1993.
10. See *New York Times*, July 22, 1984.
11. See Blumenthal, "Hart's Big Chill"; and Elizabeth Colton, *The Jackson Phenomenon* (New York: Doubleday, 1989).
12. Amiri Baraka, "What Makes Jesse Run?" *Playboy*, July 1988.
13. On the history of the Democratic Leadership Council, see Ken Baer, *Reinventing Democrats* (Lawrence, Kans.: University of Kansas Press, 2000); and interviews by authors with Will Marshall and Alvin From.
14. "Memorandum: Saving the Democratic Party," January 2, 1985.
15. See Paul Starobin, "An Affair to Remember," *National Journal*, January 16, 1993.
16. William Gallston and Elaine Ciulla Kamarck, "The Politics of Evasion: Democrats and the Presidency," Progressive Policy Institute, September 1989.
17. David Osborne and Ted Gaebler, *Reinventing Government* (New York: Plume, 1993).
18. See "The New Choice: A Progressive Agenda for the 1990s" (Washington, D.C.: Democratic Leadership Council, 1991).
19. In 1984 and 1988, male college graduates had backed the Republican presidential candidate by the same margin, 63–36 percent, but female college

graduates, who had voted for Reagan 52–47 percent in 1984, voted for Dukakis in 1988 by 51 to 49 percent. CBS/*New York Times* exit polls.

20. Clinton announcement of candidacy, July 16, 1992.
21. See Judis, *Paradox of American Democracy,* chapter 9.
22. Authors' analysis of 1994 VNS exit poll.
23. Authors' analysis of 1992 and 1996 VNS national exit polls for all figures except professionals. The latter figure is derived from authors' analysis of 1992 and 1996 National Election Studies.
24. Authors' analysis of 1992 and 1996 VNS state exit polls for Ohio and New Jersey.
25. Interview by authors.
26. Dudley Buff, Michael Hais, and Morley Winograd, "Wired Workers and the Digital Deal," *New Democrat,* November–December 1996. Later definitions of "wired workers" don't appear to include the network stipulation and may have added a specification about *preferring* to work together in a team. The slippage on the definition probably makes little difference to the usefulness (or lack thereof) of the concept.
27. Al From and Will Marshall, "Building the New Democratic Majority," *Blueprint,* fall 1998. Penn's characterization of wired workers is from "Choosing the New Economy," *Blueprint,* winter 1998.
28. See *Chattanooga Times,* January 5, 2000.
29. See Jonathan Cohn, "Play It Again, Stan," *The New Republic,* August 31, 2000.
30. Stanley Greenberg, *Middle Class Dreams* (New York: Random House, 1995, revised 1996).
31. Anna Greenberg and Stanley B. Greenberg, "Adding Values," *American Prospect,* August 2000. (Note that this essay was written before Greenberg joined the Gore campaign in late July 2000.)
32. Greenberg, *Middle Class Dreams.*
33. See "Gore's Summer Surprise," *Newsweek,* November 20, 2000; and "What It Took," *Time,* November 20, 2000.
34. A reasonable argument can also be made that Gore was hurt by distancing himself so far from the administration's very real accomplishments, especially on the economy. Note, however, that the available boost from the economy may not have been as big as commonly believed and as some political scientists asserted based on election-forecasting models. An important paper by political scientists Larry Bartels and John Zaller persuasively criticizes this viewpoint. Bartels and Zaller looked at forty-eight possible election-forecasting models using a number of standard variables, including several different economic measures. They then averaged these models' predictions, with each model's weight based on its explanatory power through the 1996 election (called Bayesian weighting). Since the historically best-performing models tended to be those based on growth in real per capita disposable income and since there had actually been a slowdown in such growth prior to the 2000 election, Bartels and Zaller found that the

weighted average prediction for Gore's percent of the two-party popular vote was only half a percentage point off the vote he actually received (as opposed to widely publicized models based on raw economic growth, which predicted anywhere from a six- to twenty-point Gore win).

35. Memo, Cadell to Carter.

36. Al From, "Building a New Progressive Majority," *Blueprint,* January 24, 2001.

37. Mark J. Penn, "Lessons of 2000," *American Prospect,* May 7, 2001; and Mark J. Penn, "Turning a Win into a Draw," *Blueprint,* January 24, 2001.

38. Press conference sponsored by Campaign for America's Future, November 10, 2000. See also Stanley Greenberg, "The Progressive Majority and the 2000 Elections," on Campaign for America's Future Web site.

39. Poll conducted November 7–8, 2000, among 2,036 respondents for the Campaign for America's Future. See also Ruy Teixeira, "Lessons for Next Time," *American Prospect,* December 18, 2000.

CHAPTER 5

1. *US News and World Report,* October 2, 2000.

2. Michael Barone with Richard Cohen and Grant Ujifusa, *The Almanac of American Politics, 2002* (Washington, D.C.: National Journal, 2001), "Introduction."

3. David Brooks, "Bush's Patriotic Challenge," *Weekly Standard,* October 8, 2001.

4. Authors' analysis of Census Bureau Historical Poverty tables, 1960–96, on their Web site.

5. John C. Green, James L. Guth, Lyman A. Kellstedt, and Corwin E. Smidt, "How the Faithful Voted: Religion and the 2000 Presidential Election," Ethics and Public Policy Center, Washington, D.C.

6. The VNS figure of 43 percent for church attendance weekly or more is much higher than the NES figure of 25 percent for every week among all adults and 30 percent among voters and the NORC figure of only 32 percent, even when combining attendance every week and almost every week. The VNS figure is probably inflated by the normative pressures of having to respond in a public place to a set of choices that are biased toward being devout (two categories that are at least weekly and another that is oddly close—"a few times a month"—among just five categories). The NES study, by contrast, actually screens people first to see if they ever attend church aside from weddings and funerals before even asking them about their level of attendance. The NORC study allows respondents to simply state their level of attendance, which is then coded into an extensive set of nine categories. The NES and NORC methods probably produce a more accurate assessment than the VNS.

7. The never-attend figure is lower in the VNS than in the other surveys—just 14 percent of voters. We believe the other surveys are more accurate for the reasons stated in the previous note.
8. Green et al., "How the Faithful Voted."
9. David Leege, "The Catholic Voter," Commonweal Foundation, June 2, 2000.
10. Peter Beinart, "The Burbs," *The New Republic,* October 19, 1998.
11. Barone et al., *Almanac.*
12. Daniel Casse, "Bush and the Republican Future," *Commentary,* March 2001.
13. NORC polling. Cited in William G. Mayer, *The Changing American Mind* (Ann Arbor, Mich.: University of Michigan Press, 1992).
14. Cited in Tom W. Smith, "Trends in National Spending Priorities, 1973–1998" (unpublished manuscript, NORC).
15. Survey conducted for Cato by Zogby polling, March 2001.
16. AARP, "Individual Accounts, Social Security, and the 2000 Election," September 2000.
17. See especially the Kaiser Family Foundation/Harvard University survey on medicare policy options, August–September 1998.
18. See John B. Judis, "Coming Attractions," *American Prospect,* December 3, 2001.
19. *Wall Street Journal,* November 14, 2001.
20. *The Bulletin's Frontrunner,* September 6, 2001.
21. David Brooks, "The Reemerging Republican Majority," *The Weekly Standard,* February 11, 2002.
22. Marshall Wittmann, Project for Conservative Reform Web site, October 23, 2001.
23. See National Resource Defense Council, "Rewriting the Rules," January 2002.

CONCLUSION

1. See John B. Judis, "Deregulation Run Riot," *American Prospect,* September–October 1999.
2. See "Negotiating Away the Environment," *Los Angeles Times,* October 30, 2001.
3. All data on health insurance coverage from Lawrence Mishel, Jared Bernstein, and John Schmitt, *The State of Working America, 2000/2001* (Ithaca, N.Y.: ILR Press, 2001).
4. Ibid.
5. See Jonathan Cohn, "Health Scare," *The New Republic,* December 24, 2001.
6. Quoted in Dionne, *They Only Look Dead.*
7. All wage data are from Mishel et al., *State of Working America.*
8. Testimony to the Senate Finance Committee, March 7, 2001.

9. *Citizens for Tax Justice,* June 18, 2001.

10. Joseph Stiglitz, "A Boost That Goes Nowhere," *Washington Post,* November 11, 2001, Sunday Outlook section.

11. See Robert McIntyre, "The $212-Billion Giveaway," *American Prospect,* November 19, 2001.

12. Quoted in Lamis, *Southern Politics.*

13. *Bergen Record,* October 1, 2001.

14. *The 700 Club,* January 8, 1992.

15. Craig Timberg, "VA GOP Attacks Democrats on Gays," *Washington Post,* August 31, 2001.

16. See Tom Willis, president of the Creation Science Association of Mid-America, quoted in the *Topeka Capital-Journal,* May 11, 1999.

17. See Ronald Bailey, "Origins of the Specious: Why Conservatives Doubt Darwin," *Reason,* July 1997.

18. See Suzanne Holland, Karen Lebacqz, and Laurie Zoloth, eds., *The Human Embryonic Stem Cell Debate* (Cambridge, Mass.: MIT Press, 2001).

19. Michael Kinsley, *Time,* June 25, 2001.

APPENDIX

1. Samuel Popkin and Michael McDonald, "Who Votes?" *Blueprint: Ideas for a New Century* (Washington, D.C.: Democratic Leadership Council, fall 1998).

2. For more discussion, see the appendix to Teixeira and Rogers, *America's Forgotten Majority.*

ACKNOWLEDGMENTS

The genesis of this book goes back to the New Synthesis lunch group that we started in Washington in early 1995 and ran more or less continuously until 2000. At the time, Democrats were fighting with each other over whether it was more important to emphasize "economics" or "values," "populist" or "quality of life" issues. We believed, then and now, that what was needed was a synthesis of the two approaches. Thanks to all who participated in these monthly luncheons.

The book would not have been possible without our editor, Lisa Drew at Scribner, who believed in the book and strongly supported it every step of the way. It would also not have been possible without a timely and generous grant that John Judis received from Bill Moyers and the Florence and John Schumann Foundation.

We received a lot of help from people who read all or part of the manuscript and provided valuable advice. Jonathan Cohn did a heroic job of making substantive comments and improving our prose. Guy Molyneux's criticisms inspired an important addition to our argument. Jo Freeman made helpful comments throughout. E. J. Dionne, Ryan Lizza, Harold Meyerson, and Mac McCorkle provided useful comments and corrections.

We also received a lot of assistance in doing our research. Dave Leip's Web site on U.S. elections provided the primary source for our county-level analysis of the presidential vote. Steve Rose shared his data on occupational change with us. Manish Patel and Melissa Corbin helped us build our database. Corbin and Natasha Udugama helped with charts and other research-related tasks. Tim Parker was invaluable in helping us with analysis of Census Bureau data. Alex Tait assisted with maps. And John Lampe helped with access to the University of Maryland library.

Others provided materials, advice, and research tips that were immensely helpful. They include Robert Atkinson, Sid Blumenthal, Ray Buckley, Jim Chapin, Frank Foer, Jim Gilbert, Stan Greenberg, David Lee, Will Marshall, Harris Meyer, Don Rose, Fred Siegel, Ken Warren, and Jason Zengerle. Glen Hartley and Lynn Chu negotiated our contract with Scribner.

We thank our families (Robin Allen, Lauren and Ian Teixeira; Susan Pearson, Hilary and Eleanor Judis) for putting up with us during the writing.

INDEX